The Impact of Idealism

Volume IV. Religion

The first study of its kind, *The Impact of Idealism* assesses the impact of classical German philosophy on science, religion and culture. This volume explores German Idealism's impact on theology and religious ideas in the nineteenth, twentieth and twenty-first centuries. With contributions from leading scholars, this collection not only demonstrates the vast range of Idealism's theological influence across different centuries, countries, continents, traditions and religions, but also, in doing so, provides fresh insight into the original ideas and themes with which Kant, Hegel, Fichte, Schelling and others were concerned. As well as tracing out the Idealist influence in the work of nineteenth and twentieth-century theologians, philosophers of religion, and theological traditions, from Schleiermacher to Karl Barth to Radical Orthodoxy, the essays in this collection bring each debate up to date with a strong focus on Idealism's contemporary relevance.

Nicholas Boyle is the Schröder Professor of German Emeritus in the University of Cambridge, and a Fellow and former President of Magdalene College.

Liz Disley is a Research Associate in the Department of German and Dutch at the University of Cambridge.

Nicholas Adams is Senior Lecturer in Theology and Ethics at the University of Edinburgh.

The Impact of Idealism

The Legacy of Post-Kantian German Thought

General editors Nicholas Boyle and Liz Disley

Associate general editor Ian Cooper

Volume I. Philosophy and Natural Sciences
Edited by KARL AMERIKS
Volume II. Historical, Social and Political Thought
Edited by JOHN WALKER
Volume III. Aesthetics and Literature
Edited by CHRISTOPH JAMME *and* IAN COOPER
Volume IV. Religion
Edited by NICHOLAS ADAMS

German Idealism is arguably the most influential force in philosophy over the past two hundred years. This major four-volume work is the first comprehensive survey of its impact on science, religion, sociology and the humanities, and brings together fifty-two leading scholars from across Europe and North America. Each essay discusses an idea or theme from Kant, Hegel, Schelling, Fichte, or another key figure, shows how this influenced a thinker or field of study in the subsequent two centuries, and how that influence is felt in contemporary thought. Crossing established scholarly divides, the volumes deal with fields as varied as feminism, architectural history, psychoanalysis, Christology and museum curation, and subjects as diverse as love, evolution, the public sphere, the art of Andy Warhol, the music-dramas of Wagner, the philosophy of Husserl, the novels of Jane Austen, the political thought of fascism and the foundations of international law.

The Impact of Idealism

The Legacy of Post-Kantian German Thought

VOLUME IV
Religion

General editors NICHOLAS BOYLE AND LIZ DISLEY

Edited by NICHOLAS ADAMS

CAMBRIDGE
UNIVERSITY PRESS

University Printing House, Cambridge CB2 8BS, United Kingdom

Published in the United States of America by Cambridge University Press, New York

Cambridge University Press is part of the University of Cambridge.

It furthers the University's mission by disseminating knowledge in the pursuit of education, learning and research at the highest international levels of excellence.

www.cambridge.org
Information on this title: www.cambridge.org/9781107039858

© Cambridge University Press 2013

First published 2013

Printed in the United Kingdom by TJ International Ltd. Padstow Cornwall

A catalogue record for this publication is available from the British Library

Library of Congress Cataloguing in Publication data
The impact of idealism.
    volumes   cm. – (The Legacy of post-Kantian German Thought)
Includes bibliographical references and index.
ISBN 978-1-107-03982-7 (v. 1) – ISBN 978-1-107-03983-4 (v. 2) – ISBN 978-1-107-03984-1
(v. 3) – ISBN 978-1-107-03985-8 (v. 4)
1. Idealism, German.   I. Ameriks, Karl, 1947– editor of compilation.
B2745.I47   2013
141 – dc23   2013017436

ISBN 978-1-107-03985-8 Hardback

Contents

Contributors

NICHOLAS ADAMS
University of Edinburgh

NICHOLAS BOYLE
University of Cambridge

PAUL FRANKS
Yale University

CYRIL O'REGAN
University of Notre Dame

JOEL D. S. RASMUSSEN
University of Oxford

DALE SCHLITT
Oblate School of Theology

JOHN WALKER
Birkbeck, University of London

MARTIN WENDTE
University of Tübingen

ROWAN WILLIAMS
University of Cambridge

GEORGE S. WILLIAMSON
Florida State University

Acknowledgements

This series of studies of the influence on the humanities of German Idealist philosophy results from the work of an International Research Network sponsored by the Leverhulme Trust, with additional support from the Newton Trust and the Schroder fund of the University of Cambridge. The editors would like to thank the Trusts and the Schroder family for their financial assistance.

Planning for the Network began in 2006, with Ian Cooper as the first Project Manager. Liz Disley took over as Project Manager in May 2010. For invaluable help and support in the early stages of the project, the general editors are grateful to the Steering Committee of the Network, whose members include: Ian Cooper, Nicholas Adams, Karl Ameriks, Frederick Beiser, Vittorio Hösle, Stephen Houlgate, Christoph Jamme, Martin Rühl, John Walker, and our patron, Onora O'Neill. A grant from Cambridge University's Department of German and Dutch enabled the Committee to meet in Cambridge in 2008. Throughout the project the staff of the Department and of the Faculty of Modern and Medieval Languages have been generous with their time and prompt with their help. Thanks are due in particular to Sharon Nevill and Louise Balshaw, and to successive Heads of the Department of German and Dutch, Christopher Young and Andrew Webber. We are also most grateful to Regina Sachers for some crucial and timely advice, and to Rosemary Boyle who has acted throughout as management consultant, and has more than once intervened decisively to keep the show on the road.

The general editors owe special thanks to the leaders of the four groups into which it was decided to divide the Network, who are also the editors of the individual volumes in this series. They agreed themes with the general editors, assembled teams to study them, and led the workshops in which they were discussed. The work of the Philosophy and Natural Science group in the University of Notre Dame was supported by the Nanovic Institute for European Studies, and that of the Aesthetics and Literature group in Leuphana University, Lüneburg, by the Thyssen-Krupp-Stiftung. For this support, and for the hospitality of both universities, the general editors would also like to express their gratitude.

Workshops met in Notre Dame, Lüneburg and Cambridge in 2010, and again in Lüneburg and Cambridge in 2011. A concluding plenary conference, open to the public, was held at Magdalene College, Cambridge, in September 2012. On all these occasions staff and students at the host institutions provided help and advice, generously and often anonymously, and to them too we express our thanks.

While we hope that our contributors feel that participation in the Network has been rewarding in itself, we thank them for giving us the benefit of their thinking, for attending the workshops and the conference, and particularly for presenting their work within the constraints of a very tight timetable. For invaluable editorial support in preparing all four volumes for the Press we are especially indebted to Jennifer Jahn. Only her intensive and always cheerful commitment to the project allowed us to meet the deadlines we had set ourselves.

The general editors and the volume editor of this volume would like to thank Magdalene College, Cambridge for hosting two workshops which formed part of the International Network, in December 2010 and 2011.

Abbreviations

FSW   *Johann Gottlieb Fichte's sämmtliche Werke*, ed. I. H. Fichte, 8 vols, Berlin: Veit & Co., 1845–6. Reprinted as vols I–VIII, *Fichtes Werke*. 11 vols, Berlin: de Gruyter, 1971.

GS   *Kant's gesammelte Schriften. Ausgabe der königlich preussischen Akademie der Wissenschaften.* Berlin: W. de Gruyter, 1900–.

GW   Hegel, Georg Wilhelm Friedrich, *Gesammelte Werke. Kritische Ausgabe*, ed. Deutsche Forschungsgemeinschaft in Verbindung mit der Rheinisch-Westfälischen Akademie der Wissenschaften, 31 vols to date, Hamburg: Meiner, 1968–.

HW   *Hegels Werke in zwanzig Bänden*, ed. Eva Moldenhauer and Karl Markus Michel, 20 vols, Frankfurt am Main: Suhrkamp, 1969–71.

KW   *Kants Werke in sechs Bänden*, ed. Wilhelm Weischedel, Wiesbaden: Insel Verlag, 1956–62.

Nachlass   *Johann Gottlieb Fichte's nachgelassene Schriften*, 3 vols, Bonn: Adolph-Marcus 1834–35. Reprinted as vols IX–XI, *Fichtes Werke*, 11 vols, Berlin: de Gruyter, 1971.

PdR   Hegel, Georg Wilhelm Friedrich, *Philosophie des Rechts: Die Vorlesung von 1819/20*, ed. Dieter Henrich, Frankfurt: Suhrkamp, 1983.

SKS   *Søren Kierkegaards Skrifter*, ed. Niels Jørgen Cappelørn *et al.*, 55 vols, Copenhagen: Gad, 1997–.

SSW   *Schellings sämmtliche Werke*, ed. Karl Friedrich August Schelling, 14 vols, Stuttgart: Cotta, 1856–61.

WM   Gadamer, Hans-Georg, *Wahrheit und Methode: Grundzüge einer philosophischen Hermeneutik*, Tübingen: Mohr, 1960.

Translations

CD, I.1   Barth, Karl, *Church Dogmatics* vol I, part 1, ed. G. W. Bromiley and
T. F. Torrance, 2nd edn, Edinburgh: T. and T. Clark, 1975.

IET   Pfau, Thomas (trans. and ed.), *Idealism and the Endgame of Theory:
Three Essays by F. W. J. Schelling*, Albany: State University of New
York Press, 1994.

NB   *Søren Kierkegaard's Journals and Notebooks*, ed. Bruce Kirmmse *et al.*,
Princeton: Princeton University Press, 2007ff.

PA   Schelling, Friedrich Wilhelm Joseph von, *Philosophy of Art*, trans.
Douglas Stott, Minneapolis: University of Minnesota Press, 1989.

PM   Hegel, G. W. F., *Philosophy of Mind*, trans. William Wallace, Oxford:
Clarendon, 1975.

PS   Hegel, G. W. F., *Phenomenology of Spirit*, trans. A. V. Miller, Oxford,
Oxford University Press, 1977.

PT   Barth, Karl, *Protestant Theology in the Nineteenth Century: its background and history*, ed. Colin Gunton, trans. Brian Cozens and John
Bowden, London: SCM Press, 2001 (first published 1947).

STI   Schelling, F. W. J., *System of Transcendental Idealism* (1800), trans.
Peter Heath, Charlottesville, VA: University Press of Virginia,
1978.

Introduction: the impact of Idealism on religion

Nicholas Adams

There are three headings under which we might consider the impact of Idealism on religion. The first concerns those areas of intellectual enquiry where the impact of Idealism is well understood in general, even if the particularities are not often in view. The second concerns those areas where the patterns of thinking are familiar, but their debts to Idealism are less often noticed. The third concerns those developments that display the impact of Idealism but are much less familiar.

The first strand, where the impact of Idealism is familiar, includes the doctrines of Christology and of the Trinity, in particular, and the transmission of idealist thought through various major theological figures in the nineteenth and twentieth centuries. The second strand, where the patterns of thinking are familiar but the debts to Idealism are less often noticed, includes developments in hermeneutics, in the relation between unity and plurality, in radical orthodoxy and non-realist theology, and in the conflict between faith and reason. These are familiar topics in theology and are central to a variety of intellectual strategies in contemporary thought. The impact of Idealism on their development and modes of expression is less often remarked; essays in this section lay special emphasis on this impact. The third strand, where the impact of Idealism is obvious when one investigates certain topics but the topics themselves are less familiar, includes the development of themes in Jewish philosophy, the rise of the category of 'myth' and some aspects of theology in the twentieth century.

The pattern followed in general by the essays is broadly tripartite. First, they establish how the topic in view is handled by particular post-Kantian figures. Second, they give some account of how this thinking is transmitted (or fails to be transmitted) through the nineteenth and twentieth centuries. Third, they suggest ways in which contemporary thinking displays the impact (or the lack of impact) of Idealism.

The essays in this volume begin the work of developing these kinds of discussion along various central intellectual axes. The first three essays rehearse topics where the impact of Idealism is well known, but whose details are rarely rehearsed in detail. Dale Schlitt's two essays on the Trinity begin with Fichte, Schelling and Hegel and show how their thinking is transmitted via Marheineke and Dorner in the nineteenth century, to Barth, Rahner and Pannenberg in the twentieth century.

Martin Wendte's essay on Christology begins with Hegel and proceeds as far as the thought of Paul Tillich via Marheineke, Baur, Strauss, Dorner, Kierkegaard and Hirsch. The aim of both Schlitt's and Wendte's essays is to tell part of the story of the impact of Idealism on these two central Christian doctrines.

They are accompanied by Joel Rasmussen's essay on Kierkegaard. Kierkegaard's work shows one of the characteristic impacts of Idealism on religious thought: a strong reaction against it. Rasmussen offers a nuanced view, rooted in the latest scholarship, showing the ways in which Kierkegaard's oeuvre is a complex appropriation as well as rejection of the thought of Hegel and Schelling and also the counter-Idealist strand of thinking found in Schlegel, Tieck and Solger.

The next four essays examine topics that are familiar and where the impact of Idealism has been noticed less often, especially by theologians. Nicholas Boyle rehearses the impact of Idealism on hermeneutics by showing the ways in which Gadamer's thought is deeply indebted to Hegel's recovery of tradition, which in turn is constituted by engagement with Kant and Herder. The core insight here is that Hegel grasps the importance of the community, of doctrine, for the interpretation of the Bible. Just as Herder offers a more historically satisfactory approach than Kant, so Hegel offers a more 'traditionally' satisfactory approach than Schleiermacher. Like several of the other authors in this volume, Boyle notes the lack of impact of Idealism – in this case in the hermeneutics of Barth and Heidegger – which means that the transmission of Idealism is marked by a long dormant period, roughly from 1831 to 1960, when Gadamer published his recognisably Hegelian *Truth and Method*. Cyril O'Regan traces the impact of Idealism on one of the central questions where theology and philosophy intersect: the relation of the one to the many. His essay has two substantial discussions, of Hegel and of Hölderlin, before considering their impact to a limited extent via Kierkegaard, and more emphatically via Staudenmaier and Baur.

It concludes with a discussion of Idealism's impact on the thought of Guardini, Przywara, von Balthasar and Marion. John Walker's essay discharges two functions. First, it sketches the way in which Hegel understands the relation between philosophy and theology, focusing on the autonomy of each. Second, it explores the way this relation plays out in the work of two British theologians, John Milbank and Don Cupitt. In this account Walker rehearses a noticeable lack of the impact of Idealism: Walker argues that certain shortcomings in the contemporary theologians' conceptions of the relation between philosophy and theology would be remedied by a deeper engagement with Hegel. My own essay on faith and reason also discharges two tasks. The first is to rehearse Hegel's account of the conflict of faith and reason in the Enlightenment and to suggest that this account is the pattern for later investigations by Amos Funkenstein, Michael Buckley, Stephen Toulmin and John Milbank. The second is to present Hegel's account of the deep bond between faith and reason in his retrieval of Anselm's ontological proof for the existence of God against Kant's critique of it. Like several of the topics addressed in this volume, Idealism has failed to have an impact here. It deserves to have an impact on discussions of the ontological argument in philosophical theology.

The final three essays explore less familiar topics where the impact of Idealism is, on closer investigation, readily visible. Paul Franks' essay on Jewish philosophy traces the mutual influence of Idealism and Jewish philosophy in its Platonic and Kabbalistic variants, focusing on Maimon, Cohen and Rosenzweig, but taking in a range of nineteenth- and twentieth-century figures. The theme of supersession, both as a topic of discussion and as a deeper structural issue (in Hegel's 'sublation', for example) plays a significant role in this account. The story of Jewish philosophy and its relation to Idealism has not been told with such clarity before. George Williamson's essay traces the impact of Idealism on understandings of mythology from Schelling, Hegel and Strauss (who make up the main body of the essay) to Heidegger, Cassirer, Landauer and Buber. The notion of 'myth' is of central importance to discussions of religion in a range of disciplines, from Biblical studies to social anthropology. The story of its genesis in the nineteenth century, and its debts to German Idealism, is not often told. Williamson offers a detailed account of the early period of its development. Rowan Williams engages a central theological topic in twentieth-century theology, the analogy of being, and shows how the rival accounts offered by Barth and Przywara make more sense when one interprets them as different displays of the impact of Idealism. He also shows that theological investigation at this high level of sophistication forces a more sophisticated engagement with figures like Hegel than is often found in theology.

German Idealism had an extraordinary impact on religion, whether one focuses on scholarly concerns with Christian doctrines or with popular understandings of atheism and evil. But it also in many cases failed to have the impact that its texts warrant. This volume begins the business of charting both the impact and the lack of impact. It is offered to today's scholars as a report of the state of play and to today's students as an encouragement and inspiration to deepen this work. There is much left to be done.

In each of the three strands identified above there are some obvious lacunae that can be acknowledged frankly and for whose omission there is no good reason beyond the contingencies surrounding a volume of this kind. These include the topics of atheism and evil, both of which were comprehensively transformed by the development of Idealism. They include the theology of Schleiermacher who, along with Schopenhauer, represents an alternative and non-Idealist reception of Kant. (Nicholas Boyle's essay discusses Schleiermacher's hermeneutics, but no essay tackles his doctrinal work.) They include the development of the thought of British Idealists.[1] They also include Idealism's impact on figures such as Marx and Nietzsche and, via them, such twentieth-century figures as Weber, Heidegger and Foucault. These latter figures have had a decisive impact on the study of religion in general and on theology more specifically. Each is in different ways a commentator on Nietzsche and each is indebted to the post-Kantian developments found in Schelling and Hegel. A volume that aimed at exhaustiveness (unlike this one) would cover these developments and many others. It would also deal with the ways in which contemporary theology is in many ways indebted to forms of thinking that explicitly critique developments in German Idealism, such as those found in early German romanticism, in pragmatism and in analytic philosophy. One would rightly expect to find discussion of various counter-movements and investigation into figures like Jacobi, Novalis and the Schlegels, and into Peirce, James and Dewey, and into the Viennese and British schools of philosophy that flourished after the Great War. Such counter-movements are negative expressions of the impact of Idealism: despite their importance such reactions against Idealism are absent from this volume and it will be up to future scholars to fill in the gaps identified here.

The most serious omission is also the most difficult to remedy. This is an account of the impact of French phenomenology on contemporary theology that, at the same time, shows the impact of Idealism on the French tradition. This is a giant undertaking because it requires a facility in the most complex intellectual discussions in contemporary theology, a grasp of the details of the development of French philosophy in the mid- to late-twentieth century, a background in the nineteenth-century German primary texts and, finally, knowledge of the history of the transmission of ideas across nearly two centuries. There is a fascinating book to be written on this difficult topic. It will require a colossus to write it: a theologian, philosopher and historian of ideas. Were it already in print, an abbreviated account might perhaps have been offered in this volume. All that exists of such an enterprise here is the following brief observation: the influence of French phenomenology on contemporary theology is itself an expression of the impact of Idealism. It will be for other scholars to investigate this complex nexus of ideas.

Two serious lacunae that can be remedied partially are the development of atheism and the development of thinking on evil in the nineteenth century. A few remarks on these topics are appropriate because they exercise a disproportionate influence on theology in the twentieth century.

Atheism after Hegel

The French atheism of the eighteenth century – of Voltaire, of Diderot, of d'Holbach – has a distinctive shape. It sets its face against rationalist developments in theology, to whose further development the atheist critiques act as a spur. Their principal features include attempts to drive a wedge between 'faith' and 'reason' in general, and between 'blind' faith and 'clear' reason in particular. They focus on the allegedly corrupt effects of ecclesial authority on belief, which are contrasted unfavourably with the liberating effects of autonomous reason. They mock the allegedly contorted rationalisations of rationalist theology (whether broadly Leibnizian–Wolffian or, later on, broadly Kantian) and offer as a contrast the illumination offered by philosophy freed from the censorship of theologians and unshackled by the burdens of doctrinal obedience. Religious belief is often cast as something obediently unthinking, wilfully dishonest or positively stupid. Certain strands of atheism in our own time mirror this French pattern, and it is by no means rare to find popular books by intelligent authors who characterise religious belief as exhibiting those features painted in such garish colours by the great French eighteenth-century atheists.

The atheist developments in German philosophy in the nineteenth century are not of this kind, by and large. The impact of Idealism on atheism is intellectually more serious, more sophisticated and in the long term more damaging or liberating (depending on one's point of view). Three figures in particular deserve thorough study: D. F. Strauss, Ludwig Feuerbach and Karl Marx. Between them they develop a range of forms of thinking that prove particularly corrosive to popular religious belief and provoke the theologians who follow them to develop new theological forms of enquiry. All three, with justification, see themselves as inheritors of Hegel's thought. The shapes of thinking of Strauss and Feuerbach are particularly noteworthy and can be sketched. For reasons of space Marx cannot be considered here.[2]

Strauss' *The Life of Jesus* (1835) is a monumental study of the Gospels that treats in detail nearly every episode of Jesus' life.[3] It is its short preface that was to prove most significant: it provides the intellectual framework for the study. Perhaps Strauss changed the way people thought, or perhaps he summarised in a decisive way changes that had already taken place. Either way, atheism (especially in relation to the Bible) looks different after Strauss' book. The preface ostensibly addresses a choice faced by the Biblical critic: either one acknowledges that modern thought requires a fundamental revision of the kinds of claim one can make about the Bible, or one buries one's head in the sand and becomes an irrelevant intellectual dinosaur. To be a modern thinker, for Strauss, is to think in a certain kind of way and either one comes to terms with this or one refuses. If one comes to terms with it, then one writes in an up-to-date modern idiom with modern insights. If one fails to do so, one remains mired in an archaic frame of mind, repeating nostrums that become increasingly meaningless to contemporary folk. The deeper influence of Strauss' preface, however, arguably lies in the way it draws certain contrasts. The principal ones are 'scientific' [*wissenschaftlich*] versus 'unscientific', 'modern' versus 'ancient', 'myth' [*Mythos*] versus 'history', and 'supernatural' versus 'natural'. (George Williamson's essay in this volume explores the significance of the category 'myth' and the ways its uses change.)[4] Strauss' categories are, one might say, binary. That is, they are oppositional and mutually exclusive. To be scientific is good; to be unscientific is bad. For one's thinking to be modern is for it to be the opposite of ancient; to be historical is to exclude the mythical. Strauss sets these binary oppositions in a way that looks almost common-sensical to those who follow him. They are the predecessors of further opposed terms that are familiar today: 'academic' versus 'confessional' approaches or 'outsider' versus 'insider' perspectives. Strauss' decisive influence (made possible in English owing to the widely read translation by George Eliot) is his success in persuading succeeding generations to deal in these binary oppositions. They are corrosive for theology for the same reason as Kant's oppositions between 'authority' and 'autonomy' and between 'tradition' and 'reason'. (Nicholas

Boyle's essay in this volume explores the ways in which a fundamental recovery of tradition is a crucial impact of Idealism on subsequent philosophical thought.)[5] Once one accepts the opposition, one is faced not with a complex historical situation but with a stark choice: this or that, yes or no, right or wrong. Once one accepts the opposition one also accepts that one must choose one way or the other. It requires great independence of mind to refuse such a choice.

Ludwig Feuerbach's *The Essence of Christianity* is, in its own words, a 'translation of the Christian religion out of the oriental language of imagery into plain speech'.[6] Its ostensible argument is that Christianity appears to be about God but really it is about humanity. His most famous formulation comes from the chapter 'The mystery of the suffering God': 'Religion is human nature reflected, mirrored in itself . . . exalted to that stage in which it can mirror and reflect itself, in which it can project its own image as God. God is the mirror of man'.[7] At a deeper level, however, Feuerbach (like Strauss) offers a series of binary oppositions: appearance and reality, imagery and plain speech, delusion and truth. These are emphatically opposed to each other. But Feuerbach goes further and suggests that certain terms that look like oppositions are in fact identical: supernatural and natural, transcendent and immanent, heaven and earth, divine and human, God and man. Feuerbach thus offers a two-pronged attack that is certainly presented as a series of arguments, but whose deeper force is felt because it functions at the level of basic categories. The first prong is to oppose certain terms and, like Strauss, to persuade the reader to choose between them. The second prong is to identify certain other terms and to persuade the reader to refuse to distinguish them. These two prongs have the same result: Christians are deluded in their speech about God; the truth is that their speech is about humanity. This is because 'God' and 'man' are the same thing. 'God' is merely imagery; in plain speech one finds that its object is 'human reason' itself.

The shapes of thinking displayed by Strauss and Feuerbach are striking. They depend for their force not upon empirical enquiry but upon the categories they bring into play. This is not what they themselves say about their work. Strauss emphasises the painstaking detail of his investigations into the Gospels; Feuerbach insists on the empirical study on which his claims rest. In reality (to use Feuerbach's idiom) it is the strong binary contrasts (Strauss) or the mixture of strong binary contrasts and emphatic identification of apparent opposites (Feuerbach) that proves decisive. Strauss' influence lies in the way his binary oppositions come to appear as common sense to his successors. It becomes obvious that one must choose between modern and ancient forms of thinking. His genius lies in the force of these oppositions. It is thus obvious to his successors that scholarship is either modern and respectable or reactionary and unscholarly. Feuerbach's appeal lies in the simplicity of his proposals: what appear to be two things (transcendent and immanent, divine and human) are in truth one thing (human thinking itself). His genius lies in the unanswerability of this identity: once one entertains this possibility, it is hard to see what argument could establish the non-identity of the divine and the human. After all, anything one says will be a display of human thinking.

These shapes of thinking in Strauss and Feuerbach are developments of aspects of Hegel's philosophy. In the *Phenomenology of Spirit*, Hegel distinguishes between representation or picture-thinking (*Vorstellung*) and the concept (*Begriff*). To simplify a sophisticated set of enquiries, Hegel suggests that religious thinking and philosophical thinking are both displays of 'spirit'. By spirit, Hegel means a form of thinking that overcomes the false opposition (very common in modern philosophy) between individual and community, between 'I' and 'we'. These two ways of thinking, the religious and the philosophical, have the same 'spiritual' substance, but they take a different form. Religious thinking deals in images. It pictures God. It thus offers an emphatic opposition between subject and object, thinking and being, sign and signified. Philosophical thinking by contrast deals in concepts. It conceptualises. It thus offers a complex relation between subject and object (where the subject acknowledges its own productivity in its apparent reception of objects), between thinking and being (where thinking is always thinking of some being and being is always mediated in thinking), between sign and signified (where what is signified is always mediated by sign, and a sign always points beyond itself to something else). Where religious thinking deals in emphatic oppositions, philosophical thought deals in complex relations. Hegel's account is both re-descriptive and reparative. In the case of 'religious' thinking he seeks to re-describe it in 'philosophical' terms. In the case of errant reasoning in modern philosophy, he seeks to diagnose the error and offer his own corrections. The emphatic oppositions of religious thought are quite normal forms of everyday thought, but they become errant when they become models for philosophy. The 'representational' opposition of subject and object (e.g. between God 'out there' and humanity 'over here') becomes errant when it is cast as a 'conceptual' opposition in philosophy between subject and object (e.g. between the object 'over there' and the subject 'in here', as one finds in Descartes) or when it becomes a purely subjective matter (e.g. the 'merely conceptual' idea of God, as one finds in Kant). Hegel sees modern philosophy as a history of false oppositions (in Descartes and his successors) or of false identities (in Kant and his successors). His repairs take the form of distinguishing oppositional forms of everyday thinking (e.g. in religion) and complex relational forms of conceptual thinking (e.g. in philosophy). He rejects oppositional forms of conceptual thinking (e.g. in Descartes) and one-sided identity thinking (e.g. in Kant).

Even in this brief sketch one can begin to see certain interesting features in the shapes of thinking displayed by Strauss and Feuerbach. Both thinkers seem to be developing Hegel's distinction between 'representation' and 'concept'. Both thinkers seem to characterise religious thought as 'representational' and philosophical thought as 'conceptual'. But, at a deeper level, matters are not quite as they seem. Hegel claims that oppositional forms of thinking are quite normal in everyday thinking; but if one wishes to think philosophically one must repair false oppositions or one-sided identities of the kind generated by Descartes and Kant, and instead deal in complex relational forms. Strauss and Feuerbach do not understand that this is a philosophical enterprise, in Hegel's sense. They take it to be a 'scientific' one.

There are some tangles here, but they are relatively easy to comb out. Hegel, at the end of the *Phenomenology*, describes his project as 'scientific' (*wissenschaftlich*). By this he means what we would call 'philosophy' rather than natural science. Hegel himself went on in his *Encyclopaedia* to explore the relation between natural science and philosophy. But when Strauss and Feuerbach say (as they do) that their work is 'scientific' (same word: *wissenschaftlich*) they mean something much closer to natural science. Both Strauss and Feuerbach make a great deal of their empirical researches, for example. But for Hegel there is no natural scientific enquiry into 'subject and object' or 'thinking and being'. These are philosophical, and not natural scientific, matters.

For Hegel 'God' can be an expression either of an opposition between subject and object (as in religion) or an expression of a complex relation between subject and object (as in philosophy). But it is a giant leap backwards to say that 'God' is an expression of illusory object A (in religion) whereas it is an expression of real object B (in philosophy). This way of thinking is a curious melding of the worst of both Cartesian and Kantian worlds. First, it generates a false opposition between subject and object. In Cartesian thinking one finds a false opposition between the world out there and the subject in here. In Feuerbach's thinking one finds a false opposition between the self out there (whether pictured as God or pictured as the thinking self) and the self in here. In Kantian thinking one finds a one-sided identification between subject and object: God is reduced to an idea of reason. In Feuerbach's thinking one finds a one-sided identification between subject and object: God is the same as reason itself. Worse, Feuerbach's shape of thinking is fully 'representational': it happens to insist on one kind of representation (the self) rather than another (God). It is not truly 'conceptual' because this would require a more relational account of subject and object, or of thinking and being. The sign of truly conceptual thinking is its ability to overcome false oppositions and one-sided identifications. Feuerbach's shape of thinking overcomes neither.

Strauss, too, takes a giant step backwards from Hegel's perspective. Instead of preserving the distinction between oppositional forms of thinking (in religion) and relational forms of thinking (in philosophy), Strauss insists one must choose between them. One must choose between representations and concepts even within religion itself. Thus he distinguishes between what is 'essential' and what is 'inessential' to the Gospels narratives, with a view to expunging the mythically 'inessential' for the sake of the dogmatically 'essential'.[8] From a Hegelian perspective Strauss mistakenly identifies 'myth' with 'representation' and 'truth' with 'concept'. But for Hegel representational and conceptual forms of thinking *both* grasp the truth. The difference lies in the forms they take: representational forms of thinking deal in oppositions between thinking and being whereas conceptual forms of thinking deal in complex relations between them. Strauss invents a new and bizarre form of thinking: an opposition between representational and conceptual thinking. The oppositional account of the representation in religion and the sophisticated relational account of the concept in philosophy is rejected in favour of a new creature undreamed of in Hegel: an oppositional account of the concept in philosophy. This is so thoroughly confused as to suggest that Strauss does not understand Hegel's philosophy.

The effects of these problematic developments of Hegel's contrast between representation and concept, in both Strauss and Feuerbach, are far-reaching for forms of atheism and they constitute an important impact of Idealism. They produce false oppositions (between subject and object, and now between representation and concept, myth and history, subject and self) and one-sided identities (between God and humanity). They fail to offer complex forms of relation of the kind Hegel so painstakingly develops. Atheist arguments come to ask questions of the form, 'what is the real object?' rather than the more Hegelian question, 'what is the relation between subject and object?' They ask of scholarly enquiry, 'is this representational or conceptual?' rather than the more Hegelian question, 'how can representational oppositions be rendered in conceptual relations?' They ask of religious formulations, 'are these representational delusions or conceptual truths?' rather than the Hegelian question, 'how can truths cast representationally be cast conceptually?' It can be seen from these examples that the atheist developments display the same oppositional form that Hegel attributes to religious thinking. That raises the possibility that one might treat them in one of two ways. One might treat them descriptively, in the same way that Hegel treats religion itself. Where atheist thinking deals in emphatic oppositions, the philosophical task is that of rendering its representational grasp of the truth in conceptual forms. Alternatively, one might diagnose them as instances of errant philosophical method, whether it deals in false oppositions (as in Descartes) or one-sided identities (as in Kant). One might then treat them reparatively, the same way Hegel treats Descartes and Kant. The philosophical task is that of overcoming false oppositions and one-sided identities through a logic that deals in complex relations.

This suggests an important impact of Idealism on how we think about atheism in our own time. After all, most scholars of Hegel are atheists. Is it being proposed that they are guilty of the missteps attributed here to Strauss and Feuerbach? Such an attribution does not follow inevitably. It may be true that some forms of contemporary atheism are versions of arguments by Voltaire, Diderot or Lessing, which seek to oppose faith to reason and which caricature religious belief as either hopelessly insouciant or dangerously deceptive. It may be that some forms of atheism display the false oppositions of Strauss, or the confused mixture of false oppositions and one-sided identities of Feuerbach. But it is also quite possible that some forms of atheism display the nuanced account of the complex relation between thinking and being that Hegel develops. Hegel's thinking does not commit him to anything other than a complex relation between thinking and being. It makes no difference, at this level, whether 'representational' forms of thinking affirm 'I believe in God' or 'there is no God'. (Obviously they have different practical consequences, but the philosophical form is not determined by them. Clearly one is true and one is false; but as we lack a God's-eye view of matters, philosophy will not decide this question.) From a Hegelian point of view, both are 'religious' forms of thinking, both are 'representational'. One affirms, the other denies, the object. Either form of thinking can be rendered conceptually. In other words, quite a lot hangs on whether atheist forms of thinking are 'religious', in Hegel's sense, in which case they will stimulate philosophical investigation and re-description, or whether they are philosophically errant, in which case they will stimulate repair. Hegel's philosophy has nothing against 'religious' atheism. But it will be utterly unforgiving against errant philosophy. One of the impacts of Idealism may well be a higher quality of atheism and a correspondingly higher quality conflict with theology.

Evil after Kant

The topic of 'evil' displays some comparable features of the impact of Idealism. In the period before the nineteenth century there are two main approaches. The first is broadly Augustinian and treats evil as inexplicable. It supposes creation is good and casts evil as a privation of the good. The second is broadly Leibnizian and treats evil as explicable. It supposes that creation is good, and it casts evil as an expression of that good. The task of theology is unending: it is one of exploring what cannot satisfactorily be explained. The task of theodicy is determinate: it is one of finding the most satisfactory explanation of evil. Kant's account of radical evil in *Religion within the Bounds of Mere Reason* is typically unusual. Instead of treating evil as an inexplicable privation of the good, or as a yet-to-be-explained expression of the good, he considers it an expression of human freedom that is simultaneously inescapable and inexplicable. Kant's account is neither Augustinian nor Leibnizian. It is curiously fatalistic, more reminiscent of ancient stoicism than Christian theology.

Approaches to evil after Kant take a variety of forms. In addition to the approaches of Augustinian theology, Leibnizian theodicy and Kantian practical philosophy, one sees two significant new developments that will have a strong impact on later thinking on evil. These are Schelling's account of human freedom and Hegel's account of natural evil. I propose here to rehearse them in the form offered by Peter Dews.[9]

First, we can consider Schelling's contribution in his *Freedom* essay of 1809. To understand Schelling, it is important to note that the conflict between good and evil is accompanied by a range of further conflicts: between freedom and necessity, between particular and universal, between love and law, between unpredictability and system. There are also at least three metaphysical locations where these conflicts play out: in the individual (as for Kant), in the world (as for the early Schelling), and in God (as for the Schelling of the *Freedom* essay, at least to begin with). The *Freedom* essay can be read as an experiment in handling these conflicts in different metaphysical locations. Each time equilibrium is found for one set of conflicts within a given metaphysical location, the discussion is displaced to another location. Schelling's *Freedom* essay models this continual ontological displacement in a way that repeatedly finds and loses equilibrium. Dews shows how this happens in a series of moves.

Schelling's most important insight guides nearly all of the developments of his thinking about evil: pairs of terms are expressions of a prior unity. That is, polarities such as subject/object, ideal/real, mind/nature etc. are subsidiary to and derivative of the 'absolute' or the 'unconditioned'.[10]

The first move in Schelling's treatment of evil is to apply this insight to the polarity freedom/necessity, and to treat the opposition expressed in this polarity as something abolished in the absolute. The metaphysical location for this moment of equilibrium is 'the world', whose process flows with necessity from its ultimate ground. This moment of equilibrium, however, is quickly disturbed by a further insight: such an understanding undermines freedom. It is no good having an equilibrium in which freedom disappears, because freedom is the *sine qua non* of all post-Kantian philosophy. The discussion is thus displaced from the world to a new metaphysical location: the subject.

In Kantian and Fichtean thought, the subject is the individual person who acts and reflects. Schelling experiments with a revision of this account of the subject. Freedom is glossed as 'pure willing' and this is attributed not to the finite agent of human action but to God, the 'absolute subject'. Rather than trying to find equilibrium between freedom and necessity in the world, Schelling attempts to make freedom dominant, but to locate it in God's being and action.

This generates two further interesting problems. The first is how to describe the world; the second is how to do justice to specifically *human* action. On the first question, Schelling experiments with describing the world as the process of God manifesting himself. On the second question, Schelling suggests that freedom must be glossed as the possibility of good and evil, and that this is best explored by thinking about God's freedom in the first instance.[11]

The question of evil thus becomes a question of the doctrine of God. Schelling identifies two unsatisfactory accounts of God. The first treats God as particular, as utterly separated from creation; the second treats God as universal, as utterly identified with creation. A more adequate account must find equilibrium between these two views: God must be understood as individual, but this individuality is to be taken as the basis of the universal. This approach marks one of Schelling's several minority reports or dissenting opinions against the majority theological consensus. The majority opinion, clarified in Aquinas' brief discussion of analogy, is that speech about God is problematic because it is human speech. The problems rest on the side of human articulation. The dissenting opinion, found here in Schelling's enquiry, is that speech about God is problematic because there is something internal to the divine life that displays the problem. Schelling attributes to God an interplay between two wills: a 'will of love' and a 'will of the basis'. Against the majority opinion, which is that God is simple, Schelling voices a dissenting opinion, which is that there is a duality in God.

The 'will of love' is expansive, outflowing, disclosing, communicative, revelatory. It seeks a merger with what is other than it. The 'will of the basis' is contractive, involuted, inward-turning. It seeks to assert its own singularity.

But Schelling does not want a bare dichotomy: he seeks something more fluid and dialectical. He thus modifies his account of these two wills so that they are not merely two discrete and opposed wills: they overlap in certain respects. The 'will of love' can only reveal itself in the particular. The 'will of the basis' strives to disclose its inward turn. Schelling thus experiments with a kind of communication of idioms between the two wills. The outcome is an oscillation: there is productive antagonism between the two wills, rather than destructive conflict. Indeed it is the dialectic between love and basis in God that, when expressed in nature, gives rise to ever more complex creatures: mineral, plant, animal. Human being stands at the apex of this ever-expanding movement. Human freedom is thus shown to be an expression of a prior divine freedom. The struggle, in human action, between particularity and universality, is bound up with a deeper struggle between the 'will of love' and the 'will of the basis' in God. Kant had understood the moral law to be the predominance of the universal over the particular. Rational action is the predominance of *Wille* (the universality of practical reason) over *Willkür* (the spontaneity of the individual self). Evil, in Kant's scheme, is the inversion of this: it is the desire for a dominance of the particular over the universal. Schelling takes this to a whole new level and locates the possibility of this inversion in God.

Evil, in this picture, is arguably not straightforwardly 'evil' any more. It is the possibility of the dominance of the 'will of the basis' over the 'will of love'. In nature the relation between the two wills is generally one of equilibrium: the universal and the particular are inextricably intertwined.[12] But in the case of human beings something distinctive is displayed: 'the particular will seeks to dominate the process to which it should surrender, to turn the universal will into the will of the basis.'[13]

The puzzle here, which confronts every commentator on evil from Augustine onwards, is that one can easily enough account for very occasional expressions of evil but it is very difficult to account for its astonishingly widespread manifestations. Sporadic perversions are one thing; almost ubiquitous perversions are arguably not perversions at all: they are the new 'normal'. The tradition's majority opinion addresses this through a doctrine of original sin. Schelling's dissenting opinion is that the groundlessness of freedom and the outflowing of love provoke fear and anxiety – the 'anguish of life'. This has a strange complexion in Schelling's account. The 'will of love' holds out the possibility of union, but this universality threatens my individuality. That individuality is thus asserted over against the universality. Put differently, the 'basis' of my being is opaque and worryingly contingent and so I deal with it by asserting it all the more strongly, giving up the freedom of love that might challenge it. The vertiginous aspect of freedom in love provokes a desire to give it up for a more secure basis.

Evil here is a way of talking about the triumph of individual identity over loving union, of particularity over universality. What is remarkable about Schelling's account is that universality is glossed as loving union rather than as impersonal moral law, as it tends to be in Kant. What makes Schelling's account a dissenting opinion in theology is not the opposition of the 'will of love' to the 'will of the basis', but the location of this opposition not in human refusal of divine love, but in God's primordial duality of wills.

Schelling's remarkable account of the two wills is quite distinct from Kant's account of *Wille* and *Willkür*. For Kant, a will is good if it is patterned to the moral law. Evil describes an inversion where the particular is made dominant over the universal. For Schelling, the 'will of the basis' is not itself evil, neither is the struggle between the 'will of the basis' against the 'will of love'; evil describes the excessive striving for individuality, for being a self, for wanting to grasp what makes one unique. This also produces a distinctive inflection of what the good is. It is not the subordination of the 'will of the basis' to the 'will of love', or of the particular to the universal. The good is, rather, the appropriate interplay of the two wills, their balance, in such a way that the drive for selfhood is preserved in the service of loving union. Neither side wins out over the other. The error of the striving self is to think that loving union can only be at the expense of individual differentiation. It is the mistaken belief that love is the abolition of selfhood rather than its fulfilment. This is what 'evil' describes.

The most interesting aspect of Schelling's account is yet to come, however. Instead of remaining content with an interrelation between the two wills, he poses a familiar question. Having established an account in which there are two terms (the will of love and the will of the basis) in opposition to each other, there is obviously the danger that this is just another dualism. Schelling's characteristic tendency is to treat pairs of terms as expressions of a deeper unity. Schelling diagnoses an equivocation in how 'being' is predicated of God. It can be 'being insofar as it is basis' and 'being insofar as it exists'. 'Basis' is the ground of being, 'existence' is the being of beings, we might say. The question is what kind of relation do 'basis' and 'existence' have. If they are merely opposed to each other, the danger of a dualism arises. But they cannot simply be subordinated to an ultimate identity, because this will once again dissolve the difference between universal and particular, freedom and necessity and even of good and evil. The principal task of the *Freedom* essay is to refuse to dissolve these differences.[14]

What is needed, Schelling suggests, is to have a ground (in the sense of something that acts as a precondition) that is at the same time not a ground (in the sense of something that overcomes the pairs of terms). He suggests that there is a prior 'un-ground'. This strange term describes a *logical* priority in which there is disjunction and at the same time refuses an *ontological* priority in which there are differences in antithetical opposition. Schelling, in fact, calls these 'non-antitheses'. Here, he clearly occupies a very rarefied theoretical atmosphere: an 'un-ground' containing 'non-antitheses'. This also, Dews suggests, has some unusual effects on speech about God. God becomes an expression of possibilities that arise as divisions from the primal un-ground. The un-ground, in other words, is in some obscure sense prior to God, and 'God himself is demoted to a secondary, dependent position.'[15] This is perhaps not a complete surprise, given Schelling's habits of thinking (and reading, including Meister Eckhart). Having ascribed to God the contrary wills of 'love' and 'basis', any logically prior condition will have to be at a higher level even than God.

This still leaves the fundamental questions in play. How can one satisfactorily describe the relation between freedom and system? How can one satisfactorily account for evil as the capacity to choose either good or evil? Schelling has an odd relation to the Augustinian proposal that evil is a privation of the good. On the one hand he explicitly denies that evil is a privation of the good. He insists that freedom is the capacity to choose either good or evil rather than the capacity to choose from a hierarchy within the good. On the other hand, he appears to contradict this by saying that evil has no independent being: 'it *is* the good, but the good regarded in its non-identity'.[16]

Dews cites Schelling's gesture towards an eschatological vision, an end-point of creation, where evil is not abolished but where it remains an unfulfilled possibility: as 'desire, as the eternal hunger and thirst for reality, but is unable to go beyond potentiality'.[17] Here evil is the perpetually available choice that is never chosen.

Quite what Schelling means is not clear. But it is not difficult to see what Schelling's intellectual strategy is in general. Schelling identifies potential false oppositions and false identities and systematically denies them. There is a potential false opposition between the will of love and the will of the basis: Schelling posits a prior condition. There is a potential false identity of ground and existence: Schelling defends against such a possibility by calling this prior condition an 'un-ground'. There is a potential false opposition of terms in this un-ground: Schelling calls them 'non-antitheses'. The instability of evil, its prioritising of particularity over the universal, undermines itself, but Schelling sees the danger of what he sees (against Augustine) as the false identity of evil and good: he deploys a strange eschatological modal logic in which there is always the possibility of evil but never its actuality and certainly no necessity either to its existence or non-existence. There is a danger that human action is conceived either as wholly external to, or as wholly internal to, God: Schelling thus insists that human action is an expression of God's own relation to himself, which is a relation between ground and existence and which is expressed as both life and becoming. Dews suggests, in a characteristically deep insight, that this strategy of affirmation, danger and denial may be a display of two different tendencies. The first is an endless displacement of the metaphysical location: from individual to world, to God, to un-ground, as each pair of terms generates a correspondingly higher logical ground of unity. But the second is more destructive: we may be seeing in Schelling's thought 'the idea of God himself being undermined by the attempt to understand him as life rather than system – and hence as vulnerable to, and indeed as imperilled by, the conflict of good and evil, whose ferocity depends on his existence'.[18] In other words, when considering the familiar triangle of God's omnipotence, God's goodness and the fact of evil, Schelling's thought may tend to undermine God's omnipotence. This is normally thought to be a characteristically twentieth-century development. It is interesting that Dews sees signs of it in Schelling's account of an un-ground that is logically prior even to God.

The impact of Idealism on the topic of evil is, in the case of Schelling, the development of forms of thinking that are neither overtly Augustinian nor Leibnizian, but not Kantian either. It is a dialectic that has the character of a slippery eel. Opposed terms generate an encompassing third, or 'ground'.

Each ground is found to contain further opposed terms that in turn generate an encompassing third, or 'ground'. Each time such a ground is grasped, the act of grasping causes it to jump out of one's hands. This could continue indefinitely, so Schelling tries out a strategy of refusing to name the third a 'ground': instead it is an 'un-ground'. But this conceptual tool is actually too powerful and causes the very idea of God to fracture.

If Schelling explicitly rejects the Augustinian account, he implicitly affirms at least aspects of it. Schelling may deny that evil is a privation of the good, but all the same he insists that evil in some sense *is* the good. Like Augustine, he insists that evil is inexplicable. It is possible that, despite his protestations, his account is a dissenting opinion within a court whose constitution is essentially Augustinian. By contrast, Hegel's account of evil, as we shall see now, is more explicitly Leibnizian in form (although not in tone): it seeks to justify God's being through treating evil as explicable, to a limited extent.

Like Kant and Schelling, Hegel views evil less as a privation of the good than as a decision to privilege the particular over the universal, or the individual's perceived good over the community's good. Like Kant and Schelling, Hegel rejects the Enlightenment belief that humanity is naturally good: he takes humanity as it comes, in all its selfishness, savagery and fearfulness. Such human displays are in a certain sense 'natural' for Hegel, and even 'inevitable': they are evidence that humanity is not what it should be, what it can be. The meaning of terms such as 'natural' or 'necessary' are not at all obvious when reading Hegel. Hegel does not mean a 'state of nature' or logical 'necessity'. He has a somewhat idiosyncratic account of them: to be 'natural' is to be undeveloped, implicit, unrealised. It has much more in common with Aristotle's *dunamis* than with medieval *natura*. At the same time, Hegel takes the Biblical account in Genesis seriously and draws attention to the fact that the fall into evil is simultaneously the acquisition of knowledge. We are creatures with moral knowledge. We have knowledge of the difference between good and evil, and for Hegel this is bound up with the fact that there is no escaping evil.[19]

Dews offers the most subtle and well-argued analysis of Hegel's account of evil in English to date. He confronts squarely the common criticisms of Hegel. It is alleged that evil is merely 'dialectical' for Hegel, in the sense that it is a necessary moment along a path to the good. It is alleged that evil is 'necessary' for Hegel, in the sense that it serves an indispensable function as humanity develops. It is alleged that Hegel is 'optimistic' in the sense that there is a pre-determined historical goal in which things breezily turn out for the best. These allegations are widespread and well known. Part of the impact of Idealism on discussions of evil is a rejection of this 'Hegelian' theodicy through a recovery of a supposedly more Kantian focus on radical evil. Dews identifies Theodor Adorno and Hans Jonas as particularly trenchant critics of Hegel.[20] There are many others, including Friedrich Tholuck, Julius Müller and Søren Kierkegaard. Dews does not dismiss these criticisms as simply false, but he shows that they do not represent a satisfactory engagement with the complexity of Hegel's texts from the *Encyclopaedia* (especially as interpreted by Michael Theunissen) or the *Lectures on the Philosophy of Religion* (which Dews himself exegetes carefully). Idealism, in Dews' interpretation, deserves to have a different impact on accounts of evil: one that understands Hegel's approach as much more concerned with confronting the failures of Kant's account of evil on the one hand, and with taking contingency and suffering with full seriousness on the other.

Dews' analysis is detailed and textually well supported: a summary of its main shape can be given relatively quickly. The important failures (as Hegel sees them) with Kant's account of evil are that it ruinously separates virtue and happiness (which had been bound together for Aristotle); it regards duty as an abstract property of self-consciousness rather than viewing it as something objective (for consciousness) as well as subjective (for self-consciousness); the moral subject for Kant is generally the individual rather than, as for Hegel, the community; Kant attributes to the individual a primordial propensity to evil that is an expression, right from the start, of its 'intelligible character', whereas for Hegel it is simply the case that one grows up more or less wicked, depending on many factors, including education; Kant's 'morality' is one in which one privileges the purity of intention over the messy business of compromise and taking responsibility for situations one did not cause; the Kantian moral subject often finds itself poised at a point of decision: shall I do good or evil? For Hegel such a question is already an expression of evil. Most interestingly, for a volume on religion, Kant plays out his moral theory in an account of reason divorced from tradition, whereas Hegel thinks it quite proper to investigate in detail the account of the fall in Genesis and to try to make sense of the doctrine of the Trinity as a model for making sense of the relation of consciousness to self-consciousness.

The theme of contingency and suffering in Hegel is one that invites serious and detailed investigation because Hegel displays contrary tendencies. On the one hand Hegel has an unusually intense focus on conflict, struggle, strife and suffering as basic to reality. This is present at a fundamental level in his concern with negativity in the system and is also displayed in such topics as the death of God, the speculative Good Friday, infinite anguish and many others. It is also manifest in Hegel's typically clear-eyed characterisation of human history: it is a slaughter-bench whose marks are bloodshed and brutality. On the other hand, Hegel always refuses to give such darkness the last word. He is insistent on the reality of recognition, of reconciliation, of movement forward, of resolution and of a final identity between the real and the rational. Good Friday is followed by Easter. Conflict is followed by forgiveness. Dews makes it plain that the task confronting the interpreter is how to relate these contrary tendencies to one another. He acknowledges that Hegel is often taken to stage a pre-arranged triumph of victory over suffering, of resurrection over crucifixion, of good over evil: the consequence of this reading is that the suffering is not 'real': it is a sham angst that secretly knows that everything will have a happy ending. Dews denies that this is Hegel's view. Through repeated exegesis of the relevant texts, he shows persuasively that Hegel's tendency is to insist on discerning movement, even in cases of apparently comprehensive breakdown. For Hegel tragedy is taken seriously, but it is never so decisive that it rules out the possibility of reconciliation. Evil is utterly real for Hegel, but it is never so powerful as finally to engulf the good. A great deal turns on whether one thinks Hegel is yet another dishonest optimist or considers him to be insisting always on hope without guarantees. Everything hangs on how one interprets his remarks about 'necessity'. If this is taken as an expression of modal logic, then Hegel is the worst kind of optimist, because he pretends to take tragedy seriously. If it is taken to be an insistence on the attraction of the always-available good, then his is the best kind of hope, because it really does take tragedy seriously.

Dews offers a salutary lesson. The impact of Idealism on discussions of evil remains unrealised so long as Hegel is not read carefully. Hegel holds together and performs the contradiction of two opposing tendencies and typically produces sober and realistic conceptions of reality, combined with an unyielding emphasis on the social dimensions of moral action. It is the societies in which we are formed that determine the quality of our ethical life, not some timelessly eternal and yet mysteriously individual moral consciousness. From time to time, the individual will subdues the universal good, catastrophes follow and from their crises new possibilities arise. This is not a statement of inevitability or a guarantee of success. It is one of the lessons of history. But it is here that Dews poses his fundamental challenge to Hegel. Against the majority opinion of the theological tradition, which places its hope in an eschaton in which all creation and all time is reconciled – even and especially the destroyed and the long departed – Hegel seems to say only that the future is marked by hope. There is no justice for the dead.[21]

Taken as a pair of contrasting approaches to evil one can see in the wake of Schelling and Hegel a variety of possible impacts of Idealism that remain largely untapped. Dews offers an invaluable starting point for fresh investigations of the texts, with a view to judging contemporary moral theory against the sophistication of the accounts found in Schelling and Hegel. Dews himself goes on to consider Schopenhauer, Nietzsche, Lévinas and Adorno: space prevents exploring those accounts here. Whether it is the Schellingian pattern of unceasing ontological displacements or the Hegelian model of logic in which opposites are held in constant mutual relation, there is a series of tasks awaiting the next generation of intellectuals who seek to take tragedy and evil seriously and a rich library of Idealist texts whose subtleties have in many cases only begun to be explored.

The impact (and lack of impact) of Idealism

One of the most remarkable features of contemporary theological study is a general awareness of the impact of Idealism accompanied by a more specific failure to say much about it. There is an implicit impact of Idealism that is rarely made explicit. This is easily demonstrated. There are many books about twentieth-century German and Swiss theologians. The latter include Barth, Tillich, Bonhoeffer, von Balthasar, Pannenberg, Rahner, Moltmann, Jüngel and many others. It is often remarked that these figures contribute to a theological heritage that stretches back to German Idealism and postgraduate students who investigate these figures quickly learn that Hegel (and to a lesser but significant extent Fichte and Schelling) are crucially important. It is not long before Kant is found to be an utterly central figure. At the same time, it is surprisingly difficult to find out what, exactly, this importance and centrality means. If one says, as many rightly do, that Pannenberg is influenced by Hegel, what exactly is this influence? If one observes, as many rightly do, that Barth's thought is in many ways a complex engagement with the Idealist inheritance, how exactly does this play out? Most students find to their immense and justified frustration that these questions are rarely answered in any detail. Similarly, if one browses the impressive array of *Cambridge Companions* to Barth, to Bonhoeffer, to von Balthasar, to Rahner and to many others, one will find in their indices a number of references to Kant and, to a lesser extent, to Hegel and others. Yet if one turns to the pages in question, they contain little more information than the index entries themselves: the names appear, in passing, but little of consequence is actually rehearsed. These are familiar and oft-remarked disappointments for students of theology.

What are the reasons for this lack of impact of Idealism in scholarship in English? They are probably not obscure. The apprenticeship of young systematic theologians includes a diet deficient in philosophy in general, and in Idealist philosophy in particular. A student who embarks on a doctorate on Barth has a formidable bibliography to master before one introduces such unwelcome suggestions as the need to read and understand Hegel's *Lectures on the Philosophy of Religion*. The latter task represents several months of scholarly labour and includes investigation into late eighteenth-century rationalist theology on the one hand, and Kantian philosophy on the other. It is a rabbit hole of daunting darkness and a wise and compassionate advisor may well caution against being dragged down it. On the other side, the apprenticeship of young continental philosophers includes a diet deficient in theology in general, and in twentieth-century German and Swiss theology in particular. A student working on Heidegger or Adorno, or on Hegel or Schelling, has a truly gigantic reading list before one suggests that it might be helpful to learn a little about the theological traditions which shape their thinking. Every advisor whose student embarks on the study of Hegel fears, with good reason, that the dissertation will never be completed because the study of Hegel affords many opportunities for endless further reading. It is a triumph to see such a dissertation to completion, without the added burden of theological enquiry. The double consequence is that systematic theologians know very little about German Idealism and continental philosophers know very little about German and Swiss theology. It is a rare conference indeed where they encounter one another; and it is a rare book that has as its author one who has served apprenticeships in both fields. Even where they exist, most students will find them unusually difficult for obvious reasons: understanding them requires precisely the double focus that most readers lack.

This volume is thus ambitious and timely. Its contributors have selected themselves in most cases: they are those whose reading has included German Idealism and German and Swiss theology. Their task is to make implicit connections explicit and to model the kinds of enquiry that will lead to deeper engagements across disciplines. They constitute a modest beginning to this endeavour. Each essay represents only the tip of the iceberg. They are, we hope, valuable iceberg tips that invite further study and stimulate deeper enquiry. This volume makes a start. There is much work to be done.

Notes

1. But see the chapter on 'Scottish Idealism' by David Fergusson in Volume I of the present work.
2. For a consideration of Marx, see Nicholas Lash, *A Matter of Hope: A Theologian's Reflections on the Thought of Karl Marx* (London: Darton, Longman and Todd, 1981).
3. D. F. Strauss, *Das Leben Jesu kritisch bearbeitet* (Tübingen: Osiander, 1835); *The Life of Jesus Critically Examined*, trans. M. Evans (London: Chapman Brothers, 1846).
4. See chapter 10. See also Nicholas Adams, 'The Bible' in Nicholas Adams, George Pattison, Graham Ward (eds.), *The Oxford Handbook of Theology and Modern European Thought* (Oxford: Oxford University Press, 2013), 545–66.
5. See chapter 5.
6. Ludwig Feuerbach, *Das Wesen des Christentums* (Leipzig: Wigand, 1841, 2nd edn 1843); *The Essence of Christianity*, trans. M. Evans (New York: Blanchard, 1855), 3.
7. *Ibid.*, 93.
8. See Adams, 'The Bible'.
9. Peter Dews, *The Idea of Evil* (Oxford: Blackwell, 2007), 61–71 (on Schelling) and 81–117 (on Hegel). Dews does not attempt to trace the antecedent sources on which Schelling and Hegel draw; I do not attempt to remedy this.
10. *Ibid.*, 62.
11. *Ibid.*, 65–6.
12. *Ibid.*, 68.
13. *Ibid.*, 68. Dews' text has 'to turn the universal will into the basis of the basis'; I take this to be a typing error, and have corrected it.
14. *Ibid.*, 74. Dews' footnotes incorrectly refer to Fichte's *Vocation of Man*. From footnote 95 onwards, the references are to the *Freedom* essay.
15. *Ibid.*, 74–5.
16. *Ibid.*, 76.
17. *Ibid.*, 76, quoting Friedrich Wilhelm Josef von Schelling, *Philosophical Inquiries into the Nature of Human Freedom*, trans. James Gutman (La Salle: Open Court Classics, 1992), 85.
18. *Ibid.*, 76.
19. *Ibid.*, 86–7.
20. *Ibid.*, 83.
21. *Ibid.*, 111–12.

1

The impact of Idealism on Christology: from Hegel to Tillich

MARTIN WENDTE

Beginning with a consideration of Hegel's Christology, this essay charts certain stages of Idealism's influence on the Christological debate within the German-speaking world up to the theology of Tillich. Two aims are to the fore. The first is a contribution to historiography. It reconstructs a chapter in the history of theology that is often overlooked in Anglo-American thought, with a particular focus on recent German-language scholarship. The second is a contribution to systematic theology. In the historical positions outlined, problems are raised and solutions are offered that current Christological debate forgets at some cost. This is true as much in questions of methodology as in matters of substance. In debates around Idealism and its impact, it will become clear that Christology is concerned not only with the person and works of Jesus Christ, but also with the very heart of theology, and thus with the categories which form the foundation and core of theological and philosophical thought as a whole. A series of questions comes into view. What are the relations between reason, faith and history, between the absolute and the relative? How are we to reconcile Christianity and other religions? What place can Christianity claim for itself in modernity? In contemporary theology these fundamental questions are rarely considered matters of Christology, but for the Idealist tradition they are, I shall show, essentially bound up with it.

The essay is divided into five sections: (1.1) Hegel's Christology, which situates Christology in the sphere of theoretical reason, redefining it in terms of speculative absolutes; (1.2) its transmission through Philipp Konrad Marheineke, Ferdinand Christian Baur and David Friedrich Strauss; (1.3) responses to it in Isaak August Dorner and Søren Kierkegaard; (1.4) its impact on Emanuel Hirsch and Paul Tillich; and (1.5) its relevance for the present. Reasons of space force certain omissions. The two most obvious are Kant and the tradition of ethical theology that followed him, and Schleiermacher's theology with its grounding in his account of consciousness and its profound historical influence on the theology of mediation. Discussion of Schelling's Christology will be limited to its influence on Tillich.[1]

1.1 Hegel's Christology

In some ways, Hegel's Christology represents the pinnacle of his thought. Hegel's system portrays the mediation of the absolute by the relative – of reason by history, of God by the world. This mediation (first) culminates in Jesus Christ, the historical person in whom the absolute is fully realised. The core methodological and categorical dimensions of Hegel's system are found in his reflections on Christology. Three are of particular interest: the dialectical mediation of reason and history, an understanding of history as process and Christology's compatibility with modernity.[2]

The mediation of reason and history reflects the rational core of Hegel's system, which finds its fullest expression in the concluding chapter of the *Science of Logic*, 'The absolute idea'.[3] Here, every apparently fixed position is shown to mediate itself through its other. The initial position, the general or thesis, does not rest within itself, but becomes its other, the particular or antithesis. This logical figure of the self-mediation of the one with its other, or the thesis with the antithesis to form its synthesis, is not merely limited to the realm of logic, but appears in natural and world history in the form of the mediation of reason with nature and history. This mediation forms the subject of religion, which in Jesus Christ is fully realised in a historical individual: Jesus Christ is the mediation between God and man. For Hegel, Jesus Christ exemplifies his fundamental claim that reality is rational. In Christ one sees the mediation of reason (God) and history (man), which, from the perspective of dialectical reason, is itself rational.[4]

This mediation is a process. This is true not only of Jesus Christ, who embodies the dialectical process itself in his life (thesis), death on the cross (antithesis) and resurrection in the Spirit (synthesis), but more broadly of the history of religion as a whole.[5] For Hegel the essence of religion consists in the reconciliation of God and man, where individual religions represent stages on the path towards the fulfilment of this reconciliation. Christianity is not primarily the end-point of historical development (other traditions, such as Islam, succeed it), but rather the absolute or consummate religion. In Christianity reconciliation is fully realised in one individual.[6] Since Jesus Christ represents the historical realisation of the fundamental structure of rational thought, Christianity itself is rational and represents the culmination of the history of religion.

Christianity is compatible with modernity. Hegel describes Christianity as justified in the eyes of modern reason precisely because of its Christological focus. This justification is dialectical in nature, too. Hegel integrates the perspective of the practising Christian into his system in such a way that he retains what he sees as the essential dogmatic substance of the Christian faith, whilst revealing its rational core; yet he also holds that the mediation of the absolute with the relative ultimately culminates not in Jesus Christ, but in individual human beings in community and, furthermore, not in the form of religious devotion but in that of speculative thought.[7] Christianity is compatible with modernity, but is not autonomous as theology; it is perfected in the speculative thought of Idealistic philosophy. The reconciliation of the Christ of faith, the rationally demonstrable unity of God and humanity and the historical Jesus which shapes Hegel's Christology – and so the reconciliation of faith, reason and history – is thus perfected not in the life, death and resurrection of the historical Son of God, nor in his appropriation by religion, but insofar as it is grasped speculatively.[8]

Hegel's account of mediation met with early opposition. Despite many differences, Hegel's critics share a concern to lend aspects of the particular, of the individual, of the antithesis, of negation a greater weight than Hegel appears to give them. It is an early criticism that Hegel failed to emphasise the full extent of the conflict between reason and history in his account of their mediation by ignoring the emerging question of the historical Jesus in his Christological thought. Some further criticised his Christology for being insufficiently ontological. These views will now be elaborated.

1.2 Hegel's early impact

Despite their differences, the four thinkers discussed in the following section – Marheineke, Baur, Strauss and Feuerbach – are participants in a single, highly dynamic and mutually influential communicative network. It displays three features. First, against a landscape of theological debate shaped by suprarationalism and rationalism, all four sought to work with Hegel's entirely new thought, whilst parts were still being published. Second, they responded to one another. Baur reacted to Marheineke and to Strauss; Strauss, as his student, was influenced by Baur. Strauss then made his name by challenging the received view of Hegelian thought. Third, the works of Baur, Strauss and Feuerbach display in various ways the antagonism between the particular and Hegel's sweeping synthesis mentioned above. Strauss and Baur, in particular, believed that Hegel's legacy had to be developed in new directions by rigorously conducted historical–critical research into Jesus, and that new work on integration remained to be done; the leading alternative came to be Feuerbach's more radical view of religion as a projection.

The question of history: Marheineke and Baur

Both chronologically and intellectually, Philipp Marheineke stands at the beginning of Hegel's historical reception. Marheineke (1780–1846) was a professor in Heidelberg from 1809 and then professor and preacher in Berlin from 1811. Initially influenced by Schelling's identity philosophy, he came to be influenced by his colleague Hegel from 1818.[9] He arranged the posthumous edition of Hegel's *Lectures on the Philosophy of Religion* and sparked animated controversies with the anti-religious left Hegelians by defending the claim that his religious right-Hegelian stance was the logical development of Hegel's fundamental approach. His *Grundlehren der christlichen Dogmatik als Wissenschaft* [*The Fundamentals of Christian Dogma as a Science*] was first published in 1819. The second edition (1827) was heavily revised along Hegelian lines and develops theology speculatively.[10] Doctrines were expounded conceptually to defend the objective truth of Christianity against modern scepticism in a way that opposed the suprarationalism and rationalism of his contemporaries.[11] Suprarationalism (e.g. in the Tübingen theologian Friedrich Gottlieb Süskind) refers to revelation in the Bible, but (against Kant) insists it cannot be deduced independently by reason; theological rationalism in this period (following Kant) seeks to limit reason to empirical phenomena, so that revelation is superfluous. By contrast, Marheineke supports the speculative compatibility of reason and revelation (and thus of philosophy and religion in a scientific theology as well). God can be located within human reason, revealed and rational. Both human and divine nature are interconnected. For human nature is in truth spirit, and thus 'the divine'.[12] Meanwhile, Marheineke maintains (initially at least) that God is only fully real when he reveals himself in the human spirit, since this in turn corresponds to his essence.[13]

The perfect historical realisation of this concept of the unity-in-difference between God and man is Jesus Christ: 'This unity of God with man is made phenomenally, or historically, manifest and tangible in the person of Jesus

Christ; in him, divine revelation is made entirely human.'[14] On the basis of this unity, Marheineke's teaching on reconciliation develops the view of Jesus Christ as the substitute for all.[15] He is the archetypal man: 'in him, all have died; all are offered in him to be a sacrifice before God.'[16] The reconciliation achieved in this way is gradually appropriated by individuals and ultimately made manifest not only in the Church, but also in the State.

Marheineke took himself to be following Hegel. His theology differs fundamentally from Hegel's, however. He conceives of God, and God's revelation, as independent of the human spirit, maintaining that what is revealed pre-exists objectively, as it were, and is apprehended entirely passively, and thus purely subjectively. God is a substance for which the relation to humanity is unnecessary: God's being-in-himself is not essentially linked to our being for ourselves. The reconciliation of the two, which is the central theme of Christology, is absent.[17]

Ferdinand Christian Baur (1792–1860), a Swabian, led the unremarkable life of a professor at Tübingen; his work, however, made him the 'greatest and most disputed' theologian, along with Schleiermacher, certainly of the nineteenth century, and the true father of historical-critical theology.[18] Baur writes as a historian of dogma, not as a constructive thinker, and his own views can often only be discerned from his portrayal of other positions.[19] Baur was initially influenced by Schleiermacher but then aligned himself somewhat more closely with Schelling in 1824 in his first major publication against the suprarational and rational (i.e. Enlightenment) forms of historiography. For whilst the suprarationalists saw the origin of Christianity as purely miraculous, Baur sought to explain its historical genesis, resembling here the rationalists. Yet the rationalists saw history as a succession of events and the history of dogma as a succession of human opinions. Baur, by contrast, sought to grasp them 'in [their] magnificent coherence as one great whole', such that world history is 'a revelation of the divine'.[20]

Following the reception of Hegel's recently published lectures, Baur portrays Hegel in his book on Gnosis from 1835 as the high point in the development of the history of religion and dogma, developing his own Idealist position in the process.[21] He regards history, especially the history of religion, as the development of the living God, in which God gives himself over to his other – to history – in order fully to become himself.[22] God in history and history itself advance through contradictions. Baur follows Hegel in developing a speculative view of history. At the same time, probably following Strauss, he departs from Hegel. He is the first historian of religion and dogma to engage in a rigorous historical-critical engagement with his sources. For Baur one can depict the reconciliation of God with humanity from the perspective of finite consciousness. Making this a principle of theological method is one of Baur's lasting achievements.

This method shaped Baur's Christology. He agrees with Hegel that, in Jesus Christ, the unity of divine and human nature appears in a historical individual.[23] Christianity thus represents the fulfilment of the history of both religion and philosophy, and is a 'turning point in world history'.[24] However, for Baur, Hegel's Christology fails to resolve a problem that already permeates the entire history of Christianity: the 'historical and the ideal Christ' are not satisfactorily reconciled to one another.[25] For Hegel recreates the ideal Christ – that is, the Christ of dogma and the speculative view of history – without drawing historical-critically on extant sources to balance him against the temporal Jesus. With Hegel, the ideal Christ is made perfect in his resurrection within humanity as a whole, which is the 'universal individual'.[26] Against Hegel, Baur privileges scholarship into the 'historically given, objective reality' of the historical Jesus, which was the very first cause from which faith developed and which is thus the true measure by which we understand the essence of Christianity.[27]

Baur's Christology can be described briefly. He treated the Gospels as historical sources for a reconstruction of Jesus' significance.[28] The heart of Jesus' teaching consists of him approaching people about their moral sense and calling for a perfect attitude, in which individuals surrender themselves entirely to God's Will, without inner division. Such a pure moral attitude places the individual in the right relationship to God.[29] For this heart of Jesus' teaching to take hold successfully as the heart of a new religion, and not to remain simply one interesting doctrine amongst many, it needed to be associated with a founder who carried exceptional significance for the people around him. Jesus saw himself as Messiah, whilst also himself embodying the moral attitude to the highest possible degree. Jesus' death called his claim to be the Messiah into question; the resurrection, grasped historically in the faith of the disciples, led the latter to claim with certainty that Jesus was the Messiah.

Baur departed from Hegel with his historical-critical reconstruction of the historical Jesus using both his own evaluation and established facts; Hegel privileged the 'witness of the spirit' above historical-critical approaches, especially in relation to the New Testament. But Baur arguably upheld Hegel's fundamental approach to Christology as the reconciliation of the spirit with historical reality, even if he located that reconciliation within the conditions of historico–critical research. More importantly, Baur's work displays a significant Kantian shift in priorities compared with both Hegel's approach and his own earlier analysis, itself shaped by Hegel, of the nature of religion, its history and Christianity. From 1852–3 onwards, Baur not only described the heart of Jesus' doctrine as a morally pure disposition, but also maintained that this morality (and not the manifestation of the unity between divine and human nature in the person of Jesus Christ) formed the inner essence of Christianity, and thus represented the 'absolutely fundamental element of its being'.[30]

The left-Hegelian collapse of Hegel's synthesis: Strauss

No theological work of the nineteenth century caused more commotion than the two volumes of *The Life of Jesus, Critically Examined*, which D. F. Strauss (1808–74) published in 1835.[31] Whilst studying at the seminary in Blaubeuren, Strauss had been taught by Baur and was introduced to Hegel's philosophy in the course of his degree. *The Life of Jesus* was so sensational that Strauss was dismissed from his postgraduate post at the Tübingen Stift, and was never subsequently employed at a university. Yet the fundamental approach taken by Strauss, which he had already formulated by 1831 and maintained until his death, displays Hegel's impact.[32] Strauss wanted first to identify the parts of the New Testament on which dogma was founded (thesis), before submitting them to a double critique (antithesis). The previous attempts to reconstruct the historical contours of the life of Jesus were subjected to the same critique as the historical forms of the content of dogma. The content of Christianity was then to be reformulated speculatively (synthesis). With this approach Strauss sought to preserve the role of criticism – explicitly in difference to and surpassing Marheineke – and to identify the true, rationally demonstrable core of the contents of Christianity.[33] *The Life of Jesus* focuses almost entirely on the critique of previous attempts to reconstruct the life of Jesus. It concludes with a brief, critical overview of the history of dogma and a sketch of the speculative reformulation of Christology (the comprehensive critical examination of the history of dogma is found in his work *On Christian Doctrine*).[34]

In the public debate at the time, readers paid attention almost exclusively to the critical factor, which was revolutionary. Strauss claimed that the majority of stories about the life of Jesus in the Synoptic Gospels are not reports of events that actually took place, but fabrications of the communities who formed in the decades directly after Jesus' death and resurrection. Strauss calls these fabrications 'myths'. To use Strauss' own definition, 'myths [are] nothing other than the historically styled guises of the earliest Christian ideas, fashioned into the inadvertently poetic fable form. All ideas which the first Christians had about their ascended master were transformed into facts.'[a,35] In the communities' stories, the life of Jesus thus accrued many aspects of the life and impact of a Messiah. Mythological interpretations were not entirely new; two aspects stood out, however. Strauss was the first to apply such interpretations to all of the material regarding the life, death and resurrection of Jesus. Furthermore, he viewed myths as poetic creations of the communities, with no historical core.[36]

By contrast, certain 'eternal truths' must be grasped in a speculative form, thus differing markedly from the tradition of dogmatic history, whilst remaining a direct link to Hegel.[37] Along with Hegel, Strauss maintains that our concept of divine nature includes the notion that it should mediate itself with the finite as its 'other', just as our concept of human nature contains its self-mediation with the divine. Thus for Christianity the union of divine and human nature occurs in history. Unlike Hegel, however, Strauss does not see how the entire fullness of the divine Spirit can pour itself out into one individual. Instead, it is more reasonable to assume that it is made incarnate in the entire human race: 'humanity represents the marriage of both natures, the God made man'[b], and all other aspects of Christology pertain to humanity as a whole.[38]

While taking himself to be following Hegel, Strauss' focus on humanity dissociates what Hegel and Baur sought to hold together, whether with or without a historical-critical method: the historical Jesus and the inner core of the faith. Instead, Strauss describes Christology's eternal truths from the speculative (Baur would have said 'ideal') perspective alone. In contrast to Hegel, Strauss understands the critic's work not as the reconstruction of speculative findings, but rather sets up his speculative insights as presuppositions that the critic must confirm.[39] From 1839 Strauss reassessed the degree to which his account was Christian.[40] He now questioned the validity of Hegel's view, according to which Christianity and the contemporary philosophy and science could be reconciled. For Strauss Christianity is shaped right down to the core by the dichotomy between God and the world, and that between Jesus Christ and all people, whilst speculative thought about these ideas leads in a monist direction. The left-Hegelian Strauss thus dissociates not only the reconciliation of the speculative Christ with the historical Jesus, but also that between modernity and Christianity: the synthesis of the

a. 'Mythen nichts Andres, als geschichtsartige Einkleidungen urchristlicher Ideen, gebildet in der absichtslos dichtenden Sage. . . . Alle Ideen, welche die erste Christenheit über ihren entrissenen Meister hatte, verwandelte sie in Thatsachen.' Strauss, *Leben Jesu*, i, 75.
b. 'Die Menschheit ist die Vereinigung der beiden Naturen, der menschgewordene Gott.' *Ibid.* ii, 735.

historical Jesus, the Christ of faith and the divine man of modern speculation collapses.

1.3 Two original outsiders between reintegration and disintegration: Dorner and Kierkegaard

Isaak August Dorner (1809–84) undertakes in his *System of Christian Doctrine* (1879–81), the impressive task of reconciling faith, speculative reason and historical consciousness, and correspondingly the Christ of faith, the unity of divine and human natures, and the historical Jesus, in a new way.[41] Dorner studied under Baur in Tübingen, was a contemporary of Strauss at the Tübinger Stift, and wrote his work as a professor in Berlin in a period that was saturated with Ritschl's Kantian understanding of Christianity: he considered himself an outsider.[42] He incorporates the thought of Schleiermacher and Hegel in a creative and original way.[43] Like Schleiermacher, he takes the Christian faith as the starting point for his work, since this represents the necessary context within which discoveries about theology can be made. Like Hegel, however, he goes on to develop the doctrine of the immanent Trinity as the context in which theology and faith itself are based, as faith points away from itself towards God as its central content and foundation. The contents of the doctrine on God and the other theological loci are, on the one hand, developed in a speculative way, and thus in such a way that the conceptual contents are themselves the subject of reflection. On the other hand, these conceptual elements are balanced by a concern with historical events.

Three of Dorner's assertions are also of particular importance when applied more closely to his Christology. First, Dorner develops the doctrine of the immanent Trinity as God's single absolute personality made manifest in the three modes of being of Father, Son as Logos and Spirit.[44] By this way of thinking, God is characterised by aseity, which is precisely what enables him to create, and open himself to, a true 'other' in freedom and out of love.[45] Second, it is speculatively speaking part of God's very nature as God to disclose himself to man, whilst man is characterised by the fact that he is receptive to God's self-disclosure; the reconciliation of the two is therefore made possible by virtue of their difference.[46] This reconciliation, written into the natures of both participants, is made manifest as revelation in religions, and Christianity is the 'fulfilment' of all religions insofar as it contains the 'absolute human incarnation of God' as its central tenet.[47] Third, the notion that the historical Jesus is the perfect revelation of God corresponds precisely to the teaching of the New Testament and Dorner expends considerable energy demonstrating the agreement between the results of his historical-critical research and the main features of his Christology.[48]

The centre of Dorner's Christology is the unity between God and man. Dorner defines this unity in such a way that the person, or the self, represents the result, not the necessary precondition, of the union of both natures.[49] He thus departed from the tradition following Chalcedon, which first placed the hypostasis in relation to divine or human nature before incorporating the other nature. In the process, however, it arguably subordinated the second nature to the first, such that a one-sided Christology (whether Docetist or anthropocentric) threatens to emerge. According to Dorner, however, the self develops out of both natures – out of human nature and the divine nature of the Logos, which is not a personality in itself, but shares in the absolute personality of God – as the self only exists as an act, and thus represents the 'eternally present self-creation' of the natures' unity.[50]

As the site of this unity between God and man, Jesus Christ is thus the 'central individual' of human history.[51] In his humanity, he is thus not merely a human like all others, but the 'second Adam', permeated by a perfect receptivity towards God.[52] Dorner takes up first Schleiermacher's and then Hegel's legacy when he further explains that Christ, as the second Adam, is the 'archetype' and head of humanity that should shape everyone.[53] He then emphasises that 'the incarnation of the Logos in its totality . . . as the centre of the world' is achieved in Christ as the human centre of the world.[54]

At the same time, Dorner insists that the formation of the unity takes place as a process that develops throughout the entire life of Jesus Christ.[55] The Logos is immutable and is therefore present in Jesus from the beginning of his life; yet it grows with the consciousness and will of Jesus' human nature, along with the unity between the divine and the human, since the human side of Jesus becomes increasingly receptive to the Logos, which can, in turn, reconcile itself ever more fully with the human side. How, precisely, to conceive simultaneously of both – the fullness of the Logos, present from the very beginning, and the ongoing process of increasing unity – was, however, considered even by Dorner himself to be a task which was almost impossible, but with which thought, in order to preserve the true humanity of Jesus, was unavoidably charged.[56]

Søren Kierkegaard (1813–55) was familiar with Idealistic philosophy after studying a year in Berlin shortly after Hegel's death, as well as from his Danish professors who were influenced by Idealism.[57] In the first period of his work, he developed the main elements of his Christology in a work that declared its opposition to Hegel's *Encyclopaedia of the Philosophical Sciences* in its very title: *Philosophical Fragments* (1844).[58] The title itself challenges speculative thought's claim to be exhaustive with the fragmentary nature of human existence and reason when faced with God and God's works.[59] In opposition to Socrates, who prefigures the Hegelian model in believing that it is possible to discover human truth and the reconciliation of God and humanity in man's act of speculative remembrance itself, the pseudonymous author of the *Fragments* insists on the impossibility of such a venture. God differs infinitely from man. The fact that God approaches humanity through revelation is thus not the expression of a movement necessary to God's nature owing to the composition of his being; rather it is the expression of his unmediated and absolute freedom, which he exercises out of pure love. In the same way, man is initially completely separated from God because of sin, so that he is able to come to God not because of his innate disposition or abilities, but only by virtue of the revelation that exists externally and prior to him.[60]

God reveals himself amidst suffering in the form of a servant in the utterly ordinary man, Jesus; and this revelation occurs ontologically as a moment, but in noetic terms as a paradox.[61] The moment refers to the single point in the present where the eternal enters into time. Here, reason reaches its limit, so that it experiences revelation as a paradox, even a double paradox. For in revelation, man first becomes aware of his sinful nature and thus the absolute contrast between him and God; at the same time he sees clearly that God standing at an infinite distance from man draws infinitely close to man. Just as man cannot fathom this act of God by reason, so he cannot respond appropriately to it with reason, but by an existential act of faith, through which man becomes contemporaneous with Christ.[62] Only this is in accordance with the truth and revelation, which must be constantly appropriated anew to give substance to life.[63]

The paradoxical Christology of the early Kierkegaard not only firmly divides the Christ of faith and all speculation about the unity between God and man from one another, but also reduces the point of contact between the Christ of faith and the historical Jesus to the mere fact that Jesus once existed historically. For the early Kierkegaard faith in Christ is not the product of historical study.[64] In his main work on Christology, *Practice in Christianity*, and other writings from the same period, meanwhile, the late Kierkegaard sketches a more detailed image of Jesus Christ within history as a paragon and a reconciler, on whom man seeks to model himself in imitation and faith.[65] Here, Christ meets man in a dialectic that cannot be sublated: as the suffering Christ he is, according to his human nature, the model man, whom the individual seeks to imitate in his own life. Yet the individual discovers that he is not able to imitate, but is a sinner in need of grace. At this point, Christ meets him as the reconciler who, according to his divine nature, adopts the individual by grace. Once adopted, however, the man in faith is instantly charged once again with the imitation of suffering following Christ's example, in the course of which he soon becomes conscious of the need for a new gift of grace from Christ the reconciler. Despite the fact that the late Kierkegaard enriches his Christology with the motifs of the suffering Jesus Christ, thereby reconciling it with the historical Jesus Christ, even this late Christology remains a thorn in reason's side. For if reason seeks to conceive of the unity between God and man in Christ, it can only apprehend it as an absolute, overlooking in particular the sinfulness of man and the particularity of this historical situation:

> The God-man is not the union of God and man – such terminology is a profound optical illusion. The God-man is the unity of God and an individual human being. That the human race is or is supposed to be in kinship with God is ancient paganism; but *that* an individual human being is God is Christianity, and this particular human being is the God-man. . . . and no relation to the God-man is possible without beginning with the situation of contemporaneity.[66]

Kierkegaard therefore is led by theological, hamartiological, christological and anthropological concerns to explode the Idealist synthesis between the historical Jesus and the Christ of faith and to reject the speculative reconciliation of God and man. Kierkegaard insisted that Christ should remain an outsider in the supposedly Christian modern world.

1.4 The impact of Idealism on the Christological thought of Emanuel Hirsch and Paul Tillich

In Hirsch and Tillich we find Idealism's influence on two of the most important German theologians of the first half of the twentieth century. Faced with an attitude towards intellectual history in Germany which was permeated by the biased favouring of historicising, anti-speculative thought, the early Hirsch and Tillich turned to Idealistic thinkers. Through their own research into Fichte and Schelling, respectively, Hirsch and Tillich contributed to the renaissance of Idealism in the 1910s and 1920s. The fundamental insights that they attained would especially shape their approaches to Christology.

Emanuel Hirsch (1888–1972) was a National Socialist, rightly stripped of his chair at Göttingen after 1945. In his central work on systematic theology, *The Christian Account*, he put forward what some see as the most ambitious neo-Protestant work of the twentieth century.[67] This work is taken by contemporary scholars to be more than far-right pseudo-scholarship and is currently experiencing a renaissance in Germany. Christology forms the core subject matter of the work. Hirsch links the historical Jesus both with reflections on the nature of knowledge in the wake of Fichte and with the Christ of faith (cast in Hirsch's distinctive idiom).[68] In so doing, Hirsch seeks to develop a Christology that can withstand the crisis of transformation in the modern era. All Christian beliefs are taken to have to justify themselves before the modern consciousness' concept of truth and they thus change their medieval, but also their older Protestant forms (and partly contents as well), and have to be grasped in a new form so that the man of the present can be a Christian with an honest heart.

Hirsch translates all statements about Christ-in-himself into statements about Christ-for-us. Jesus Christ is the revelation of God only in his relation to the faithful conscience, not independently of it.[69] Hirsch takes a theory of subjectivity, developed from Fichte, as the starting point of his *Account*. Hirsch also rejects a speculatively integrated discussion of Christ and arranges his central Christological investigations into the discussions of the word and of faith. The 'Word of God' is divided into the 'Word as Revelation', 'the Word as reconciliation' and the 'Word as new creation'. As space is limited, we will focus on the first of these in what follows. Hirsch follows Luther in that he only ever recognises the Word of God as revelation in the double structure of the law and the Gospel. The concept of law is grasped broadly and signifies the 'ethico-religiously reflected interaction with reality in general'.[c] Through the revelation of law, man becomes transparent to himself as one who does not determine himself, but nonetheless desperately tries to do so. The lasting truth of the revelation of law consists of bringing man face to face with this aporetic simultaneity of creatureliness and sinfulness. It is, however, untrue in that it further urges man to justify himself before God by his own efforts. The truth of the Gospel resides in the

---

c. 'Ethisch-religiös reflektierten Umgang mit Wirklichkeit überhaupt.' Ulrich Barth, *Die Christologie Emanuel Hirschs* (Berlin and New York: de Gruyter, 1992), 596.

fact that, instead of the untruth of the law, it reveals the truth of the loving God, who saves out of mercy alone.[70]

According to Hirsch, this classification of the underlying concepts of revelation can be developed purely theoretically. Of course, revelation itself never occurs purely theoretically; rather, it is only realised when 'a human-historical reality becomes an encounter with God in my mind, heart and conscience'.[d] The human-historical reality in which Christian revelation takes place is the life of the man Jesus, which should be researched closely following the historical-critical method, which should also thematise Jesus' consciousness of God along with his despair upon the Cross. Jesus' life is not the revelation: 'Only insofar as the living God makes our encounter with him into the Word which determines his own presently divine, and our human, consciousness can it be said that God is made manifest in Jesus, his Word and his history'.[e] Continuing to consider the historical Jesus, this occurs when Jesus appears as the teacher of and witness to the good news, which bears witness to his doctrine in his life. Thanks to revelation, the individual looking on can appropriate existentially what he perceives historically in such a way that he 'receives Jesus' knowledge of the Father as the basis of his own life'.[f]

The antinomian structure of the revelation of the law and the Gospel, embodied by Jesus, corresponds to the general human consciousness of truth. In the wake of the late Fichte, the structure of knowledge as such is also understood in an antinomian way, and thus displays the structure of absolute negativity. Knowledge becomes transparent to itself precisely because it does not grasp itself as an absolute, for it is preceded by being, where it also finds its limit and negates itself. At the same time, knowledge knows itself to be established in being as well.

> Hirsch's Christology thus forms the systematic centre of his theology, because it is the version of a theory of absolute negativity and reconciliation which is consistent with the theory of subjectivity, and which [derives from Fichte and (MW)] finds its religious counterpart in the image of Jesus from the *theologia crucis*.[g]

d. 'Daß eine menschlich-geschichtliche Wirklichkeit mir zur Begegnung mit Gott in Sinn, Herz und Gewissen wird.' E. Hirsch, *Christliche Rechenschaft*, ed. Hayo Gerdes (Tübingen: Katzmann, 1989), ii, 9 (§73).
e. 'Nur indem uns der lebendige Gott die Begegnung mit ihm zu seinem eignen gegenwärtig göttlichen, unsre menschliche Subjektivität bestimmenden Worte macht, wird es wahr, daß Gott in Jesus, seinem Wort und seiner Geschichte, offenbar ist.' *Ibid.*, 11 (§73).
f. 'Jesu Erkenntnis des Vaters zum eignen Lebensgrund empfängt.' *Ibid.*, 23 (§74).
g. 'Hirschs Christologie bildet darum das systematische Zentrum seiner Theologie, weil sie die konsequent subjektivitätstheoretische Fassung einer Theorie absoluter Negativität und

In Hirsch's Christology, the Christ of faith, the historical Jesus and the rational structure of knowledge itself thus find a form of reconciliation which has passed through the modern crisis of transformation, and which is therefore capable of being integrated into the general consciousness of truth.

Hirsch's theory of knowledge is influenced by Fichte, but the form of Hirsch's theory diverges from the versions put forward by the three great Idealists, Hegel, Fichte and Schelling, in that he posits the theory of subjectivity as the site of integration, not a system which transcends and encompasses the subject, i.e. the absolute. Hirsch clarifies in particular the difference between him and Hegel and Schelling. He stresses that modern conditions require a system also to function as a philosophy of history. Following Kierkegaard, Hirsch maintains, amongst other things, that an overarching philosophy of history levels all particulars within history. On this point, he diverges fundamentally from Tillich, with whom he was in dialogue for many years, and who sought to produce a comprehensive system which met twentieth-century intellectual demands.[71]

Paul Tillich (1886–1965) was the son of a priest from Breslau. He studied in Breslau and Berlin and devoted his philosophical doctoral thesis of 1910, as well as his theological thesis of 1912, to Schelling's philosophy. Both works are not only situated at the beginning of Schelling's contemporary reception, but are entirely original in that they present the first discussion of Schelling's later 'positive' philosophy. Schelling fundamentally shaped Tillich's theological thought, and his Christology above all. This is evident both in the *Systematic Theology* of 1913, which is the central work of his early phase whilst also paving the way for his later thought, and also in his major late work of the same name, the *Systematic Theology* which appeared between 1955 and 1966. In his *Systematic Theology* of 1913, Christology provides a structure that forms the point of intersection between a philosophy of mind, an analysis of the nature of Christianity, a philosophy of history and a theological cosmology.[72] These levels are all linked by the concept of paradox. Tillich inherits this concept from Kierkegaard, yet employs it less as an anti-speculative concept than as the principle of integration between the various levels.[73] As Tillich states in the introductory section on the philosophy of religion, the nature of the mind is fundamentally shaped by a basic Christological structure, since it consists of the irreconcilably different but nevertheless interrelated elements of intuition and reflection.[74] Intuition's role is to make a start; reflection is at once written into the intuition, whilst

Vermittlung ist, die [von Fichte herkommt und (MW)] ihre religiöse Entsprechung im Jesus-Bild der *theologia crucis* findet.' Barth, *Christologie*, 629.

nevertheless struggling against it, despite depending upon it, and eventually it returns to it. Tillich describes the relationship between intuition and reflection as a paradox.[75] The place where the paradox – and therefore the structural centre-point of the mind – enters history is religion. The essence of Christianity is the fact that the absolute (or the intuition) has entered into the relative (the reflection). In Jesus Christ the paradox is made manifest in an individual being, and that makes Christianity the absolute religion.[76] The paradox is realised in a radical way on the cross, where the moments at which the relative transcends itself, and returns to the absolute, are acted out simultaneously.

Tillich's reconstruction of the reconciliation of the absolute with the relative is shaped by Schelling in three ways, and in the third, at least, decisively surpasses Hirsch.[77] First, he defines the central question that is considered in Christology as the relation of tension between speculation and history. Second, the rationality of this relation corresponds to Schelling's later theory of potencies. In contrast to Hegel, Tillich emphasises the relative isolation of the moment of reflection (or the moment of the particular, the antithesis, the individual, etc.) as opposed to intuition (the general, the thesis, the absolute, etc.), and so also sees Schelling as the father of existentialism.[78] Third, the realisation of the paradox occurring within history can be seen in two ways. It appears when the self-descent of the absolute is emphasised, as a history of revelation, when the relative and its ascent to the absolute are emphasised, as a history of humanity. Tillich follows Schelling by strengthening the history of revelation and even places it within a broad framework of the philosophy of history: the entirety of history was striving towards the moment of the Incarnation and this has consequences not only for the faithful subject but for the entire cosmos. Accordingly, it requires a comprehensive system, in order to discuss the various levels and the broad scope of the Christ-event.

For reasons of space, Tillich's late Christology can only be mentioned in passing here.[79] It represents the centre of the *Systematic Theology* not only in terms of structure, but also content, for it also lends the system as a whole its characteristic identity.[80] Tillich thus defines the task of his entire system by assimilating the driving desire of Schelling's thought to reconcile the eternal truth of the Christian message and the respective historical situation.[81] In Tillich's system, this reconciliation is achieved by means of the method of correlation, which – like all methods – needs to be suited to its subject matter, and which also has a Christological character. It seeks to establish a mediation between the human situation and eternal truth by explaining 'the contents of the Christian faith through existential questions and theological answers in mutual dependence'.[h,82] Christology is not only considered – as in the early Systematic Theology – within the framework of a universal history of revelation and in its meaning for the whole cosmos, but from an existential-theological perspective: as an answer to the alienation of humans under the conditions of their fallen existence, so that Christology is conceived as a function of soteriology.[83] Unlike the 1913 account, but still taking up Schelling's influences, the Christ-event is later grasped explicitly in ontological categories, namely as the new being. Hence Tillich's definition: 'Jesus as the Christ is the bearer of the new being in the totality of his being',[i] who overcomes alienation. As such, the Christ-event, which represents the reconciliation of the absolute with the contingently finite, is further understood as a paradox.

In the light of Tillich's confusing statements about the historical Jesus, however, one could question, in relation to both method and content, whether Tillich emphasises the finite moment as he intended. In terms of content, what is distinctive about Jesus is the fact that he constantly gives everything away; this is simply the Jesus who is the Christ.[84] In terms of methodology he makes two claims. On the one hand, the faithful adoption of Christ becomes illusory for the faithful when it cannot be connected to historical facts. On the other hand, however, faith can extricate itself from the historical Jesus, since it is grounded in its own image of Jesus Christ. As a result, the quest for the historical Jesus, which for Tillich is certain to fail, is necessary in itself and unproblematic for him.[85]

Tillich thus presents a comprehensive system shaped by Christology, which demonstrates the possibility of reconciling Christianity with the modern through the relation between philosophy and theology, insofar as it emphasises the uncompromising rationality of the phenomenon of revelation, without covering up the contingent and often contradictory character of human existence. Tillich therefore links reflections on the nature of reason with the Christ of faith and a profound appreciation of the emptiness of the historical situation into which Christ comes. It is however questionable whether he relieves the pressure from problems which arise with the question of the historical Jesus.

This problem links him to his great antagonist, the Swiss theologian Karl Barth. With Barth, the history of Idealism's influence enters a new, influential chapter, which, in many contexts of Barth's reception, also signals its

---

h. 'Die Inhalte des christlichen Glaubens durch existentielles Fragen und theologische Antworten in wechselseitiger Abhängigkeit.' P. Tillich, *Systematische Theologie* I/II (Berlin and New York: de Gruyter, 1987), i, 74.

i. 'Jesus als der Christus der Träger des Neuen Seins in der Totalität seines Seins ist.' *Ibid.* II, 132.

end. At the same time, Barth's attitude towards Idealism is itself ambivalent (perhaps even dialectical). Despite emphatically excluding philosophy from the fundamental questions of theology, and despite his uncompromising critique of the modern, Barth painted a sympathetic portrait of Hegel in his *Protestant Theology in the Nineteenth Century*.[86] More significantly, the basic direction of his thought around the doctrine of the Trinity can further be understood as his own recasting of the theory of the absolute, and at least the late Barth's mode of thinking is dialectically shaped, as is clear, for example, from the Christology of his *Church Dogmatics*, right down to the section headings. He is also linked to Hegel by an approach to historical-critical research that mirrors Hegel's concern with the witness of the spirit, and possibly also by the Platonism and docetism discernable in his theology.[87] A comprehensive investigation of Barth's relation to Hegel has yet to be undertaken; it will be challenging owing to the relatively few references to Hegel in the *Church Dogmatics*. At any rate, it lies outside the scope of this essay.

1.5 The relevance of Idealist Christologies today

Two lines of enquiry in particular might fruitfully display the relevance of the impact of Idealism on our theme. First, a Hegelian approach to this impact should be encouraged: one that highlights its rationality. Second, the importance of the questions that this history poses should be summarised. Various problems and areas of thought have to be brought together in dialogue, in the contemporary context, in such a way as to respond to the issues in Christology. These can be briefly outlined.

From a Hegelian (all too Hegelian?) perspective, the impact of Hegel's Christology could be seen as the historical realisation of its rational contents. It therefore does not necessarily have to be read – as sometimes happens – as the straightforward collapse of a synthesis, achieved by Hegel alone, into right- and left-Hegelian camps of less-gifted epigones. Rather, disintegration can itself be understood as a rational figure, namely as the pneumatological transcendence of the centre of Christology through a phase of negation. According to Hegel, at its centre, the historical realisation of reason is fulfilled in Jesus Christ in its dialectical motion between thesis, or the general (the incarnation and his life), antithesis, or the particular (the cross), and synthesis or unity (the resurrection). This three-fold step that forms the material core of Christology is experienced as impact of Christology itself: after Hegel and Marheineke provided the thesis, the appeal of the particular arises as an antithetical constellation as Strauss emphasises the meaning of the historical Jesus and Kierkegaard the meaning of the individual person Jesus, as well as the existential appropriation of Christianity in the conditions of the fall. With Baur and Dorner in the nineteenth century, and with Hirsch and Tillich in the twentieth, attempts at a new synthesis appear, which seek to integrate the antithetical arguments in their own way (and thus partly by returning to other Idealists). Finally, today we are faced with the task of developing new forms of this synthesis.

Perhaps this way of reading the effective history is overly harmonised and fails to do justice to the polyphony or even dissonance of its historical development. Yet the positions mentioned within this approach nevertheless reveal the problems and questions which, in terms of systematic theology, are of central importance for any contemporary Christological debate. The studies of the impact of Idealistic Christologies are decisively directed towards a goal in systematic theology: they highlight dimensions of Christology that are vital for current theological models. A contemporary Christology that ignores the questions tackled in the nineteenth and early twentieth centuries is deficient.

The following questions seem to be unavoidable: from the generations following Hegel down to the present day, it has been accepted in scholarly practice that a Christology that ignores the results of historical-critical research may show signs of Docetism. Similarly, in the wake of Kierkegaard's insights, and also those of Karl Barth, many contemporary theories show an awareness that Christologies need to be existentially or ecclesiastically appropriated: they develop out of these practical contexts. It is therefore often recognised that a contemporary Christology must draw both the historical Jesus and the Christ of faith into discussion. The question is how to relate them. There are two further approaches that Hegel himself and a few Hegelians pursued, but which have largely vanished from current Christological debates, particularly in the Anglo-American sphere. First, Hegel emphasises that the rationality of Christology is not only explicable from a perspective coming from within the Church; it can also be established through the primarily philosophical illumination of the underlying structures of reason itself. Second, Hegel emphasises that Jesus Christ can only be understood when he is seen as the culmination of the history of religion (and the world), which develops in phases. The historical Jesus and the Christ of faith must, therefore, also be linked with the rationally established unity between God and man and the reconciliation of God with man that can be discerned in the history of religion.

This can be expressed in terms of disciplines. Currently, Christology is mostly discussed within the sphere of systematic theology whilst the formulation of Christological questions is considered with recourse to a position informed by the history of dogma and drawing on results of research into the New Testament. Idealism would insist on considering the results of scholarly research into other religions in the formulation of Christological questions. In addition, it would establish a relation to philosophy: not only the philosophy of religion, but also fundamental, or first philosophy. In other words: even if it seems foreign to the Anglo-Saxon tradition, strongly shaped as it is by the philosophy of language analysis, Christological questions do not only concern a discourse internal to religion. They bear on the deepest subjects of philosophy itself. This applies in relation to philosophy's current hermeneutic task, since it can hardly contribute to the enlightenment of the present in the age of the return of religions, unless it also addresses the central questions of Christianity. This is true in relation to the questions that plague philosophy itself about its own foundations and limitations. It also raises the related question of the validity of reason as it functions outside particular situations – its absolute dimension – in its respective relations to history.

In the light of today's demands, in today's university, we cannot expect or want the questions and subjects addressed here to be reconciled as thoroughly as they are in Hegel's thought. It is perhaps simply the nature of the beast that the categorically diverging fundamental approaches, the respective methods employed and the material results of historical-critical research, existential appropriation, speculative reconstruction and the insights of the history of religion cannot be integrated as perfectly as Hegel envisaged. In particular, the foundation in first philosophy and theories of the absolute, and the (re)construction of a comprehensive history of religion throw up a variety of difficult problems. At the same time, however, we can learn from Idealism and its impact that Christianity in modernity demands from its very heart – from Jesus Christ – that none of the disciplines and questions considered here be excluded from Christological discussion.

Translated by Lyndon Webb

Notes

1. For Schelling's Christology, see for instance Georg Neugebauer, *Tillichs frühe Christologie: Eine Untersuchung zu Offenbarung und Geschichte bei Tillich vor dem Hintergrund seiner Schellingrezeption*, Theologische Bibliothek Töpelmann 141 (Berlin and New York: de Gruyter, 2007), 36–145, as well as Malte Dominik Krüger, *Göttliche Freiheit. Die*

Trinitätslehre in Schellings Spätphilosophie [Religion in Philosophy and Theology], 31 (Tübingen: Mohr Siebeck, 2008), esp. 231–72.

2. For a summary of Hegel's Christology, see Peter C. Hodgson, *Hegel and Christian Theology: A Reading of the Lectures on Philosophy of Religion* (Oxford: Oxford University Press, 2008), esp. 155–76, and also Martin Wendte, *Gottmenschliche Einheit bei Hegel: Eine logische und theologische Untersuchung*, Quellen und Studien zur Philosophie 77 (Berlin and New York: de Gruyter, 2007).

3. See G. W. F. Hegel, *Wissenschaft der Logik. Zweiter Band. Die subjektive Logik* (1816), Friedrich Hogemann and Walter Jaeschke (eds.), *Gesammelte Werke*, vol. XII (Hamburg: Felix Meiner, 1981), 237–47.

4. See Hegel, *Vorlesungen über die Philosophie der Religion. Teil 3: Die vollendete Religion*, Walter Jaeschke (ed.) (Hamburg: Felix Meiner, 1995), 1.

5. See here the masterfully succinct Hegel, *Enzyklopädie der philosophischen Wissenschaften im Grundrisse (1830)*, W. Bonsiepen and H.-C. Lucas (eds.), *Gesammelte Werke*, vol. XX (Hamburg: Felix Meiner, 1992), §569.

6. On developmental history (*Entwicklungsgeschichte*) see broadly Hegel, *Vorlesungen über die Philosophie der Religion. Teil 3*, and on its consummation in Christianity see particularly *ibid.*, 177.

7. See Hegel, *Enzyklopädie*, §§571–3.

8. This is perfected in the idea's reflexive thinking of itself; see Hegel, *Enzyklopädie*, §577.

9. For a biography, see Eva-Maria Rupprecht, *Kritikvergessene Spekulation: Das Religions- und Theologieverständnis der spekulativen Theologie Ph.K. Marheinekes* (Beiträge zur rationalen Theologie, vol. III) (Frankfurt a.M. and Berlin: Peter Lang, 1993), 12–34.

10. Philipp Konrad Marheineke, *Die Grundlehren der christlichen Dogmatik als Wissenschaft* (2nd edn, completely revised) (Berlin: Duncker and Humblot, 1827).

11. See Marheineke's programmatic thought, *Grundlehren*, 5–30.

12. *Ibid.*, 180ff. (§306).

13. *Ibid.*, 184 (§312).

14. *Ibid.*, 193 (§326).

15. In addition, see Gunther Wenz, *Geschichte der Versöhnungslehre in der evangelischen Theologie der Neuzeit*, vol. I (Munich: Kaiser, 1984), 318–21.

16. Marheineke, *Grundlehren*, 239 (§398).

17. Here, primarily see Falk Wagner, 'Der Gedanke der Persönlichkeit Gottes bei Ph. Marheineke: Repristination eines vorkritischen Theismus', *NZSTh* 10 (1969), 44–88, esp. 75ff.; this critique is developed expansively by Rupprecht, summarised in Rupprecht, *Spekulation*, 312–21.

18. Emanuel Hirsch, *Geschichte der neuern evangelischen Theologie im Zusammenhang mit den allgemeinen Bewegungen des europäischen Denkens*, 3rd edn, vol. V (Gütersloh: Gütersloher Verlagshaus, 1964), 518.

19. See, for example, Peter C. Hodgson, *A Study of Ferdinand Christian Baur: The Formation of Historical Theology* (New York: Harper and Row, 1966), 91.

20. Ferdinand Christian Baur, *Symbolik und Mythologie oder die Naturreligionen des Alterthums* (Stuttgart: Metzler, 1824), V.

21. Baur, *Die christliche Gnosis oder die christliche Religionsphilosophie in ihrer geschichtlichen Entwicklung* (Tübingen: Osiander, 1835), 686ff.

22. See Wolfgang Geiger, *Spekulation und Kritik. Die Geschichtstheologie Ferdinand Christian Baurs* (Munich: Kaiser, 1964), 45.

23. See, for example, Baur, *Die Epochen der kirchlichen Geschichtsschreibung* (Tübingen: Fues, 1852), 251.

24. Baur, *Gnosis*, 716.

25. *Ibid.*, 711.

26. *Ibid.*, 715, see also Geiger, *Spekulation*, 70f.

27. *Ibid.*, 712.

28. Baur himself summarises his results in *Das Christenthum und die christliche Kirche der ersten drei Jahrhunderte* (Tubingen: Fues, 1853), 21–40; for a comprehensive overview, see also Hodgson, *Study*, 100–21 and 221–37.

29. Baur, *Christenthum*, 31.

30. *Ibid.*, 35. On this point of criticism, see in particular Geiger, *Spekulation*, 76–95.

31. D. F. Strauss, *Das Leben Jesu, kritisch bearbeitet*, vols. I and II (Tübingen: Fues, 1835).

32. See Friedrich W. Graf, *Kritik und Pseudo-Spekulation: David Friedrich Strauß als Dogmatiker im Kontext der positionellen Theologie seiner Zeit* (Munich: Kaiser, 1982), 53–69. On the Christology of Strauss see also Dietz Lange, *Historischer Jesus oder mythischer Christus: Untersuchungen zum Gegensatz zwischen Friedrich Schleiermacher und David Friedrich Strauß* (Gütersloh: Gütersloher Verlagsanstalt, 1975).

33. See Graf, *Kritik*, 55f.

34. See Strauss, *Die christliche Glaubenslehre in ihrer geschichtlichen Entwicklung und im Kampfe mit der modernen Wissenschaft*, vol. I (Darmstadt: WBG, 2009).

35. See George Williamson's essay in this volume, chapter 10.

36. *Ibid.*, 41–51.

37. *Ibid.* and VII; II, 729–44.

38. For a comprehensive account of Strauss' Christology, see Graf, *Kritik*, 574–606.

39. See Graf, *Kritik*, 490–7.

40. See Werner Zager, 'Einführung', in: Strauss, *Die christliche Glaubenslehre*, 18ff., as well as Strauss, *Glaubenslehre*, 1–4, and for a comprehensive account, Strauss, *Der alte und der neue Glaube: Ein Bekenntnis* (Gesammelte Schriften von David Friedrich Strauss), Eduard Zeller (ed.), vol. VI (Bonn: Strauss, 1877), 8–97.

41. Isaak August Dorner, *System der Christlichen Glaubenslehre. Band I und II* (Berlin: Hertz, 1887). For more on this three-fold mediation in Dorner's thought, see also Hirsch, *Geschichte*, 386, and Uwe Gerber, *Christologische Entwürfe*, vol. I: *Von der Reformation bis zur Dialektischen Theologie* (Zürich: EVZ, 1970), 189ff.

42. See here Christine Axt-Piscalar, *Der Grund des Glaubens. Eine theologiegeschichtliche Untersuchung zum Verhältnis von Glaube und Trinität in der Theologie Isaak August Dorners* (Tübingen: Mohr Siebeck, 1990), 5.

43. On this, and the following reflections, see Axt-Piscalar, *Der Grund*, 34–7.

44. See Dorner, *System* I, 430–47.

45. On this aspect and its incorporation within Christology, see Jonathan Norgate, *Isaak A. Dorner: The Triune God and the Gospel of Salvation* (London: T. & T. Clark, 2009), 52–64, 165ff.

46. Dorner, *System* I, 542ff. and Dorner, *System* II, 410.

47. *Ibid.*, 718.

48. *Ibid.*, II, 257–300.

49. *Ibid.*, 411–21, and Axt-Piscalar, *Der Grund*, 236–44.

50. Dorner, *System* II, 416.

51. *Ibid.*, 422.

52. *Ibid.*, 422.

53. *Ibid.*, 423.

54. *Ibid.*, 427.

55. *Ibid.*, 431–42, also Axt-Piscalar, *Der Grund*, 244–7.

56. *Ibid.*, 438.

57. See Joel Rasmussen's essay in this volume, chapter 4.

58. Søren Kierkegaard, *Philosophical Fragments*, trans. H. Hong and E. Hong (Princeton: Princeton University Press, 1985).

59. On the following, see Toshihisa Hachiya, *Paradox, Vorbild und Versöhner: S. Kierkegaards Christologie und deren Rezeption in der deutschen Theologie des 20. Jahrhunderts* (Europäische Hochschulschriften, Reihe XXIII, vol. 836) (Frankfurt a.M.: Lang, 2006), 43–83.

60. See Kierkegaard, *Philosophical Fragments*, 37–43, 55ff.

61. For a detailed analysis of the way in which Kierkegaard's concept of paradox distances him from the movements towards reconciliation of Hegel and the Danish Hegelians, see Jon Stewart, 'The paradox and the criticism of Hegelian mediation in *Philosophical Fragments*', in *Kierkegaard Studies* 2004, 184–207.

62. See Kierkegaard, *Philosophical Fragments*, 79–86.

63. On the anti-Hegelian thrust of Kierkegaard's thought, see Merold Westphal, 'Kierkegaard und Hegel', in Alastair Hannay, Gordon Marino (eds.), *The Cambridge Companion to Kierkegaard* (Cambridge: Cambridge University Press, 1998), 101–23, esp. 115.

64. See also Hermann Deuser, 'Religious dialectics and Christology', in *ibid.*, 392ff.

65. Søren Kierkegaard, *Practice in Christianity*, trans. H. Hong and E. Hong (Princeton: Princeton University Press, 1991). See also Hachiya, *Paradox*, 171–232.

66. Kierkegaard, *Practice in Christianity*, 82.

67. Hirsch, *Christliche Rechenschaft*, ed. Hayo Gerdes, 2 vols. (Tübingen: Katzmann, 1989).

68. See here the authoritative work: Ulrich Barth, *Die Christologie Emanuel Hirschs: eine systematische und problemgeschichtliche Darstellung ihrer geschichtsmethodologischen, erkenntniskritischen und subjektivitätstheoretischen Grundlagen* (Berlin and New York: de Gruyter, 1992). Whilst Barth also reconstructs Hirsch's early Christology, we are concentrating on his later, mature version.

69. *Ibid.*, 582.

70. *Ibid.*, 599.

71. See Hans-Walter Schütte, 'Subjektivität und System: zum Briefwechsel E. Hirsch (1888–1972) und P. Tillich (1886–1965)', in Christian Danz (ed.), *Theologie als Religionsphilosophie. Studien zu den problemgeschichtlichen und systematischen Voraussetzungen der Theologie Paul Tillichs* (Tillich-Studien 9) (Wien: Lit, 2004), 3–22.

72. On the following, see G. Neugebauer, *Tillichs frühe Christologie: Eine Untersuchung zu Offenbarung und Geschichte bei Tillich vor dem Hintergrund seiner Schellingrezeption* (Theologische Bibliothek Töpelmann 141) (Berlin and New York: de Gruyter, 2007), 252–89.

73. See also Hermann Fischer, 'Die Christologie als Mitte des Systems', in Hermann Fischer (ed.), *Paul Tillich. Studien zu einer Theologie der Moderne* (Frankfurt a.M.: Athenäum, 1989), 214–17.

74. See Paul Tillich, *Systematische Theologie von 1913*, in: *Paul Tillich, Gesammelte Werke: Supplementary and Unpublished Volumes*, vol. IX, Doris Hummel and Gerd Lax (eds.) (Berlin and New York: de Gruyter, 2009), 273–434; the position of the intuition is developed more closely in §§1–15 of the introduction, that of the reflection in §§16–21.

75. *Ibid.*, 314 (§22).

76. *Ibid.*, 348 (§9).

77. On these three points, see Neugebauer, *Tillichs*, 278–83.

78. See Tillich, *Schelling und die Anfänge des existentialistischen Protestes (1955)*, in *Paul Tillich, Gesammelte Werke*, vol. IV: *Philosophie und Schicksal*, Renate Albrecht (ed.) (Stuttgart: Evangelisches Verlagswerk, 1961), 133–44.

79. See Anne Marie Reijnen, 'Tillich's Christology', in Russell Re Manning (ed.), *The Cambridge Companion to Paul Tillich* (Cambridge: Cambridge University Press, 2008), 56–73.

80. See also Fischer, *Christologie*, 207.

81. See Tillich, *Systematische Theologie* I/II (Berlin and New York: de Gruyter, 1987), 9.

82. See also Neugebauer, *Tillichs*, 354–62.

83. Tillich, *Systematische Theologie*, II, 98ff. and 163.

84. *Ibid.* I, 161; for more on this complex, see also Fischer, 'Die Christologie', 217–21.

85. Tillich, *Systematische Theologie*, II, 108, 111–18 as well as Gunther Wenz, 'Die reformatorische Perspektive: Der Einfluss Martin Kählers auf Tillich', Hermann Fischer (ed.), *Paul Tillich. Studien zu einer Theologie der Moderne*, 62–92, esp. 76–81.

86. Karl Barth, *Die protestantische Theologie im 19. Jahrhundert: Ihre Vorgeschichte und ihre Geschichte* (Zürich: EVZ, 6th edn, 1994), 343–78.

87. For an initial comparison between Barth and Hegel see for example Martin Wendte, 'Lamentation between contradiction and obedience: Hegel and Barth as diametrically opposed brothers in the spirit of modernity', in Eva Harasta and Brian Brock (eds.), *Evoking Lament: A Theological Discussion* (London: T. and T. Clark, 2009), 77–98.

2

German Idealism's Trinitarian legacy: the nineteenth century

Dale Schlitt

Fichte, Hegel and Schelling have had an enormous impact on the development of Trinitarian thought. Hegel and Schelling, in particular, have profoundly influenced Trinitarian thinking from their day until today. The root reason for this influence can be traced back to the way in which these three German Idealists embraced, from early on and each in his own way, what they understood to be the triadic structure of dynamically developing subjectivity.

2.1 The Idealist adventure

J. G. Fichte: setting the stage

Fichte (1762–1814) was the earliest of the three to focus so intensely on what came to be this Idealist trademark; namely, the triadic structure of subjectivity. In his search to find a way to ground all experience and knowledge, he rejected Kant's notion of the thing-in-itself and argued at length that all we had to deal with was consciousness as such. In his ground-breaking work of 1794–5, *Science of Knowledge*, he laid out a basic principle followed by two further principles – all three were then to ground all science and thinking.[1]

Fichte argued that all there is to start with is the basic principle: I = I; I am I; I am. This is a principle of initial identity since the 'I' does not adhere to anything else and underlies all experience. With the affirmation of this first principle, he was setting up philosophy as a scientific knowing of knowing, a doctrine of knowledge based on one starting point.[2] However, though this initial identity of the I is the certainty of one's relation with oneself, it does not explain its own reality, free as it is and yet limited. For Fichte, then, as a second principle the I posits or sets against itself a not-I or not-self which limits the initial I.[3] The third principle is the recognition that each of these first two principles determines the other. The I posits the not-I as limiting itself and the I limits the not-I. The I, as limited by the not-I, is passively posited. The I, as knowing it limits the not-I, or object, is active. With this third principle Fichte accounts for the reciprocal interaction between self and other.[4] These three principles underlie and ground the further elaboration of his systematic thought. Though he will go on later to work with a form of Trinitarian expression, it is really his initial insight into the dynamic triadic structure of subjectivity which, as modified by Hegel and Schelling, has had an impact through their thought on subsequent Trinitarian thinking.[5]

G. W. F. Hegel: a daring claim

Hegel (1770–1831) acknowledged that Fichte followed in the tradition of Descartes and Kant when he identified the I as an initial unity and, along with Kant, as the source of the categories of thought. He praised Fichte for taking the tremendous step of trying to show how the categories of thought arise in necessary fashion out of the initial I itself. But, with the ever-recurring presence of the not-I, Hegel claimed that Fichte proposed what Hegel called an absolute contradiction since the not-I should have been absolute and inclusive in its own right. For Hegel, Fichte ended merely with the infinite of infinite progression, in which limit constantly recurs without an enriched return to a renewed identity. Fichte was not able to reintegrate subjectivity and objectivity in a true concept of spirit as movement of inclusive subjectivity.

Over the years Hegel himself worked out his mature concept of spirit and presented that concept on the level of religion as a movement of inclusive Trinitarian divine subjectivity. He first presented his philosophical reading of Trinity in his 1807 *Phenomenology of Spirit*.[6] He then sketched out his readings of Trinity in the 1817, 1827 and 1830 editions of his *Encyclopaedia of the Philosophical Sciences in Outline*.[7] He filled in these sketches with his 1821, 1824, 1827 and 1831 lectures on the philosophy of religion.[8] Hegel saw his concept of spirit bringing to explicit formulation the necessary movement of logical thought categories, from the point of view of his system, in the first sphere of logic, formally speaking, as a movement of inclusive subjectivity whose realisation then occurs in the second and third spheres of nature and spirit. These second and third spheres are, in contradistinction to the first sphere of logic, the real-philosophical spheres. The distinction here is between the 'real-philosophical' spheres of nature and spirit, on the one hand,

and the sphere of logic as the movement of pure thought, on the other. 'Real-philosophical' refers to all the spheres of Hegel's systematically developed philosophy other than that of logic. In his *Encyclopaedia* sketches of this over-all movement of spirit, his presentations of Trinity stand as the penultimate moment, which he identifies as revealed religion, just before his presentation of philosophy. Focusing on the overall structure of his encyclopaedic system as a whole and referring to selected elements in his presentation of Trinity in the 1830 *Encyclopaedia* and his lectures will help in gaining an appreciation of his philosophically informed efforts to reconceptualise Trinity, namely, to develop a philosophy of absolute, inclusive divine subjectivity.

The *Encyclopaedia* begins with logic, understood as movement of pure thought whose initial moment is the thought determination or category of pure being, the being of pure thought. It ends in an enriching advance that, in the philosophy of absolute spirit, is an equally enriched resultant return to what was the initial movement of logic. But now, at the end of this self-developing movement of spirit, the logical concept has become the philosophical concept where form and content are truly and fully adequate. Hegel would say that concept and reality are united in the absolute idea. Absolute spirit is then the idea developing from the immediacy of logic to the logical idea's self-othering in nature and finite spirit. This development of spirit continues as enriching, advancing return through finite spirit in philo-sophic thought to the renewed and enriched immediacy, or identity, of the idea. This overall movement from logic to the real-philosophical spheres, culminating in philosophy, is a process of self-determination by absolute spirit. It occurs in logic as inclusive subjectivity, in nature as self-othering of the idea and in and through art, religion and philosophy as absolute sub-jectivity. Within this overall process Hegel places revealed religion, which he identifies with Christianity and especially Lutheran Christianity, as the penultimate sphere in which the content is true but the form as yet burdened with pictorial representation rather than conceptual clarity. He presents revealed religion schematically in the form of an 'immanent' and 'economic,' so to speak, divine self-revelation as self-development of Trinitarian divine subjectivity, the movement of spirit in the realm of revealed religion. He employs an explicitly religious or representational, but nevertheless always philosophically informed, language to lay out 'immanent' and 'economic' Trinity in three moments, namely, those of universality, particularity and individuality. It could be argued that each of these moments is syllogistically structured, and without doubt he clearly develops the last of these, individ-uality, as a movement explicitly formulated in terms of three self-mediating syllogisms.[9] In the *Encyclopaedia* this moment of individuality climaxes as the effective self-revelation of absolute spirit in and through finite spirit in community, the final moment of syllogistically structured divine Trinitarian reconciliation. In the sphere of religious representation, this reconciliation remains the movement of self-determining divine subjectivity. It has not yet been explicitly established as mediation of the absolute self or concept in the form of philosophical thought where the otherness indicated by reference to God would be overcome.

In his encyclopaedic system as a whole, this final moment – namely philosophical thought – is for Hegel the truth or perfect correspondence of subject and object, or better, of self and concept. It is this perfect correspondence or absolute spirit, infinite or inclusive totality, only insofar as it is the end result inclusive of the whole process. As the final moment, philosophy is for Hegel the grounding return to the immediacy of logical thought. This enriched, grounding return finally justifies seeing Hegel's real-philosophical spheres themselves, and in particular his philosophical thought or concept, as his re-conceptualisation of Trinity. Moreover, this grounding return warrants recognising his logic as the appropriate logical reformulation of 'immanent' Trinity, with 'immanent' carefully nuanced so as not to insinuate an independently *existent* reality. This grounding return on the part of philosophical thought explains why Hegel can use philosophically reinterpreted representational language to describe logic as the presentation of God, as God is in the eternal divine essence before the creation of nature and finite spirit.

In his encyclopaedic system Hegel, appropriately, from the perspective of his system, deals with 'immanent' Trinity twice. First, he presents it as movement of self-determining inclusive subjectivity in the form of pure thought or logic and, second, as moment of universality in the real-philosophical sphere of the philosophy of religion. Likewise, he examines 'economic' Trinity twice. He does this, first, in the same real-philosophical sphere as including the 'immanent' Trinity. Second, he again examines 'economic' Trinity in philosophical thought as the grounding return both to the immediacy of 'immanent' Trinity on the level of philosophy of religion, and to the immediacy of logic on the level of spirit as a whole. The encyclopaedic system is, in its totality, Hegel's philosophically reinterpreted presentation of 'economic' Trinity, inclusive of 'immanent' Trinity. Hegel rather humbly, though daringly as well, ends his 1827 and 1830 editions of the *Encyclopaedia* with the famous quote from Aristotle's *Metaphysics*: 'For it is this, what God is.'[a][10]

---

a. 'Τοῦτο γὰρ ὁ θεός.' Hegel, GW xx, §577; PM §577.

In this overall sweep of spirit, identified by Hegel as what God is, 'immanent' Trinity is the initial moment structuring the overall dynamic of divine self-development as self-revelation. From the perspective of his system in its speculative presentation, this overall dynamic is a movement from initial identity to difference to grounding return as renewed, inclusive identity. It is a movement from initial infinite, to finitude, to inclusive or true infinite. In this way, logically reformulated as inclusive subject, religiously represented as absolute divine subjectivity and philosophically re-conceptualised as absolute spirit, Trinity is for Hegel the whole truth.

So Hegel saw religion as the consciousness of the all-encompassing object or God, which has become the inclusive self-consciousness of absolute spirit. This inclusive self-consciousness is given fullest expression as a movement of Trinitarian divine self-positing subjectivity in what he refers to in the *Encyclopaedia* as the revealed religion and in his *Lectures on the Philosophy of Religion* as the consummate religion. It is a movement, in and through finite spirit, from universality to particularity to individuality. The first element, characterised by universality and identified in 1831 as the kingdom of the Father, is the appearance of the divine idea in the realm of thought. It is 'in itself' the moment of initial identity. It contains this otherness within itself as moment of judgement or separation as negation, the begetting, so to speak, of itself as the Son, but it does this only as a sort of play. With otherness as moment of negation, he thinks together, dialectically, initial identity (God the Father) with the other (God the Son) of that initial identity in their momentary contradiction (positive and negative, universal and particular). When the contradiction of universal and its negation or its other is thought through they are seen to have become a new identity, traditionally referred to theologically as the Holy Spirit. For the other is the other of this initial identity, which it thus includes.

The second element in the development of the consummate religion as movement of spirit is the appearance of the divine idea in the doubled movement of diremption and reconciliation. It is the sphere of particularity, difference and objectivity, identified as the kingdom of the Son. It appears as the movement of judgement in which the divine idea comes into existence 'for itself'. This element is characterised by contradiction. The divine idea others itself as an independent world in and out of which finite spirit arises as that which is both good and bad. Finite spirit is thus self-estrangement and reconciliation has to occur in an exclusive individuality. It has to take place in an individual divine–human self, in the mediating death of Christ resulting in an immediate existence spiritually interpreted as the risen Christ.

As this historical appearance of the divine idea, the second element of the consummate religion is the moment of objectivity in the overall development of God as spirit. This historical appearance occurs as a triadically structured movement from God, as presupposed universality, to the particularity of the community's spiritual consciousness of the risen Christ by means of mediating individuality.

In the third element of the consummate religion, namely, in spiritual community, the objective reconciliation achieved in Christ has become for Hegel the subjective relationship of the individual subject to this objective reconciliation with the truth. The previous two elements of the consummate religion, and now this third element, are for Hegel the very progression of the idea of God and, indeed, of God as spirit. They are the absolute eternal idea 'in itself,' 'for itself' and now 'in and for itself'. These elements are the life and activity of God consummated in the third element as the community or unity of the individual empirical subjects who are filled by the Spirit of God, the Holy Spirit or reconciling return of the divine idea out of the self-othering of judgement. The third element of the consummate religion is the movement of inclusive, and now absolute, divine subjectivity, the dynamic movement of spirit both as grounding return to the immediacy or identity of 'immanent' Trinity in the real-philosophical sphere of revealed religion and as advance to philosophical thinking. It is the moment of individuality identified as the kingdom of the Spirit.

According to Hegel the Trinity of religious representation retains the characteristics of three independently represented subjects in an inadequately purified parental and filial relationship. His re-conceptualisation negates such a representation. It negates as well the continuing projection of reconciliation insofar as it is achieved in a divine subject over against the self. The true content of this religious reconciliation is preserved, for Hegel, in the move to philosophical thought as the full mediation of subject and object, self and concept, in self-determining conceptual thought. As purification this transition not only negates but preserves in a truer form and, therefore, develops the true content expressed as Trinity. Nowhere can this sublation be seen more clearly than in Hegel's proposal to translate what appears on the level of religious representation as divine freedom; namely, to create or not to create, into a logically necessary self-othering of the absolute idea in, and as, nature. Hegel called this self-othering, as logically necessary self-determination, 'free self-release'.[b]

b. 'Die *unmittelbare Idee* als ihren Widerschein, sich als *Natur* frei *aus sich zu entlassen.*' GW xx §244; PM §244.

Hegel argued that a great deal was at stake in his effort to re-conceptualise God as Trinity and in his claim that God can be conceived adequately as Person, subject and spirit only if God is conceived as Trinity. Were God not conceived as Trinity, God would be for Hegel an empty word.[11] His speculative dialectical re-conceptualisation of Trinity was his post-Kantian response to the problems of the one and the many and of the relationship between identity and difference. By means of this re-conceptualisation he was able to give content to the term 'God'. In his philosophy of religion, he traced the development of the concept of God through the various religions of the world, arriving ultimately in Christianity at an explicit understanding of the Trinitarian God as absolute subjectivity and subject, with the spiritual community becoming the locus of spirit's self-realisation. He saw in the Trinitarian divine self-othering and sublation of that otherness a movement of progression which is both development and enriched return, the principle and axis upon which not only the history of religions but history itself turns. World history is then for Hegel the history of God. He understood freedom ultimately as logically necessary but truly self-determining. Knowledge of God, Christianity's truth-claim and truth itself, were likewise grounded immediately in his re-conceptualisation of Trinity as movement of self-determining divine subjectivity. In eliminating the need for a distinction in 'immanent' Trinity between divine essence and divine person, Hegel continued the modern turn to the subject. He was able to avoid a Cartesian appeal to God to guarantee truth and certainty in knowledge by making of the Trinitarian God the very structure of truth itself. He claimed to recognise in Trinity in general, and in the 'inner' or 'immanent' Trinity in particular, a congruity with his fundamental, speculatively formulated dialectic of positive/negation/negation-of-negation. He found in the Christian doctrine of Trinity the means to give religious expression to mediation in the self as concept, his philosophical response to personal and social alienation so prevalent in his day. Hegel might well argue that in the future it would still be this philosophical response, in the form of the true infinite as inclusive totality which, when appropriately adapted, would prove most fecund for a further re-conceptualisation of Trinity as the whole truth.

F. W. J. Schelling: the radically free and personal Trinitarian God

Schelling (1775–1854) judged Hegel's philosophy in general, and philosophical re-conceptualisation of Trinity in particular, to be too rationalist, not allowing sufficiently for the freedom and the personal nature of God. He called Hegel's philosophy negative philosophy, namely, a transcendental reflection which could lead to the idea of God but which could never really capture the reality of existence. He identified his own philosophy as positive, as recognising the 'facticity' and 'priorness' of being. His positive philosophy included philosophy and theology, with the latter's reference to revelation, in a creative philosophical construction taking into consideration the un-prethinkable God of Exodus 3:14.[12] Schelling found in Christianity this affirmation of the facticity and priorness of God as being. In emphasising this facticity and priorness, he gave his notion of ground an interesting reformulation in the context of his discussion on God.

Schelling made his philosophically formulated presentation of Trinity the core theme of his positive philosophy, bringing together Trinitarian theological traditions, Scriptural references and philosophical reflection. In Trinity he found the speculative foundation for his stress on the radical freedom of God and for his insistence that God is in some way personal from the very beginning of God's self-development. He interpreted Trinity as movement focused on the Father as source of Trinitarian unity, presented the Son as subordinate to the Father, though not a created reality, and envisioned the Holy Spirit as the final re-establishment of the initial divine unity previously disrupted in creation.

In 1811 and 1813 Schelling had presented a certain Trinitarian speculation in *Die Weltalter*.[13] In his 1831–2 lectures, published in 1992 as *Urfassung der Philosophie der Offenbarung* (*Original Version of the Philosophy of Revelation*), he develops in great detail his positive philosophical presentation of Trinity.[14] He seems to have dictated this *Urfassung*, which will serve here as text of reference.[15] After 1832, he continued lecturing on his positive philosophy. For example, his 1841–2 lectures, published by Paulus during Schelling's lifetime and without Schelling's authorisation as *Philosophie der Offenbarung* (*Philosophy of Revelation*), are particularly well known.[16] Though Trinitarian thinkers before 1992 would normally have been familiar with the 1841–2 writings and not with the *Urfassung* text, the latter is a more reliable text of reference. The two versions are sufficiently coherent to permit working with the *Urfassung* and then moving from it to a consideration of possible influences by Schelling on later Trinitarian thinkers.

Schelling's lectures on the philosophy of revelation follow upon his lectures on the philosophy of mythology, with the two together making up his philosophy of religion. In the philosophy of mythology Schelling examined the world of religion, characterised by necessity, though the Trinity was already at least implicitly at work in the various religions in a movement toward the realm of Christian revelation, a realm characterised by freedom. The key then to understanding Schelling's lectures on the philosophy of religion, and especially his philosophical re-conceptualisation of Trinity, is the notion and reality of freedom. At crucial points in his lectures Schelling refers to and works with 'will' in its ability to decide to be or not to be, to act or not to act.[17] He shows the way in which God's unity is actual in the freedom of the Father that comes to fruition in the Son. Then he explains the arising and the result of the generation of the Son through the Father in the Spirit. Finally, he affirms that the creator has become one God in three Persons.

To affirm the most radical sense of divine freedom, Schelling asserts the priority and given-ness of God's essence as pure being. In his essence, God is for Schelling pure actuality and unity, so that God as such is absolute subjectivity. God is the Lord even of being, so God could will either to be or not to be. As this pure unity, God presumes no prior potentiality. But unity implies the notion of difference and, thus, the possibility of becoming and development. As this beginning, this unity and this source of potential development, God can appropriately be named Father. So for Schelling, at this stage in the presentation of his thought on Trinity, Father refers to God as such in his original and potentially originating unity. He then identifies this potency as the first of three potencies residing in God as Father, with this latter taken in a wider sense to refer to what today is often called 'immanent' Trinity. Schelling is quick to note that God does not at this point become this or any following potencies, since such an understanding would imply necessity in God. Rather, the first potency and further potencies reveal what God is, namely, the Lord of being. The first potency for further development gives rise to a second potency, which is the potentiality to become real or actual. The second potency is not one that gives rise to but to which rise is given. It is the arising of an essence homogeneous with the first potency but in such a way that it needs to actualise itself. Schelling calls 'giving rise to' generation and refers to 'being given rise to' as generated. This second potency can only be given the name 'Son'. He brings this his initial reflection together with the assertion that these two potencies find their renewed unity in the third and final potency. Already now, by way of anticipation, this third potency can be described as the realisation, in and through creation, of the actuality of the two first potencies in the renewed unity of the being of the Father. Schelling names this final potency Spirit.

The three-fold structure at which Schelling arrives not only will come to lay the groundwork for his later affirmation of three Persons in God but also to characterise and undergird his thought on such religious themes as Trinity, creation, incarnation, reconciliation and what might more traditionally be referred to as the Parousia. He is introducing, in his own systematic way and with a special emphasis on the radical freedom of God, Boehme's notion of movement in God into his own understanding of God.

Schelling reiterates that the point of departure in the unity of God and freedom of the Father itself implies the differentiation of the Son established in the Father. He gives further precision to his presentation of the arising of the Son by distinguishing three perspectives on that arising: the originary form of divine being in which the Son is revealed within the absolute immanence of the Father, then the Son insofar as he is for the Father and as he is posited outside the Father.

From the first perspective, the Son is willed by the Father as the possibility of being outside of the Father though, at this point, in referring to the Son Schelling is speaking of pure eternity unaffected by temporal considerations. From the second perspective, the Son stands against the Father. Here Schelling says that the Father is indeed free only in the Son for it is in willing the Son that the Father intends through the Son to will, in creation, that which is external to the Father. The Father loves the Son as the possibility of this creation. So, the glory of the Father, which is his freedom, is also the glory of the Son who will freely bring into being a world of which the Father will ultimately be Lord. From the third perspective, Schelling further spells out the idea that the generation of the Son can only be properly spoken of in relation to the act of creation. It is not a question of the Son being created but rather, given the will of the Father to create, that in and through that creation the Son as second potency begins his process of self-development through nature, history and religion toward personhood. With these distinctions Schelling argues that his philosophical presentation of the arising of the Son assures a certain notion of 'eternal generation' from the first perspective while also from the third perspective taking into consideration various Trinitarian theological traditions and scripture which, for example, recognise in the Son one who has received all from the Father and who consequently shows a certain dependence on and subordination to the Father. For Schelling the Son becomes Person only through self-development in creation, a self-development in which the Son ultimately hands over all to the Father.

In speaking of the dialectical process of the arising of the Son hidden in the Father, Schelling says that the arising of the Son from originary being involves negation (the Son is not the Father) and being rendered potential (able to develop) and especially being posited as non-being, then being. This

generation of the Son is more of an exclusion leading to the need for the
Son to develop, since the Son is not the original pure being. The Son is that
which can be, a potency received from the Father. As such, the Son is selfless
self because he does not have his own will. He fulfils the will of the Father.
His essence is thus selfless will and his work is to reveal the will of the Father
toward unity. So the Son makes the Father develop or be actual in the real
world, but does not make the Father as such develop or be actual.

Schelling speaks of the external generation of the Son, in the full sense,
as the establishment of divinity outside of God. He spells out the continuing
process, and then result, of the generation of the Son that takes place in the
Son's kenosis, an act and process occurring in, through and as creation. He
acknowledges the eternity of the Son as possibility hidden within the Father,
whom he identifies with God who is pure being. But he refuses to accept
eternal generation as such in any full sense. The Son will be fully avowed
as Son only at the end of creation. Eternal generation would mean the Son
arises by necessity of the divine nature rather than through the free act of
the Father. For Schelling, this would not be a true generation since it would
lack the spontaneity of freedom. A necessary generation would not result in
the possibility of development and actualisation on the part of the Son. For
it is by the Father's will that the Son is obliged to develop and realise his
potential to become Person.

In creation, being appears as truly other to God and as needing to evolve
and develop. It was the intention of the Father already with the internal
'generation' of the Son to give rise to a world external to him; and it is
this appearance of an external world which Schelling identifies with the
generation of the Son, for in each case the result is a form of being external to
God the Father. The generation of the Son is both appearance of the world
and the Son's appearance in the world. However, for Schelling the demiurgic
Son internal to the Father is of course the cause of the being of the world,
the means by which creation occurs. So in creation, the Father, as cause,
remains outside the tension characteristic of the world and the Son is the
cosmic cause which brings forth the world and acts in it. In this creation
as externalisation the Father is in effect giving up his divinity in a form of
kenosis that begins with creation. With creation the Son is no longer hidden
within the Father. Rather, the Son is excluded from the Father. With this
externalisation the Son is no longer divine, for he is not in the Father who is
pure being. This obliges the Son to develop on his own and to work to bring
the world back to God. He is at work in the world, slowly re-establishing its
unity with the Father. In this work the Son reveals to the world not his own
but the Father's will, which he has received from him.

Schelling conceives of human consciousness as external result of the generation of the Son. Human consciousness is the ultimate level at which the drama of reconciliation between God as pure being and the loss of that being in the externalisation of creation takes place. Human sinfulness disrupts the reconciliation begun by the Son at the moment of creation. It does this by turning away from the unification being brought about by the Son. So the Son must begin a new creation in his appearance as an individual human being. But even this interruption of the Son's glorification does not hinder the final outcome of the Son's work in the world. Schelling acknowledges that the glorification of the Son in this new creation is, with the resurrection, a full glorification before the Father but not before the world. The Son overcomes the second self-emptying but has not as yet arrived at the full glorification that is the goal of creation as such and will only come about at the end of things. For this to occur, both the Son's and the Father's glorification have to become evident and known to human consciousness. God as such, the Father, remains outside the world and the Son is first fully actualised as Son when he has completely overcome his own potency that had excluded divinity. Only at this point is the true will of the Father revealed, namely, the will to overcome externally posited non-being in the renewed and fuller realisation of the fullness of being. The Father is completely revealed only when he is present to the self, to and in human consciousness, as the fullness of being that he is. This revelation only takes place when Father and Son are, together, fully actualised as divine Persons.

Creation's goal is the external glory of the Father become immanent in creation through its recognition in human consciousness. This is a mutual glorification in which both Father and Son are in possession of the true being of the Father. In the end all of creation will, through human consciousness, be aware of the fullness of being which the Father was from the beginning. Both Father and Son will have equal right to this finally established being and this is the final unity of Father and Son. The realisation of this shared possession of being in and through its revelation to human consciousness is the goal and purpose of creation. Here Schelling identifies the kingdom with being, which the Father had given over to the Son. The role of the Son is then to transform this being external to God into divine being. The transformation is ongoing, meaning that handing over the kingdom to God does not imply that the Son gives up his lordship. The Father's receiving of the re-divinised being from the Son is the beginning of the Father's now having this being in common with the Son. The Son's exclusionary lordship over being outside of God ends, and lordship over being is common to Father and Son. Now each potency, as Person, is the whole divinity.

The Father's and Son's sharing of being in itself cannot be accomplished by the Son, whose role is to develop and actualise. It can only be accomplished by a third potency, namely, that of the Holy Spirit, which goes out from the Father and Son as final potency. Schelling justifies this assertion by saying that the Holy Spirit is the inner result of the Father's generation of the Son, that is, active in nature and especially in human consciousness. The Father's willing the tension between his own divine being and the being of the world is not only a negation of the Son's divine being within the Father but also that of the Spirit. The Spirit's being is mediated through the Son. The Spirit does not work immediately but, rather, urges, incites and prompts prophets to speak out and individual persons to establish, perhaps better re-establish, the world and themselves in divine being. There are three sides to what the Spirit does: the role of demiurgic potency working with the Son in the creation of a tension between divine being and the being of the world, the role of cosmic potency in the development of creation and the role of unifying the Father and Son in their glorification at the end of time. This Spirit can only come fully upon humankind with the glorification of the Father that, in turn, can only come through the glorification of the Son. If Christ does not go, the Spirit will not descend upon the disciples. In bringing together in human consciousness the glory of the Father and the Son, the Spirit becomes fully individualised divine Person.

For Schelling the decisive insight into the doctrine of the Trinity is that human seeking after the free origin of actual being finds its answer in God in three Persons. At this point, God as a whole has become actual in three different Persons, with each one being the whole God. Father, Son, and Spirit remain three objective differences whose independence is not lost in resultant unity. Each returns into the divine unity with its own subjective character, and this is the highest expression of the idea of Trinity. Re-constituted divine unity is rooted in the interpersonal relations among the three divine Persons.

Schelling has in his own unique way affirmed the radical freedom and personal character of God. He does this by insisting that God develops from an initial unity in the Father, a variant on his fundamental philosophical notion of ground, in which God is initially both free and absolute personality. This development takes place as three divine potencies becoming three divine Persons who, in their interaction through the Spirit, together glory in renewed and enriched divine unity previously lost with creation. For Schelling this development takes place in and through creation, culminating in the free recognition by human persons that God is one God in three divine Persons characterised by their ongoing, varied lordship of being, by spontaneity, free movement of will and shared final glory.

In their Trinitarian thinking, Hegel and Schelling have then, following upon Fichte's early initial insights into the triadic structure of subjectivity, each worked out an inclusive philosophical theology or philosophy of God. Each in his own way has characterised God as a dynamically developing triadically structured movement occurring in and through history that has become the history of God. This movement toward a unity of human and divine brings the human into the divine, enriching both. Each has indeed pushed this notion of the development of God considerably beyond what more orthodox traditional Trinitarian thinking had embraced.

2.2 A Trinitarian legacy already in the nineteenth century

Once Hegel and Schelling arrived on the scene, nineteenth-century thinkers reflecting more creatively on Trinity found themselves dealing with a whole host of new or at least newly phrased questions raised by the Idealists concerning God's self-consciousness and being, the possibility of God's becoming something different or more than God was, divine freedom and Personhood, and the possibly enriching nature of God's relationship with creation.[18] Two such thinkers in particular, Philipp Marheineke and Isaak August Dorner, entered more directly and explicitly into dialogue with Idealist approaches to Trinity. (It would be most interesting to complement these references to Marheineke and Dorner with a review of the influence of Idealism, and especially of Schelling, on the Russian religious philosopher, Vladimir Solovyov [1852–1900] and, through him, on Russian Trinitarian thinking.[19]) The explicitly formulated Idealist thrust to their Trinitarian thinking makes it relatively easy to identify the impact Hegel and Schelling had on that thinking. Marheineke and Dorner thus give clear witness to a more positive though varyingly critical reception of Idealist Trinitarian thought, and they do this both by the ways in which they approached the question of Trinity and through the very language they employed in their own Trinitarian reflection. Though they did not, in the shorter run, have a perduring positive impact on nineteenth-century Trinitarian thinking, they, and especially Dorner, served to help mediate Idealist understandings of Trinity and, particularly, that of Schelling to those who followed in the twentieth century.

Philipp Marheineke: a mixed dialectic of being and thought

Marheineke (1780–1846), Hegel's friend and professorial colleague, quickly edited Hegel's works after his death.[20] His own *Die Grundlehren der christlichen Dogmatik (Fundamental Doctrines of Christian Dogmatics)*, published in 1819, showed more influence by Schelling.[21] But Marheineke turned to Hegel as resource and special source of inspiration in his second edition, *Die Grundlehren der christlichen Dogmatik als Wissenschaft (Fundamental Doctrines of Christian Dogmatics as Science)*, published in 1827 during Hegel's lifetime.[22] It may well be that these theological studies, especially that of 1819, influenced Hegel as he developed a more explicitly Trinitarian structure for the Christian or consummate religion in his lectures on the philosophy of religion.[23]

In the 1827 edition, Marheineke describes Trinity as a dialectical movement of being when he interweaves Idealist and more traditional theological terminology. He speaks of the moments of God in which God is being in itself and being for itself. In the eternal mediation of these two, God is Spirit. The mutual negation of being in itself, the being of the Father, and being out of itself, the being of the Son, is the negation of this negation and thus their positive positing. God is the identity of identity and difference, Trinity. The being of the Father and of the Son is contained and sublated in this actuality of God as Spirit.

With his regular reference to Father, Son and Spirit Marheineke is determined to retain certain basic terms common to various Christian Trinitarian theological traditions. At the same time, he constantly works with a number of terms and ideas clearly taken from Hegel, terms such as 'in itself', 'for itself' and the sublation of these two in the Spirit. Though Marheineke works a great deal with Hegelian terms and dynamics, his positing of an initial moment of being that is prior to thought is quite foreign to Hegel, who presented being as the being of thought and first thought determination in his science of logic. Though Marheineke tries to bring being and thought together, his regular reference to being, and especially to a first moment of being before thought, rather harks back to Schelling. Marheineke's references to being may well be not only the result of his effort to remain coherent with more orthodox Trinitarian theological traditions but a continuing indication of his earlier attachment to the thought of Schelling. That Marheineke spoke more fundamentally of knowing rather than willing does clearly throw him into the Hegelian camp. Still he may, perhaps not fully self-consciously, be mediating not only between more orthodox traditions and Hegel but also between Hegel and Schelling.

In the end, Marheineke seemed to satisfy neither philosophers nor theologians. However, Marheineke represented a major first effort to work theologically with insights and dynamics around a variety of themes that Hegel and Schelling had introduced systematically into reflection on the notion of God as Trinity. In his 1827 effort to rethink Trinity creatively, Marheineke drew inspiration especially from Hegel but his reference to being surely recalls Schelling as well.

Isaak August Dorner: the ethical Trinity

Dorner (1809–84) published the first volume of his important study, *A System of Christian Doctrine*, in 1879.[24] While showing in his own thought similarities to Schleiermacher and Kant, it is especially in his notion of the ethical Trinity that he brought together elements from both Hegel and Schelling. With Hegel, Dorner does not speak of Father, Son and Holy Spirit as Persons. Yet, closer to Schelling, he refers to them as perduring modes of being through which absolute divine personality expresses itself. But, in a rather telling phrase one can sense Dorner's rejection of Schelling's notion of potencies as such while retaining some other aspects of Schelling's thought regarding, for example, the idea that the three remain distinct even in the result of the movement toward, for Schelling, personhood:

> Because of the Christian consciousness (§31, 2), and in accordance with scripture, it is requisite to know that these three modes of the divine Being do not become extinct in their product, the divine Personality, but that they eternally endure, in such a way indeed that God can reveal Himself in the world according to each of the three modes of Being, and that in each of them God knows Himself and wills Himself according to its distinction from the other modes, that in each of them He exists as a person and not merely as a power.[c,25]

With Schelling, Dorner stresses the importance of will in his idea of an ethical Trinity as, more specifically for him, the unity of necessity and freedom. Dorner maintains this notion of will in tandem with the need for reference to necessity, a Hegelian theme, in his then more inclusive idea of a truly ethical Trinity. In that ethical Trinity, the Father was necessity, the

---

c. 'Für das christliche Bewußtsein (§31, 2) und gemäß der H. Schrift ist noch erforderlich zu erkennen, daß jene drei Seinsweisen Gottes in ihrem Producte, der göttlichen Persönlichkeit, nicht verlöschen, sonder ewig fortdauern, so zwar daß Gott nach jeder der drei Seinsweisen sich offenbaren kann in der Welt, und daß er in jeder derselben nach ihrem Unterschied von den andern sich will und sich weiß, in jeder derselben als persönlich und nicht bloß als Kraft ist.' Dorner, *System der christlichen Glaubenslehre*, vol. i (Berlin: Wilhelm Hertz, 1879), 431 (i.e. §32, 1).

necessarily good moment of being. The Son is the free or volitional form of goodness in God. The agency of the Holy Spirit eternally affects the unity of the self-knowledge and the self-volition of the free in the necessary and that of the necessary in the free. For Dorner this is a metaphysics of love, a process of eternally absolute personality. He claimed that Trinity so understood was the archetype and principle assuring the unity of necessity and freedom that is experienced in evangelical Christian freedom, itself an essentially ethical matter. In what he calls ethical love, there is a self-preserving love of God-self in God and a communicative form of love by God for what God has brought about. In this communicative love, God is ethically immutable and as God is ever faithful in relations with the world and in history as the history of God's deeds.[26]

During the course of his own presentation of Trinity, Dorner himself pointed out the importance of the Trinitarian thought of both Hegel and Schelling: 'It is impossible to deny that these systems [Hegel's and Schelling's] have done the service of having achieved something for the metaphysical foundations of the concept of the Trinity.'[d,27] Though Dorner himself incorporated a number of identifiably Hegelian elements into his own thinking, it is hard to escape the feeling that he was finally closer to Schelling than to Hegel. There are clear 'family resemblances' between Dorner's Trinitarian thought and that of Hegel and Schelling, but especially that of Schelling. Sadly for Dorner, despite the high quality of his theological reflection, it represented in its speculative character more the thinking of the 1840s than that of the 1870s. For there had already occurred, especially with Albrecht Ritschl from 1865 onwards, a shift from metaphysics toward historical studies carried out in an increasingly neo-Kantian philosophical context.[28] Still, Dorner, in the long run, did help mediate Idealist thinking on Trinity to twentieth-century theologians. These theologians, often themselves greatly influenced by that Idealist thought, would return with a vengeance, so to speak, to reflections on Trinity. The German Idealist Trinitarian legacy would become ever more evident in the twentieth century.

Notes

1. The 1794–5 German text of the critical edition of Fichte's *Science of Knowledge: Grundlage der gesamten Wissenschaftslehre*, is available in J. G. Fichte, *Gesamtausgabe der Bayerischen Akademie der Wissenschaften*, vol. 1. 2: *Werke 1793–1795*, Reinhard Lauth and Hans Jacob

d. 'Man wird auch ihren [Hegels und Schellings] Systemen das Verdienst nicht absprechen dürfen, für die metaphysischen Grundlagen des Trinitätsbegriffs etwas geleistet zu haben.' Dorner, *System der christlichen Glaubenslehre* i, 383 (i.e. §30b, 2).

(eds.) (Stuttgart: F. Frommann, 1965). However, references here are to the *Grundlage* as found in Immanuel Hermann Fichte (ed.), *Johann Gottlieb Fichtes sämmtliche Werke*, 8 vols. (Berlin: Veit and Co., 1845–6), vol. I, 83–328. Reprinted as vols I–VIII, *Fichtes Werke.* 11 vols. (Berlin: de Gruyter, 1971). English translation: *Science of Knowledge*, Peter Heath and John Lachs (eds. and trans.) (Cambridge: Cambridge University Press, 1982), 89–286.

2. On this first principle see Fichte, *Grundlage*, §1, 91–101/*Science*, §1, 93–102.

3. On this second principle see *ibid.*, §2, 101–5/*Science*, §2, 102–5.

4. On this third principle see *ibid.*, §3, 105–23/*Science*, §3, 105–19.

5. See Cyril O'Regan, 'The Trinity in Kant, Hegel, and Schelling', in *The Oxford Handbook of the Trinity*, Gilles Emery, O. P. and Matthew Levering (eds.) (Oxford: Oxford University Press, 2011), 256, with further reference to Fichte's *Die Anweisung zum seligen Leben* (1806).

6. G. W. F. Hegel, *Phänomenologie des Geistes*, Wolfgang Bonsiepen and Reinhard Heede (eds.), *Gesammelte Werke*, vol. IX (Hamburg: Felix Meiner, 1980), 409 line 37 to 421 end; *Phenomenology of Spirit*, trans. A. V. Miller (Oxford: Clarendon Press, 1977), 464 line 37 to 478 end.

7. For Hegel's presentation of Trinity in the 1830 *Encyclopaedia* edition being referred to here, see *Enzyklopädie der philosophischen Wissenschaften im Grundrisse (1830)*, Wolfgang Bonsiepen and Hans-Christian Lucas (eds.), with Udo Rameil, *Gesammelte Werke*, vol. XX (Hamburg: Felix Meiner, 1992), §§564–71, explicitly on Trinitarian syllogisms §§567–71 (hereafter *GW* XX)/Hegel's *Philosophy of Mind*, trans. William Wallace (Oxford: Clarendon, 1975), §§564–71 (hereafter *PM*), explicitly on Trinitarian syllogisms §§567–71.

8. The various lecture-series texts are clearly identified in *Vorlesungen: Ausgewählte Nach-schriften und Manuskripte*, Walter Jaeschke (ed.), vol. V: *Vorlesungen über die Philosophie der Religion, Teil 3: Die vollendete Religion* (Hamburg: Felix Meiner, 1984). English translation: *Lectures on the Philosophy of Religion*, Peter C. Hodgson (ed.), trans. R. F. Brown, P. C. Hodgson and J. M. Stewart with the assistance of H. S. Harris, vol. III: *The Consummate Religion* (Berkeley: University of California Press, 1985). For fuller remarks on Hegel on Trinity and for bibliography, see: Dale M. Schlitt, *Hegel's Trinitarian Claim: a Critical Reflection* (Leiden: Brill, 1984; Albany, NY: State University of New York Press, 2012); *Divine Subjectivity: Understanding Hegel's Philosophy of Religion* (Scranton, PA: Scranton University Press, 1990, 2009); 'Hegel's reconceptualization of trinity: further reflections', in Erwin Schadel and Uwe Voigt (eds.), *Sein – Erkennen – Handeln: Interkulturelle, ontologische und ethische Perspektiven. Festschrift für Heinrich Beck zum 65. Geburtstag* (Frankfurt a.M.: Peter Lang, Europäischer Verlag der Wissenschaften, 1994), 559–65.

9. See Hegel, *Sämtliche Werke. Jubiläumsausgabe in zwanzig Bänden*, Hermann Glockner (ed.), vol. XVIII: *Vorlesungen über die Geschichte der Philosophie* (Stuttgart: Frommann, 1928), 253; *Lectures on the History of Philosophy*, trans. E. S. Haldane and F. H. Simson, vol. II (New York: Humanities, 1955), 76; Review of 'Über die hegelsche Lehre oder: absolutes Wissen und moderner Pantheismus', 2. K. E. Schubarth and L. Carganico, 'Über Philosophie überhaupt und Hegels *Enzyklopädie* der philosophischen Wissenschaften insbesondere. Ein Beitrag zur Beurteilung der Letzteren', in Johannes Hoffmeister (ed.), *Berliner Schriften 1818–1831*, Philosophische Bibliothek, vol. CCXL (Hamburg: Felix Meiner, 1956), 352.

10. The English translation of the quote is that of Walter Jaeschke, 'Philosophical theology and philosophy of religion', in *New Perspectives on Hegel's Philosophy of Religion*, David Kolb (ed.) (Albany, NY: State University of New York Press, 1992), 7.

11. Hegel, *Vorlesungen: Ausgewählte Nachschriften und Manuskripte*, Walter Jaeschke (ed.), vol. III: *Vorlesungen über die Philosophie der Religion, Teil 1: Einleitung. Der Begriff der Religion* (Hamburg: Felix Meiner, 1983), 43 lines 292–310 (1824 lecture series). English translation: *Lectures on the Philosophy of Religion*, Peter C. Hodgson (ed.), R. F. Brown, P. C. Hodgson and J. M. Stewart with the assistance of J. P. Fitzer and H. S. Harris (trans.), vol. I: *Introduction and The Concept of Religion* (Berkeley: University of California Press, 1984), 126–7 (1824 lecture series).

12. See Douglas Hedley, 'Review of *Göttliche Freiheit. Die Trinitätslehre in Schellings Spätphilosophie*, by Malte Dominik Krüger' in *Modern Theology* 27 (2011): 193–4. In reading and presenting an overview of Schelling's Trinitarian thought I have taken guidance first and foremost from Malte Dominik Krüger, *Göttliche Freiheit. Die Trinitätslehre in Schellings Spätphilosophie* (Tübingen: Mohr Siebeck, 2008), whose study includes a full bibliography and extended discussion of relevant historical, textual and systematic studies. Also most helpful: Emilio Brito, 'Trinité et création. L'approche de Schelling', *Ephemerides Theologicae Lovanienses* 62 (1986), 66–88, who provides helpful references to several classical studies on Schelling on God; Émile-Alfred Weber, *Examen critique de la philosophie religieuse de Schelling* (Strasburg: Truttel et Wurtz, 1860), 36–73; for a wider presentation of Schelling on God, see Rowland Gray-Smith, 'God in the philosophy of Schelling. A dissertation in philosophy', PhD dissertation, University of Pennsylvania, Philadelphia, PA, 1933.

13. Emilio Brito, 'Trinité et création', 67–9, provides a helpful summary of Schelling's Trinitarian thought as found in *Die Weltalter. Fragmente. In den Urfassungen von 1811 und 1813*, M. Schröter (ed.) (Munich: Beck, 1946).

14. Teilband 1, *Philosophische Bibliothek*, Walter E. Ehrhardt (ed.), vol. 445a (Hamburg: Felix Meiner, 1992), lectures 16–30, 95–213, and especially lectures 23–30, 150–213. Cited as *Urfassung* with page number.

15. On the importance and reliability of this text, see: Walter E. Ehrhardt, 'Nachwort des Herausgebers', in W. J. S. Friedrich, *Urfassung der Philosophie der Offenbarung*, Teilband 2, Walter E. Erhardt, *Philosophische Bibliothek*, vol. 445b (Hamburg: Felix Meiner, 1992), 729–42; see also Krüger, *Göttliche Freiheit*, 25–9.

16. The text is available in *Philosophie der Offenbarung 1841/42*, with an introduction by Manfred Frank (Frankfurt a.M.: Suhrkamp, [1993] 1977). The editor's long introduction provides an ideal entry into the questions surrounding an understanding of Schelling's later philosophy and especially into its complex relationship to that of Hegel. Among the various printings of this volume, ISBN number 978-3-518-27781-2 includes Kierkegaard's notes on Schelling's lectures, providing an interesting reading of the lectures that is relatively easy to follow: 'Kierkegaards Nachschrift der Schelling-Vorlesung von 1841', 391–467. There is also the collected-works text of these lectures in *Friedrich Wilhelm Joseph von Schellings sämmtliche Werke. Zweite Abtheilung. Dritter Band und Vierter Band: Philosophie der Offenbarung* (Stuttgart: J. G. Cotta, 1858). They are often referred to as vols. XIII and XIV respectively. One or more versions of Schelling's philosophy of revelation lectures will also be included in the *Historisch-kritische Ausgabe*, 40 vols. (Reihe I: *Werke*, II: Nachlass, III: *Briefe*), Thomas Buchheim and Hans Michael Baumgartner (eds.) (Stuttgart-Bad Cannstatt: Frommann-Holzboog, 1976ff.).

17. For example, Schelling, *Urfassung*, 190.

18. On nineteenth-century Trinitarian thought see, for example, the following more recent overviews: Samuel M. Powell, 'The doctrine of the Trinity in nineteenth-century German Protestant theology: Philipp Marheineke, Isaak Dorner, Johann von Hofmann, and Alexander Schweizer', PhD dissertation, Claremont Graduate School, 1987; *The Trinity in German Thought* (Cambridge: Cambridge University Press, 2001), esp. 104–72; 'Nineteenth-century Protestant doctrines of the Trinity' in *The Oxford Handbook of the Trinity*, Gilles Emery, O. P. and Matthew Levering (eds.) (Oxford: Oxford University Press, 2011), 267–80; Aidan Nichols, 'Catholic theology of the Trinity in the nineteenth century', in *The Oxford Handbook of the Trinity*, 281–93; Christine Helmer, 'Between history and speculation: Christian Trinitarian thinking after the Reformation', in *The Cambridge Companion to the Trinity*, Peter C. Phan (ed.) (Cambridge: Cambridge University Press, 2011), 149–69.

19. See David Brown, 'Solovyov, the Trinity and Christian Unity', *Dialogue and Alliance* 4 (1990), 42. Brown refers especially to Vladimir Solovyov, *Lectures on Godmanhood* (London: Dennis Dobson, 1948; now available in a second facsimile edition, San Rafael, CA: Semantron, 2007).

20. See Samuel M. Powell, 'The doctrine of the Trinity in nineteenth-century German Protestant theology', 62–104, esp. 88–104; 'Nineteenth-century Protestant doctrines of the Trinity', 272–4.

21. Philipp Marheineke, *Die Grundlehren der christlichen Dogmatik* (Berlin: F. Dummler, 1819).

22. Marheineke, *Die Grundlehren der christlichen Dogmatik als Wissenschaft* (Berlin: Duncker und Humblot, 1827). On Trinity, see §§413–436, esp. §§413, 422–36.

23. Observation by Walter Jaeschke in *Reason in Religion: The Foundations of Hegel's Philosophy of Religion* (Berkeley, CA: University of California Press, 1990), 296 n. 45.

24. Isaak A. Dorner, *System der christlichen Glaubenslehre, vol. I: Grundlegung oder Apologetik, vol. II: Specielle Glaubenslehre* (Berlin: Wilhelm Hertz, 1879–81, 1st edn; Berlin: Wilhelm Hertz, 1886, 2nd edn) with various editions available online. English translation: *A System of Christian Doctrine*, revised edition in 4 vols., trans. Alfred Cave and J. S. Banks (Edinburgh: T. and T. Clark, 1888–91, vol. I: 1888) with various editions available online. Reference will be made to volume one of the English text, trans. by Alfred Cave and cited by page after the following initial reference by numbered section as well. On Trinity, see especially the section entitled 'The doctrine of the Holy Trinity, or of God as the essentially triune', subsection, C, 'Positive statement of the doctrine of God as the essentially triune', *A System of Christian Doctrine*, §§31, 31b, and 32, 412–65.

    In this presentation of Dorner, I am working especially with Powell, 'The doctrine of the Trinity in nineteenth-century German Protestant theology', 105–50, esp. 126–50; 'Nineteenth-century Protestant doctrines of the Trinity', 274–5; Jonathan Norgate, *Isaak A. Dorner: The Triune God and the Gospel of Salvation* (London: T. and T. Clark, 2009), esp. 1–47, with a very helpful overview of *A System of Christian Doctrine*, on 1–9; and John W. Cooper, *Panentheism: The Other God of the Philosophers: From Plato to the Present* (Grand Rapids, MI: Baker Academic, 2006), 122–4. It should be noted that Wolfhart Pannenberg has described Dorner as 'the most important champion of an essential Trinity in Protestant theology during the second half of the 19th century' in *Systematic Theology*, vol. I, trans. Geoffrey W. Bromiley (Grand Rapids, MI: William B. Eerdmans, 1991), 295.

25. Dorner, *A System of Christian Doctrine*, 448–9. For Dorner on Schelling's understanding of divine potencies in relation to Trinity, see *A System of Christian Doctrine*, 406–7. Also see Isaak Dorner, 'Über Schellings neues System, besonders seine Potenzenlehre' (1860), reprinted in Isaak Dorner, *Gesammelte Schriften* (Berlin: Wilhelm Hertz, 1883), 378–431.

26. Dorner, 'Dogmatic discussion of the doctrine of the immutability of God' (1856), in Claude Welch (ed. and trans.), *God and Incarnation in Mid-Nineteenth Century German Theology* (New York: Oxford University Press, 1965), 115–80. On Dorner's view of ethical immutability as compared with ontological immutability, see Norgate, *Dorner*, 45–6.

27. Dorner, *A System of Christian Doctrine*, 400.

28. Karl Barth, *Protestant Theology in the Nineteenth Century: Its Background and History*, Colin Gunton (ed.), trans. Brian Cozens and John Bowden (London: SCM Press, 2001) (first published 1947), 577–8. See also Emanuel Hirsch, *Geschichte der neuern evangelischen Theologie* (Gütersloh: C. Bertelsmann, 1951), 211, cited by Norgate, *Dorner*, 5 n. 23.

3

German Idealism's Trinitarian legacy: the twentieth century

DALE SCHLITT

Hegel presented Trinity as a dialectically developing movement of divine subjectivity and Schelling proposed an understanding of Trinity as the dynamic interaction of three divine potencies becoming three divine Persons in a renewed fullness of divine being.[1] This presentation and this proposal were so impressive, even in various aspects persuasive, that it would be hard to delimit their influence on twentieth-century Trinitarian thought.[2] The impact these German Idealists have had on subsequent Trinitarian thinking, and especially on that of the twentieth century, should come as little surprise, given the insight, industry and intention toward inclusiveness with which they have creatively handled so many universal themes of ongoing human and religious importance in their Trinitarian considerations. These themes include, for example, subjectivity and objectivity, personhood, spontaneity, freedom and necessity, alienation, spirit, history, universality and particularity, community, infinity, revelation, being as becoming, spirit, and experience and knowledge of God.

3.1 Tracing the Idealist Trinitarian legacy

Tracing the twentieth-century Idealist Trinitarian legacy at a farther remove from the first half of the nineteenth century involves a process of interpretation, at times more art than science, than would be the identification of Idealist influence and resultant impact in the nineteenth century. This process requires paying attention to more general considerations as well as factors related to the self or the one interpreting and to the other or that which is the subject of interpretation.

Among more general factors there is the need to take into consideration both the intrinsic importance of what Hegel and Schelling had to say about Trinity and the growing chronological distance between them and twentieth-century Trinitarian thinkers. This process of interpretation requires recognising, at least in principle, the possibility of a certain 'lineage' among Trinitarian thinkers who will have influenced those following after them. One has to recognise that Idealist philosophers, and those whom their thought has influenced, have conditioned, irrevocably, the overall intellectual and cultural context within which especially western thought as such finds itself and thinking about Trinity in particular takes place. For example, it would be hard not to acknowledge the impact the Idealists have had on contemporary understandings of experience and of the relationship between self and other. This context surely affected and conditioned, at times overtly and at other times less consciously, those thinking creatively about Trinity in the twentieth century and continues to be an important factor in such reflection now into the twenty-first century.

In this interpretative process, from the side of the self, the one or ones doing the interpreting need a good acquaintance with and knowledge of what Hegel and Schelling actually said if they wish to be sensitive to themes, approaches and directions characteristic of Idealist Trinitarian thinking. Being sensitive in this way will permit them, with creative insight and careful judgement, to identify and point out the presence of such themes, approaches and directions in the thought of philosophers, theologians and others who come after the German Idealists. They need as well to profit from previous study of the influence of Idealism on various Trinitarian thinkers and to recognise, perhaps critically, consensuses formed or forming around the Idealist Trinitarian lineage in general and with regard to particular forms of Idealist influence noted in the positions developed by specific Trinitarian thinkers.

To carry out this process of interpretation permitting one to trace the twentieth-century Idealist Trinitarian legacy means of course that one must focus directly on the other or others whose thought is to be interpreted. One will want to consider whether various Trinitarian thinkers have themselves acknowledged a debt to Idealist thinking, or even whether they have rejected such thinking. Of utmost importance, there must be something in a given Trinitarian thinker's way of approaching Trinity and the themes addressed which makes of those thinkers at least potential witnesses to an ongoing Idealist Trinitarian legacy.

3.2 Witnesses to Idealism's Trinitarian legacy

Following upon these more general remarks, the next step is to work with them in identifying the Idealist Trinitarian legacy more concretely by referring to several carefully chosen twentieth-century Trinitarian thinkers who, in their understanding of Trinity, are witness to that legacy. Three major theologians, namely, Karl Barth, Karl Rahner and Wolfhart Pannenberg, will serve as such witnesses. They, in turn, have influenced, often quite directly, Trinitarian thinkers who followed after them. Focusing on selected aspects of their thought will help recognise what might be called 'family resemblances' between their thought on Trinity and that of Hegel or Schelling, or both. 'Family resemblances' refers here to likenesses similar to those noticed in a multi-generational family portrait when one rather spontaneously focuses on facial and other features passed on from one generation to another.

These 'family resemblances' are similarities of thought identifiable in a variety of ways and which can, when examined, often be traced to the influence of German Idealist thinking on subsequent Trinitarian thought. At times such influence and its resultant impact can be noted on the basis of explicit statements made by the Trinitarian thinkers themselves. At other times, however, it will be necessary to single out important themes similarly focused on, thought patterns ordered in like fashion and dynamics according to which, in comparable fashion, relationships between human and divine develop. In some cases, there is a rather clear and established consensus concerning a relationship of what might be referred to as Trinitarian thinkers' creative dependence on Idealist approaches to the question of Trinity. In other cases, the link may be less evident and establishing it will depend on a certain more spontaneous insight into the influence and impact of Idealist thought on a specific Trinitarian thinker. Identifying Hegelian influences will be easier since more work has been done on Hegel's direct and indirect influence on subsequent Trinitarian thought. Tracing Schelling's direct and indirect influence will be more difficult since there is much detailed research still to be done on ways in which Schelling's thought may have come to influence later Trinitarian thinking. Though occasionally it will be helpful to note specific ways in which one or the other Trinitarian thinker rejected or, from his perspective, corrected a position taken by Hegel and/or Schelling, the following remarks will focus primarily on the more positive reception of Idealist thinking by selected subsequent Trinitarian thinkers and, through them, the impact that thinking has had on Trinitarian thought in general.

Already now, in a sense by way of anticipation, it can be said that German Idealist thinkers, and especially Hegel and Schelling, have indeed left in their aftermath a cultural and intellectual context especially conducive to reflecting creatively on the notion of God as Trinity. They provided many specific insights and novel approaches that subsequent Trinitarian thinkers have often found helpful, whether as such or in modified form, as these thinkers worked to give more contemporary expression to the ancient understanding of God as Trinity. Among these is, first of all, Karl Barth.

Karl Barth: the self-revealing Trinity

Barth (1886–1968) burst on to the twentieth-century theological scene with his understanding of Trinity as movement of divine self-revelation. He argued this position vigorously in his monumental *Church Dogmatics*, especially volume I.1, published in 1932.[3] There Barth famously analyses the phrase, 'God reveals Himself as the Lord', to reveal the triadic structure of divine revelation as such: a Revealer, Revelation and Revealedness.[4] '*God* reveals Himself. He reveals Himself *through Himself*. He reveals *Himself*' – God the Father who reveals, God the Son who is revelation and God the Holy Spirit who makes possible the reception of the revelation.[5] Barth presents a three-fold yet single divine lordship, which he identifies with God's freedom, and speaks three times of one divine I as absolute divine personality.

Many have recognised here a more direct, as well as a more indirect or mediated, influence of Idealist thought on Barth's interpretation of revelation in Trinitarian terms. To help in identifying this influence, one can do no better than turn first of all to an important article by Wolfhart Pannenberg.[6] In this article, Pannenberg brings to the fore several elements of Hegelian thought to interpret various aspects of Barth's thought as reflecting parallels between that thought and what Hegel had said. He does this in part as a way of critiquing both Hegel and Barth while he seeks to create a space for his own Trinitarian reflection.

Pannenberg opens his discussion on the relationship between Barth and Hegel by acknowledging that there is a growing consensus that Barth's theology is a variation on modern themes of subjectivity and autonomy.[7] After a review of certain aspects of the development of Barth's thought in the 1920s, he draws attention to several content-wise parallels between Barth and Hegel in that thought from 1927, but especially from 1932, onwards.

For instance, as Barth himself had mentioned, Hegel had almost single-handedly reintroduced the notion of the Trinity into philosophical and at least Protestant theological discussion. In his own passionate and inimitable way, Barth did this again for theology in the twentieth century. Indeed, Barth found in Trinity, and especially immanent Trinity, a way not only to begin his theological reflection but, in reaction to Hegel, to assure the independence of God who as Father stands in relation to the Son and not then in a necessary relation with the world as a condition for divine self-development. In both Hegel and Barth the notions of revelation and Trinity are closely linked, and ultimately are part of the same formal movement. Hegel speaks more radically of the movement as one of divine self-development while Barth focuses more on the movement as one of self-revelation, though of course Hegel had spoken of both. Hegel and Barth both worked with and gave great emphasis to Anselm's ontological proof for the existence of God.[8] Despite these more material similarities, Barth never ceased to recall ambiguities in Hegel's thought that, at least for Barth, ultimately finitised Hegel's supposed infinite movement of thought when Hegel tied it necessarily with finite human subjectivity out of which it never escapes. For Pannenberg, Barth seems to have found, in his encounter with Kierkegaard's thought, confirmation of his own basic hesitancy vis-à-vis the thought of Hegel.[9]

Pannenberg then refers to Dorner, whom he sees as falling under the influence of Hegel. He does not, however, specifically mention Schelling. As Pannenberg stresses, Barth greatly appreciated Dorner, especially for the latter's insistence on the importance of the Christian doctrine of the Trinity and the way in which it permitted Dorner to move beyond both pietism and rationalism.[10] Also, Dorner had insisted that human personality had its grounding in the Trinity, a theme dear to Barth. Pannenberg notes that Dorner had already spoken of divine modes of being, a phrasing that Barth made his own. Surely then Dorner is a theologian who mediated between the thought of both Hegel and the later Schelling and that of Barth and those subsequently influenced by him. Idealist thought influenced Barth both directly through his own reading, especially of Hegel, and indirectly through Dorner.

Pannenberg sees difficulties in the idea of establishing the divine I as already realised with God the Father. Among these difficulties, he points to the almost inevitable subordination of Son and Spirit when one so begins. This, for Pannenberg, was a problem that Dorner, but not Barth, had resolved by establishing the divine I as absolute personality resulting from the interaction of the three divine modes of being.[11] For Barth the divine I of absolute personality expresses itself from the beginning in and as each of the three divine modes of being.

Among the further points Pannenberg makes in his dense but insightful article, is the claim that Barth does not really work out his Trinitarian thought on the basis of scriptural exegesis. Rather, he does so more on the basis of an analysis of the inner logic of the concept of revelation.[12] Barth would respond that his very notion of revelation was, for him at least, witnessed in scripture. Pannenberg goes on to refer to Barth's saying that God already, in eternity, is not without his other and is himself insofar as he is with and in that other. He then insightfully asks the rather astute question as to whether this is not, at least in its structure, the very understanding of subjectivity that Hegel worked out in the development of his understanding of Trinity based on the concept of the Spirit. Pannenberg goes on to ask if even the form of this argument is not similar to that of Hegel. For, while there are real differences between Hegel and Barth, both had, each in his own way, worked out the notion and structured movement of Trinity from and as one of divine self-revelation.[13]

With this remark Pannenberg comes to the essence, so to speak, of the similarity between the thought of Barth and that of Hegel. The structured movement of Barth's thought on Trinity as a movement of subject, predicate and object, or Revealer, Revelation and Revealedness, parallels that of Hegel with his notions of 'in itself', 'for itself' and 'in and for itself'. This is, according to Pannenberg, for both Hegel and Barth a self-objectivising movement as divine self-revelation, though Hegel articulates this movement in a more radical formulation including creation as necessary moment of divine self-development and self-revelation, whereas for Barth the movement of divine self-revelation occurs freely in Jesus Christ.[14] Spirit is for Hegel an ultimately necessary movement of thought formulated in various ways appropriate to the successive moments in his encyclopaedic system while for Barth Trinity is a triply exercised movement of lordship as the free acting of the one divine personality in three distinct divine modes of being. The movement Barth proposes then reflects the structure of that of Hegel. But the way in which he sees it developing reflects more the thought of Schelling as mediated through Dorner. For once Dorner and Barth have veered away from Hegel's project of identifying God as a movement of conceptual thought occurring in and through human thinking. The natural next step within the overall Idealist framework constituting at least a partial context for Barth's thought is to think more, as Schelling did, in terms of will and decision. This is precisely what Barth does, at least indirectly, to the extent that he identifies the essence or being of God with the acts of God within the Trinity and in further revelation through creation, reconciliation, and redemption.

Other authors have indicated further similarities between Barth's Trinitarian thought and that of Idealist thinkers, similarities which are harder to address more directly here given the present focus on the first volume, part one, of Barth's *Church Dogmatics*. An example of such authors would be Samuel M. Powell, who draws attention to what he describes as resonances between Barth's thought and that of Hegel. He speaks of the 'centrality and Christocentric character of revelation in Barth's theology', which resembles Hegel's view of revelation. He also speaks of Barth's presentation of 'the dialectical relationship between Father and Son' in volume IV of the *Church Dogmatics*.[15] In this relationship God passes over into the negation of God without ceasing to be God. Then too, Eberhard Jüngel has, with regard to Barth's Trinitarian thought, written that God's being is in becoming, a theme Hegel himself had in a systematic and determined way introduced into philosophical and theological reflection on God.[16] In addition, Allan Torrance refers to a 'similarity of pattern between Barth's concept of the Word and Hegel's pan-unity of "Absolute Spirit, the one and universal self-thinking thought."' He also speaks of strong parallelisms between Barth's actualism and Hegel's dynamic conception of 'Being'.[17]

Barth, then, has followed in the footsteps of Hegel in that he has, like Hegel, thought Trinity without having, at least in principle, to identify a divine essence beyond or underlying what are for Hegel the moments constituting the movement of divine subjectivity or the modes in and through which absolute divine personality expresses itself. This one movement, whether in Hegel or Barth, permitted each of them to bring together and identify a number of theologoumena such as Trinitarian divine subjectivity or personality, divine self-revelation and the Kingdom of God. With respect to the Kingdom of God, each of these thinkers identified it with what can be termed more loosely the being itself of God. In this move to identify God's being and kingdom, Hegel set up and Barth reinforced a pattern and an approach toward understanding the kingdom or reign and realm of God, employed also by Pannenberg, which serves as an alternative to the more ethically oriented Kantian understanding of the Kingdom of God. These two alternatives, with the former more easily incorporating the latter, have conditioned and established the general parameters of further twentieth-century philosophical and theological reflection on the notion of the Kingdom of God.

In evaluating the greatness of Hegel's philosophy, Barth had written, 'it is possible to bypass Fichte and Schelling, but it is as impossible to pass by Hegel as it is to pass by Kant'.[18] Yet at least in regard to Trinitarian thinking, Barth seems himself in his emphasis on divine freedom and divine modes of being to recall the continuing influence of the later Schelling on Trinitarian thinking. In the case of Barth, one recognises at least the indirect influence of Schelling through Dorner. And through Barth, in one way or another, both Hegel and Schelling continue to influence subsequent Trinitarian thinking. It would be well to recall again Barth's evaluation of Hegel as 'a great problem and a great disappointment, but perhaps also a great promise'.[19] Barth fulfils his own prophecy by showing in his Trinitarian thought something of the great promise of Hegel and, indeed, even Schelling.

Karl Rahner: the self-communicating Trinity

Rahner (1904–84) is arguably the most influential twentieth-century Roman Catholic theologian.[20] He is a complex thinker, a theologian who has incorporated elements from various philosophical traditions into his thinking as he addressed a wide-ranging series of theological questions. Among them, he presented Trinity as a movement of free divine self-communication, especially in his study, *The Trinity*, originally published in 1967, whose title in German translates as, significantly, *The Trinity as Transcendent Ground of Salvation History*,[21] and in two articles, 'Trinity, divine', and 'Trinity in theology', in the theological encyclopaedia, *Sacramentum Mundi*, which he co-edited.[22]

In line with his transcendental theological anthropology and consequent understanding of the structure of the Christian experience of God, Rahner stresses the need for a double mediation in his understanding of Trinity as free divine self-communication. There is the Father's self-communication through the presence of the Spirit at the transcendental level of human experience and through the appearance of the historical saviour, Jesus Christ, at the categorical level of that experience. Trinity is, then, for Rahner a movement of self-communication of the Father as holy mystery, Son as divine self-gift, and Spirit as the one who enables the acceptance of this self-gift. The unoriginate Father mediates himself to himself, the Son is in truth uttered for himself and is the symbol of the Father in which the Father is other than himself and through which he possesses himself.[23] The Spirit is the one who is received and accepted in love for himself. These are three distinct ways or manners of divine subsisting making up one movement of divine self-communication. In this self-communication, the immanent Trinity is the economic Trinity and vice versa, otherwise it would not be self-communication and self-gift.[24] Rahner is quick to stress that this divine self-communication arises out of abundance and not as a movement from potencies to actualities,[25] surely a reference to Schelling's idea of potencies becoming persons through their action in creation.[26] Though Rahner's and Barth's notions of self-communication and self-revelation, respectively, are similar in formal structure to each other and both to Hegel's notion of spirit as self-development, Rahner's shows greater affinities with Roman Catholic theological outlooks while Barth's is more compatible with Protestant sensitivities.

Winfried Corduan has argued to a similarity, to use his word, in the understanding of knowing that undergirds both Hegel's and Rahner's thought in general and, it could be added, their Trinitarian thinking in particular.[27] Hegel and Rahner, each in his own way, turn to the subject and then establish the other or object of knowing out of the 'self'. Hegel begins his dialectically developing movement of logical thought with a first moment, the being of thought. Rahner, for his part, starts from the thought of being and observes that in knowledge the subject becomes the object known, what Rahner calls, to use a Thomistic phrase, the conversion to the phantasm. More specifically, regarding Rahner on Trinity and the experience of God, this initial Rahnerian moment is the pre-thematic awareness of God as the mysterious horizon of being. In his Trinitarian thought, he further identifies God, as absolute mystery, with God the Father. While remaining within a certain overall Kantian context, Rahner has in effect moved from Kant's unacceptable distinction between knower and the unknowable thing-in-itself to a pre-thematic moment of union of self and other. He continues this move in his discussion of the finite human self and its transcendental awareness of being, which being in its absoluteness he identifies with God and, finally again, with God the Father within the Trinity. Given this identification of the horizon of being as mystery with God the Father, Rahner has likewise transformed both the Kantian thing-in-itself and, seemingly, Schelling's notion of ground into a notion of God the Father as absolute mystery. Nicholas Adams, in turn, speaks more generally of Rahner's working with a German understanding of ground as being mediated to Rahner from Schelling by contact with Heidegger. He writes, 'the main point is that the "ground" of thinking is itself unthinkable, yet must be presupposed if one acknowledges that thinking nonetheless happens.'[28]

Many other authors have commented on possible influences of various thinkers, and especially Hegel, on Rahner. Among them, for instance, Milton Michael Kobus explores more especially the influence of Heidegger and Maréchal on Rahner's Trinitarian thought, but without reference to Hegel.[29] Anne Carr speaks of Hegelian ideas as only 'occasionally present' in Rahner's thought, though she does point out several such ideas:

> Chief among these are Hegel's use of the transcendental method to show the grounding of contingent experience in the absolute; his criticism of Kant in showing the ability of the human intellect not only to establish its own limits but simultaneously to transcend those limits in doing so; the dialectical unity of knowing and being; and the turn to history as the realm of the realization of transcendent spirit.[30]

In speaking more generally of Hegel's influence on contemporary theology and on Rahner, Stanley J. Grenz and Roger E. Olson have left the following, rather colourful, remark:

> The specter that haunts Rahner's theology begins to look more and more like the ghost of Hegel, whose pantheistic philosophy of the 'true infinite' that includes the finite in itself blurred the distinction between God and humanity. The house of contemporary theology has been haunted by Hegel's ghost ever since the great German philosopher lectured at Berlin, and Rahner's theology has not been completely exorcised of it.[31]

Whether the notion of the true infinite is considered more negatively or positively, Hegel and Rahner, each in his own way, see Trinity as a movement from initial 'self' to other on to recognition and realisation of the initial 'self' in the other, a mono-subjectively formulated movement of inclusive divine subjectivity. For each of them, Trinity indeed bears the structure of what Hegel called the true infinite. With regard to Rahner in particular, it will be helpful to note that he argues God is immutable in God-self but mutable in God's plenitude in and through creation and human history, whereas Schelling, for example, had insisted only that God the Father, taken here as God 'before' the recognition of initial divine potencies, did not evolve and develop.[32]

Rahner has, with his fundamental notion of divine self-communication, picked up on and run with an idea rather more latent in Hegel's thought. In that thought in general and at times in a more explicit way, especially with reference to the death of Christ, there is a sense of self-sacrifice and self-gift.

From the point of view of Hegel's speculative dialectic, the movement of thought is always one from an initial moment to a second moment and then an enriched return to the first moment. In each of these moves, the prior moment involves a going over into appearance as, or development into, an other, in effect a giving over to another, a sort of formally structured idea of self-gift. So, despite the fact that these moves are described by Hegel as moves from unrealised to realised, his philosophy is at least implicitly in its formal structure of 'going over into' a philosophy of generosity. What Rahner has done, especially in his Trinitarian thought, has been to bring to the fore and reformulate this generous move of self-gift so that his theology of the Trinity becomes a theology of divine generosity.

Wolfhart Pannenberg: Trinity as reciprocally self-distinguishing Father, Son and Spirit

Pannenberg (né 1928) has long been thought of as having maintained Hegel's notion of history as the history of God while transforming Hegel's final-causality-oriented notion of God as movement of spirit into an eschatological understanding of God as the power of the future proleptically active in the present, and especially in the resurrection of Jesus.[33] But Pannenberg is not simply a Hegelian. Schelling as well had worked out an end-oriented and indeed future-oriented understanding of Trinity moving toward a renewal, in his case, of an initial unity of being lost with creation. While Pannenberg clearly reflects this general Idealist thrust toward a culminating end, he interacts with many different theological, philosophical, anthropological, sociological and scientific traditions. To some extent at least these traditions have themselves mediated various Idealist themes and approaches to Pannenberg and others of his generation. On the theological scene, for example, post-idealist thinkers such as Dorner and Barth, themselves influenced by Idealist thought, have in turn had great influence on Pannenberg who is deeply cognisant of such theological traditions. For present purposes, however, it will be sufficient to focus briefly on several examples of 'family resemblances' between Pannenberg's thought on Trinity and that of German Idealists, whether available to Pannenberg more directly or as mediated through others. While admiring Pannenberg's true theological virtuosity and admitting the need for a great deal more study of the relationships between the thought of Pannenberg and that of Hegel and especially Schelling, one quickly comes to recognise as well the great-great-grand paternity, so to speak, of Hegel and Schelling in Pannenberg's theology.[34]

Pannenberg himself spells out his vision of Trinity, in thorough discussion with earlier and then contemporary Trinitarian thinkers, in the first volume of his *Systematic Theology*, published in German in 1988, though his Trinitarian thought pervades all three volumes of his study.[35] Following his critique that Barth did not really let scripture provide the content of his notion of revelation, Pannenberg works, in a way reminiscent of Schelling, extensively with a wide variety of scriptural witnesses to describe the mutual and inter-relational activity of Father, Son and Spirit, to whom he refers as centres of action whose distinctive features emerge more clearly in the world-historical move from creation to eschatological consummation. His proposal to follow the development of Father, Son and Spirit in their relationships with creation recalls Schelling's way of conceiving the three divine potencies on their way to personhood, as does his affirmation of divine unity fully established only at the eschaton. For Schelling, this is the re-establishment of full divine being which had been lost at the moment of creation. For Pannenberg this is the divine unity established through the loving mutual relations of Father, Son and Spirit. It is interesting to note that in *Systematic Theology* Pannenberg refers to Hegel and to the earlier Schelling in the course of his history of the notion of divine revelation but no longer to the later Schelling as he had done in *Revelation as History*. He continues to refer to Hegel over the course of his presentation on the history of the notion of the Trinity in his *Systematic Theology* but does not there refer explicitly to Schelling. Nor does he seem to refer explicitly to Schelling in developing his own theology of the Trinity.[36]

In emphasising the variety of ways in which the three divine Persons interact in divine revelation, Pannenberg takes an important step beyond what is for so many Trinitarian thinkers the more traditional way of understanding the three Persons more or less exclusively in terms of relations of origin.[37] Without denying these relations, he goes on to explore the richness with which he sees scripture describing mutual relations between each of the divine Persons in their multiform interaction with one another.[38] But whereas Schelling spoke of shared divine being, Pannenberg speaks more of shared kingdom and lordship. The Father indeed gives rise to the Son and yet depends on the Son to carry out the reign of the Father. The Son both accepts lordship from the Father and submits himself to the Father's lordship. Each bears witness to the other. And the Spirit not only comes from the Father but bears witness to the Father in bringing to fullness the Son's revelation of the Father. In and through this analysis of these and other mutual relations witnessed in the scriptures, Pannenberg brings to the surface an interrelated movement among the three Persons that is formally but not materially common to them. Though each remains truly different from the other, this formally common movement is one of self-constitution through self-gift one to the other and discovery, in love, of who one is in and through the other.[39] Here Pannenberg has in fact transferred Hegel's overall idea of subjectivity as self-development through otherness from God as such, essentially a mono-subjectivally formulated development, to each of the three divine Persons in their mutual, intersubjectival action. For Pannenberg the triune God is not one subject acting in three distinct ways but is, rather, three distinct divine centres of action moving through their mutual relations and interaction to a final consummation at the end of time. In this final consummation Pannenberg insists on the continuing distinction among the three centres of action, thus recalling Dorner's insistence that the three divine modes of being remain distinct as Persons in the final divine unity. In fact, Schelling, Dorner and Pannenberg each finds it important, in the working out of his thought on Trinity, to emphasise this ongoing and finally perduring distinctness of the three.

In describing this consummation, Pannenberg employs the scientific notion of a field.[40] This field is God's essence as movement of interpersonal love acting in and through the divine Persons. It comes, cumulatively through and as the Holy Spirit, to full realisation as the triune unity of love. This triune unity finally includes all that has occurred in history. Pannenberg then sees history as the history of God, who becomes what Hegel had called the true infinite. For Hegel this true infinite took the form of an inclusive movement of love on the level of religion and of self-thinking thought in philosophy. For Schelling this was an inclusive movement of three freely willing divine potencies-become-Persons through restoring and sharing in the fullness of divine being, and now, for Pannenberg, a field constituted through the interpersonal love of three divine Persons.

The identification here of 'family resemblances' between Pannenberg's Trinitarian thought and that of Hegel and Schelling, a sort of intellectual kinship, can be grounded further and justified at least indirectly by acknowledging his great familiarity with this thought. One can do this by noting, for example, the remarks Pannenberg makes concerning Hegel and Schelling in some of his own writings and then by citing several attestations by others to his profound knowledge of the thought of these two.

Early on Pannenberg referred to Hegel and both the earlier and the later Schelling in his introduction to the volume he edited, *Revelation as History*.[41]

That Pannenberg continued to have an intense interest in Hegel can be seen by the fact that he invited Ludger Oeing-Hanhoff to work on the theme of the reception and critique of Hegel's Trinitarian thought in a presentation to the Protestant Theological Faculty of the University of Munich in 1976.[42] His deep understanding of Hegel is evident in his impressive 1970 study, 'The Significance of Christianity in the Philosophy of Hegel'.[43] One should note as well his later study, 'La Doctrina de la Trinidad en Hegel y su recepción en la teología alemana'.[44] In this article Pannenberg first provides a helpful overview of Hegel on Trinity and then reviews the history of western Trinitarian thought, referring back briefly but insightfully to Augustine, Aquinas and Spinoza, then forward from Hegel through Marheineke and especially Dorner to Barth, Rahner, Jüngel and Moltmann. He stresses Dorner's mediation of Hegel to Barth, who then influences Rahner in his affirmation that the economic Trinity is the immanent Trinity and vice versa. Jüngel links Barth's thought on Trinity and revelation more explicitly with the cross and Moltmann takes this linkage up in the form of a social model of the Trinity.[45]

Along with these references to several of Pannenberg's studies on Idealist thought and especially that of Hegel, there are enlightening personal anecdotes concerning Pannenberg and his great interest in Idealist thought. Robert W. Jensen, for example, provides a particularly pertinent witness to Pannenberg's knowledge of and being at home in Idealist thought:

> I began my study at Heidelberg just as Pannenberg was beginning his teaching. My first semester, he lectured on nineteenth-century Protestant theology, which for most of the semester meant Fichte and Schelling and Schleiermacher and Hegel . . . It was apparent that here was the lecturer's intellectual and even spiritual milieu; for all his sometimes pointed critique, he was at home with and indeed loved these thinkers. When he disagreed with any of them, it was in the way that they disagreed with each other.[46]

I myself also remember fondly the time, at the beginning of my working on a doctoral dissertation on Hegel on Trinity, when I submitted a series of questions, written in my best German and also in English, to Prof. Dr Pannenberg. Later, when he kindly received me in his office in Munich, he thanked me for sending the questions in both English and German because he was not sure he would have understood my written German. In any case, it was clear from our conversation that he had a deep and detailed understanding of Hegel. Still, Winfried Corduan recounts that in discussion

Pannenberg was uncomfortable with the idea of identifying Hegelian roots in his thought, referencing instead Duns Scotus.[47]

Barth, Rahner and Pannenberg – three scholars who in their Trinitarian thought give clear witness to German Idealist influence over the course of the twentieth century. The ways in which the German Idealists have exercised this influence are surely multiple. They have, for example, with their profound and wide-ranging reflection given rise to an overall cultural and intellectual milieu that takes for granted many of their insights and which, at times at least, various Trinitarian thinkers may simply have presupposed and embraced without focusing explicitly on it. The German Idealists have of course created specific works and given lectures that these and other Trinitarian thinkers have often read directly. The Idealists have surely influenced various Trinitarian thinkers more indirectly, with their thought being mediated through theologians such as Dorner and philosophers of the calibre of Heidegger.

Barth, Rahner and Pannenberg, but especially Pannenberg with his profound knowledge of Idealist Trinitarian thought, are witnesses to both Hegelian and Schellingian influences and similarities. They exemplify and thereby give more specific content now to what has been referred to as 'family resemblances' between their thought and that of the Idealists. Generally speaking, Barth and Rahner lean more toward the Hegelian essentially monosubjectival approach to understanding Trinity, while Pannenberg tends more toward the Schellingian, to some extent 'intersubjectival', approach to Trinity. Traditionally, it has been said that western Trinitarian thought stressed more the oneness of God whereas eastern Trinitarian thought emphasised more the three-ness in God. But now Barth, Rahner and Pannenberg have in their own ways continued a move begun by Hegel and Schelling, when considered together, of introducing into the heart of western Trinitarian thinking itself these two different approaches to Trinity; namely, of stressing the oneness or the three-ness. Western Trinitarian thinking can never again be described so monolithically in terms of focus on oneness.

It would be worthwhile as well to explore German Idealist influence, whether more direct or through now classic nineteenth- and twentieth-century Trinitarian thinkers, on other important philosophers and theologians. Among them, for example: the Russian philosopher, Vladimir Solovyov, so strongly influenced by Schelling; the liberationist theologian, Leonardo Boff; the post-Rahnerian Catherine Mowry Lacugna; the feminist theologian Elizabeth Johnson and the process thinker Joseph A. Bracken who, while working with process thought was also influenced by Schelling.[48]

I would refer as well to my own recent reflection on the trajectory of development of the notion of experience from Hegel to Peirce, on to Royce, James, Dewey and John E. Smith, with an initial effort on my part to think of Trinity in terms of experience against the background of Hegel's philosophical reading of Trinity.[49] As the review of three now classic Trinitarian thinkers and reference to others over the course of the twentieth century has shown, German Idealist Trinitarian thinking has indeed proven fecund and its cumulative impact quite significant.

3.3 A challenging legacy

The history of reflection on the experience and notion of God as Father, Son and Holy Spirit is marked by three major efforts to provide, in systematic form, a coherent and comprehensible understanding of Trinity. First, Eastern Church fathers such as Gregory of Nyssa and Basil of Caesarea modified the neo-Platonic view of reality so that Son and Spirit were on the same divine level with the Father rather than emanating, as the neo-Platonic intellect (*nous*) and world soul (*psychē*) did, in a descending and deterministic way from the initial One (*hen*). With this modification, the Eastern Church fathers protected divine freedom and transcendence by saying that the Father freely sends the Son and the Spirit into the world. With this modification they created a space within which human freedom could be exercised.[50] Second, in Augustinian–Thomistic traditions there was a turn inward to the self to find analogies with which to shed light on the relationships of origin of Son to Father and Spirit to Father and Son. Third, in something of a tectonic shift the Idealists proposed in a systematic and formal way to think of Trinity not from a substance-based understanding of reality but as one rooted in a dynamic notion of subjectivity. Though Hegel and Schelling would in a sense say they were simply bringing to explicit consideration the notion of self that is latent in previous Trinitarian thinking, they did in dramatic fashion highlight the developing self as a movement of becoming and introduced in a systematic way the consequent notion of history as the history of God into their understandings of Trinity as movement of inclusive divine subjectivity. They, but especially Hegel, formally and effectively freed themselves from the need to refer to a substantial substratum underlying that which was distinct in God, whether such distinction would be conceived as moment or potency or mode of being. This permitted them to give primacy to the notion of relation and opened the door to a consideration of variously formulated mutual relationships between God and the world in line with and culminating in the idea of the true infinite as inclusive whole.[51]

Impressive as this re-envisioning of Trinity in a more dynamic and developmental mode was, it posed a number of serious challenges to which Trinitarian thinkers coming after Hegel and Schelling have had to respond. Many of these challenges remain 'out there', so to speak, even today. These challenges will surely oblige future Trinitarian thinkers to continue paying attention to and addressing often difficult and complex questions as they work toward an ever-deeper understanding of the communal and individual experience of God as Father, Son and Holy Spirit. Among such challenges facing those who would continue serious efforts to think creatively of Trinity, there is then the need to:

(1) return ever again to a fresh reading of scriptural texts and especially those of the New Testament, which are witnesses to early community and individual experiences of God as Father, Son and Holy Spirit;

(2) develop an understanding of divine 'self', perhaps rooted in the notion of the expressivist self, which allows them to come to terms with the tendency in religious communities to address one God while praying to Father, Son and Holy Spirit;

(3) find coherent and comprehensible ways in which to think of becoming and developing in relation to God in such a manner that religious communities, their theologians and leaders can recognise those ways as helping them give faithful expression to what they experience;

(4) continue to build upon the Idealists' insights into the importance of working with internally interrelated elements in furthering thought on Trinity, including, as a consequence, the bringing together of and treating in a more integrated way various theological themes such as Kingdom of God, revelation and grace, in a more dynamic understanding of Trinity;

(5) recognise, as Hegel and Schelling did in their own ways, that Trinitarian philosophical and theological reflection must take into consideration the religiously pluralist world in which such reflection takes place today;[52]

(6) explore whether, after having seen the Idealists and those following them work with notions of being, thought and will, it would be helpful and indeed the next logical step to look into the notion of experience which, as a more inclusive reality, might better serve to bring together various Idealist insights, along with insights from older Trinitarian

traditions and scripture, in a renewed and enriched, indeed enriching, understanding of Trinity.

German Idealist thinkers, especially Hegel and Schelling, have had such an enduring impact on so many areas of thought and reflection, including in a special way creative Trinitarian reflection, that they have forever changed the intellectual context within which such reflection will be carried out. In particularly impressive moves, they not only dialogued with, critiqued and modified various more generally philosophical as well as more specifically Trinitarian traditions, but they actually themselves worked out their own understandings of dynamically developing subjectivity with which they could then carry out their creative Trinitarian reflection. In so doing, they carved out for themselves an important Trinitarian legacy continuing into the twenty-first century.

Notes

1. On Hegel's and Schelling's Trinitarian thought, see chapter 2 in the present volume.
2. On twentieth-century Trinitarian thought see, for example, the following more recent overviews: Samuel M. Powell, *The Trinity in German Thought* (Cambridge: Cambridge University Press, 2001), 173–259; Veli-Matti Kärkkäinen, *The Trinity. Global Perspectives* (Louisville, KY: Westminster John Knox Press, 2007), 67–380; Gilles Emery, O. P. and Matthew Levering (eds.), *The Oxford Handbook of the Trinity* (Oxford: Oxford University Press, 2011), esp. 294–345; Peter C. Phan (ed.), *The Cambridge Companion to the Trinity* (Cambridge University Press, 2011), 173–290.
3. Karl Barth, *Church Dogmatics*, vol. I.1 (*CD*, I.1), G. W. Bromiley and T. F. Torrance (eds.), trans. G. W. Bromiley, 2nd edn (Edinburgh: T. and T. Clark, 1975).
   There have been several recent review studies, in English, of Barth on Trinity. For a summary of Barth's thought on Trinity, following the order in which Barth presents it in *CD*, I.1, see George Hunsingen, 'Karl Barth's doctrine of the Trinity, and some Protestant doctrines after Barth', in *The Oxford Handbook of The Trinity* (Oxford: Oxford University Press, 2011), 294–313, esp. 294–309. For a presentation referring to a wider range of citations from the various volumes of the *Church Dogmatics*, see Peter Goodwin Heltzel and Christian T. Collins Winn, 'Karl Barth, reconciliation, and the Triune God', in Phan, *Cambridge Companion to Trinity*, 173–91. Also: R. D. Williams, 'Barth on the Triune God', in S. W. Sykes (ed.), *Karl Barth: Studies of his Theological Method* (Oxford: Clarendon, 1979), 147–93; Alan Torrance, 'The Trinity', in John Webster (ed.), *The Cambridge Companion to Karl Barth* (Cambridge: Cambridge University Press, 2000), 72–91; Powell, *The Trinity in German Thought*, 183–93, 216–26, 243–8. For an older, favourable and quite developed consideration of Barth on Trinity, see Claude Welch, *In His Name* (New York: Scribner's, 1952), 161–213. Bibliographies and references in these studies open on to what are seemingly innumerable further studies on Barth on Trinity.
4. *CD*, I.1, 295.

5. *Ibid.*, 296.

6. Wolfhart Pannenberg, 'Die Subjektivität Gottes und die Trinitätslehre: ein Beitrag zur Beziehung zwischen Karl Barth und der Philosophie Hegels', in *Kerygma und Dogma* 23 (1977), 25–40; Jürgen Moltmann, *The Trinity and the Kingdom of God: The Doctrine of God* (New York: Harper and Row, 1981), 241 n. 22, draws attention to the similarity of Barth's doctrine of the Trinity with Hegel's, as indicated by L. Oeing-Hanhoff in 'Hegels Trinitätslehre', *Theologische Quartalschrift* 159 (1979), 287–303.

7. Pannenberg, 'Die Subjektivität Gottes', 25.

8. *Ibid.*, 27.

9. *Ibid.*, 28.

10. *Ibid.*, 28.

11. *Ibid.*, 29.

12. *Ibid.*, 30–6.

13. *Ibid.*, 31. In noting this reflexive structure of subjectivity or, here in Barth, personality, Moltmann, *The Trinity and the Kingdom of God*, 142 with 242 n. 37, refers as far back as Fichte, who 'talked about "being", about "the existence of being" and about "the bond of love" or of reflection, which permits the two to be one'. Moltmann cites J. G. Fichte, *Die Anweisung zum seligen Leben oder auch Die Religionslehre* (1812).

14. Pannenberg, 'Die Subjektivität Gottes', 30–1.

15. Samuel M. Powell, 'Nineteenth-century Protestant doctrines of the Trinity', in Emery and Levering, *Oxford Handbook of Trinity*, 279.

16. Eberhard Jüngel, *God's Being Is in Becoming: The Trinitarian Being of God in the Theology of Karl Barth*, trans. John Webster (Grand Rapids, MI: Eerdmans, 2001).

17. Allan Torrance, 'The Trinity', 89–90 n. 7, quotes R. D. Williams, 'Barth on the Triune God', 188. He also cites Horst Georg Pöhlmann in *Analogia entis oder Analogia fidei? Die Frage der Analogie bei Karl Barth* (Göttingen: Vandenhoeck & Ruprecht, 1965), 117. See also Torrance, *Persons in Communion: An Essay on Trinitarian Description and Human Participation* (Edinburgh: T. and T. Clark, 1996), 244ff.

18. Karl Barth, *Protestant Theology in the Nineteenth Century: Its Background and History*, Colin Gunton (ed.), trans. Brian Cozens and John Bowden (London: SCM Press, 2001) (first published 1947), 396.

19. *Ibid.*, 421.

20. See John W. Cooper, *Panentheism: The Other God of the Philosophers: From Plato to the Present* (Grand Rapids, MI: Baker Academic, 2006), 224; more specifically regarding Rahner's influence on Catholic Trinitarian theology, Peter C. Phan, 'Mystery of grace and salvation: Karl Rahner's theology of the Trinity', in Phan, *Cambridge Companion to Trinity*, 192; concerning Rahner's more indirect influence in Protestant theology, Nicholas Adams, 'Rahner's reception in twentieth-century Protestant theology', in Declan Marmion and Mary E. Hines (eds.), *The Cambridge Companion to Karl Rahner* (Cambridge: Cambridge University Press, 2005), 211–24.

21. Rahner's study on the Trinity: 'Der dreifaltige Gott als transzendenter Urgrund der Heilsgeschichte', in *Mysterium Salutis. Grundriß heilsgeschichtlicher Dogmatik*, Johannes Feiner and Magnus Löher (eds.), vol. II (Einsiedeln: Benziger, 1967), 317–401; *The Trinity*, trans. Joseph Donceel (London: Burns and Oates, 1970), with particular focus on the third part, 80–120. For helpful recent English-language presentations of Rahner on Trinity

see, for example: Vincent Holzer, 'Karl Rahner, Hans Urs von Balthasar, and twentieth-century Catholic currents on the Trinity', in Emery and Levering, *Oxford Handbook of Trinity*, 318–23; Phan, 'Mystery of grace and salvation', 192–207; on certain aspects of Rahner's thought, see Cooper, *Panentheism*, 224–6; David Coffey, 'Trinity', in Marmion and Hines, *Cambridge Companion to Rahner*, 98–111. An earlier study: Thomas F. Torrance, 'Toward an ecumenical consensus on the Trinity', *Theologische Zeitschrift* 6 (1975), 337–50.

22. Vol. VI, Karl Rahner *et al.* (eds.) (New York: Herder, 1970), 295–308, esp. 298–303.

23. Rahner, 'The theology of the symbol', in *Theological Investigations*, trans. Kevin Smyth, vol. IV (London: Darton, Longman and Todd, 1966), 236–7. See Winfried Corduan, 'Elements of the philosophy of Hegel in the transcendental method of Karl Rahner' (PhD dissertation, Rice University, 1977), 191.

24. Rahner, *The Trinity*, trans. Joseph Donceel (London: Burns and Oates, 1970), 22.

25. Rahner, 'Trinity, divine; Trinity in theology', in Rahner *et al.*, *Sacramentum Mundi*, vol. VI, 300–1.

26. Still, it is interesting to note that Schelling had spoken of the Son's causality in terms of formal causality. Rahner himself refers to this causality as quasi-formal causality and later on simply as formal causality.

27. Winfried Corduan, 'Elements of the philosophy of G. W. F. Hegel in 'The transcendental method of Karl Rahner; Hegelian themes in contemporary theology', *Journal of the Evangelical Theological Society* 22 (1979): 351–61, esp. 357–8.

28. Adams, 'Rahner's reception', 217.

29. Milton Michael Kobus, 'The doctrine of the trinity according to Karl Rahner' (DTh dissertation, Graduate Theological Foundation, 2007).

30. Anne Carr, *The Theological Method of Karl Rahner* (Missoula, MT: Scholars Press, 1977), 11 with n. 1.

31. Stanley J. Grenz and Roger E. Olson, *20th Century Theology: God and the World in a Transitional Age* (Downers Grove, IL: IVP Academic, 1991), 254.

32. See Rahner's *Foundations of Christian Faith: An Introduction to the Idea of Christianity* (New York: Crossroad, 1978–87), 219–23 where, in a section entitled 'Can the immutable "become something?"' Rahner discusses this point in some detail. See also Rahner, 'Jesus Christus, Systematik der kirchl. Christologie', in J. Höfer and K. Rahner (eds.), *Lexikon für Theologie und Kirche*, vol. V (Freiburg: Herder, 1956–65), columns 957–8, and Corduan, 'Hegelian themes', 357, where he cites this latter text but indicates as reference p. 956 and refers to Hans Küng's analysis in *Menschwerdung Gottes* (Freiburg: Herder, 1970), 648–52. Kärkkäinen's remarks in *The Trinity. Global Perspectives*, 79–80, are quite helpful. In regard to this question of an immutable God changing, he also refers, on p. 79 n. 20, to Karl Rahner, 'On the theology of the Incarnation', in *Theological Investigations*, vol. IV, trans. Kevin Smyt (New York: Crossroad, 1982), 105–20.

On the relationship between the thought of Rahner and that of Hegel, I have so far not been able to consult the following: H. Striewe, '*Reditio subjecti in seipsum*. Der Einfluss Hegels, Kants und Fichtes auf die Religionsphilosophie Karl Rahners' (doctoral dissertation, Faculty of Philosophy, Freiburg-im-Breisgau University, 1979); James W. Harvey, 'Hegel, Rahner and Karl Barth. A study in the possibilities of a Trinitarian theology' (DPhil thesis, University of Oxford, 1989).

33. On Pannenberg's reading of Hegel's focus on the inclusive end-moment, see Nicholas Adams, 'Eschatology sacred and profane: the effects of philosophy on theology in Pannenberg, Rahner and Moltmann', *International Journal of Systematic Theology* 2 (2000): 283–306, discussion of Hegel and Pannenberg on 286–92.

34. See Iain Taylor, *Pannenberg on the Triune God* (London: T. and T. Clark, 2007), 14–21.

35. Wolfhart Pannenberg, *Systematic Theology*, trans. Geoffrey W. Bromiley, vol. I. (Grand Rapids, MI: William B. Eerdmans, 1991), esp. 259–336. Pannenberg, 'Die Subjektivität Gottes', 25–40. See Powell, *The Trinity in German Thought*, 202–10, 233–9, 243–5, 253–8; Veli-Matti Kärkkäinen, 'The Trinitarian doctrines of Jürgen Moltmann and Wolfhart Pannenberg in the context of contemporary discussion', in Phan, *Cambridge Companion to Trinity*, 223–42, esp. 229–42; Cooper, *Panentheism*, 278–82; Kärkkäinen, *The Trinity: Global Perspectives*, 123–50; and somewhat more broadly, Grenz and Olson, *20th Century Theology*, 186–99; Christiaan Mostert, 'From eschatology to Trinity: Pannenberg's doctrine of God', *Pacifica. Australasian Theological Studies* 10 (1997), 70–83, available online at www.pacifica.org.au/volumes/volume10/issue01/; Roger E. Olson, 'Trinity and eschatology: the historical Being of God in the theology of Wolfhart Pannenberg' (PhD dissertation, Rice University, 1984).

36. Pannenberg, *Systematic Theology*, vol. I, 223.

37. See, for example, Pannenberg, *Systematic Theology*, 307, 318–21.

38. *Ibid.*, 308–19 and throughout the three volumes of *Systematic Theology*.

39. For a particularly inspiring reference to 'Person', see *ibid.*, 422–32, under subtitle 'The love of God' and especially 425–32.

40. See, for example, *ibid.*, 382–4.

41. Wolfhart Pannenberg and Ulrich Wilkens (eds.), *Revelation as History* (London: Collier-Macmillan, 1968, [German edition 1961]), 16–17.

42. The text of this important study is available in Ludger Oeing-Hanhoff, 'Hegels Trinitätslehre. Zur Aufgabe ihrer Kritik und Rezeption', in Theo Kobusch and Walter Jaeschke (eds.), *Metaphysik und Freiheit: Ausgewählte Abhandlungen* (Munich: Erich Wewel, 1988), 91–120, with reference to Pannenberg's invitation on p. 115.

43. In Wolfhart Pannenberg, *The Idea of God and Human Freedom* (Philadelphia: The Westminster Press, 1973), 144–77.

44. Wolfhart Pannenberg, 'La Doctrina de la Trinidad en Hegel y su recepción en la teología alemana', *Estudios trinitarios* 30 (1996), 35–51.

45. *Ibid.*, 35–41 for the overview of Hegel on Trinity and 41–51 for the more historical review.

46. Robert W. Jensen, 'Parting ways?', *First Things*, Issue Archives, May 1995, available online at www.firstthings.com/article/2008/09/001-parting-ways-22.

47. Winfried Corduan, 'Some facts about Pannenberg', Corduan's blog, 13 May 2009, available online at http://win_corduan.tripod.com/theologians.html/#pannenberg/.

48. For example, Vladimir Solovyov's lectures delivered in 1876 at the University of St Petersburg and the (Institute of the) Higher Courses of Studies for Women, and available in translation: *Lectures on Godmanhood* (San Rafael, CA: Semantron, 2007, facsimile edition of the first edition: Dennis Dobson Limited, 1948); see Peter Peter Zouboff, 'Introduction', in *Lectures*, 9–66; Leonardo Boff, *Trinity and Society*, trans. Paul Burns (Maryknoll, NY: Orbis, 1988); Catherine Mowry Lacugna, *God for Us: The Trinity and Christian Life* (New York: Harper, 1991); Elizabeth Johnson, *She Who Is: The Mystery of God in Feminist*

Theological Discourse (New York: Crossroad, 1993). Among Joseph A. Bracken's many studies on Trinity see, for example: *The Triune Symbol: Persons, Process and Community* (Lanham, MD: University Press of America, 1985); *Society and Spirit: A Trinitarian Cosmology* (London: Associated University Presses, 1991); *The One and the Many: A Contemporary Reconstruction of the God-world Relationship* (Grand Rapids, MI: William B. Eerdmans, 2001).

49. Dale M. Schlitt, *Experience and Spirit: A Post-Hegelian Philosophical Theology* (New York: Peter Lang, 2007), esp. 205–59.

50. Ekkehard Mühlenberg suggested these points regarding neo-Platonism and Christian Trinity several years ago.

51. More specifically on Hegel, see Ludger Oeing-Hanhoff, 'Die geschichtliche Notwendigkeit des Hegelschen Gottesbegriffs', in *Metaphysik und Freiheit. Ausgewählte Abhandlungen*, Theo Kobusch and Walter Jaeschke (eds.) (Munich: Erich Wewel, 1988), 123–4.

52. Martin Wendte helpfully brought my attention more fully to the relationships Hegel and Schelling developed between their thought on various religions of the world and their Trinitarian thought.

4

Kierkegaard, Hegelianism and the theology of the paradox

JOEL D. S. RASMUSSEN

In the decades following the First World War, there emerged first in Germany and France, and then spreading outward, what has aptly been called a Kierkegaard 'craze' in which the Danish thinker Søren Kierkegaard (1813–55) was excavated from his relative obscurity and heralded in an era of deep cultural malaise as a 'protesting' thinker on one hand, and as a 'rousing' thinker on the other.[1] With respect to the former, Kierkegaard was supposed to *protest* against the absolute Idealism of G. W. F. Hegel (1770–1831), a philosophy of evolutionary necessity, which, in the words of Michael Theunissen, 'identifies the beginning as the wrapped-up end and the end as the unwrapped beginning'.[2] With respect to the latter, Kierkegaard is said to *rouse* readers about 'existentialism'. But what is existentialism? Generally, it is characterised as the philosophical commitment to understanding oneself subjectively in life's concrete, contingent and ultimately absurd specificity, instead of pursuing the always-elusive universal knowledge of a totalising objective metaphysical system. Kierkegaard – in the pseudonymous works *Fear and Trembling*, *The Concept of Anxiety*, *Concluding Unscientific Postscript* and *The Sickness unto Death*, among others – is often reckoned to be the father of this existentialism, a distinctively modern philosophical tradition in which figures as otherwise diverse as Karl Jaspers, Martin Heidegger, Gabriel Marcel and Jean-Paul Sartre were all supposed to be related. Kierkegaard's prioritisation of subjectivity over objectivity, along with his rejection of the alleged abstractions of Hegelianism, was embraced by those who regarded the most important questions of philosophy as bearing not on the philosophy of history, the identity of meaning and being or absolute knowing, but rather on the concrete actuality of existing human beings. His analyses of such affective dimensions of human experience as anxiety, boredom and despair were supposed to signal a decisive break with philosophical traditions that regarded reason as the principal psychological faculty. Such analyses chimed well with the phenomenology of twentieth-century existentialists, just as Kierkegaard's emphasis on the importance of freely choosing one-self in one's concrete existence harmonised with their discussions of human authenticity.

This 'existentialist' reception of Kierkegaard came under criticism in the second half of the twentieth century, however. In Paul Ricoeur's view, for example, 'existentialism', conceived as a cohesive philosophical school, does not exist.[3] To purge Kierkegaard's authorship of its deeply Christian character and reconcile it with the atheism of Sartre or, alternatively, to read Sartre's works as compatible with the religious themes in Kierkegaard's writings, misinterprets both thinkers. Accordingly, recent scholarship has sought to liberate Kierkegaard from the existentialist caricature and to attempt a re-evaluation of his works in their own context, especially with respect to Kierkegaard's complex relationship both to Christianity and to Hegelianism. This essay will focus on the latter.

4.1 Kierkegaard's response to Hegel

The first major reassessment of Kierkegaard and Hegel is best regarded as a false start. Niels Thulstrup's *Kierkegaard's Relation to Hegel* crystallised and grounded in scholarship the widely held view that 'Hegel and Kierkegaard have in the main nothing in common as thinkers, neither as regards object, purpose, or method, nor as regards what each considered to be indisputable principles.'[4] Merold Westphal takes a less one-sided view: 'There is appropriation as well as negation, and Kierkegaard is never simply anti-Hegelian.'[5] Westphal's claim is echoed in Jon Stewart's prodigious scholarly rejoinder to Thulstrup and the 'standard view'. Stewart demonstrates that 'there are many more points of comparison and similarity between the two thinkers than are generally recognized', and that, far from being a simple 'relation' between the two, 'Kierkegaard had several different *relations* to Hegel that evolved over time.'[6] On Stewart's telling, this evolution passes through three distinct stages. The first is characterised as a period during which Kierkegaard was 'strongly and positively influenced by Hegel and Hegelian philosophy'.[7] The titles *From the Papers of One Still Living* (1838), *The Concept of Irony* (1841) and *Either/Or* (1843) all appear during this period. The middle period, beginning with *Fear and Trembling* in 1843 and culminating with *Concluding Unscientific Postscript* in 1846, constitutes a phase during which Kierkegaard through his pseudonyms developed a sustained critique of Hegelian philosophy. Stewart shows how in many cases where it has been assumed that Kierkegaard had Hegel in his sights, the main targets are rather the Danish Hegelians Johan Ludvig Heiberg (1791–1860) and Hans Lassen Martensen (1808–84). However, it remains unclear whether Kierkegaard took himself to be criticising Hegel himself as well. Finally, Stewart dates the third period from after Kierkegaard left off work on his unpublished *Book on Adler* in 1846 until his death in 1855. During this period, according to Stewart, 'Kierkegaard dropped his polemic and for one reason or another made his peace with Hegelianism.'[8]

I shall contest the claim that in this last period Kierkegaard 'made his peace with Hegelianism', if this means Kierkegaard no longer finds elements of Hegel's thinking profoundly objectionable. Granted, he writes less frequently and less antagonistically against 'the system' in the last period, but the tension remains and sometimes surfaces. For example, in *Practice in Christianity* (1850), Kierkegaard's pseudonym Anti-Climacus alleges critically that Hegel has 'deified the established order'.[a,9] And in 1854, the year before Kierkegaard died, he complains in a journal entry discussing God and history that 'the Hegelian rubbish that the actual is the true is just like the confusion of thrusting the words and actions of the dramatic characters upon the poet as his own words and actions'.[b,10] Such statements attest to something other than having made peace with Hegelianism. It is clearly correct, as Stewart has shown, that in *The Sickness unto Death* Kierkegaard deploys Hegelian concepts and methodologies. But, as I shall elucidate in section 4.4, the dialectic at work in *The Sickness unto Death* functions differently from the productive mediation of Hegelian dialectic. It is rather what Ricoeur has aptly named 'broken-off dialectic' and as such is a form of dialectic that maintains the tension of a theological paradox, rather than consummating in the conceptual mediation of Hegelian absolute knowing.[11] In view of the centrality of this paradox, I will show in sections 4.2–4.6 how Kierkegaard's relations to Hegelianism are creative, dialectical and sometimes appreciative, while also highly critical – even in the final years of his life.

4.2 A truth in irony

Speculative philosophy in a Hegelian key was the dominant movement in Danish intellectual life during Kierkegaard's university years; when the

---

a. 'Forgudede det Bestaaende.' Søren Kierkegaard, Niels Jørgen Cappelørn *et al.* (eds.), *Søren Kierkegaards Skrifter.* 55 vols. (Copenhagen: Gad, 1997–), XII, 96 [hereafter SKS].
b. 'Det Hegelske Sludder om, at det Virkelige er det Sande, er derfor aldeles ligesom den Forvexling, at paanøde en Digter, at hans dramatiske Personers Ord og Handlinger ere hans personlige Ord og Handlinger.' SKS, XXVI, 266–7 (NB, 33:24).

young Kierkegaard was hoping to break into the cultural elite of Copenhagen, Hegel was widely regarded as the greatest and most influential philosopher of the age.[12] Copenhagen's first Hegelian, Heiberg, was the leading figure in Danish cultural life and Kierkegaard early on assumed that recognition by Heiberg and his circle was the sure path to intellectual esteem in what has come to be called Denmark's 'Golden Age'.[13] If Heiberg was Denmark's prominent figure in the literary sphere, then the 'Hegelianising theologian' Martensen stood at the centre of the religious sphere.[14] Martensen tutored Kierkegaard in the theology of Friedrich Schleiermacher and later recalled that although as a pupil Kierkegaard was 'not an ordinary intellect', he nonetheless 'also had an irresistible urge to sophistry, to hairsplitting games, which showed itself at every opportunity and was often tiresome'.[15] The feeling was mutual, as Kierkegaard's journals make abundantly clear. So while Kierkegaard might initially have hoped Heiberg would become his 'mentor', as Stewart puts it, from the very beginning he perceived Martensen as a 'rival'.[16]

Kierkegaard's actual mentor and favourite teacher during his university years was the poet and philosopher Poul Martin Møller (1794–1838). Møller sometimes lectured on Hegelian philosophy, but 'saw evident limitations in the sheer abstractness of Hegel's speculative philosophy'.[17] When Kierkegaard's pseudonymous author of *Concluding Unscientific Postscript* reflects on Møller almost a decade after his death, he claims that at a time 'when everything here at home was Hegelian, [Møller] judged quite differently, [and] that for some time he first spoke of Hegel almost with indignation, until his wholesome, humorous nature made him smile, especially at Hegelianism, or, to recall P. M. even more clearly, made him laugh at it heartily'.[c,18] It is nonetheless clear, however, that when Kierkegaard was Møller's student, both were in many respects sympathetic to Hegel's philosophy.

Kierkegaard's own closest scholarly engagement with Hegel's philosophy may well have been precipitated as early as 1835.[19] A conversation with Møller, which Kierkegaard records as having to do with the concepts of irony and humour, may well have been an occasion for Møller to show Kierkegaard a draft of his short essay 'On the concept of irony'. It is likely this essay influenced Kierkegaard's choice of topic for his master's thesis *On The Concept of*

---

c. 'P. M., medens Alt var hegeliansk, dømte ganske anderledes, at han først en Tid lang næsten med Indignation talte om Hegel, indtil den sunde humoristiske Natur, der var i ham, lærte ham at smile især af Hegelianismen, eller, for endnu tydeligere at erindre om P. M., ret hjertelig at lee af den.' SKS, VII, 41.

Irony, with Continual Reference to Socrates. Møller's short piece foreshadows Kierkegaard's critique of romantic irony.[20]

Kierkegaard derived much of the method and substance of his critique from Hegel who, Kierkegaard notes, regarded romantic irony as 'an abomination'.[d,21] In his *Lectures on Aesthetics*, Hegel alleges that 'moral depravity' was 'made into something sacred and of the highest excellence' through the movement associated with Schlegel.[e,22] And in the *Philosophy of Right* (in a remark that anticipates the section of Kierkegaard's *Either/Or* entitled 'The Seducer's Diary') Hegel remarks:

> Friedrich von Schlegel in his *Lucinde* . . . [has] argued that the marriage ceremony is superfluous and a formality which could be dispensed with, on the grounds that love is the substantial element and that its value may even be diminished by this celebration. [The surrender to sensual impulse is represented] as necessary in order to prove the freedom and intensity of love – an argument with which seducers are not unfamiliar.[f,23]

In *The Concept of Irony* Kierkegaard cites directly and draws upon both Hegel's *Philosophy of Right* and his *Lectures on Aesthetics*, as well as his *Lectures on the Philosophy of History*, his review of Solger's posthumous writings and most especially from his *Lectures on the History of Philosophy*. However, while Hegel is clearly Kierkegaard's primary interlocutor throughout the work, *The Concept of Irony* nonetheless manifests a deep ambivalence not simply towards irony, but also toward Hegel's critique of it.

In part 1, 'The position of Socrates viewed as irony', Kierkegaard deploys the Hegelian dialectical triad of possibility, actuality and necessity to reach a conception of Socrates as an ironist of 'infinite absolute negativity': 'it is negativity because it only negates; it is infinite, because it does not negate this or that phenomenon; it is absolute, because that by virtue of which

---

d. 'En Vederstyggelighed.' SKS, I, 321.
e. 'Liederlichkeit zur Heiligkeit und höchsten Vortrefflichkeit gemacht werden, wie zur Zeit von Friedrich von Schlegels *Lucinde*.' G. W. F. Hegel, Eva Moldenhauer and Karl Markus Michel (eds.), *Hegels Werke in zwanzig Bänden*. 20 vols. [HW] (Frankfurt a.M.: Suhrkamp, 1969–71), XIV, 116.
f. 'Daß die Zeremonie der Schließung der Ehe überflüssig und eine Formalität sei, die weggelassen werden könnte, weil die Liebe das Substantielle ist und sogar durch diese Feierlichkeit an Wert verliert, ist von *Friedrich von Schlegel* in der *Lucinde* . . . aufgestellt worden . . . Die sinnliche Hingebung wird dort vorgestellt als gefordert für den Beweis der Freiheit und Innigkeit der Liebe, eine Argumentation, die Verführern nicht fremd ist.' HW, VII, 317 (§164).

it negates is a higher something that still is not.'[g,24] Although Socrates is unable to reach a positive conception of a 'higher something', nonetheless it becomes clear through Kierkegaard's comparative analysis of Socratic irony and romantic irony in the second part of the dissertation that this is the key to establishing the 'world-historical validity' of the former over the unjustifiable character of the latter. The rationale of Kierkegaard's argument is expressly Hegelian. He reasons that the irony of Socrates signals the first emergence in history of a valid form of individual subjectivity that asserts itself over against the objective social structures and norms (viz., the institutions of the Athenian city-state) in fidelity to a 'higher something', whereas according to Kierkegaard (following Hegel) romantic irony manifests the arbitrary, extravagant and unjustified attempt by such figures as J. G. Fichte, Friedrich Schlegel, Ludwig Tieck and K. W. F. Solger to assert the subjective 'I' as 'the constituting entity' that wants 'to construct the world'.[h,25] Kierkegaard's dissertation supplements the Hegelian philosophy from within a Hegelian framework:

> Finally, here irony also met its master in Hegel. Whereas the first form of irony [Socratic irony] was not combated but was pacified by subjectivity as it obtained its rights, the second form of irony [romantic irony] was combated and destroyed, for inasmuch as subjectivity was unauthorized it could obtain its rights only by being annulled.[i,26]

Thus in 1841 he was still highly reliant upon Hegel.

But Kierkegaard is already seeking to distinguish his method of 'contemplation' from Hegelian 'speculation'.[j,27] Kierkegaard argues that, although Hegel has rightly anathematised romantic irony, the weakness of Hegel's treatment is that 'by his one-sided attack on the post-Fichtean irony he has overlooked the truth of irony, and by his identifying all irony with this, he has done irony an injustice'.[k,28] In the short concluding section of *The Concept of Irony*, he begins to sketch his own alternative to romantic irony.

g. 'Her have vi altsaa Ironien som *den uendelige absolute Negativitet*. Den er *Negativitet*, thi den negerer blot; den er *uendelig*, thi den negerer ikke dette eller hiint Phænomen; den er *absolut*, thi det, i Kraft af hvilket den negerer, er et Høiere, der dog ikke er.' SKS, I, 299.

h. 'Construere Verden. Jeget blev det Constituerende.' SKS, I, 310.

i. 'Endelig traf ogsaa Ironien her sin Mester i Hegel. Medens den første Form af Ironi ikke blev bekjæmpet, men *beroliget* derved at Subjectiviteten skete *sin Ret*, saa blev den anden Form af Ironi bekjæmpet og *tilintetgjort*; thi da den var uberettiget, kunde den kun skee *sin Ret* derved, at den blev ophævet.' SKS, I, 282.

j. 'Contemplationens Form.' SKS, I, 281.

k. 'Hegel, ved eensidig at vende sig mod den efterfichtiske Ironi, har *overseet Ironiens Sandhed*, og idet han identificerede al Ironi med denne, har gjort Ironien Uret.' SKS, I, 303.

Kierkegaard does not wish to deny the importance of the romantic longing for something higher and more perfect than historical existence. Rather, he advocates a role for a controlled form of irony within a fuller view of life, where irony is employed to relativise life's actual, historical features as 'a genuine and meaningful element in the higher actuality whose fullness the soul craves'.[l,29] Instead of pursuing the negative freedom of romantic imagination, controlled irony is supposed to help one achieve a positive freedom within actuality by contextualising one's finite historical existence within the infinite. And it is especially in an age of such prodigious speculative achievement and scientific scholarship that the mastered form of irony is particularly important, Kierkegaard insists, because 'in our joy over the achievement in our age, we have forgotten that an achievement is worthless if it is not made one's own.'[m,30] Kierkegaard's critique is an attempt to preserve a role for irony in the face of Hegel's 'one-sided' repudiation of it.[31] In this respect, although *The Concept of Irony* is 'Hegelian' in the way it draws upon Hegel's critique of irony, it is also already critical.

4.3 *Either* aesthetic irony *or* ethical Hegelianism?

In 1841 Kierkegaard journeyed to Berlin to attend lectures on the 'positive philosophy' of F. W. J. Schelling (1775–1854). Although initially excited by the lectures, Kierkegaard soon tired of them and devoted much of his stay in Berlin to composing what would become *Either/Or*, his first pseudonymous book. The preface to this work opens with a dictum he expects readers to recognise:

> It may at times have occurred to you, dear reader, to doubt somewhat the accuracy of that familiar philosophical thesis that the outer is the inner and the inner is the outer. Perhaps you yourself have concealed a secret that in its joy or in its pain you felt was too intimate to share with others . . . I myself have always been rather heretically minded on this philosophical point and therefore early in my life developed the habit of making observations and investigations as well as possible.[n,32]

l. 'Et sandt og betydningsfuldt Moment i den høiere Virkelighed, hvis Fylde Sjælen attraaer.' SKS, I, 356–7.

m. 'Man har i vor Tid af Glæde over Resultatet glemt, at et Resultat dog ingen Værdi har, naar det *ikke er erhvervet*.' SKS, I, 356.

n. 'Det er maaskee dog stundom faldet Dig ind, kjære Læser, at tvivle en Smule om Rigtigheden af den bekjendte philosophiske Sætning, at det Udvortes er det Indvortes, det Indvortes det Udvortes. Du har maaskee selv gjemt en Hemmelighed, om hvilken Du følte, at den, i sin Glæde eller i sin Smerte, var Dig for kjær til, at Du kunde indvie Andre i den . . . Jeg for min Part har

The thesis in question here derives from Hegel's *Science of Logic*, but Victor Eremita (the pseudonymous editor of *Either/Or*) formulates this passage so that the implications of the thesis can be explored not at the level of speculative logic, but rather in terms of personal existence.[o,33] Cast in terms of Kierkegaard's theory of the 'stages' or 'spheres' of existence, the two volumes of *Either/Or* explore the larger implications of living one's life under the criteria of either the 'aesthetic sphere' or the 'ethical sphere', respectively – criteria which, in the former case, resist the full disclosure of subjective interiority on the paradigm of romantic irony and, in the latter case, mediate personal identity into the larger social forms in a way bearing a striking resemblance to Hegelian ethics.

The first volume of *Either/Or* contains the papers of a young aesthete known to us only as A, and through the arbitrary jumble of the genres of aphorism, essay, diary and epistle they embody the form of romanticism that Hegel and Kierkegaard both criticise as arbitrary, extravagant and unjustifiably subjective. By contrast, the writings of B – known to be a judge named William – appear in the form of two long letters to A in which he argues that the ethical sphere sublates the aesthetic and thereby preserves the most important aesthetic elements within it. Marriage paradigmatically exemplifies the ethical sphere according to William and equally enables one to cultivate the life-long commitment in love that he calls 'the summit of the aesthetic'.[p,34] But to achieve this, one must affirm oneself in one's given social-historical context. The aesthete's desire to live in worlds of his own imaginative creation, he says, lacks the substantiality needed to make the marriage vow and nurture the kind of love that preserves the aesthetic within the ethical. A vow, however, is not a matter of mere aesthetic interest or enjoyment; it is a matter of ethical decision. Thus, 'the ethical' is the sphere from which one derives one's 'idea' of what it is to live and this idea governs one's 'mode' of living. But William makes it clear that thinking ethically is not equivalent to being good, but rather 'designates the choice by which one chooses good and evil or rules them out'.[q,35] The ethical question thus turns on whether an individual will or will not view existence in ethical categories. Westphal shows how William's emphasis on 'self-choice'

altid været noget kjættersk sindet paa dette Punkt af Philosophien, og har derfor tidlig vant mig til, saa godt som muligt, selv at anstille Iagttagelser og Efterforskninger.' SKS, II, 11.

o. 'Das *Innere* ist als die Form der *reflektierten Unmittelbarkeit* oder des Wesens gegen das *Äußere* als die Form des *Seins* bestimmt, aber beide sind nur *eine* Identität'. HW, VI, 180.

p. 'Det Høieste I det Æsthetiske.' SKS, III, 136.

q. 'Det betegner det Valg, hvorved man vælger Godt of Ondt eller udelukker dem.' SKS, III, 165.

entails appropriating the actual social institutions within which one lives, and doing this most concretely by taking upon oneself the mantle of 'married individual'.[36] William affirms the validity of *Sittlichkeit* (ethical life), but he also critiques speculative philosophy alongside romantic aestheticism in terms that strongly echo Møller. Without mentioning Hegel's name, but in an obvious allusion to his philosophy of 'mediation', Judge William restates Møller's insight into the similarity between speculative philosophy and romantic irony when he writes to A:

> The polemical conclusion, from which all your paeans over existence resonate, has a strange similarity to modern philosophy's pet theory that the principle of contradiction is cancelled. I am well aware that the position you take is anathema to philosophy, and yet it seems to me that it is itself guilty of the same error . . . You mediate the contradictions in a higher lunacy, philosophy in a higher unity. You turn toward the future . . . Philosophy turns toward the past, toward the totality of experienced world history; it shows how the discursive elements come together in a higher unity; it mediates and mediates. It seems to me, however, that it does not answer the question I am asking, for I am asking about the future.[r,37]

According to William, then, neither speculative philosophy nor romantic irony gives orientation regarding individual ethical action, the question of how one should conduct oneself in personal life, 'for if one admits mediation, then there is no absolute choice, and if there is no such thing, then there is no absolute Either/Or'.[s,38]

Hegelian philosophy and romantic irony alike tend toward a version of nihilism (ethically speaking) wherein the individual fails to become a self in freedom. Key to understanding how William envisions becoming an ethical self, therefore, is 'choice', the personal freedom and responsibility to decide between competing alternatives for how one should live. The precise reason he thinks speculative philosophy is just as ethically impotent

r. 'Det polemiske Resultat nemlig, hvoraf alle Dine Seirshymner over Tilværelsen gjenlyde, har en underlig Lighed med den nyere Philosophies Yndlings-Theori, at Modsigelsens Grundsætning er hævet. Vel veed jeg, at det Standpunkt, Du indtager, er Philosophien en Vederstyggelighed, og dog forekommer det mig, at den selv gjør sig skyldig i den samme Feil . . . Du medierer Modsætningerne i en høiere Galskab, Philosophien i en høiere Eenhed. Du vender Dig mod den tilkommende Tid . . . Philosophien vender sig mod den forbigangne Tid, mod hele den oplevede Verdenshistorie, den viser, hvorledes de discursive Momenter gaae sammen i en høiere Eenhed, den medierer og medierer. Derimod synes den mig slet ikke at svare paa det, hvorom jeg spørger; thi jeg spørger om den tilkommende Tid.' SKS, III, 166–7.

s. 'Thi indrømmer man Mediationen, saa er der intet absolut Valg, og er der ikke et saadant, saa er der intet absolut enten – eller.' SKS, III, 169.

as romantic irony has to do with its confusion of the sphere of freedom with that of thought. Philosophy (presumably Hegelian philosophy) views the external history of effects 'under the category of necessity' and ignores the inner deed that must be viewed 'under the category of freedom'.[t,39] Like the pseudonymous editor of *Either/Or*, William doubts that the outer is the inner and the inner is the outer, affirming instead the ethical priority of the 'interior deed': for 'in this world there rules an absolute Either/Or, but philosophy has nothing to do with this world'.[u,40] In William's view, therefore, selfhood is a double existence of both the 'inner deed' of choice and the 'external deed' of an action's historical effects, but this dialectic does not admit mediation into a higher conceptual unity.[v,41] This denial of any logical mediation of the outer and the inner, of essence and existence, becomes a hallmark of Kierkegaard's authorship. So, if we still wish with Westphal to characterise Kierkegaard's relations to Hegel in terms of 'an *Aufhebung*', then we should also be mindful that the Kierkegaardian sublation is an idiosyncratic one.[42] Ricoeur aptly names it a 'broken-off dialectic',[43] and instead of tending toward a culmination in the ostensibly objective consummation of what Hegel names 'Absolute knowing', the Kierkegaardian broken-off dialectic increasingly insists upon 'subjectivity', 'the absurd', 'the paradox' and 'faith'.

4.4 The teleological suspension of Hegelian *Sittlichkeit*

In Kierkegaard's 1843 work *Fear and Trembling*, his pseudonymous author Johannes de Silentio depicts the purported contrast between 'the world of the inner deed' and that of the 'external deed' in even deeper relief. Only here, the contrast is not between 'the aesthetic' and 'the ethical', but between 'the ethical' and 'the religious'. On de Silentio's telling, religious faith

> is precisely the paradox that the single individual as the single individual is higher than the universal, is justified before it, not as inferior to it but as superior – yet in such a way . . . that the single individual as the single individual stands in an absolute relation to the absolute. This position cannot be mediated, for all mediation takes

---

t. 'Philosophien seer Historien under Nødvendighedens Bestemmelse, ikke under Frihedens.' SKS, III, 170.

u. 'I denne Verden hersker der et absolut enten – eller; men denne Verden har Philosophien ikke med at gjøre.' SKS, III, 171.

v. 'Den indvortes Gjerning . . . den udvortes Gjerning.' SKS, III, 170.

place only by virtue of the universal; it is and remains for all eternity a paradox, impervious to thought.[w,44]

By contrast, 'the ethical' represents the Hegelian theme of mediated totality:

> The ethical as such is the universal, and as the universal it applies to everyone, which from another angle means that it applies at all times. It rests immanent in itself, has nothing outside itself that is its τέλος [end, purpose] but is itself the τέλος for everything outside itself, and when the ethical has absorbed this into itself, it goes not further.[x,45]

De Silentio's way of developing this contrast is to compare tragic heroes from classical and Biblical literature – Agamemnon, Brutus and Jephthah – with the Biblical figure of Abraham, the paradigmatic person of faith. Regarding the former three, their cases are tragic precisely because despite the fact they all end up killing their children, the *Sittlichkeit* that supposedly justifies these killings (and ostensibly makes them sacrifices rather than murders) is the ethical expectation of their people. Said another way, the three tragic cases all turn on a conflict between parental responsibilities to one's child and civic duties to one's society, where the latter duties tragically trump the former ones. In the case of Abraham's apparent willingness to sacrifice Isaac, by contrast, there is no such social requirement, 'It is not to save a nation, not to uphold the idea of the state that Abraham does it', de Silentio writes: 'there is no higher expression for the ethical in Abraham's life than that the father shall love the son.'[y,46] This is why the binding of Isaac is ethically indefensible and why Abraham must be regarded as a murderer unless he, in fact, has some still higher responsibility that in turn trumps the ethical. In this connection, de Silentio poses the question of whether

w. 'Troen er netop dette Paradox, at den Enkelte som den Enkelte er høiere end det Almene, er berettiget ligeoverfor dette, ikke subordineret, men overordnet, dog vel at mærke saaledes, at det er den Enkelte, der efter at have været som den Enkelte det Almene underordnet, nu gjennem det Almene bliver den Enkelte, der som den Enkelte er det overordnet; at den Enkelte som den Enkelte staaer i et absolut Forhold til det Absolute. Dette Standpunkt lader sig ikke mediere; thi al Mediation skeer netop i Kraft af det Almene; det er og bliver i al Evighed et Paradox, utilgængeligt for Tænkningen.' SKS, IV, 149–50.

x. 'Det Ethiske er som saadant det Almene, og som det Almene Det, der er gjeldende for Enhver, hvilket fra en anden Side lader sig udtrykke saaledes, at det er gjeldende i ethvert Øieblik. Det hviler immanent i sig selv, har Intet uden for sig, der er dets τέλος, men er selv τέλος for Alt, hvad det har udenfor sig, og naar det Ethiske har optaget dette i sig, da kommer det ikke videre.' SKS, IV, 148.

y. 'Det er ikke for at frelse et Folk, ikke for at hævde Statens Idee, at Abraham gjør det . . . Der er intet høiere Udtryk for det Ethiske i Abrahams Liv, end dette, at Faderen skal elske Sønnen.' SKS, IV, 153.

there might be some interior deed of faith, a 'teleological suspension of the ethical', that would vindicate Abraham's external deed in the absence of any societal justification. That the operative conception of the ethical is Hegelian here is clear when de Silentio writes:

> If the ethical – that is, social morality – is the highest and if there is in a person no residual incommensurability in some way such that this incommensurability is not evil (i.e., the single individual, who is to be expressed in the universal), then no categories are needed other than what Greek philosophy had or what can be deduced from them by consistent thought. Hegel should not have concealed this, for, after all, he had studied Greek philosophy.[z,47]

Even if de Silentio had not mentioned Hegel in this connection, his gloss of 'the ethical' here with the phrase 'social morality' is the giveaway, since the Danish term he uses '*det Sædelige*' is equivalent to Hegel's German term for 'ethical life', namely '*Sittlichkeit*', as distinguishable from Kantian '*Moralität*'.

Now, the main point of *Fear and Trembling* is not that faith *necessarily* contradicts 'social morality'. Rather, the claim is that authentic religiousness entails the recognition that the laws and customs of a society are historically contingent and that if there *is* a teleological suspension of the ethical – any affirmation of which is only ever made 'by virtue of the absurd' – then one's highest responsibility is not to society but to God.[aa,48] Thus, the *Sittlichkeit* that stands in tension with faith 'is not a life that revolves around some eternally valid moral laws, knowable by a timeless ahistorical reason', as C. Stephen Evans puts it. Instead, 'it is an ethical life that sees the highest life as one that is devoted to the furtherance of social institutions and socially sanctioned values. Furthermore, this life is conceived, in Hegelian fashion, as in some sense absolute or final.'[49] To recall de Silentio's words, 'It rests immanent in itself, has nothing outside itself that is its τέλος [end, purpose] but is itself the τέλος for everything outside itself, and when the ethical has absorbed this into itself, it goes not further.'[bb,50] Because of such claims to absoluteness or finality, it has been suggested that 'this ethical life sees itself in religious terms as providing salvation'.[51] Yet this is to view things wrongly,

---

z. 'Hvis det Ethiske: det Sædelige er det Høieste, og der intet Incommensurabelt bliver tilbage i Mennesket paa anden Maade, end at dette Incommensurable er det Onde: det Enkelte, der skal udtrykkes i det Almene, saa behøver man ikke andre Kategorier end hvad den græske Philosophi havde, eller hvad der ved en consequent Tænkning lader sig uddrage af disse. Dette burde Hegel ikke have lagt Skjul paa; thi han har dog havt græske Studier.' SKS, IV, 149.

aa. 'I Kraft af det Absurde.' SKS, IV, 131.

bb. 'Det hviler immanent i sig selv, har Intet uden for sig, der er dets τέλος, men er selv τέλος for Alt, hvad det har udenfor sig, og naar det Ethiske har optaget dette i sig, da kommer det ikke videre.' SKS, IV, 148.

he insists. On this, at least, even if not on other matters, Kierkegaard's later pseudonym Anti-Climacus agrees with de Silentio. As Anti-Climacus puts it in *Practice in Christianity* (1850), 'Why has Hegel made conscience and the state of conscience in the single individual "a form of evil" (see *Rechts-Philosophie*)? Why? Because he deified the established order.'[cc,52] The point of de Silentio's notion of a teleological suspension of the ethical, then, we can take to be his fundamental distinction between the universal [the social] and the absolute:

> The paradox of faith, then, is this: that the single individual is higher than the universal, that the single individual – to recall a distinction in dogmatics rather rare these days – determines his relation to the universal by his relation to the absolute, not his relation to the absolute by his relation to the universal. The paradox may also be expressed this way: that there is an absolute duty to God.[dd,53]

This prioritisation of the single individual stands in considerable tension with what Hegel writes in his *Philosophy of Right* (which is precisely where Anti-Climacus directs his readers when he alleges that Hegel deifies the universal or, rather, the established order). There, after introducing the notion of a stage of consciousness at which 'subjectivity claims to be absolute', Hegel writes:

> This last and most abstruse form of evil, whereby evil is perverted into good and good into evil and the consciousness, knowing that it has the power to accomplish this reversal, consequently knows itself as absolute, is the greatest extreme of subjectivity from the point of view of morality. It is the form to which evil has advanced in our time – thanks to philosophy, i.e., to a shallowness of thought which has twisted a profound concept into this shape and has presumed to call itself philosophy, just as it has presumed to call evil good.[ee,54]

cc. 'Hvorfor har Hegel gjort Samvittigheden og Samvittigheds-Forholdet i den Enkelte til «en Form af det Onde» (jvf. *Rechts-Philosophie*), hvorfor, fordi han forgudede det Bestaaende.' SKS, XII, 96.
dd. 'Troens Paradox er da dette, at den Enkelte er høiere end det Almene, at den Enkelte, for at erindre om en nu sjeldnere dogmatisk Distinction, bestemmer sit Forhold til det Almene ved sit Forhold til det Absolute, ikke sit Forhold til det Absolute ved sit Forhold til det Almene. Paradoxet kan ogsaa udtrykkes saaledes, at der er en absolut Pligt mod Gud; thi i dette Pligtforhold forholder den Enkelte som den Enkelte sig absolut til det Absolute. Naar det da i denne Forbindelse hedder, at det er Pligt at elske Gud.' SKS, IV, 162.
ee. 'Diese letzte abstruseste Form des Bösen, wodurch das Böse in Gutes und das Gute in Böses verkehrt wird, das Bewußtsein sich als diese Macht und deswegen sich als absolut weiß, ist die höchste Spitze der Subjektivität im moralischen Standpunkte, die Form, zu welcher das Böse in unserer Zeit und zwar durch die Philosophie, d.h. eine Seichtigkeit des Gedankens, welche

Although not explicit, the target of Hegel's critique of independent subjectivity here is once again surely the post-Fichtean irony of early German romanticism. The fact that he attacks a form of independent subjectivity that conceives of *itself* as absolute, however, means Hegel is attacking a view different from the one Kierkegaard, through his pseudonyms, defends. The notion of a teleological suspension of the ethical, for example, is supposed to work through faithfully relating the self to the absolute, not by recognising itself as absolute. Yet even so, insofar as de Silentio claims the teleological suspension of the ethical cannot be mediated through some universal rationality, Hegel would regard it, at best, as a form of what in his *Phenomenology of Spirit* he calls 'unhappy consciousness'; at worst, he would regard any attempt to suspend the *Sittlichkeit* of concrete universality as a manifestation of evil, or sin, itself. For 'Evil', he maintains, 'is nothing other than the self-centredness of the natural existence of Spirit.'[ff,55]

De Silentio has little to say about evil, except a brief remark about sin. 'Up until now,' he notes, 'I have assiduously avoided any reference to the question of sin and its reality.'[gg,56] This is because, as he says, the whole work is centred on Abraham insofar as he can be understood in 'immediate' rather than in dogmatic categories.[hh,57] Hegel, by contrast, insists that evil – represented religiously [pictorially] in the story of 'the Fall' – can be mediated conceptually and thus the experience of alienation can be understood as a necessary stage in the inexorable process of universal reconciliation, consummating, ultimately, in what he calls 'absolute knowing'.[ii,58] In effect, then, on a Kierkegaardian reading, Hegelianism is the ultimate hubris: the claim that one can know the mind of God.

Kierkegaard protests at Hegel's naturalisation of evil through the category of necessity, along with his *Aufhebung* of religious representations into philosophical concepts. In Kierkegaard's view, by making evil 'nothing other than' a necessary moment in the world-historical process of universal self-consciousness, Hegel's philosophy of Absolute Spirit makes subjective freedom nothing more than an illusion, and in the process he reduces ethics to a sham discourse. As de Silentio puts it, an ethics that ignores sin is a completely

---

einen tiefen Begriff in diese Gestalt verrückt hat und sich den Namen der Philosophie, ebenso wie sie dem Bösen den Namen des Guten anmaßt, gediehen ist.' HW, VII, 265–6 (§140).

ff. 'Das Böse nichts anderes ist als das Insichgehen des natürlichen Daseins des Geistes.' HW, III, 564 (§777).

gg. 'I det Foregaaende har jeg med Flid holdt ethvert Hensyn til Spørgsmaalet om Synden og dens Realitet borte.' SKS, IV, 188.

hh. 'Umiddelbare.' *Ibid.*

ii. 'Das Absolute Wissen.' HW, III, 575–91 (§§788–808).

futile discipline, but if it affirms sin, then it has *eo ipso* exceeded itself.[jj,59] In *The Concept of Anxiety* and *The Sickness unto Death*, Kierkegaard's pseudonymous authors Vigilius Haufniensis and Anti-Climacus, respectively, affirm and develop de Silentio's point about the futility of any ethics that ignores sin, doing so from the point of view of an 'ethical–religious' sphere of life that (ostensibly, at least, and by faith alone) teleologically suspends the view of ethical life represented as 'social morality' in *Fear and Trembling*, and as *Sittlichkeit* in the writings of Hegel. Between Haufniensis and Anti-Climacus, we find Johannes Climacus – the vociferously anti-speculative pseudonymous author of *Philosophical Fragments* and *Concluding Unscientific Postscript* – for whom the noetic effects of sin mean that even the highest accomplishments of human rationality are in important respects still broken and limited.

For Kierkegaard, the phenomena that give rise to thought at the same time exceed what we think about them and in that respect escape the total comprehension of absolute knowing. In particular, one's concrete existence and experience of the world cannot be fully narrated and to that extent at least it is non-rational. Insofar as it is non-narratable, it remains unknown, and this unknown gets symbolised as 'other' or 'alien' in one's understanding of the world. Human experiences of this alienation from the natural world, from other human beings, from ourselves and perhaps most fundamentally the alienation experienced as 'sin' or 'radical evil', cannot ultimately be explained through any conceptual system.

4.5 The theology of paradox and the denial of conceptual mediation

Kierkegaard's later pseudonyms never engage Hegel's writings in the detailed way Kierkegaard did in *The Concept of Irony*. Instead, the critique is always made at a general level and often obliquely. Through his indirect polemic Kierkegaard is attempting to indicate a sphere of existence opaque to any speculative system of knowledge and intimated only through faith. This puts him at odds not simply with the Danish Hegelians, as Stewart claims, but with Hegel as well.

In *Concluding Unscientific Postscript*, Climacus insists upon the strict opposition between an objective logical system and subjective existence: '(a) *a*

---

jj. 'En Ethik, der ignorerer Synden, er en aldeles ørkesløs Videnskab, men gjør den Synden gjeldende, saa er den eo ipso ude over sig selv.' SKS, IV, 188.

logical system can be given; (b) *but a system of existence cannot be given*'.[kk],[60]
He allows that if one nonetheless wishes to construct a logical system, then
'special care must be taken not to incorporate anything that is subject to the
dialectic of existence'.[ll],[61] In particular, Climacus insists that the attribute of
'movement' is a feature exclusive to existence, along with the 'dialectic of the
beginning', and neither can be smuggled into logic; abstract categories *are*,
they do not *become*. But Hegelians do not observe such caution, he thinks,
and in particular, 'Hegel's matchless and matchlessly admired invention –
the importation of movement into logic (not to mention that in every other
passage one misses even his own attempt to make one believe that it is there) –
simply confuses logic'.[mm],[62] However, while on one side of the opposition
speculative philosophy has the world of actuality against it, on the other side
Climacus thinks Christianity answers to this analysis in a way that calls each
individual deeper into his or her subjective existence through faith. And, he
remarks, it was through reading *Fear and Trembling* (along with reading G. E.
Lessing) that he learned how Christian existence is 'rooted in the paradox'
that can never be mediated by historical reasoning or speculative logic.[nn],[63]

One finds Climacus' most potently charged expressions of 'the paradox'
in the third chapter of *Philosophical Fragments*. Paradox, as Johannes Climacus
here characterises it, is manifest in three expressions: the *ultimate paradox of
thought*, the *absolute paradox* and the *paradox of faith*. Climacus characterises
'the ultimate paradox of thought' as the desire 'to discover something that
thought itself cannot think'.[oo],[64] This is the speculative aporia issuing from
the longing for absolute knowledge which, because absolute, exceeds human
noetic capacities. Although thought craves comprehension, the closest one
can come to understanding the absolute is to discover that it is incomprehensible. Still, human understanding is drawn in 'paradoxical passion' to
this frontier, an 'unknown' that Climacus also calls 'the god', but (ostensibly) merely to signify 'that it is the unknown'.[pp],[65] This paradox of thought
is a fervent 'incentive' because human understanding is drawn to what is

kk. '(a) *et logiske System kan der gives*; (b) *men der kan ikke gives noget Tilværelsens System*.' SKS, VII,
105, italics in the original.

ll. 'Skal der imidlertid construeres et logiske System, saa maa der fornemligen agtes paa, at Intet
optages, som er underkastet Tilværelsens Dialektik.' SKS, VII, 106.

mm. 'Hiin mageløse og mageløst beundrede Opfindelse af Hegel, at bringe Bevægelse ind i Logiken
(ogsaa fraseet, at man paa hvert andet Sted savner endog blot hans eget Forsøg paa at bilde En
ind at den er der), netop er at forvirre Logiken.' SKS, VII, 106.

nn. 'Ligger . . . i Paradoxet.' SKS, VII, 103.

oo. 'Dette er da Tænkningens høieste Paradox, at ville opdage Noget, den ikke selve kan tænke.'
SKS, IV, 243.

pp. 'At det er Guden betyder os jo kun, at det er det Ubekjendte.' SKS, IV, 249.

unknown;[qq],[66] yet it is a frustrating 'torment' because understanding always falls short of the absolute to which it is drawn.[rr],[67] This incapacity is not simply a matter of finite limitation but is, Climacus indicates, a consequence of sin: 'In this way', he at one point puts it, 'the Socratic principle that all sin is ignorance is correct; sin does not understand itself in the truth'.[ss],[68]

From a Christian point of view, the divine response to human sin is to 'become flesh' and dwell among a broken and alienated humanity in such a way as to take on sin and effect reconciliation. 'The heart of the matter', Climacus says, is 'the historical fact that the god has been in human form.'[tt],[69] But to think 'the eternalizing of the historical and the historicizing of the eternal' is supposed to constitute an infraction of human understanding's conception of what is possible.[uu],[70] Thus, of this 'absolute paradox' Climacus writes, 'The understanding certainly cannot think it, cannot hit upon it on its own, and if it is proclaimed, the understanding cannot understand it and merely detects that it will likely be its downfall.'[vv],[71] Its very absurdity creates the possibility of 'offence'.[ww],[72] Precisely because of the enduring noetic effects of sin on human understanding, according to Climacus, the divine response to human sin cannot be rationalised and speculatively understood.

Kierkegaard's fullest treatment of the dialectic of sin and salvation is found in his 1849 work *The Sickness unto Death*, published under the pseudonym Anti-Climacus. The question in *The Sickness unto Death* is not how the alienating evil of sin entered the world in the first place (the animating question of *The Concept of Anxiety*), but rather how not to despair over the apparent impossibility of ever escaping sin. Although Hegel is never mentioned in the work, commentators have long noted how it evidences a deep relationship to Hegelian dialectic. This is clear in the following: 'The human self is . . . a derived, established relation, a relation that relates itself to itself and in relating itself to itself relates itself to another.'[xx],[73] Moreover, as Stewart notes, Anti-Climacus refers to his methodology as a dialectical movement and to his central term, namely 'despair' (*Fortvivelse*), as a dialectical concept.[74] But while the terminology is Hegelian, its logic is not. For

---

qq. 'Incitament.' SKS, IV, 249.   rr. 'Qval.' SKS, IV, 249.
  ss. 'Saaledes er det Socratiske rigtigt, at al Synd er Uvidenhed; den forstaaer sig ikke i Sandheden.' SKS, IV, 254.
  tt. 'Det Historiske, at Guden har været i menneskelig Skikkelse, er Hovedsagen.' SKS, IV, 300.
  uu. 'Det Historiskes Eviggjørelse of det Eviges Historiskgjørelse.' SKS, IV, 263.
  vv. 'Forstanden tænker det vel ikke, selv kan den ikke falde paa det, og naar det forkyndes, kan den ikke forstaae det, og mærker blot, at det nok bliver dens Undergang.' SKS, IV, 252.
ww. 'Forargelse.' SKS, IV, 253.
  xx. 'Et . . . deriveret, sat Forhold er Menneskets Selv, et Forhold, der forholder sig til sig selv, og i at forholde sig til sig selv forholder sig til et Andet.' SKS, XI, 130.

Hegel, 'despair' is the negative moment of transition in the 'serial progression' from one manifestation of consciousness to the next.[75] By contrast, on Anti-Climacus' treatment, despair is sin and it is no mere moment in a speculative logic but is 'the continuance of sin' in human existence.[yy,76]

Accordingly, instead of evil overcome through a logical process, Anti-Climacus substitutes an unresolved either/or dialectic. This is a static, 'broken-off dialectic', as Ricoeur names it, insofar as it denies any higher comprehension through some rationally mediating third term.[77]

In *The Sickness Unto Death* reason is powerless to escape or transform the persisting evil of sin by mediating these antinomies of despair into a higher reconciliation. Moreover, while *The Sickness unto Death* might have initially looked like a purely 'psychological' phenomenology of sin, we now recognise that it is more fittingly understood in terms of a theology of paradox. Anti-Climacus endorses the thesis of what he takes to be orthodox dogmatics, and with this the conviction that no one could ever scientifically demonstrate and thereby comprehend the reality of alienating sin as an enduring condition in which human subjects dwell.[78] Such a demonstration would entail a demonstration of God's reality as well, for 'that it is *before God* is the definitively positive element in it'.[zz,79] The very possibility of an indubitable philosophical demonstration of God's reality, however, is what Kierkegaard consistently denies across his entire authorship. God's reality is not a matter for the seemingly inexorable logic of objective necessity, but for the movement of faith made in subjective freedom.

4.6 On making peace with Hegelianism

Kierkegaard's writings display an evolution in his attitude toward Hegelianism. However, there are two arguments against Stewart's suggestion that in a final post-1846 period Kierkegaard 'for one reason or another made his peace with Hegelianism'.[80] First, while *The Sickness unto Death* deploys elements that show his familiarity with Hegel's method of analysis, he deploys these elements in a theology of paradox that is fittingly characterised by Ricoeur as a 'grimacing simulacrum' of Hegelian phenomenology.[81] Second, while 'Kierkegaard dropped his polemic' after 1846, it does not follow that he 'made his peace with Hegelianism'.[82] There is evidence to the contrary. An 1847 piece of writing that went unpublished during Kierkegaard's lifetime

---

yy. 'Syndens Continueerlighed.' SKS, XI, 218.
zz. 'At det er *for Gud* er just det Positive i den.' SKS, XI, 212.

indicates less a 'peace with Hegelianism' than a cultural eclipse of Hegel's speculative 'system' and a changed focus on the 'single individual.'[aaa],[83]

Thus, in this final period Kierkegaard still understood himself in terms of the 'single individual' formula he first developed to take aim at 'the system'. The reason why he no longer polemicises against it is not due to a softening in his viewpoint toward 'the system', but because it had become less culturally relevant than it previously had been. This should not mean that from 1847 Kierkegaard's writing 'can be characterized by its absence of a relation to Hegel'.[84] In those few later places where Kierkegaard does mention Hegelianism, the earlier oppositional attitude clearly remains. For example, in one 1847 journal entry Kierkegaard alleges that the 'fundamental flaw of Hegelian philosophy' is the 'ungodliness' of wanting to abolish the role of individual conscience in the God-relationship, and thereby working to 'deify the judgment passed by the world and one's contemporaries'.[bbb],[85] In 1850, Anti-Climacus echoes this view when in *Practice in Christianity* he alleges that Hegel has 'deified the established order'.[ccc],[86]

Granted, in this last period Kierkegaard writes less frequently about Hegelianism than previously, but usually when mention is made, it is to protest. For example, in 1849 he alleges that 'all the Hegelian talk about doubting and then arriving at certainty' is simply 'rubbish'.[ddd],[87] In 1850, he reprises his old refrain saying, 'Christianity begins about where Hegel ends; the misunderstanding is only that Hegel thought that he was through with Christianity at that point – had even gone beyond it.'[eee],[88] In that same year, he chastises himself for having relied so positively on Hegelian methodology and categories in *The Concept of Irony* – 'What a Hegelian fool I was!'[fff],[89] Another 1850 entry seems to betray a touch of *Schadenfreude* when he writes, '"The system" has just about disappeared. When two students converse and mention the system, they almost involuntarily smile.'[ggg],[90] And in 1851 he asserts, 'The danger in Hegel was that he altered Christianity – and thereby

---

aaa. 'Den Enkelte.' SKS, XVI, 99.

bbb. 'At ville forgude Verdens og de Medlevendes Dom . . . Det er denne Ugudelighed (at afskaffe Samvittigheds-Forholdet) der er den hegelske Philosophies Grundskade.' SKS, XX, 207 (NB, 2:166).

ccc. 'Forgudede det Bestaaende.' SKS, XII, 96.

ddd. 'Vaas som alt det Hegelske, om at tvivle og saa kommer man til Vished.' SKS, XXII, 405 (NB, 14:101).

eee. 'Der, hvor Hegel ender, der omtrent begynder det Xstlige [Christelige] Misforstaaelsen er blot, at Hegel mener *der* at være blevet færdig med det Christelige, ja at være gaaet langt videre.' SKS, XXIII, 68 (NB, 15:96).

fff. 'O, jeg hegelianske Daare.' SKS, XXIV, 32 (NB, 21:35).

ggg. '"Systemet" er som forsvundet; naar to Studerende tale med hinanden og nævne Systemet, komme de næsten uvilkaarligt til at smile.' SKS, XXIV, 17 (NB, 21:13).

achieved agreement with his philosophy', an alteration Kierkegaard characterises as 'infinitely treacherous'.[hhh],[91] Finally, in 1854, the year before Kierkegaard's death, he protests at the 'Hegelian rubbish that the actual is the true',[iii],[92] and characterises Hegel personally in a way that is hardly gracious: 'But Hegel – O, let me think as a Greek! – How the gods must have grinned! Such a repulsive professor who had completely seen through the necessity of everything and got the whole thing down by rote – ye gods!'[jjj],[93] Kierkegaard had hardly made his peace with Hegelianism in his later years.

Yet despite Kierkegaard's enduring hostility toward Hegelianism, its impact on his thinking is obviously deep and extensive, issuing in a number of 'relations' that warrant ongoing reconsiderations. Indeed, even to make sense of Kierkegaard's writings requires that we contextualise them in terms of Hegelian philosophy. In doing so, the temptation to assign Kierkegaard a place within the logical development of the *Phenomenology* will be a perennial one. This is because in Hegelian terms Kierkegaard's unwillingness to represent the unity of spirit through the movements of mediation manifests an 'unhappy consciousness', which is to say, 'the consciousness of self as a dual-natured, merely contradictory being'.[kkk],[94] This final temptation, however, meets with still another Kierkegaardian challenge, for any such incorporation makes the leap of presupposing the reality of the system without ever obviously or finally demonstrating it. Despite Hegel's efforts to disarm this challenge, it can be argued that he also recognised its weight. As Ricoeur writes, 'we need to rediscover that the possibility of the system is both a presupposition and a question for Hegel himself'.[95] In this view, Kierkegaard's relations to Hegelianism should be understood in the light of Hegel's own questioning of the system. So long as the very possibility of the system remains an open question, so too the possible reality remains open of the 'unknown' that transcends philosophy, and which philosophy does not yet, and arguably never could, incorporate. In the words of the Kierkegaardian theology of paradox, this 'frontier' remains both the 'torment' and the 'incentive' of every unfinished philosophy.

---

hhh. 'Uendelig lumskt.' SKS, XXIV, 443 (NB, 25:7).

iii. 'Det Hegelske Sludder om, at det Virkelige er det Sande.' SKS, XXVI, 266 (NB, 33: 24).

jjj. 'Men Hegel – o, lad mig tænke græsk! –: hvor har Guderne griint! En saadan ækel Professor der ganske havde gjennemskuet Alts Nødvendighed, og faaet det Hele paa Ramse: I, Guder!' SKS, XXV, 388 (NB, 30: 11).

kkk. 'Das *unglückliche Bewußtsein* ist das Bewußtsein seiner als des gedoppelten, nur widersprechenden Wesens.' HW, III, 163 (§206).

Notes

1. Paul Ricoeur, 'Doing philosophy after Kierkegaard', in Joseph H. Smith (ed.), *Kierkegaard's Truth: The Disclosure of the Self* (New Haven: Yale University Press, 1981), 325.

2. Michael Theunissen, *Kierkegaard's Concept of Despair*, trans. Barbara Harshaw and Helmut Illbruck (Princeton: Princeton University Press, 2005), 117.

3. Ricoeur, 'Doing philosophy after Kierkegaard', 326.

4. Niels Thulstrup, *Kierkegaard's Relation to Hegel*, trans. George L. Stengren (Princeton: Princeton University Press, 1980), 12.

5. Merold Westphal, 'Kierkegaard and Hegel', in Alastair Hannay and Gordon D. Marino (eds.), *The Cambridge Companion to Kierkegaard* (Cambridge: Cambridge University Press, 1998), 101.

6. Jon Stewart, *Kierkegaard's Relations to Hegel Reconsidered* (Cambridge: Cambridge University Press, 2007), 14.

7. *Ibid.*, 33.

8. *Ibid.*, 34.

9. Søren Kierkegaard, *Practice in Christianity*, Howard V. Hong and Edna H. Hong (eds.) (Princeton: Princeton University Press, 1991), 87.

10. Kierkegaard, *Søren Kierkegaard's Journals and Papers*, Howard V. Hong and Edna H. Hong (eds.), 7 vols. (Bloomington: Indiana University Press, 1967–1978), II, 147 (no. 1445).

11. Ricoeur, 'Doing philosophy after Kierkegaard', 336.

12. Carl Henrik Koch, *Den Danske Idealisme* (Copenhagen: Gyldendal, 2004), 100.

13. See Bruce Kirmmse, *Kierkegaard in Golden Age Denmark* (Bloomington: Indiana University Press, 1990), 136–97.

14. George Pattison, *The Philosophy of Kierkegaard* (Montreal: McGill-Queen's University Press, 2005), 28.

15. Quoted in Bruce Kirmmse (ed.), *Encounters with Kierkegaard: A Life as seen by his Contemporaries* (Princeton: Princeton University Press, 1996), 196.

16. Stewart, *Kierkegaard's Relations to Hegel Reconsidered*, 64.

17. Alastair Hannay, *Kierkegaard: A Biography* (Cambridge: Cambridge University Press, 2003), 48.

18. Kierkegaard, *Concluding Unscientific Postscript*, Howard V. Hong and Edna H. Hong (eds.) (Princeton: Princeton University Press, 1992), 34.

19. Kierkegaard, *Kierkegaard's Journals and Notebooks*, Niels Jørgen Cappelørn *et al.* (eds.) 11 vols. (Princeton: Princeton University Press, 2007–), vol. I, 216.

20. Poul Martin Møller, 'Om Begrebet Ironie', in *Efterladte Skrifter*, 2nd edn, 3 vols. (Copenhagen: Reitzel, 1848), vol. III, 158 [translation JDSR].

21. Kierkegaard, *The Concept of Irony*, Howard V. Hong and Edna H. Hong (eds.) (Princeton: Princeton University Press, 1989), 286.

22. G. W. F Hegel, *Hegel's Aesthetics: Lectures on Fine Art*, trans. T. M. Knox, 2 vols. (Oxford: Clarendon Press, 1975), I: 508.

23. Hegel, *Elements of the Philosophy of Right*, Allen W. Wood (ed.), H. B. Nisbet (trans.) (Cambridge: Cambridge University Press, 1991), 205 (§164).

24. Kierkegaard, *The Concept of Irony*, 261. Kierkegaard takes the phrase directly from Hegel (see p. 254), who uses the phrase 'unendliche absolute Negativität' once in passing to characterise the irony of Solger. See *Hegel's Aesthetics*, I, 68; HW, XIII, 98.

25. Kierkegaard, *The Concept of Irony*, 273.

26. *Ibid.*, 242.

27. *Ibid.*, 241.

28. *Ibid.*, 265.

29. *Ibid.*, 328.

30. *Ibid.*, 327.

31. *Ibid.*, 265.

32. Søren Kierkegaard, *Either/Or*, Howard V. Hong and Edna H. Hong (eds.), 2 vols. (Princeton: Princeton University Press, 1987), vol. I.3.

33. 'The *inner* is determined as the form of *reflected immediacy* or of essence over against the *outer* as the form of *being*; the two, however, are only one identity.' Hegel, *The Science of Logic*, George di Giovanni (eds. and trans.) (Cambridge: Cambridge University Press, 2010), 460.

34. Kierkegaard, *Either/Or*, vol. II, 137.

35. *Ibid.*, 169.

36. Merold Westphal, 'Kierkegaard and Hegel', in Alastair Hannay and Gordon D. Marino (eds.), *The Cambridge Companion to Kierkegaard*, 106.

37. Kierkegaard, *Either/Or*, vol. II, 170.

38. *Ibid.*, II, 173.

39. *Ibid.*, II, 175.

40. *Ibid.*, II, 175.

41. *Ibid.*, II, 174.

42. Westphal, 'Kierkegaard and Hegel', 101.

43. Ricoeur, 'Doing philosophy after Kierkegaard', 336.

44. Kierkegaard, *Fear and Trembling*, Howard V. Hong and Edna H. Hong (eds.) (Princeton: Princeton University Press, 1983), 55–6.

45. *Ibid.*, 54.

46. *Ibid.*, 59.

47. *Ibid.*, 55.

48. *Ibid.*, 35.

49. C. Stephen Evans, *Kierkegaard on Faith and the Self: Collected Essays* (Waco: Baylor University Press, 2006), 215–16.

50. Kierkegaard, *Fear and Trembling*, 54.

51. Evans, *Kierkegaard on Faith and the Self*, 215–16.

52. Kierkegaard, *Practice in Christianity*, 87.

53. Kierkegaard, *Fear and Trembling*, 70.

54. Hegel, *Philosophy of Right*, 170 (§140).

55. Hegel, *Hegel's Phenomenology of Spirit*, A. V. Miller (trans.) (Oxford: Clarendon Press, 1977), 469–70 (§777).

56. *Fear and Trembling*, 98.

57. *Ibid.*

58. Hegel, *Phenomenology of Spirit*, 479–93 (§§788–808).

59. Kierkegaard, *Fear and Trembling*, 98–9.

60. Kierkegaard, *Concluding Unscientific Postscript*, 109.

61. *Ibid.*, 109.

62. *Ibid.*, 109.

63. *Ibid.*, 105.

64. Kierkegaard, *Philosophical Fragments*, Howard V. Hong and Edna H. Hong (eds.) (Princeton: Princeton University Press, 1985), 37.

65. *Ibid.*, 39.

66. *Ibid.*, 44.

67. *Ibid.*, 44.

68. *Ibid.*, 50.

69. *Ibid.*, 103.

70. *Ibid.*, 61.

71. *Ibid.*, 47.

72. *Ibid.*, 49.

73. Kierkegaard, *The Sickness unto Death*, Howard V. Hong and Edna H. Hong (eds.) (Princeton: Princeton University Press, 1980), 13–14.

74. Stewart, *Kierkegaard's Relations to Hegel Reconsidered*, 572.

75. Hegel, *Phenomenology of Spirit*, 49.

76. Kierkegaard, *The Sickness unto Death*, 105–6.

77. Paul Ricoeur, 'Kierkegaard and evil', in Joseph H. Smith (ed.), *Kierkegaard's Truth: The Disclosure of the Self*, 320.

78. Kierkegaard, *The Sickness unto Death*, 98.

79. *Ibid.*, 100.

80. Stewart, *Kierkegaard's Relations to Hegel Reconsidered*, 34.

81. Ricoeur, 'Kierkegaard and evil', 320.

82. Stewart, *Kierkegaard's Relations to Hegel Reconsidered*, 34.

83. Kierkegaard, *The Point of View*, Howard V. Hong and Edna H. Hong (eds.) (Princeton: Princeton University Press, 1998), 118–19.

84. Stewart, *Kierkegaard's Relations to Hegel Reconsidered*, 613.

85. Kierkegaard, *Kierkegaard's Journals and Notebooks* IV, 206.

86. Kierkegaard, *Practice in Christianity*, 87.

87. Kierkegaard, *Journals and Papers* IV, 297 (no. 4457).

88. *Ibid.*, II, 225 (no. 1615).

89. *Ibid.*, IV, 214 (no. 4281).

90. *Ibid.*, III, 322 (no. 2957).

91. *Ibid.*, II, 226 (no. 1618).

92. *Ibid.*, 147 (no. 1445).

93. *Ibid.*, 227 (no. 1620).

94. Hegel, *Phenomenology of Spirit*, 126 (§206).

95. Ricoeur, 'Doing philosophy after Kierkegaard', 336–7.

5

Biblical hermeneutics: from Kant to Gadamer

NICHOLAS BOYLE

'The approach to the Christian religion that is flourishing in our time', the young Hegel wrote in 1795, '...takes reason and morality as the basis of its analysis and as an aid to elucidation calls on the spirit of the nations and the ages.'[a] Two figures above all must have been in his mind as representative of the two great currents that he thought were renewing Christian thinking: Kant ('reason and morality') and Herder ('the spirit of the nations and the ages'). In Kant's treatise, *Religion within the Boundaries of Mere Reason*, published two years previously, the heritage of critical and rationalist deism had been given newly powerful expression through its fusion with a moral theory centred on human freedom and autonomy. Herder, both pupil and declared adversary of Kant, whom he surpassed both in learning and in linguistic ability, had for over two decades been attempting to synthesise the rapidly growing wealth of historical, philological and anthropological knowledge about the nations, literatures and religions of the world into a universal history that both respected human variety and explained the unique position he, as an ordained minister, attributed to Christianity. Hegel himself soon came to realise that two such potent and antagonistic thinkers could not, by a mere verbal gesture, simply be waved together into a single contemporary 'approach to the Christian religion'. On the contrary, they represented two conflicting forces, both of which, from different, perhaps opposite directions, threatened the Bible-based, Lutheran Christianity in which he, like them, had been brought up.[1]

---

a. 'Die Behandlungsart der christlichen Religion, die zu unseren Zeiten im Schwange steht, die Vernunft und Moralität zur Basis ihrer Prüfung und den Geist der Nationen und Zeiten in der Erklärung zu Hilfe nimmt...' Moldenhauer, Eva and Michel, Karl Markus (eds.), *Hegels Werke in zwanzig Bänden*. 20 vols. (Frankfurt a.M.: Suhrkamp, 1969–71), [hereafter HW] [All translations are my own].

Kant had given extraordinary new effectiveness to a hermeneutic dilemma deployed, implicitly or explicitly, by Toland, Tindal and other radical followers of Locke, and more recently given currency by Lessing: either the theological propositions said to be contained in the Bible were rationally based, in which case they could be known without recourse to the Bible, or they were not, in which case it was difficult to see why a rational person should give them any credence. The scriptures, on which alone Lutheran theology had claimed to be based since the Formula of Concord of 1577, were either superfluous or wrong.[2] Herder could counter this sophistry by questioning its glib use of the notion of rationality: there was more to the human mind than 'reason', whatever that was. There was, for example, poetry and there was certainly a great deal of that in the Bible. In the course of history and across the range of nations and civilisations, past and present, humanity had done considerably more than merely progress to the 'so-called Enlightenment' of a 'little northern corner of the world'.[b] But if reason was, as we should now say, culturally determined, Herder faced another problem, at least as intractable as the threat of deism, the problem of historicism. By what universal standard could he compare and evaluate the achievements of different 'nations and ages', and so claim for the Christian scriptures the status not of 'a' book, but of 'the' book, and for Christianity a place at the summit of history, as the one means by which all human beings could be saved? If Herder maintained the irreducibility of human variety, he risked compromising the uniqueness of Christianity. If, after all, he asserted some general measure of human value ('reason' perhaps?), he risked falling back into deism. As Hegel elaborated his mature system, he discovered a means of interpreting the Christian scriptures, which avoided, or reconciled, the dilemmas both of Kantian deism and of Herderian historicism.[3] His solution found little echo in the nineteenth century but was revived to great effect in the twentieth by Hans-Georg Gadamer. Even in Gadamer's version, however, Hegelian hermeneutics bear the mark of their Lutheran origin and still stand in need of revision. In what follows, I shall consider first the specifically hermeneutic aspects of Kant's philosophy of religion and the alternatives to Kant offered by Herder and Schleiermacher, before outlining Hegel's solution and its creative development by Gadamer.

b. 'Sogenannte Aufklärung . . . kleiner nordischer Weltteil.' Johann Gottfried Herder, *Auch eine Philosophie der Geschichte zur Bildung der Menschheit* in: *Schriften zu Philosophie, Kunst und Altertum 1774–1787*, Jürgen Brummack and Martin Bollacher (eds.) (Frankfurt: Deutscher Klassiker Verlag, 1994), 87.

In the later years of his life Kant gave much attention to religious questions. In his childhood he had suffered from the intellectual tyranny exercised in Prussia by pietist Lutheranism under King Frederick William I. From 1740 onwards, aged 16, he had lived under the open-minded regime of Frederick William's son, Frederick the Great, and the years from 1740 to 1786 could be called the heyday of the German Enlightenment. In 1786, however, Frederick the Great died and Frederick William II had a very different attitude to religion from his predecessor. In 1788 the new king's minister for Church affairs, Johann Christoph Wöllner, issued what became known as the 'Religionsedikt', requiring strict orthodoxy in the preaching of all pastors and expressing distress at the spread of the 'errors' of Socinians and deists, and the decline in respect for the revealed word of God in the Bible, all under 'the excessively abused name of Enlightenment'.[c] Five months later another edict announced the re-establishment of strict religious censorship. It must have seemed to Kant that the oppressive religious atmosphere of his youth under Frederick William I was being restored. Almost as if he was determined to resist this new royal policy, or as if he wanted to test its limits, or perhaps felt morally bound to defend the principles of 'Aufklärung' to which he had devoted his life, Kant now began to write more, and more directly, about religion than ever before. The last sections of the *Critique of Judgement* are explicitly theological. Immediately after its publication, Kant wrote a number of short essays on religious topics for the main organ of the Prussian Enlightenment, the *Berlinische Monatsschrift*, and in 1793 he published *Religion within the Boundaries of Mere Reason*. The Berlin censors seem not to have dared to prohibit Kant's writings, but the king was angered. In October 1794 he wrote to Kant through Wöllner, accusing him of 'distorting and belittling' major doctrines 'of holy scripture and of Christianity', specifically in his treatise on religion and 'in other shorter essays', and threatening his 'supreme displeasure' and 'disagreeable steps' if Kant continued.[d] Kant replied by denying that he had passed any negative judgement on Christianity, but giving his personal assurance that he would obey Frederick William's wishes. He published no more on religion for three years. In 1797 Frederick William II died. Kant felt released from a promise, which had been made to the king personally, and published an essay on the relation between

c. 'Den äußerst gemißbrauchten Namen: Aufklärung.' Manfred Kühn, *Kant. Eine Biographie* (Munich: Beck, 2003), 392.
d. 'Entstellung und Herabwürdigung . . . der heiligen Schrift und des Christentums . . . in anderen kleineren Abhandlungen . . . Unserer höchsten Ungnade . . . unangenehme . . . Verfügungen.' KW, VI, 268.

theology and philosophy that he had written in 1794 but had suppressed in accordance with his undertaking. This appeared in 1798 as the first section of the three-part work *Der Streit der Fakultäten* [*The Conflict of the Faculties*].[4]

In *The Conflict of the Faculties* each of the three so-called 'higher' faculties of the eighteenth-century German university, theology, law and medicine, is envisaged as involved in a boundary disagreement with the 'lower' faculty of philosophy, the newcomer in the university that covered not only logic, metaphysics and ethics, but also mathematics, natural science, ancient languages, rhetoric, poetry and history. As solutions to each of the three conflicts Kant presents three essays, of which the 1794 essay on theology and philosophy is the most substantial and the one that clearly mattered most to him. His preface to the whole work published Frederick William II's letter and Kant's reply to it, which explained his recent silence on religious matters and his return to them, drawing attention to the conflict between theology and philosophy as the central issue in the collection. Kant is quite open about the social and political aspect of this conflict. He distinguishes the 'higher' faculties from 'philosophy' as faculties that have an acknowledged social role as vocational subjects: those who study them know they have a future in a structured profession that performs a useful function, or one which is generally regarded as useful. They are therefore protected by the state power, which has an interest in their success. 'Philosophy' is not so protected, or not yet. In the long term and in its own way Kant's intellectual polemic contains a political threat to the privileged position of the established clergy and is a direct riposte to the dead king.

Kant opens the essay with a systematic statement of the opposition between the religion of the philosopher and the religion of the theologian. On the one hand, in the theology faculty there is 'the Biblical theologian' who is a 'scriptural scholar' – one who builds his science of theology on the foundation of Biblical scripture. On the other, in the philosophy faculty, there is the 'rational' theologian who is a 'rational scholar' – one who builds his theology on the basis of reason. The Biblical theologian serves 'ecclesiastical faith', the faith of a particular Church, articulated simply as the rules you have to obey to belong to that Church or sect. The rational theologian serves what Kant a little tendentiously calls 'religious faith', the faith of pure religion as defined in his own treatise on religion within the boundaries of mere reason, which is common, Kant believes, to all human beings. The faith of the Biblical theologian is based on 'statutes' – the laws contained in and issued with the authority of a book and declared to the world as 'revelation'. The faith of the rational theologian is based on 'inner laws' – the laws all rational agents internally impose upon themselves.[e] The faith of the Biblical theologians is therefore dependent on the arbitrary will of someone outside themselves. The faith of the rational theologians develops within themselves and within all human beings simply through the exercise of their own reason. When the Biblical theologian and the rational theologian engage in discussion, therefore, they each have symmetrical anxieties: the Biblical theologian fears that the rational theologian will 'philosophise away' the dogmas that have to be accepted simply as revealed in the Bible, while the rational theologian fears that his Biblical counterpart will lose sight of the true, internal nature of religion.[f] Kant's aim in the essay, he claims, is to show that the conflict between these anxieties can be resolved if we have the right principles for the interpretation of scripture. Therefore, his answer to the conflict of the faculties is to put forward a new hermeneutic.

However, in his search for a resolution of the conflict, Kant admits no compromise in respect of the nature of religion. 'Religion is in no respect distinct from morality.'[g] The central concept in Kant's thinking about morality is freedom, and therefore freedom is the central concept in his thinking about religion, too. Freedom for Kant is the freedom to give myself rational laws for my conduct – laws for my conduct that accord with my reason – rather than receiving laws from outside myself. This principle of autonomy is opposed by Kant to any principle of heteronomy: any suggestion that the laws determining our moral conduct come from any source other than, or outside, ourselves. But it is not only materialist determinism that offers a heteronomous account of moral obligation. Any religious system that derives moral commands from something outside ourselves is also heteronomous: for example, a system that says we are obliged to do what God commands us or what our holy books tell us to do. Even the laws of a secular regime, of a king, for instance, have moral authority over us only because our reason tells us that we must obey properly constituted state authority. For Kant, we could say, only autonomous acts are good and heteronomy is the root of all evil. The definable content of religion is the morally good; that is, autonomous conduct of life – the free observance of universal, rational law – and to suggest it is anything other or more than that is already immoral.

e. 'Der biblische Theolog . . . Schriftgelehrte . . . der rationale . . . Vernunftgelehrte . . . Kirchenglaube . . . Religionsglaube . . . Statuten . . . Offenbarung . . . innern Gesetzen.' KW, VI, 300–1.
f. 'Wegzuphilosophieren.' KW, VI, 303.
g. 'Religion unterscheidet sich nicht . . . in irgend einem Stücke von der Moral.' KW, VI, 301.

'In religion everything depends on what we actually do': religion is a matter not of what is said – e.g. in prayers and creeds – but of what is done.[h] Religion is essentially about moral practice: it is nothing other than a way of being morally good. To be precise, it is that way of being morally good that understands our specific moral obligations as originating in God.[i] The nature of our obligations does not change in the least when they are regarded as religious obligations; we are obliged not to lie and not to murder whether or not we regard those obligations as originating in divine commandments communicated on Mt Sinai. There can never be a case where a religious commandment, properly understood, would be in conflict with a moral commandment, let alone where it might take precedence over it: a religion that commanded us to lie or murder for the sake of God would simply be immoral and a usurpation of the name of religion: it would not be religion at all.

In terms of the great Reformation conflict between justification by faith and justification by works, Kant seems to come down firmly on the side of works. Indeed, Kant directly opposes the central Lutheran concept of justification by faith, if that is understood to mean that it is of any religious – that is moral – significance simply to utter words asserting that one believes something. This is especially so if the supposed object of belief is not an object of possible experience, for example, the assertion that so-and-so is the Son of God. If that assertion is merely a claim to know something – in Kant's terms, if it is 'theoretical' – it has nothing to do with making the believer a better person and so is no part of religion.[5] Indeed, to assert either in general that faith alone could make one better or, in particular, that faith in so-and-so could do as much, would be *contrary* to religion if one's motive for professing one's general belief in faith alone, or for claiming one had that particular faith in a particular person, were simply the desire for heaven or the fear of hell.[6] For concern with one's own comfort is not a moral, and so not a religious, motive. Even if there appear to be arguments for such a belief drawn from the testimony of others – the scriptures *say* so-and-so was the Son of God or an inspired prophet, etc. – or even if it appears that the historical evidence can only be explained on the basis of such a belief – e.g. only if this belief is true can such and such miracles be explained – in those cases such arguments do not do what they intend to do – they cannot prove anything of moral relevance because morality is not a matter

---

h. 'Alles kommt in der Religion aufs Tun an.' KW, VI, 307.
i. 'Der Inbegriff aller unserer Pflichten als göttlicher Gebote.' KW, VI, 300–1.

of what we know but of what we do, and what is not moral is not religious either.

The Lutheran (and indeed Calvinist) appeal to the authority of holy scripture as the ground of belief is therefore repugnant to Kant in two ways. First, it obscures the one true ground of religious concepts, namely their basis in morality, by suggesting that we have them because they are communicated to us in a book. We know about God, Kant believes, not because of what the Bible or indeed any extraneous authority tells us – whether that authority is a Church, a tradition or the local priest – we know about God from our rational reflection on our moral life – that is, through our attempt to live rationally and make reason practical. Second, and worse still, the Lutheran conception of the prime authority of the Bible might lead us to the conclusion that morality itself is what the Bible tells us to do – not what our reason tells us to do through laws that we impose on ourselves. Indeed, as an example of a certainly wicked act, Kant cites the case of Abraham who prepares to offer his son as a human sacrifice – an action which all reason and all nature must tell him is wrong – on the sole ground that he has received a command to do so from an external authority, a God. The conclusion is manifest: to do something because God or the Bible or the Koran tells you to do it, and not because you know that reason requires it, is actually to do evil.[7]

Thus the only possible resolution of the conflict between the faculties of theology and philosophy is unconditional surrender by theology. Kant's new hermeneutic is a set of principles for making rational sense of the Bible; that is, for translating its meaning into conclusions that a rational person can come to anyway, without reading the Bible at all. He expounds these 'philosophical principles of scriptural exegesis' in two stages.[j] First, he distinguishes two elements in the content of the Bible: the 'canon' and the 'organon'. The 'canon' consists of the parts of the Bible that express 'pure religious faith', the rational religion of morality as Kant understands it. The 'organon' consists of the parts that express 'ecclesiastical faith', in the form of statutes that do not and cannot derive from 'mere reason' but have to be accepted simply as a matter of 'revelation'. Evidently there is no problem of interpretation posed by the 'canon' in the Bible as Kant understands it – that consists anyway of the rational religion that is identical with morality. The new hermeneutic is needed for the 'organon', the parts that reason cannot reach.

Kant's second step therefore is to divide the material in the Biblical 'organon' in two. First, there are the 'theoretical' assertions that claim to

---

j. 'Philosophische Grundsätze der Schriftauslegung.' KW, VI, 303.

provide knowledge about things which go beyond the limits that the *Critique of Pure Reason* has laid down. Statements, for example, that are or are held to be about the nature of God, the Trinity, the Incarnation, the Resurrection, about what happened before the beginning of the world or what will happen after its end. Then there are 'practical' assertions – that is, assertions about the moral life – which contradict, or appear to contradict, rational moral law. (If they coincided with the moral law, of course, they would be part of the 'canon'.) An example would be the doctrine of predestination, which seems to Kant directly contradictory to his fundamental principle of moral freedom.

As for the 'theoretical' assertions that go beyond what human beings can know, in a sense Kant thinks that these are not important. Since they are theoretical, they have no practical consequences. Religion is about practice and therefore they are no part of religion. As for their theoretical status, they have none – they are meaningless. However, and this is Kant's first hermeneutical rule, it must be *permissible* for the philosophy faculty to give such doctrines a moral meaning that is in accordance with reason: the theology faculty must not object to this procedure. In other words, some sense can be found even in the most irrational parts of scripture, provided they are made relevant to our moral life. The process of making relevant may involve a fairly robust treatment of the Biblical text. Paul clearly argues that our belief in our own resurrection is dependent on our belief that Christ has risen from the dead. However, Kant says, if we want to retain any meaning for the concept of resurrection at all we must have the courage, and be allowed, to say that in that respect Paul was wrong.[8] If resurrection means anything at all, we believe in Christ's resurrection because of our belief in our own, not the other way round. Our reason, Kant assures us, tells us that a morally perfect person ought to live forever. We need no Bible, and no historical account of any past prophet, to come to that conclusion. Once we have come to it, we may see in the Biblical narrative, and in Paul's commentary on it, an expression of our conclusion. We can see Christ as a morally perfect person whose eternal life was guaranteed by the God in whom we believe on moral grounds. (Alternatively, we may dismiss Biblical talk of resurrection – Christ's or anyone else's – as harmless nonsense, irrelevant to the moral life.)

As for the 'practical' – moral – assertions in the Bible that run counter to rational morality, Kant says it is not merely permissible to interpret these so that they harmonise with reason, it is obligatory to do so. Kant does not specify the means – we may allegorise the text, say it was not meant literally or does not need to be taken literally now – but one way or another we have to acknowledge reason as 'the supreme interpreter of the scripture'.[k] This has clearly been done, Kant remarks with evident relish, by Christian churchmen themselves in the case of the doctrine of predestination: it was plainly adhered to by St Paul and was at the time of the Reformation made into a pillar of the doctrine of 'a great Protestant Church'. It has since been abandoned by most of them because reason finds it 'incompatible with morality'.[l]

If there is an obvious weakness in Kant's new hermeneutic, it lies in his neglect of history. What a particular person or a particular nation did or said or thought about God or the moral law – or indeed anything else – cannot, in Kant's view, be of fundamental importance because it can only be a matter of fact, something that happens to have happened. It cannot express a universal law because a universal law can only be formulated by our reason. The formulation in words of matters of fact will always belong to the 'organon', never to the 'canon' of a holy book. Even if we do see a particular event or person as a perfect example of a universal law – as Kant sees Jesus – it is the law itself that matters.[9] It is because we have first recognised the law that we are able subsequently to recognise the example of it furnished by history and recorded in the scriptures.

The strength and weakness of Kant's approach are both visible in an essay, *Hypothetical Beginning of Human History*, published in January 1786, well before Prussia's religious crisis, when Frederick the Great was still on the throne.[10] It nonetheless perfectly exemplifies the principles of interpretation later formulated in *The Conflict of the Faculties*. At the same time it is an amusing *jeu d'esprit*, characteristic of the halcyon days of the German Enlightenment, before the French Revolution.

In this essay Kant takes the example of a historical Biblical narrative, chapters 2 to 6 of Genesis, and seeks to show that the story it tells follows the lines that rational reflection, operating without any historical evidence at all, deduces as the necessary first stages in human moral development: 'Step by step, the reader . . . will observe whether the path taken by philosophy in accordance with [abstract] concepts coincides with that alleged by history.'[m] These are Kant's hermeneutic priorities in a nutshell: first, the rational concepts, provided by philosophy, and only after them the examples – the evidence – provided by history. So Kant proceeds in this essay by analysing in the abstract the steps by which human beings might have begun

---

k. 'Die oberste Auslegerin der Schrift.' KW, VI, 306.

l. 'Einer großen protestantischen Kirche . . . mit der ganzen Moral unvereinbar.' KW, VI, 306–7.

m. 'Der Leser wird . . . Schritt vor Schritt nachsehen, ob der Weg, den Philosophie nach Begriffen nimmt, mit dem, welchen die Geschichte angibt, zusammentreffe.' KW, VI, 86.

to be aware of their rational powers and their capacity for rational moral behaviour, their freedom, as he calls it, and then appending a reference or allusion to the Biblical text, sometimes just the number of a chapter or verse, which shows that the Bible tells the same story. Both major specific principles of Kant's Biblical hermeneutics expressed in *The Conflict of the Faculties* can here be seen at work.

The first principle was that where theoretical assertions are made about things that go beyond human understanding they *may* (but do not have to) be interpreted in a fashion consonant with reason. They may of course also be left uninterpreted altogether, in which case they simply do not figure in a reasoned account of the contents of the Bible. That is what happens here with chapter one of Genesis – the story of the creation, which was to cause so much grief to nineteenth-century Englishmen (and twentieth-century Americans). Kant simply omits it because it deals with matters that he has shown in his first *Critique* to lie outside the domain of what is knowable. Kant begins his rational history of the human race not with the beginnings of the natural world, nor with the first solitary human being, which would be a biological absurdity, but with the first breeding pair. The nucleus of humanity – that is, of human society – is not a man, but a man and a woman. He therefore also begins his reading of Genesis at chapter 2, with Adam and Eve already in existence (though not named of course, because historical particularities such as names are not rationally determinable): this is as far back in human history as reason can go. If the Bible purports to go back further, it has gone outside the realm in which what it says can be paraphrased rationally.

Kant's second major hermeneutic principle was that assertions in the Bible that contradict practical reason – i.e. immoral assertions – *must* be given a rational re-interpretation, a re-interpretation that brings them back into harmony with reason. Kant's principal concern in his 1786 essay is of this kind. For the Biblical narrative in these chapters of Genesis was the basis for a central dogma in Lutheran and Reformed orthodoxy, the doctrine of inherited original sin: since the sin of Adam and Eve, it was held, had been handed down by physical inheritance to the entire human race, human beings were incapable of doing good on their own initiative but – at least in the most rigorous forms of the belief – could only ever do good as a consequence of the exceptional influence of divine grace.[11] Kant held this belief to be fundamentally immoral, a denial of the basic moral principle of freedom. His hermeneutical rules therefore require that the Biblical narrative be interpreted to mean not this but the opposite. The three conclusions of his hermeneutical exercise have to be, he writes (with evident satisfaction):

that the readers of this text cannot attribute any of the evils that oppress them to God (an appearance of pious theodicy that in reality denies God any influence at all over human affairs), that they have no right, either, 'to ascribe their own delinquency to some original transgression of their ancestors' and that they must therefore attribute only to themselves and their free choice the evil consequences of any misuse of their own power of reason.[n] Kant achieves this extraordinary inversion of the Protestant Christian tradition by an equally extraordinary inversion of the apparent significance of the Biblical narrative.

The Biblical story tells of the expulsion of the first human couple from the garden, in which they are at one with nature and their every need is met without any pain or effort, into a world in which they have to toil for a living and face pain and death, while their descendants develop a social and economic life which creates opportunities for immorality, violence and war. Kant interprets this story as the story not of a decline, not of a fall from grace, but of the liberation of the human species. The so-called fall releases human beings from the state of heteronomous animals driven by instinct, by an external power, whether we call it the law of nature or the will of God. Potentially, they can now rise by their own efforts to the state of rational beings, freely ordering their affairs in accordance with universal, self-imposed law, and thus can be said to be fulfilling the ultimate purpose of creation. It follows of course that if human beings are now free to do good they are also free to do evil. The Biblical story may show us human beings doing evil, but thereby, and more importantly, it shows us that they are free. For the individuals concerned, it may be called the story of a fall because with the attainment of their freedom they become capable of misusing it – that is, they become liable to sin and to all the miserable consequences that flow from sin. For the human species as a whole, however, leaving the Garden of Eden is the first step in progress – it is 'a progression from the worse to the better'.[o] It is as a species, not as individuals, that human beings are called to achieve that fully rational state of affairs that is the goal of creation, and the misfortunes of an individual life should not prevent us from seeing our efforts, however slight or futile they seem, as part of that grand collective endeavour.

The amusing, ingenious or possibly deceitful aspect of Kant's procedure in this essay is that, although it pretends not to be an exercise in the

n. 'Seine eigene Vergehung ... einem ursprünglichen Verbrechen seiner Stammeltern zuzuschreiben.' KW, VI, 101.
o. 'Ein Fortschritt vom Schlechteren zum Besseren.' KW, VI, 102.

hermeneutics of which *The Conflict of the Faculties* would later contain the principles, that is not to be a reading of the text and asking what the rational sense of it might be, what we are given is exactly that. Kant initially presents his account of human origins to us as a rational analysis, supposedly independent of the text, which only at the end is shown to be congruent with what is contained in scripture. Overtly, he is not showing us how to read a Biblical text. Covertly of course he is, for it surpasses credibility that Kant should give us this particular rational sequence of concepts unless 'step by step' he were first reading the text, using it as his guide, 'as a map', he says.[p] But all the time he pretends that he has not read the text and then feigns the surprise, or satisfaction, of finding his ideas confirmed by it. The serious justification for this procedure is that, in Kantian terms, the only religious – that is, moral – sense to be found in scripture will be a sense that we have already determined by our moral reflection before we start to read. The satirical implication is that the right way to read this text is not to read it at all, but to treat it as the material for playful speculations, 'Mutmaßungen', which are all that its bizarre and irrational features deserve, while the weighty matters of human freedom, moral behaviour and guilt are best dealt with by abstract reasoning, without assistance, or rather without interference, from historical narratives. One might think that even in Nietzsche there is nothing to match the satirical effrontery with which, under the cover of an academic amusement, a philosopher's speculation, Kant overturns the central myth of Protestant Christianity – the myth of the Fall of Man – and makes of it a parable of Enlightenment.[12]

Amusing though Kant's speculations might be, his hermeneutics were a threat to all who looked to scripture for the word of salvation, and in particular to the ministers called to preach that word, whether of the Lutheran tradition, like Herder, or the Reformed, like Schleiermacher. Between them, Herder and Schleiermacher built up an alternative hermeneutic, which for a century held at bay the Kantian deconstruction of Bible-based Protestantism, or, in the words of Karl Barth, Herder was 'the inaugurator of nineteenth-century theology before its actual inauguration by Schleiermacher'.[13] Herder's response to the deist reduction of scripture to either a 'republication of the religion of Nature' or irrelevant and meaningless 'mysteries' was a step of great imagination and influence.[14] He broke with the Lutheran and Reformed requirement that the Bible be regarded as a book unlike any other, possessing visible characteristics that clearly

p. 'Als Karte.' KW, VI, 86.

demonstrated its supernatural origin, but avoided the trap laid by deists such as Toland, who had roundly declared: 'Nor is there any different rule to be followed in the Interpretation of *Scripture* from what is common to all other Books'.[15] Unlike Toland, Herder grasped that books were of many kinds and, whether or not they were of divine origin, needed many different 'rules' of 'interpretation'. He was probably the first thinker to make constructive theological use of the idea that the Bible could, and should, be read 'as literature', but he was able to do so because he had already laid the foundations for a creatively new understanding of the nature of literature. Literature appears in Herder's theoretical works of the 1770s as the expression of the spirit of a 'nation' and an 'age', but an expression that has passed through and is owed to the unique experience of a 'genius'.[16] Applied to the literature of the Bible, this principle gave a wholly new importance to the concept of the Biblical 'authors' – now a plurality of religious geniuses, rather than the unitary Holy Spirit whom orthodoxy still claimed to have dictated the scriptural text and whose words were therefore expected, by friend and foe, to be the voice of universal reason. It was of the essence of poetry as Herder conceived it that it emerged from the direct contact between the life surging in the universe and the individual source of life within the poet and so it was, he held, in the Bible. The 'feelings' and 'characteristics' of individual human beings are, he says, what we find in the psalms,[17] and the 'genius' of Biblical literature, as of all poetry, lies originally in the putting into words of this moment of contact between the historically specific individual and the animator of the universe, a process that 'can be called human and divine, since it is both'.[q] Named or unnamed, the authors of the scriptures have for Herder an individuality that is inseparable from their inspiration, their privileged access to divinity.

While Kant's hermeneutic requires us to deploy the concepts of morality and religion within the boundaries of mere reason, in order to determine the *rational* meaning of the scripture, Herder's requires us to deploy knowledge of scripture's historical and literary context in order to determine its *original* meaning. Herder's insistence on the individuality and the variety of the Biblical authors transforms the Bible from an allegedly divine monologue into a recognisably human text with a meaning at least as complex as its own history. The transformation however creates new problems if scripture is to retain its status as the sole fount of authority in Church matters. The truth that scripture contains resides for Herder not in some rationally paraphrasable meaning that could be substituted, without remainder, for the

---

q. 'Man kann diesen also menschlich und göttlich nennen, denn er ist beides.' Herder, *Vom Geist der ebräischen Poesie* in: *Schriften zum Alten Testament*, ed. Rudolf Smend (Bibliothek deutscher Klassiker, 93) (Frankfurt: Deutscher Klassiker Verlag, 1993), 661–1308, here 962.

written text, but in the moment of contact between the religious genius and the divine life, of which the text is a record and representation. But what tells us that all these different geniuses have had access to the same divinity? How are such moments of sacred inspiration, and their textual records, to be distinguished from the inspiration of pagan poets? And how adequate is the record anyway? It is essential, Herder tells us, to clear away the accumulated misuse of the texts over the centuries by churches and sects, so that we can return to the situation and emotions of the writer and hear, for example, the songs of the psalmist as for the first time. But, like Calvin and Luther before him, he is unwilling to recognise that the entire text of the Old and New Testaments has been selected and authenticated for him by the very Church whose traditions of interpretation he is seeking to discard (though he does go so far as to acknowledge that it is thanks to the liturgy of the temple that we have the Book of Psalms at all and can distinguish the sacred literature of Israel from the profane literature of ancient Greece). Herder has to treat the first chapter of Genesis as the direct word of God Himself – the only witness of most of the events described – but otherwise the Bible has become for him a report at one remove of experiences that are now almost infinitely distant and perhaps in principle ineffable.[18] We have too little in common with the world of Moses, he writes, to be able to relive the moment when the patriarch saw the finger of God inscribe the covenant on tablets of stone.[19] And when he comes to write the history of Christianity, he excludes from consideration the life of its founder: that 'silent figure' is completely unrepresented by the Church that claims to have preserved his memory.[r] Herder's attempt to found a historical hermeneutic for the Christian scriptures, as an alternative to Kantian deism, leaves Christian truth floating in an a-historical void.

Schleiermacher's response to the Kantian challenge is more systematic than Herder's but in the end he entangles himself in the same contradictions. He follows Herder's example in seeking an alternative to 'reason' as the basis for the universal significance of the scriptures, and in his early *Addresses on Religion to its Cultured Despisers* finds it, like Herder, in the founding experience of the divine that individual religious geniuses have mediated to the rest of the human race. He is better able than Herder to justify the unique claims of Christianity, which he argues is the only religion to make the principle of mediation into its central insight, but his concept of the mediating genius is restricted to the religious field – he explicitly shrinks from extending it into secular culture and aesthetics – and so it lacks

---

r. 'Stille Gestalt.' Herder, *Ideen zur Philosophie der Geschichte der Menschheit. Text* in: *Werke*, ed. Wolfgang Pross, iii/1 (Munich: Hanser, 2003), 653.

something of the general explanatory power that it has for Herder.[20] However, in his later dogmatics, *The Christian Faith*, Schleiermacher develops this appeal to a privileged experience of the divine so that it becomes a clear rival to Kant's principle of rational autonomy. In place of universal 'reason' and its postulate of freedom, we are told that there is, at least potentially, a universal 'feeling' of our absolute dependence on something outside ourselves.[s] In his review of the second edition of *The Christian Faith*, Hegel's pupil, Karl Rosenkranz (1830), objected that a Church, or rather sect, formed out of individual believers united only by their personal feeling of dependency was far too 'subjective' a structure, and that an ecclesiology with such a basis could not do justice to the role of religion in articulating the identity of an ethical, cultural and political collective such as a nation or a state.[21] A similar objection could be made to Schleiermacher's lectures on *Hermeneutics and Criticism*, published posthumously in 1838. Indeed, conceptually speaking, Schleiermacher's hermeneutics show less advance on Herder than his dogmatics. Schleiermacher shares both Herder's concern to locate the original moment of the Biblical writer's inspired insight, the writer's own distinctive 'feeling' of the divine, and Herder's belief that to do so it is necessary to strip away the accretions of ecclesiastical tradition; he takes both to an extreme at which they become self-defeating.

If hermeneutics is 'the art of understanding the utterance of another',[t] or more specifically 'understanding the utterance at first as well as its originator and then even better',[u] Schleiermacher argues, it must then draw both on 'grammatical interpretation', which is guided by 'the language-stock common to the author and his original public',[v] and on 'psychological interpretation', which requires one to 'regard any given complex of thought as a moment in the life of a specific human being'.[w] The Bible therefore is not to be regarded as a single work, with one author, the Holy Spirit, and addressed generally to a Church which took on its institutional form long after the books were committed to writing: it is the work of particular individuals, in particular circumstances, addressing particular audiences. The books of

---

s. 'Gefühl.' F. D. E. Schleiermacher, *Der christliche Glaube nach den Grundsätzen der evangelischen Kirche* i (Berlin: Reimer, 1822), 173.

t. 'Die Kunst, die Rede eines andern richtig zu verstehen.' F. D. E. Schleiermacher, *Hermeneutik und Kritik*, ed. Manfred Frank (Frankfurt a.M.: Suhrkamp, 1977), 75.

u. 'Die Rede zuerst ebensogut und dann besser zu verstehen als ihr Urheber.' Schleiermacher, *ibid.*, 94.

v. 'Die grammatische Auslegung ... aus dem dem Verfasser und seinem ursprünglichen Publikum gemeinsamen Sprachgebiet.' *Ibid.*, 101.

w. 'Die psychologische Auslegung ... jeden gegebenen Gedankencomplexus als Lebensmoment eines bestimmten Menschen aufzufassen.' *Ibid.*, 167, 178.

the Bible are occasional writings, 'Gelegenheitsschriften', *pièces d'occasion*.[x] Indeed, Schleiermacher not only sees the Bible as broken down into individual texts by individual authors, but he regards even the experience of the individual authors to which those texts give expression as broken down into individual occasions, moments or foci of concentration. He goes so far as to invent the word 'speech-act'[y] to describe the individual units into which he regards a text as broken down for the purposes of interpretation. As far as the New Testament is concerned, Schleiermacher thus sends off his successors in hectic pursuit of an unattainable goal, on a chase dubbed by one of the participants 'the quest for the historical Jesus' – the search for the speech-act or set of speech-acts, whether of Jesus or of his disciples, the meaning of which, either correctly understood in context or fatefully misinterpreted by being taken out of context, must have been the foundation of Christianity.[22] That the search necessarily has to be fruitless is, however, already determined by the nature of the historicising and atomising hermeneutic mechanism that has set it in motion. Schleiermacher has shattered the Reformation Bible, the one and only *Scriptura*, into a constellation of historically contextualised and ever more finely divisible speech-acts in which it is impossible to discern the 'original' moment of insight, the single central utterance that comes directly from the mouth of God.

Schleiermacher's search for the original meaning, for the original audience, of the original words in the original language leads him, like Herder, to exclude from consideration the role of the Church in writing, selecting, interpreting or using the Biblical texts. The Church has no role to play, for example, in helping us to understand such statements in the New Testament as 'this is my Son' or 'God was in Christ' by reference to its own later doctrinal formulations; no role in helping us to interpret what John's Gospel says about eating Christ's flesh by reference to the practice of the Eucharist; nor can the Church's incorporation of the Exodus story into the Easter liturgy shed any light on the concepts of liberation and redemption to be found in the Hebrew narratives. The subjectivism identified by Rosenkranz thus reduces Schleiermacher's ecclesiology to paradox: through the Church the faithful mediate to one another their feeling of absolute dependency on God, but the same Church has no role in mediating to them the texts in which that feeling is expressed in words, is made historically and locally specific, and so becomes accessible to the world at large. Because, like the

---

x. *Ibid.*, 88.   y. 'Sprechakt.' *Ibid.*, 89, and see Frank's footnote, 100.

sixteenth-century Reformers, Herder refused a role to the Church in determining the canon of Biblical writings, he lacked a criterion for distinguishing between sacred and secular literary geniuses. Schleiermacher, in his
philosophical–theological *Addresses*, hesitated to follow that example. In
his hermeneutics, however, the legacy of Herder is fully apparent when
he insists, like Toland before him, that there is no 'special hermeneutic'[z]
necessary for the Judaeo–Christian scriptures, and that the same principles
of interpretation apply equally to sacred and to secular texts.[23] But he can
maintain that position only because his account of interpretation is defective
in one crucial respect: he overlooks that the interpreter of the utterance, as
much as its originator, has a language-stock on which to draw and a particular
audience of his or her own, and that he or she conducts the interpretation in
a particular historical, ethical and political context. Surely, the act of reading
is a collision not just between a person and a text or between a reader and
an author, but between two spirits, the spirits of two worlds, the spirit in
which the text was written and the spirit in which it is read. By contrast,
Schleiermacher's account of reading is intensely individualistic: he sees the
reader as a solitary, male, all-powerful interrogator of the text, of the pris-
oner and victim to which the instruments of 'scholarship' ('Wissenschaft')
are applied.[24] This conception of reading appealed to the churchmen, particularly the academic churchmen, of the nineteenth century, even though,
by failing to resolve either the deist antithesis of reason and revelation or
the historicist antithesis of the particular and the universal, it left their liberal religion defenceless against the criticisms of Kant, whose moral theory
they were often enough willing to identify as the 'essence of Christianity'.[aa]
Adolf von Harnack, doyen of German liberal theology, professor in Berlin,
personal friend of the Kaiser and signatory in 1914 of the manifesto of
ninety-three intellectuals who called on 'German militarism' to defend 'German culture',[25] including specifically the legacy of Kant, wrote in his own
Essence of Christianity: 'the Gospel is in no way a positive religion like the
rest . . . it contains no statutory or particularistic elements . . . *it is, therefore,
religion itself*'.[bb,26] With such support from the German institutional establishment, Schleiermacher's hermeneutics were for nearly a hundred years
able to marginalise Hegel's critique both of Kantian moral religion and of

---

z. 'Spezielle Hermeneutik.' Schleiermacher, *Hermeneutik*, 90.
aa. 'Das Wesen des Christentums.'
bb. 'Daß das Evangelium überhaupt keine positive Religion ist wie die anderen, daß es nichts
    Statutarisches und Partikularistisches hat, *daß es also die Religion selbst ist*.'

Schleiermacher's attempted alternative and to hand on to the Biblical criticism of the twentieth century the deist presuppositions first formulated in the eighteenth.[27]

In his *Lectures on the Philosophy of Religion*, first delivered in 1821, Hegel made it plain that in his view, hermeneutics was a science of limited value in the study of theology, if indeed it was a science at all. 'Commentaries on the Bible' he says, 'do not only acquaint us with the content of scripture but rather themselves contain the attitudes of their time.'[cc] That does not matter, Hegel believes; what does matter is that the ideas and attitudes that the commentaries contain should be the right ones, the doctrines affirmed in the creeds, the triune nature of the Godhead, the divinity of Christ, the eternal judgement to come.[28] The criterion for the interpretation of scripture has to be dogmatic, Hegel asserts: anything else turns scripture into a wax nose that can be given any shape you like.[29] He rejects the antithesis of reason and revelation on which Kant's hermeneutic depends and the consequential belief that there is a rational theology that can be opposed to a Biblical theology. There are not two paths to God, one 'positive', imposed from outside, and one rational and internal. There is one divine spirit that operates in us particular human beings and the truth that comes to us in the form of a positive, historically specific, revelation is a rational truth. 'That it is positive', Hegel says, 'in no way detracts from its quality of being rational, of being our own.'[dd] On the contrary, anything rational is met by us in sensuous experience in a positive form: the laws of our own country are positive, they are historical accidents, but we recognise in them a higher rationality than accident, we recognise them as an expression of our own freedom. With one blow, Hegel's understanding of 'spirit' renders obsolete both the conception of freedom that underlies Kant's moral religion and Schleiermacher's conception of the hermeneutic relationship between interpreter and text. For Hegelian 'spirit' is something common to (at least) two subjectivities, two parties to a conversation – their shared presumptions and procedures and goals – and Hegel defines 'freedom' as 'the essence of the spirit'.[ee] Our participation in a shared society, in a shared linguistic, ethical, political or religious structure is an expression and exercise of our shared freedom and

---

cc. 'Die Kommentare über die Bibel machen uns nicht sowohl mit dem Inhalt der Schrift bekannt, sondern enthalten vielmehr die Vorstellungsweise ihrer Zeit.' HW, XVI, 36.

dd. 'Daß es positiv ist, benimmt seinem Charakter, vernünftig, unser eigenes zu sein, ganz und gar nichts.' HW, XVII, 195.

ee. 'Das Wesen des Geistes.' HW, XII, 30.

the term 'freedom' has no meaning outside such a context (there is no freedom of the press in a desert, and Robinson Crusoe is not a free man until
Friday becomes his slave). The autonomy that Kant wishes to make central to
rational religion can exist only within a specific historical and institutional
framework, as part of the continuing interaction of human subjectivities.
Similarly, the process of interpretation is not, as Schleiermacher seems to
imagine, a one-sided interrogation, but a conversation between the ethical,
political and religious spirit that produced the text and the different spirit
that produced the reader. The one spirit of God operates in our reading of
the scriptures as it also operated in the writing of them. Hegel says that:

> The story of Christ has been narrated by those on whom the spirit had
> already been poured. The miracles were received and narrated in this
> spirit and the death of Christ was understood by that spirit as meaning
> that in Christ God was revealed, as was the unity of the divine and
> human natures.[ff]

The scriptures must be read in the light of the dogmatic categories, for in
that light they were written.

The moment of Pentecost, the outpouring of the spirit that first constituted the Christian community, is as central to Hegel's philosophy of
religion as autonomous freedom is to Kant's. The Church is not for him the
embarrassment that it is for Herder, the malign source of heteronomy that
it is for Kant or the irrelevance that it is for Schleiermacher's hermeneutics. The moment in which the Church comes into being is the moment in
which words are first found to express the truth of the divinity of Christ
and with it the truth that in Christ God and man have become one. It is
therefore also the moment in which the historicist antithesis of the universal
and the particular is overcome. For the universal significance of Christianity
proves to reside in its proclamation that God can be and has been revealed
in particular, historically specific, human life: finite individuality can be, and
has been, and in the Church continues to be, of absolute and eternal importance. Christianity is not a set of documents about one past event among
many others, but the life of the spirit in a potentially universal community,
the Church, which preaches the self-revelation of God in humanity and has

---

ff. 'Die Geschichte Christi ist auch von solchen erzählt, über die der Geist schon ausgegossen war.
Die Wunder sind in diesem Geiste aufgefaßt und erzählt, und der Tod Christi ist von
demselben wahrhaft so verstanden worden, daß in Christus Gott geoffenbart sei und die
Einheit der göttlichen und menschlichen Natur.' HW, XVII, 289.

expressed its own self-understanding in various ways, including by the composition of documents about its founding events. The antithesis between written scripture and oral tradition – so essential to Calvin's understanding of the Reformation[30] – is said by Hegel to be trivial,[31] for both scripture and tradition are subordinate to the activity of the spirit and are manifestations of it: tradition requires to be grounded in an authority that only the spirit can provide; scripture requires to be interpreted and interpretation is the spirit in action. Scripture and tradition then are equally expressions of the identity of the community which comes into being with its recognition of Christ as both God and man, and which is given full power by the spirit to define and refine its teaching. Since, in the Church, the spirit in which the sacred texts are read is also the spirit in which they were written, it makes no sense to pursue their 'original' meaning. The reading of them is as much a part of the process of God's self-revelation as was the writing of them.

Hegel, then, has produced a powerful argument for the view that hermeneutics cannot be an independent science with a competence of its own. To put it bluntly, he has shown that how you interpret a text depends on what it says and who you are. Schleiermacher may have been right to demand that you should interpret a text as, in a conversation, you might seek to understand the speech of another. But he attempted to base his hermeneutics largely on the analysis of only one element in the conversation, the mind and linguistic resources of the interpreter's conversation partner, thus overlooking two further vital elements: the mind and linguistic resources of the interpreter him- or herself, and what the conversation is about.[32] If the texts to be dealt with are about God, then your interpretation of them will be influenced by your conception of God, of God's revelation to you and of the mediation of that revelation through all the structures of meaning that you inhabit. The question of how to read a text about God is an ethical and political, historical and philosophical question: it cannot be reduced to a problem in hermeneutics. Maybe, then, 'hermeneutics' is simply the name that is given to the evasion of all the substantial issues that a text raises: in the case of texts about God, any substantial issue whatever.

The catastrophe of the First World War transformed all aspects of German culture, including theology and philosophy. Both Karl Barth and Martin Heidegger turned away from the 'liberal' legacy of the nineteenth century in an attempt to address directly the substantial issues. As Heidegger, initially a Catholic outsider to the academic establishment, sought to return philosophy from its preoccupation with the theory of knowledge to the question of 'being', so Barth, an academically unqualified Swiss pastor, and thus initially an outsider too, reacted against his teacher Harnack's betrayal of Christianity to this-worldly powers. He reformulated his Pauline commentary, *The Letter to the Romans*, as a critique of Schleiermacher, and refocused his theological enterprise on the question of 'God'.[33] Neither Barth nor Heidegger, however, showed any interest in recovering Hegel's hermeneutical perspective. For Barth, hermeneutics offered no access to the fundamental reality of the triune God, and whatever Heidegger may have meant by a 'hermeneutics of *Dasein*', it had very little to do with reading the Bible, while his later exegetical work on philosophers and poets was too idiosyncratic to be susceptible of imitation. Only in the work of his pupil, Hans-Georg Gadamer, did Heidegger's thought become productive of new developments in the art of interpreting texts.

Gadamer's *Truth and Method* (1960)[34] is devoted, among other things, to reinstating Hegel's hermeneutics at the expense of Schleiermacher's: Hegel, he says, is 'fundamentally superior'.[gg] Gadamer sees Schleiermacher's hermeneutics – somewhat misleadingly described as 'Romantic hermeneutics'[hh] – as the attempt at a recovery of the original process by which the writer wrote the text, 'a second creation, the reproduction of the original production'.[ii] Such a project he thinks impossible, even absurd. Given that our being is essentially historical, that we are finite creatures that live in time and eventually die, any attempt to restore things to their past state is doomed to fail. What is thought of as recovered or restored – a painting cleaned, for example, or a piece of music played on period instruments – is by that token necessarily at least one stage removed from its original: eighteenth-century music was not played on instruments that were, or pretended to be, two hundred years old. Similarly, the original meaning of a text is irrecoverable: the result of an attempt to recover what Paul originally meant to say to the Romans could not be meaningful to a modern audience in the way that what Paul said was meaningful to his. Paul was not passing on to the Romans a reconstruction of something said two thousand years before. Hermeneutic archaeology offers the modern audience only 'the communication of a meaning that has died',[jj] and when Gadamer says that 'the real meaning of a text, as it speaks to the interpreter, does not depend on such occasional factors as the writer and his original public',[kk] his use of the word

gg. 'Grundsätzlich überlegen.' WM, 161.
hh. 'Romantische Hermeneutik.' WM, 162ff.
ii. 'Eine zweite Schöpfung, die Reproduktion der ursprünglichen Produktion.' WM, 159.
jj. 'Die Mitteilung eines erstorbenen Sinnes.' WM, 160.
kk. 'Der wirkliche Sinn eines Textes, wie er den Interpreten anspricht, hängt eben nicht von dem Okkasionellen ab, das der Verfasser und sein ursprüngliches Publikum darstellen.' WM, 280.

'occasional' is clearly directed at Schleiermacher's belief that all writings are 'Gelegenheitsschriften'. The 'real meaning' is 'always also determined by the historical situation of the interpreter'.[ll] Gadamer therefore puts forward the deliberately provocative argument that prejudices are essential to the process of understanding in order to counter Schleiermacher's principle that we should approach a text without any preconceived notions of our own. That principle, handed down to Schleiermacher from the Enlightenment, is itself a prejudice, 'a prejudice against prejudices'.[mm] The Enlightenment regarded the claims of authority and tradition to determine interpretation, whether of sacred or secular texts, as a prejudice. Herder and Schleiermacher thought it essential to their programme of returning to the original moment of a writer's inspiration that they should sweep away interpretations based on authority or tradition, which were no more than obstacles hindering the process of recovery. But Gadamer sees it as perfectly reasonable to allow the personal authority of a 'teacher' or an 'expert' a role in determining our reading of a text:[nn] they may after all know more about the subject than we do, just as a tradition of interpretation may preserve a truth that is otherwise inaccessible to us. Some prejudices may be right.

Behind the hostility to prejudices, however, in Gadamer's view, there lurks an even more important error, a false notion of the identity of the interpreter. An interpreter is neither detached from a historical context nor possessed, in fact or in potential, of infinite knowledge and wisdom or of infinite life in which to acquire them. If we were infinite in that way, we might be able to afford the luxury of starting the work of interpretation with a blank sheet. But we are historically determined, like the texts we are reading – determined, that is, 'by family, society, and state'.[oo] The contribution of the authority and traditions of family, society and state to our interpretations of the past is probably greater, and certainly more fundamental, than our personal resources of responsiveness or inventiveness. 'Therefore an individual's prejudices are to a far greater extent the historical reality of his being than his personal judgements'.[pp] According to Gadamer, it is that 'historical reality' of the interpreter's being which, in the act of interpretation, enters into dialogue with the historical reality of the text, just as for Hegel the spirit that reads the scriptures confirms, and is confirmed by, the

ll. 'Ist immer auch durch die geschichtliche Situation des Interpreten mitbestimmt.' *Ibid.*
mm. 'Das Vorurteil gegen die Vorurteile.' WM, 255.
nn. 'Der Erzieher . . . der Fachmann.' WM, 264.
oo. 'Familie, Gesellschaft und Staat.' WM, 261.
pp. 'Daher sind die Vorurteile des Einzelnen weit mehr als seine Urteile die geschichtliche Wirklichkeit seines Seins.' WM, 261.

spirit that wrote them. By contrast, Gadamer thinks, Schleiermacher forgets that the interpreter has his own psychology and grammar, his linguistic and cultural context, his prejudices, and that these are as intrinsic to the process of 'understanding' ('Verstehen') as their equivalents in the author of the text. Schleiermacher therefore falsifies the position of the interpreter, even though he too claims to be involved in a conversation with another whose speech he is simply trying to understand. Gadamer accuses Schleiermacher of involving himself rather in a bogus conversation of the kind held by interviewers or oral examiners or certain doctors, who are not really trying to talk with and to someone but are getting them to talk in order to size them up.[35] This falsification results from Schleiermacher's failure to note the full implications of two simple facts about speech: that it is always uttered *to someone* and always *about something*.

As to the first point, Schleiermacher certainly noticed that interpretation involved trying to identify the original audience for an utterance, but he did not recognise that any utterance is also comprehensible by, and in that sense intended for, many more than its original audience: its audience can quite legitimately be defined as anyone who *can* understand it. And Schleiermacher did not, therefore, notice the consequence: that any utterance, since it can have meaning for those in quite different circumstances from any that the original speaker could possibly imagine, potentially always means *more* than the original speaker intended; 'the meaning of a text always outstrips its author'.[qq] Or, in William Empson's words: '"What is conceivable can happen too," / said Wittgenstein, who had not dreamt of you.'[36] An essential part of the process of understanding, Gadamer believes, is seeking to 'apply' the meaning of the text in the new context provided by the world, the time and the circumstances of the interpreter.[rr] He shows how the idea of applying a law to the circumstances of a particular case, or of applying a Biblical text to contemporary events, can be extended to include similar procedures in the study of secular literature or of history. There is nothing improper about seeking to apply a text written in one set of circumstances to concerns created by another. On the contrary, that is what understanding and interpretation always involve. Why else would one hold a conversation if not to learn something of interest? 'Understanding', Gadamer says, is a 'miracle, which is not a mysterious communion of souls [as Schleiermacher's attempt to re-experience the original

qq. 'Immer übertrifft der Sinn eines Textes seinen Autor.' WM, 280.
rr. 'Die Applikation.' WM, 312.

moment of inspiration implies it is] but a shared participation in a common meaning'.[ss]

Second, therefore, the 'common meaning', the meaning that a conversation has for both parties to it, is the thing that the conversation is about.

> To understand means, in the first place, to agree about the matter in
> hand, and only secondarily to isolate and understand the opinion of
> the other. The first of all hermeneutical conditions is the prior
> understanding that derives from having to do with the same thing.[tt]

To understand someone ('verstehen') is to come to an understanding with them ('sich verstehen') about a matter of shared concern.[37] The relationship of interpretation involves two equal partners with common interests, not, as for Schleiermacher's school, the interrogation of a text by a detached and dispassionate observer. Questions are asked, certainly, in the course of interpretation, but Gadamer stresses that the basic structure of a conversation is the exchange of questions (and answers), the reciprocity between the parties that is guaranteed by their relating to a third factor, the issue of common concern. Indeed, before interpreters can ask any questions at all, they have to face the primary question represented by the text itself: what kind of a world do they inhabit, what kind of horizon bounds them, such that they can face this text and undertake to interpret it, that is, address this new common concern? Every time we start to try to understand a text, however old, we are confronted with the question: can we open ourselves to this thing, new to us, and if so, how?

In reading any text we confront what Gadamer calls our own historicity. Gadamer generously acknowledges that in what he says about historicity he is building on the insights of Heidegger, and particularly on the concluding sections of *Being and Time I*. But while Heidegger in those sections slides into making the historicity of our existence into a matter of our choice, as if we could decide what historical significance our life is to have, Gadamer is truer to Heidegger's exposition in the earlier pages of *Being and Time* vol. I of our finitude and mortality. Thanks to Heidegger, Gadamer claims, the historical time in which all life is lived towards death no longer needs to be seen – as it was seen in the hermeneutics of Schleiermacher and the nineteenth-century

---

ss. 'Dies Wunder des Verstehens . . . das nicht eine geheimnisvolle Kommunion der Seelen, sondern eine Teilhabe am gemeinsamen Sinn ist.' WM, 276.

tt. 'Daß Verstehen primär heißt: sich in der Sache verstehen, und erst sekundär: die Meinung des anderen als solche abheben und verstehen. Die erste aller hermeneutischen Bedingungen bleibt somit das Vorverständnis, das im Zu-tun-haben mit der gleichen Sache entspringt.' WM, 278.

historians – as an 'abyss' that separates us in the present from the alien past and prevents us from understanding it.[uu] Instead, time is the 'ground' which supports all human happenings and in which the present is rooted.[vv] Time is not there to be conquered, it is not an empty space between us and the past, it is 'filled out by the continuity of tradition' and resembles a bridge rather than a void.[ww] For suspicious historicists the passage of time merely increased the possibilities of error in interpreting the past. For Gadamer, it is continuously creating new sources of understanding, as new consequences of the text emerge, new events cast a retrospective light on it and so what might be called new prejudices are created that help understanding rather than hindering it. (We might, for example, say that what has happened in German poetry since Goethe may in some respects make it more difficult for us to see his poetry as his contemporaries saw it, but it has also revealed far more of what was in it than Goethe's contemporaries could understand.) The tradition through which a text is mediated to us is a part of that text itself and we distort or reduce it if we think there is such a thing as the 'unmediated' – the original – 'phenomenon'.[xx] Conversely, the view that we have of the past is part of our present situation and in that sense the past interprets us as much as we interpret the past – we are its creatures and that mutual dependence of past and present is our historicity: 'to be historical is never to be exhaustively characterised by one's own self-knowledge.'[yy]

Tradition, in Gadamer's sense of the term, is therefore not simply a hermeneutical tool, one instrument among others that we can call on to understand a text. Tradition is the process of understanding itself. Understanding is not ultimately – whatever it may be in the first instance – a matter of an individual's understanding. 'Understanding is not to be thought of so much as an act of subjectivity, but rather as an insertion into a process of handing on, in which past and present are continuously mediated to each other'.[zz] My understanding, let us say, of a novel of Dostoyevsky is a bringing alive of that work and its meaning not just in my own mind but in the whole world that I inhabit and that has made me. That resurrection of Dostoyevsky's meaning in our time is not some inappropriate imposition on his

uu. 'Abgrund.' WM, 281.   vv. 'Grund.' WM, 281.
ww. 'Ausgefüllt durch die Kontinuität . . . der Tradition.' WM, 281.
xx. 'Die unmittelbare Erscheinung.' WM, 284.
yy. 'Geschichtlichsein heißt, nie im Sichwissen aufgehen.' WM, 285.
zz. 'Das Verstehen ist . . . nicht so sehr als eine Handlung der Subjektivität zu denken, sondern als Einrücken in ein Überlieferungsgeschehen, in dem sich Vergangenheit und Gegenwart beständig vermitteln.' WM, 274-5.

text but what the text was written for in the first place: to be meaningful with a meaning that it was beyond the author or any of his original audience to imagine. The medium of that transmission, in which past meaning becomes a different and present meaning, is tradition. Tradition is what links text and interpretation together and so intimately that in Gadamer's view, the reader 'is a part of the text that he understands'.[aaa] Gadamer's concept of tradition, in short, resurrects, interprets and hands on to our age, and in the context of hermeneutics, Hegel's concept of 'spirit'.

There are of course limitations to the achievement of *Truth and Method*, which is hardly surprising since the limitations on any interpretative venture are one of its major themes. It is a constraint, perhaps even a prejudice in a non-Gadamerian sense, that in respect of intellectual history the German terminology of Gadamer's time and place, 'Enlightenment' and 'Romanticism', for example, are used with little attempt to enquire into their legitimacy, or that the term 'Art' ('Kunst') is deployed with a freedom unfamiliar to Anglo-Saxons, who do not necessarily think of literature as art or of art as a quasi-religious activity (as Gadamer believes it to be).[38] Gadamer speaks the language of an early twentieth-century academic brought up in a largely Idealist tradition. It is also a language sufficiently secularised to limit his ability to address what he admits to be a central issue, theological hermeneutics.[39] Modern hermeneutics, he argues, came into existence as a defence against Enlightenment attacks on the truth of scripture, but he is reluctant to accept the full range of Hegel's responses to those attacks, perhaps because they imply a far more institutional and social conception of religion than the private concern with personal salvation that he sees as the proper 'application' of theological texts.[40] His own defence of tradition is clearly capable of being extended into the ecclesiological field, but that is not a direction in which he seems willing to take it. Unfortunately, he thereby compounds his own most serious historical misrepresentation. Gadamer's identification of the Enlightenment as the source of various nineteenth-century errors and diremptions has had a wide and misleading influence. It has obscured that the roots of the hermeneutic dilemmas he discusses lie not in Schleiermacher, nor even in Herder, whose contribution he rather undervalues, but in Luther and Calvin. But it would not be right to dwell in conclusion on the putative defects of a masterpiece that has done so much to transmit the legacy of Idealism to the modern age and to demonstrate the theological potential of that legacy even for those outside the tradition, if we may call it that, of the sixteenth-century Reformation.

---

aaa. 'Gehört mit zu dem Text, den er versteht.' WM, 323.

Notes

1. On Hegel's theological education in the Tübingen *Stift* see in particular: H. S. Harris, *Hegel's Development: Toward the Sunlight, 1770–1801* (Oxford : Clarendon Press, 1972), 72–96; Mark Ogden, *The Problem of Christ in the Work of Friedrich Hölderlin* (London: Modern Humanities Research Association for The Institute of Germanic Studies, University of London, 1991); Michael Franz (ed.), *'An der Galeere der Theologie': Hölderlins, Hegels und Schellings Theologiestudium an der Universität Tübingen* (Schriften der Hölderlin-Gesellschaft 23/3) (Tübingen: Hölderlin-Gesellschaft; Eggingen: Edition Isele, c2007).

2. On the deist fork, see my 'Lessing, biblical criticism and the origins of German classical culture', *German Life and Letters* 34 (1981), 196–213.

3. I have developed this theme at greater length in my *Sacred and Secular Scriptures: A Catholic Approach to Literature* (London: Darton, Longman and Todd, 2004; Notre Dame: University of Notre Dame Press, 2005), on which some parts of the following argument are based.

4. Wilhelm Weischedel (ed.), *Kants Werke in sechs Bänden* (Wiesbaden: Insel Verlag, 1956–62) [henceforth KW], VI, 261–393.

5. *Ibid.*, VI, 307.

6. *Ibid.*, V, 842–5, cf. VI, 188–9.

7. *Ibid.*, V, 839.

8. *Ibid.*, VI, 305.

9. *Ibid.*, V, 714–19.

10. *Ibid.*, VI, 83–102.

11. See e.g. the first chapter of the *Formula of Concord* of 1577: J. T. Müller (ed.), *Die symbolischen Bücher der evangelisch-lutherischen Kirche, deutsch und lateinisch* (Gütersloh: Bertelsmann, 1900), 519–23, esp. 573–87.

12. Even Nietzsche's own retelling of the Genesis story in *Der Antichrist*, §48, makes no secret of its polemical intention, and thereby reduces its effectiveness.

13. Karl Barth, *Die protestantische Theologie im 19. Jahrhundert* (Zurich: Zollikon, 1947), 302.

14. Matthew Tindal, *Christianity as Old as the Creation: Or, The Gospel, a Republication of the Religion of Nature* (London: [s.n.], 1730).

15. John Toland, *Christianity not Mysterious Or, A Treatise shewing, that there is Nothing in the Gospel Contrary to Reason, Nor above it: And that no Christian Doctrine can be Properly call'd a Mystery* (London: [s.n.], 1702), 49.

16. See Johann Gottfried Herder, *Über den Ursprung der Sprache*, in: *Frühe Schriften 1764–1772*, Ulrich Gaier (ed.) (Bibliothek deutscher Klassiker, I) (Frankfurt: Deutscher Klassiker Verlag, 1985), 695–810.

17. Herder, *Vom Geist der ebräischen Poesie*, in: *Schriften zum Alten Testament*, Rudolf Smend (ed.) (Bibliothek deutscher Klassiker, 93) (Frankfurt: Deutscher Klassiker Verlag, 1993), 661–1308, 1194.

18. *Ibid.*, 495.

19. *Ibid.*, 1097.

20. Schleiermacher, *Über die Religion. Reden an die Gebildeten unter ihren Verächtern*, H.-J. Rothert (ed.) (Philosophische Bibliothek 255) (Hamburg: Felix Meiner, 1970), 79, 93.

21. Karl Rosenkranz, review of Schleiermacher, *Der christliche Glaube*, in: *Jahrbücher für wissenschaftliche Kritik* (1830) 2, coll. 841–59, 865–87, (1831) 2, coll. 824–44, 924–52.

22. The phrase seems to have been invented in 1910 by Albert Schweitzer's English translator, W. Montgomery, to render 'Leben-Jesu-Forschung,' a concept unfamiliar, presumably, to either an academic or a general public in England at the time.

23. F. D. E. Schleiermacher, *Hermeneutik und Kritik*, Manfred Frank (ed.) (Frankfurt: Suhrkamp, 1977), 85–90. Schleiermacher makes only a partial exception for the New Testament, on the grounds that, he asserts, the language of these writings is an 'unnatural' ('nicht naturgemäß') mixture of Greek and Hebrew (*ibid.*, 90).

24. E.g. *ibid.*, 213 ff.

25. 'Ohne den deutschen Militarismus wäre die deutsche Kultur längst vom Erdboden getilgt.' www.nernst.de/kulturwelt.htm accessed 18 October 2012: 15:08.

26. Quoted in J. C. O'Neill, *The Bible's Authority: A Portrait Gallery of Thinkers from Lessing to Bultmann* (Edinburgh: T. and T. Clark, 1991), 222.

27. See O'Neill, 'The Study of the New Testament', in: Ninian Smart (ed.), *Nineteenth-Century Religious Thought in the West* (Cambridge: Cambridge University Press, 1985), III, 143–78.

28. HW, XVII, 200; XVI, 46.

29. *Ibid.*, XVI, 37.

30. See e.g. Jean Calvin, *Institution de la religion chrétienne* (Geneva: Labor et Fides, 1967), I, 7, 38–41.

31. HW, XVII, 321.

32. For a more sympathetic account of Schleiermacher, see Andrew Bowie, 'The philosophical significance of Schleiermacher's hermeneutics', in Jacqueline Mariña (ed.), *The Cambridge Companion to Friedrich Schleiermacher* (Cambridge: Cambridge University Press, 2005), 73–90. Bowie rightly stresses the contribution Schleiermacher's *Dialectics* can make to an understanding of his hermeneutics, but it seems to me that the claim that interpretation is conversation (as Gadamer believes) is different from the claim that texts can contain propositions of 'general validity in the name of universal agreement' (as Bowie states Schleiermacher believes, *ibid.*, 84).

33. Karl Barth, *Der Römerbrief*, 2nd edn (Munich: Christian Kaiser, 1922).

34. Hans-Georg Gadamer, *Wahrheit und Methode. Grundzüge einer philosophischen Hermeneutik*, 4th edn (Tübingen: Mohr, 1975), henceforth WM.

35. *Ibid.*, 345–6, 363.

36. William Empson, 'This last pain', *Collected Poems* (London: Chatto, 1977), 32.

37. WM, 168.

38. Cf. *ibid.*, 142–3.

39. *Ibid.*, 162–5, 294.

40. *Ibid.*, 292, 404, 492–9.

6

Aesthetic Idealism and its relation to theological formation: reception and critique

Cyril O'Regan

Under the heading of 'aesthetic Idealism' I mean to investigate accounts of becoming, plurality and division as well as being, unity and totality. My concern is not with aesthetic theory: 'aesthetic' qualifies and inflects a determinate slice of post-Kantian enquiry whose attention has shifted from issues of the applications of categories to the manifold of appearance to a set of meta-philosophical issues. These involve the reception of Spinoza.[1] Obviously, there are some figures with claims to be counted as German Idealists to which the adjective 'aesthetic' fairly clearly applies. Given the rich commentary tradition on the evolution of the thought of both Hegel and Schelling, it is evident that the agenda, which H. S. Harris refers to as the 'resumption of the whole into one', engages both forms of thought, even if Schelling gets off to a much quicker start.[2] There are other thinkers to whom the attribution of 'aesthetic Idealism' also applies, even if less obviously so. Dieter Henrich has made the case that one better appreciates Hölderlin by seeing him among the Idealists.[3] The central justification, Henrich offers, for counting Hölderlin with or among the Idealists are the poet's fragmentary metaphilosophical reflections, which antedate the creation of his major poetry, and which seem to elect literature as the more appropriate venue to attempt to comprehend time and history felt as burden and opportunity, plurality experienced as a profound but intriguing challenge and division acknowledged to be a potential blessing even if immediately it is experienced as a curse.[4]

For reasons of space I shall consider just Hegel and Hölderlin. In the case of Hegel, I privilege the *Phenomenology of Spirit*, *Encyclopaedia of the Philosophical Sciences* and *Lectures on the Philosophy of Religion*, although I will treat other texts of Hegel in passing.[5] In the case of Hölderlin, the foundational texts include the metaphilosophical text fragments 'Judgement and being' (*Urteil und Sein*), representative poems such as 'When on a holiday', 'Patmos',

142

'Bread and Wine', and 'The Only One', although again, on a need basis, I will extend discussion beyond these poems.[6]

Aesthetic Idealism, in my account, displays five characteristic marks:

(1)   A perception of a whole and a conception of truth that sees the particular in terms of its fit within the whole. The whole plays a regulative role even when – or especially when – there is recognition of division as well as plurality and evanescence. There is no reason to suppose in all cases of aesthetic Idealism that the power of unification is stressed equally or in the same way. We will see that such is not true in the pair under analysis.

(2)   This holism encourages the use of the terms 'life' (*Leben*) and 'love' (*Liebe*) as terms for forces of integration that, nonetheless, respect temporality, plurality and division. Their standing in for a holistic commitment can be sustained over time as fundamentally adequate or come to be displaced by other terms considered to be more adequate. It turns out that Hegel provides an example of the latter, Hölderlin of the former.

(3)   These underdetermined pre- or metaphilosophical terms are deployed in different discourses, whether actual philosophy in the case of Hegel, or poetics and actual poetry in the case of Hölderlin.

(4)   This choice in turn reflects some basic decisions about the hierarchical arrangement of the discourses of philosophy, art and religion. At the same time, there is a range of tolerance allowed for the blurring of the boundaries between discourses.

(5)   Religion in general remains important, and Christianity especially important, even if there is general agreement that most historical forms of Christianity are deficient and require critique. Still, the reconstruction of Christianity or the possibility of a reconstructed Christianity is not ruled out. There is significant agreement concerning the resources available for the refurbishing of Christianity, should that be deemed possible or advisable. Art, non-Christian religions and speculative philosophy are all felt to be genuine candidates. Which of these come to be regarded as providing the most assistance, or what combination of these (re)sources are called on, helps the students of the period to distinguish between the different paths taken by Hegel and Hölderlin and thus their different inflections of dialectical holism.

The main thrusts of this essay are, on the one hand, to see the history of effects in theological discourse of these different forms of aesthetic Idealism and, on the other, to see how they interact with each other on the contemporary theological scene broadly defined. No historically literate theologian will deny that Hegel's influence has been considerable and continues apace in theologians such as Hans Küng, Jürgen Moltmann, Ebehardt Jüngel, but also in Wolfhart Pannenberg and Hans Urs von Balthasar.[7] I shall also argue that Hölderlin has a theological influence. I will not make the case via the theological influence of the 'late' Heidegger whose mystagogical philosophy is reinforced – if not constituted – by a reading of Hölderlin. Rather, I will argue that Hölderlin's thought and poetry have a direct influence on Catholic theology in and through culturally literate, Catholic German theologians, but also indirectly on contemporary theology in and through a variety of postmodern discourses from Benjamin to Derrida and Marion.

6.1 The Hegelian modality of aesthetic Idealism

I begin with a general point about Hegel's own development in the post-Kantian horizon of thought that is characterised above all by a grasp of a contemporary need to provide coherence to a diffusive plurality and to overcome the divisions within consciousness and between consciousness and reality. In Hegel's early 'theological' writings the horizon is more existential and social than epistemological or metaphysical.[8] Hegel is concerned with vetting modern discourses and forms of life regarding their integrative function or lack thereof. Even as he uses Kantian philosophy to critique historical and confessional forms of Christianity, Hegel is asking where one can find a model for this wholeness. The well-known answer is that the basic template is provided by Greek religion, which more successfully than historical forms of Christianity illustrates a positive relation between the individual and the community and a more integral interconnection between discourse, practice and forms of life. In due course, Hegel comes to think that Christianity has a greater facility for universality and for requisitely re-enchanting the world, which also involves in significant measure its disenchanting. Unfortunately, however, Christianity is crippled by a number of more or less self-inflicted wounds. Some are coincidental with its emergence such as its parochial nature, its impossible ethic and its penchant to subject its founder to apotheosis. Others develop over time as Christianity – despite itself – becomes a world religion. In the early Frankfurt and Jena years, Hegel uses 'love' as an integrative concept, the same term also favoured in his meta-philosophical phase by Hölderlin.[9] A number of Hegelian commentators have remarked on the early prominence of 'love' and those particularly concerned with the development of Hegel's thought have spoken both to the continuity and discontinuity between it and the later term 'spirit'.[10] Of course, 'love' continues to have currency in the texts of the later Hegel. It serves, for example, more or less as a functional equivalent for *Geist* in the preface to the *Phenomenology* and throughout Hegel's treatment of Christianity in *Lectures on the Philosophy of Religion*.[11]

Some light can be shed on the contrast between Hölderlin and Hegel. From a historical point of view there is the disciplinary threshold that Hegel essentially crosses in his *Differenzschrift* (1802) and *Glauben und Wissen* (1802) in which the central issue becomes that of adequate conceptual formation, which it turns out can only represent a critique of Kant's categories, their relations, and the scope of their application. From a comparative point of view, one can espy in Hegel the movement from the meta-philosophical sphere in which one is not committed to favouring a particular form of language, whether art, religion or philosophy, to a commitment to philosophy but one more apt to deal with those issues that appear to be named – if only inchoately – in a meta-philosophical discourse that is relatively underdetermined. With respect to plurality, division and temporality, resolution comes to be seen as tied up with the ability to follow a self-generating series of concepts of considerably greater integration and plasticity than that observable in Kant.[12]

'Life' is in precisely the same situation as 'love'. In Hegel's mature work *Leben* still has the ability to illuminate *Geist* to the extent to which *Leben* is defined by dynamic movement from potentiality to actuality, is capable of surviving and flourishing in different states, can tolerate disunity or disruption and, finally, is capable of renewing itself in and through death. In the *Encyclopaedia* Hegel has a firm conceptual grasp of a relation that was somewhat associative earlier on. Life lays down the formal structure of spirit, which has its maximal zone of operation in consciousness and self-consciousness. Hegel's disagreements with Kant, on the one hand, and Spinoza, on the other, had to do with livingness of spirit, which renders the intimacy of time and eternity, resolves plurality and overcomes diremption.[13] The move to philosophy carries the conviction that the matrix of the philosophical concepts and the governing concept of spirit can penetrate more deeply into the structural and historical challenges to reason and present a satisfying answer to both sets of challenges. A condition of the possibility of both, however, is that a conceptual framework is not a dead aggregate of notions, but in effect shows the motility and aim associated with living matter. Philosophy, however, will not fail to see that religion and art will also exhibit something of this livingness in their respective attempts to represent but also participate in a reality that unites being and becoming in a becoming that has inbuilt finality. Thus in a sense philosophy repeats – in non-identical fashion – what is exhibited or can be exhibited in these two meaning and truth-giving domains. There are successes and failures in both of these domains. When it comes to successes in art, Hegel thinks that linguistic art demonstrates the greatest capacity to manifest life, and of the three forms of linguistic art he thinks it worth talking about – epic, drama and lyric – it is drama (tragic) which, in his view, is the highest.[14] Yet even after the waning of his unrestricted enthusiasm for ancient Greece, which issues in qualifications similar to those of Schiller,[15] Hegel continues to recognise the general superiority of Greek tragedy, based largely on his understanding of the priority of plot over character and structural agonism over the event of illumination.[16] Here we find grounds for disagreement as well as agreement with Hölderlin, to which we will return later.

As suggested already, in his earlier period Hegel tolerated well the blurring of the domains of art and religion. In the works of the mature Hegel, however, there comes to be a gradual assertion of boundaries. The *Phenomenology* illustrates a stage in the development of the autonomy of the two representational spheres. At first, this may seem paradoxical, since Hegel finds a place for a 'religion of art' (*Kunstreligion*).[17] On further inspection, however, the trumping of this form of religion by Christianity in the *Phenomenology* suggests that the blurring of the domains of art and religion is a handicap that needs to be overcome. In chapter 7, the prerogatives of Christianity are laid bare: its mode of representation is sharper, its historical sense deeper, its sense of the divine and the human both more intense and its grasp of their intimacy more transparent. The emergent evaluative as well as conceptual distinction between Christianity and Greek religion is preserved in *Lectures on the Philosophy of Religion*, even as the account of the Greek ethos tends to be viewed solely as religion rather than a mixed form of art and religion.[18] Conversely, in his *Aesthetics*, Hegel comes to think of the contributions of Greek art as analytically separate from its contributions to religion. Hegel models, then, an evolution never made by Hölderlin for whom Greek art and religion forever remain mutually porous.

Of course, for Hegel, beyond religion, even or especially Christianity, lies philosophy or at least speculative philosophy. Philosophy also provides the criteria for judging which religions are more or less successful. In his later works Hegel provides a taxis of at least a good cross-section of those religions known to intellectuals and scholars at the beginning of the nineteenth century. If intimations of the extent of Hegel's knowledge can be found in the section on religion in the *Phenomenology*, its full expression is to be found in the section on 'determinate religion' (*bestimmte Religion*) in *Lectures on the Philosophy of Religion*.[19] Hegel essentially adjudicates (a) between Judaism, Greek religion and Christianity and (b) between inadequate and adequate forms of Christianity. Relative to his early entirely hostile construction of Judaism as a religion of alienation, in his mature work Hegel views Judaism more positively.[20] Nonetheless, in general Judaism falls well below Greek religion whose measure of unification of opposites is in turn surpassed by Christianity. From the *Phenomenology* onwards, Christianity is taken to have no serious rivals. Problems with Christianity have to do with the discrepancy between the putative essence of Christianity and its actual forms, for time and again historical forms of Christianity fall well short of what Christianity can be and ought to be. Again, although the polemical edge to Hegel's remarks disappears in his later work, the judgements made about historical forms of Christianity in such early essays as 'Positivity' and 'The Spirit of Christianity and its Fate' are not revoked. Early forms of Christianity fetishise the founding figure of Christianity; Catholicism represents a repression of the Christian spirit in a double and even contradictory form: it represents within Christianity something like a re-Judification in that its stress on otherworldliness condones alienation and its authoritarian polity represses freedom.[21] At this stage Hegel does no more than develop Kant's critique of historical forms of Christianity in *Religion within the Boundaries of Mere Reason*.[22] As is well known, Hegel insists that the realisation of Christianity happens in the Reformation. Only in Protestantism, with its insistence on the freedom of all and its democratisation of what is to be considered holy, does a historical form of Christianity correspond to its concept.[23] Protestant Christianity in turn remains the basis for the modern secular world in that it provides not only the bases for, but also the legitimation of the structures of family, ethical life and the State.[24]

While Hegel takes the sensible view that, as with any religion, Christianity is defined by its practices (e.g. Eucharist) and forms of life (institutions and organisations), he does put significant emphasis on beliefs and more specifically Christian beliefs as they are tied to and express the meta-narrative of Trinitarian prologue, creation, fall, redemption, sanctification and eschaton. Hegel is not simply saying that Christianity has a story with episodes linked together by conjunction and temporal markers of now and then. Nor is he insisting that this story is directly extractable from a reading of the Bible which, in terms of interpretation, he is prepared to say functions like a 'wax nose', thus infinitely malleable and supportive of widely various interpretations.[25] Without showing from whence the meta-narrative derives, Hegel is convinced that it provides the religious form of apprehending the unification of a reality marked by history, difference and contradiction. This is the narrative shape presented in the *Phenomenology*, *Lectures on the Philosophy of Religion*, and presented in synoptic form in the religious syllogism in the *Encyclopaedia* (§564–71). The well-known contrast between Schleiermacher's lack of support for the Christian doctrine of the Trinity and Hegel's support is often overstressed, since, on the one hand, it might exaggerate the extent to which Schleiermacher does marginalise the doctrine of the Trinity and, on the other, it might fail to highlight the function the Trinity plays in Hegel's construction of Christianity.[26] It should be noted that in Hegel's mature works the Trinity is not a theological construction in any straightforward sense. In terms of sources Hegel keeps quite strange company. For example, he appeals neither to Augustine nor Aquinas. Instead, in *Lectures on the Philosophy of Religion*, it is figures outside the mainline theological traditions such as Valentinus the Gnostic, the Platonic Jewish philosopher Philo and the Lutheran mystic, Jacob Böhme (1575–1624) who are mentioned.[27] In important respects, Hegel rejects the Nicene view of the Trinity of three Persons and one essence and suggests in all three texts that classical Trinitarianism is tritheistic.[28] Hegel's organic – but also dramatic – development of the whole rules out positing three Persons. Conversely, Hegel's texts encourage thinking of the entire movement as a movement towards a single divine personality (*Persönlichkeit*), which necessarily will involve the elevation of the human community to the divine. In the three texts we are examining, the Trinity is in effect the triadic synopsis for the Christian meta-narrative, which tells the story in a symbolic medium of the development into unity of a fragmented and fractured reality.

That the Christian symbol of the Trinity has this utility is the essential reason for Hegel's interest. It most certainly is not nostalgia. Hegel assumes with the Enlightenment that most Christian doctrines are dogmatic in the pejorative sense of being obscurantist and authoritarian. Yet he also agrees with the Kant of *Religion* that some of these doctrines can be saved, specifically those that prove adequate to experience and admit of being justified by reason. Of course, early on Hegel critiqued Kant's notion of reason (*Verstand*) in the name of a speculative form of reason (*Vernunft*), which has more than heuristic application. It is Hegel's different sense of the scope of reason that allows him to think that the Trinity is the prime candidate for conceptual rehabilitation. In this rehabilitation what, in the theological tradition, would be referred to as the immanent Trinity of Father, Son and Spirit gets assigned to kingdom or sphere of the Father or more abstractly the sphere of Universality (*Allgemeinheit*). The fact that Hegel feels entitled to do the former shows how far he is from the theological tradition and how little the Biblical text functions as a constraint to philosophising. In the *Phenomenology*, *Lectures on the Philosophy of Religion*, and the *Encyclopaedia*, the kingdoms or spheres of the Son and the Spirit, associated respectively with Particularity (*Besonderheit*) and Individuality (*Einzelheit*), variously cover the fields of creation, fall and redemption, the Church, sanctification and eschaton. The emphasis falls here not on divine agency, but always on the ratio of connection between the divine and the human. And with respect to this, the kingdom of the spirit in which we see the divine reflected in the community is more important than Christ, especially a Christ who secures redemption on our behalf and thus at the expense of our autonomy.[29]

The proper medium of the Christian meta-narrative, even its triadic synopsis, remains 'representation' (*Vorstellung*). At its highest level, however, thought must transcend all representation and thus all narrative with its suggestion of tensed relations. The move from representation to concept (*Begriff*) therefore is not simply a move from pictorial to abstract thought, but a move from discourse, which is bogged down in the finite and the temporal, to one which is not. The goal in Hegel is eternity, even as his eternity – the echo of Boethius is startling – is dynamic life.[30] In Hegel's oeuvre there are many discussions of this process, the two most famous being Hegel's discussion of 'absolute knowledge' (*absolutes Wissen*) at the end of the *Phenomenology* and his even more condensed – but marvellously lucid – discussion of the relation between the religious syllogisms and philosophical syllogisms that conclude the *Encyclopaedia* (§§564–74).

6.2 The Hölderlinian model of aesthetic Idealism

We now turn to Hölderlin with a view to seeing how he, too, represents a form of aesthetic Idealism and a pre-philosophical commitment to a project of 'reunification philosophy' (*Vereinigungsphilosophie*), which respects time, plurality and difference, while resolving the pathos that belongs to each. I follow Dieter Henrich closely in his description of Hölderlin's meta-philosophical elaborations and how and why these elaborations will necessarily lead to Hölderlin's poetics and finally his major poetry. I will also follow the broad outline of Henrich's sense of the developing differences between Hegel and Hölderlin with regard to their understanding of the nature of the whole, their discursive priorities, philosophy, on the one hand, poetry on the other, and the relation between art and religion. I, necessarily, will have to supplement Henrich when it comes to coming to grips with Hölderlin's embrace of Christianity, and his sense of its relation to Greek thought in general and Greek religion in particular. However much, in *The Course of Remembrance*, Henrich wants to combat Heidegger's interpretation of Hölderlin, compromised as it is by Heidegger's lack of attention to general cultural context and, specifically, to the emergence of German Idealism, since he repeats its tendency to exclude by failing to acknowledge the existence of a Christian strain in Hölderlin's poetry.[31]

Deeper even than the mutual friendship of Hegel and Hölderlin, according to Henrich, is their insertion in a constellation of discursive needs in excess of the Kantian problematic and not capable of being satisfied by operating within its terms. The discursive needs of the 1790s are not the same as the discursive performances of either or both. Hölderlin tries to think through the issues of how time, plurality and division can be accepted without the reduction to naturalism and hallowing the status quo. What is crucial, as Henrich has shown,[32] is a deep reading of Fichte's *Wissenschaft-slehre*, which, arguably, is the Idealist text that most clearly operates within the parameters of Kant's epistemological descriptions and strictures, and thus the least affected by the Romantically laced Spinozism whose dissemination is aided by Jacobi's very attempt to root it out.[33] The latter clearly is an important lens for Hölderlin in the mid-nineties as he critically engages Fichte's transcendental thought. As suggested already, the pivotal text is the fragment 'Judgment and Being' (*Urteil und Sein*). Fichte is important for Hölderlin because he points to the intrinsic connection between consciousness and opposition, and articulates a problematic in which one can look beyond opposition to a pre-given unity or see through opposition to resolution. Hölderlin's adoption of Fichte is in effect an adaptation of the pattern articulated in the first three propositions of the *Wissenschaftslehre*, which concern respectively the positing of the I, the positing of the not-I and the opposition which points to a resolution – which is asymptotic – between I and not-I. Hölderlin rings a number of changes on the Fichtean model.[34] First, the major key is being rather than consciousness. Second, while in Hölderlin there is an analogue for the first proposition, which suggests a kind of intimacy beyond opposition that marks time and a world of plurality, this note is not stressed as much as the note of the dynamics of resolution struck in the third proposition. A third difference is that Hölderlin seems to hold out more hope for actual resolution than Fichte does, whose position in the *Wissenschaftslehre* has rightly been described as an 'unrealized eschatology'.[35] We are talking here about a minor twist or torque of Fichte, since Hölderlin is not proposing the constitutive kind of resolution that gave purpose to Hegel's search and eventually got ratified in and by the Hegelian system. Hölderlin's 'reunification philosophy' lies, therefore, between Fichte's heuristics and Hegel's self-validating movement, which results in a fully transparent totality.

When Hölderlin applies the language of 'modulation', 'tone' and 'harmonics' to resolution, it suggests that more is going on than a preference for Spinoza over Fichte, which is typical of Schelling's *Naturphilosophie*. Rather, it intimates a groping for the proper register for resolution, which reflects the level of claim being advanced.[36] The language qualifies the resolution hoped for by suggesting that the totality aimed at cannot be comprehended fully and thus remains elusive to a significant extent. Fichte's third proposition, and thereby his constitutive finitism, remains at least a subtext.[37] In this early period, Hölderlin thinks in terms of associated pairs: total comprehensibility and closure, on the one hand, and apprehension and an ungraspable hint of totality on the other. Although not in 'Judgment and Being', 'interruption' is an important concept for the early Hölderlin, and he intimates that while a purely finite mode of seeing and knowing can be breached, it cannot be transcended completely.[38] Totality can be glimpsed. This alone is possible; and this is enough. The aesthetic horizon becomes transparent when it is beauty that comes to characterise this appearance of totality. Hölderlin has no theory of the transcendentals, but for him it would be a mistake to separate beauty from truth and perhaps even from goodness. But this means that beauty and truth are best considered as events suspending time rather than involving the transplanting of wounded selves into the domain of the infinite and the eternal, the 'longing' (*Sehnsucht*), which Hölderlin thinks is noxious.[39]

Once the term 'beauty' appears, there is a sense in which the inchoate aesthetic Idealism becomes fully explicit. And once beauty appears, it is also the case that questions put into circulation by Schiller, such as where in history can we find the clearest historical instantiation of beauty, whether it is possible to create beauty in the modern age and what is the proper language for the exposure of a beauteous truth and a truthful beauty, gain urgency and require addressing. In his great hymns and odes Hölderlin is on his way, if not precisely to answering these questions, then to bringing out their full dimensions. As with his friend Hegel, for Hölderlin, the Greeks suggest themselves as plenary. They are the ones who glimpse the whole, but also in important respects find it imponderable. If other philhellenes are drawn to the plastic arts, Hölderlin is drawn to its epic, lyric and tragic literature. Here it is worth recalling his reflection on Sophocles as well as his cryptic reflection on Oedipus, so loved by Heidegger. Sophocles' vocation – which now is also every poet's vocation – is to open a sense of being in the midst of the inexplicable. And Oedipus, in a mesmerising but inscrutable saying, 'has one eye too many perhaps' (*hat ein Auge zuviel vielleicht*).[40] Hölderlin means more than that Oedipus' (everyman's) ordinary perception wreaks havoc, for this is to say that he has 'two eyes too many' and that he comes to see better without them. It is obvious that Hölderlin understands that ordinary perceiving needs to be insulted in order for seeing to happen. But he seems to want to say that in and through suffering there is a kind of perception that could be thought of as a third eye that has a glimpse of the totality that never fully gives itself.

To mirror in the modern world the vocation of Sophocles and to have something like 'one eye too many' is precisely, and non-accidentally, to have a poet's vocation. This point is expressed time and again throughout Hölderlin's poetry. Still, there is nothing wrong with considering Hölderlin's poem, 'Dichterberuf', as exemplary. In that poem the poet is not characterised as someone who exercises a craft, but rather as someone struck by lightning and creative genius. Moreover, genius is not talent or a state; it is an event, something that comes 'over us' (*über uns*).[41] One can find a similar statement in 'The Journey' ('Die Wanderung').[42] The last lines read: 'Oft überraschet es einen / Der eben kaum es gedacht hat.' Hamburger's translation of 'Yet often it takes by surprise / A man whose mind it has hardly entered' is not inaccurate, but it is flat and fails to capture both the sense of being subject to an event and the lack of anticipation in *überraschen*. There seems to be here a general recall of the Greek 'suddenly' (*exaiphnes*), found in the theophanies of Homer and Plato's description of the ecstatic experiences of the good and the beautiful, as well as a particular recall of Pindar's celebration of events of glory that are overwhelming. The rooting of poetry then in ancient Greece is deep, although this is not to say that Hölderlin thinks – anymore than the early Hegel – that a straightforward retrieval is possible. Greece as Greece is not possible in the modern age; what might be possible is Europe or more specifically Germany as a non-identical repetition. Still, even with an obvious reversion to Greece, it seems difficult to suppress in 'comes over us' the echo of the overshadowing of Mary at the Annunciation.

I should briefly address the commonality and difference between the philosopher Hegel and the poet Hölderlin on Sophocles who, for both, sums up Greek tragedy. When Hegel speaks of Greek tragedy, he tends to concentrate upon plot and structure rather than character and the exorbitant price of insight. For him the central play is *Antigone*.[43] By contrast, Hölderlin thinks that character is more important than determinate structure and more important than plot. What truly matters is coming to the moment of 'letting be', which, if ecstatic, has suffering as its other side. Neither judgement is disinterested. Hölderlin and Hegel are dealing with the issue of resolution and the role discourse plays regarding either its hope or its reality. Both are also asking the question whether and how much Greek non-philosophical thought, and especially tragedy, illuminates the modern situation and is capable of being re-inscribed in a discourse more apt for the age. Hegel's answer is that insofar as tragedy is about structural conflict and movement it offers a model for a dialectical philosophy that is alone adequate to represent reality as truly actual (*wirklich*). Hölderlin's answer is that tragedy offers a pre-script for a new form of lyric poetry, because tragedy is in the end always about blinding insight that gets to the height and depth of reality. A similar relation exists between their respective uses of *Liebe*. Both authors associate love with the Greek ethos, while also using it as a meta-philosophical principle about integration into a totality. But the differences are salient: *Liebe* is a key term throughout Hölderlin's major poems whereas it is essentially replaced by *Geist* in Hegel's major work. In addition, as Henrich underscores, *Liebe* indicates a kind of resolution that is less structural and static than that aspired to by the later Hegel.[44]

Philosophy is for Hegel the supreme discourse as it can speak about art and religion; the supreme discourse for Hölderlin is a form of poetry broad and deep enough to mime the idioms of philosophy and religion without being identical with either. We have spoken already of the hallowing of Greek thought, and of Pindar and Sophocles in particular, which suggests Hölderlin's incapacity or unwillingness to distinguish between Greek religion and Greek art – here linguistic art. Hegel, as we noted, in due course separated one from the other, even if they remained fused up to the *Phenomenology*. But beyond this, Hölderlin's poetry illustrates a fusion that for some interpreters and commentators is one to be ignored: that is, his remembrance of the past in order to go forward into the imponderable future involves a recollection of Christianity as well as Greek religion/art, albeit a form of Christianity cleansed of dogmatic encrustation, prescription and dictate. Throughout his major poems, one finds not only recalls of both, but the Greek and the Christian are imbricated with the consequence that Christianity is Hellenised, and Greek religion/art is Christianised. Neither Heidegger nor Henrich draws attention to this feature of Hölderlin's thought, which separates him decisively from the mature Hegel who draws a clear line of demarcation between both, not only in terms of description, but also in terms of evaluation. Hegel is adamant in the texts of his mature period that Christianity is higher than any religion, Greek religion included, and that religion is higher than any form of art, Greek art included.

Gadamer rightly underscores the difference between Hölderlin's appeal to Greece and the other German enthusiasts, including Schiller and Goethe.[45] The 'holy remembrance' (*heilig Gedächtnis*) speaks to an untoward intimacy with regard to what he recalls. The connection is made deeper at the linguistic level if one recalls Hölderlin's use of the alcaic meter typical of the classical ode. The Greek world brings together theophany and fragile human being and rarely, if ever, gestures to the kind of transcendence represented in Greek philosophy by its divide (*chorismos*) between the One and the Many, struggle and unity, and time and eternity. To the degree to which most forms of historical Christianity support a view of transcendence beyond the world, they, too, are rejected by the German poet. While Hölderlin's great poetry is continuous with his original grasping of the aesthetic whole in the fragment 'Judgment and Being', in his poetry the whole is more polymorphously than amorphously divine. It can take masculine or feminine forms, can speak of Father Aether or refer to the divine mother and can articulate a whole range of semi-divine beings, in particular Bacchus and Dionysius, who are more earthy and relevant than most of the historical and ecclesial figurations of Christ. But in the end there is none of the kind of segregation that we find in Hegel. Hölderlin's mature poetry provides evidence of the attraction of the Biblical figure of Christ. In 'Bread and Wine' and 'Patmos', Christ is a theophanous figure as are Zeus and Demeter, Apollo and Dionysus.[46] In 'The Only One' ('Der Einzige') Christ is the brother of Heracles.[47] The belonging together of Christ and the Greek gods is not coincidental. It is a fundamental decision that has folded within it the decision not to decide. 'The Only One' is a poem that very much strains in the direction of giving Christ superiority over the Greek gods, but Hölderlin can only draw back. He finds it intolerable 'That if I serve one I / must lack the other.' (*Das, dien' ich einem, mir / Das andere fehlet.*)[48] In the case of Hegel, decision is required. Christ is that form of theophany that does not remain other. He does not disclose the fragile, but the titanic self, or better, he discloses the titanic self that rises to divine status precisely in and through the fragile, historical and embodied self that is capable of death and thus disappearance. This difference is illustrated in and by the difference between the eclipse of the sacred in Hölderlin, which is vouched for so aggressively by Heidegger, and the 'death of God' in Hegel, articulated in the *Phenomenology* and *Lectures on Philosophy of Religion*, which has proved so influential in modern theology. In the case of the former, the poet is painfully experiencing the disenchantment of a world that, nonetheless, does not completely suspend the promise of the appearance of the divine at least in moments, traces and hints. In the case of the latter, the 'death of God' functions as the overcoming of the God who is 'beyond' (*Jenseits*) and thus transcendent in a noxious way that bleeds meaning and truth from the world. The death of this God involves his emptying into the world and especially into human being and thus carries the implication of the divinisation of the world and the apotheosis of human being.[49]

The mixing of the Christian and the Greek recurs throughout Hölderlin's poems, even those – or perhaps especially those – most clearly advertised as Christian, for example, 'Bread and Wine', 'Patmos', 'The Only One', 'Celebration of Peace' and 'To the Madonna'.[50] The Christian elements are strong both in terms of figuration and content. The figure of Christ is crucial in the first four poems, and Mary (even if not Mary alone) to the last. Yet Christ not only has a relation to the Greek gods due to a similarity of function (mediatorship), but a relation to the Father. And, as in the Gospels, the Father is essentially the object of the address of the Son.[51] There is nothing doctrinal in Hölderlin's account, whether provisional or ultimate. Rather, in 'Bread and Wine' and 'Patmos', the figuration is deeply Johannine. This is not to gainsay that Father and Son are blended figures and that the Father can be associated with Zeus as well as the God who says in Exodus 3:14 'I am who am', and the Son with a host of Greek demi-gods. Still, this granted, Hölderlin's figuration differs decisively from that found in Goethe's famous 'Prometheus' (1773), and differs considerably from the empty transcendence of the Biblical God who in Hegel's early writings is depicted as alienating and repressive.[52] Hegel's early view remains within Goethe's orbit. We find this position somewhat modified in the section on 'Unhappy consciousness' (*unglückliches Bewusstsein*) in the *Phenomenology*. Nonetheless, the change is, arguably, largely cosmetic. It is still the case that the Biblical Father must die if the human being is to live fully. In contrast, Hölderlin's Father is totally benign and giving. 'Patmos' renders him best: 'and what the Father / Who reigns over all loves most / Is that the fixed letter / Be given scrupulous care, and the remaining / Be well interpreted.'[53]

The above passage not only reflects a God who is profoundly providential, perhaps just that Father addressed by Christ, but seems to point to the function of the Holy Spirit as hermeneut. Speaking of the Spirit, Hölderlin finds a place for him/her, even if there is no attempt to integrate the activities of the Father, Christ and Spirit in anything resembling a formal Trinitarian scheme found either in the theological tradition or in Hegel's revisionist schema. The connection between fire and spirit is well established, and although fire has Greek resonances as well as Biblical, the Biblical resonances can be heard even in 'Der Ister', one of those poems adopted by Heidegger as connecting Hölderlin exclusively to the Greeks and essentially bypassing the Bible and the Christian tradition.[54] The apostrophising of fire: 'Fire, come now!' (*Jetz komme, Feuer!*), recalls the *maranatha*, which concludes the book of Revelation (22:20).[55] In Hölderlin's hymns and odes, to the extent to which there is Christian material, it shares space with Greek material, and to the extent to which the figures of Father, Son and Spirit are in play, they remain at once entirely Biblical in their mode of evocation and their relations enigmatic.[56] Unlike Hegel, Hölderlin does not seem to think that the Bible is a wax nose that admits of any kind of interpretation. Nor is the Bible replaceable by a meta-narrative in which the accent falls on resolution and closure in and by a conceptual matrix that can articulate the logos of reality and thus to all intents and purposes articulate a theodicy.[57] For Hölderlin, the Bible is a text of epiphany and relation like the best of Greek literature. The Bible keeps the modern self grounded in remembrance and hope, whereas meta-narrative and concept, or meta-narrative and syllogism, are devices of recollection (*Erinnerung*), which elevate human beings to the divine point of view where they are unfaithful to the world and the human condition characterised by finitude and epistemic limitation. Within a Hölderlinian frame of reference, *Erinnerung* pretends a resolution that is an absolution from these constraints seen as obstacles to realisation rather than situations of grace. For Hölderlin the world remains enigmatic, and there are at best hints (*Spuren*) that make waiting precious and give life to hope.

6.3 The impact of aesthetic Idealism

It might be thought that the history of reception of aesthetic Idealism in theology is necessarily a one-sided affair in which philosophical figures are the only possible subjects of discussion. I think this is a mistake and will shortly sketch trajectories that suggest that the Hölderlinian brand of aesthetic Idealism not only has had influence in modern aesthetics, literary theory and poetic practice, but that this influence is felt throughout religiously interested philosophy and also in theology proper. Contrariwise, the history of effects of Hegel's thought is so vast and multi-varied that what is required is a narrowing of focus that gives determinacy. I am convinced, however, that the aesthetic Idealist designation of Hegel's thought, and its close relation to Christianity as rendered by a meta-narrative and by the representation of the Trinity, provides sufficient determinacy to enable the interpreter to proceed. Not all right-wing Hegelians affirm Hegel on grounds of his aesthetic dialectical holism, or on the basis of his affirmation of speculative philosophy as the master discourse, or, again, on the basis of what he takes to provide the definition of Christianity. Similarly, not all left-wing Hegelians understand that there are peculiarities in Hegel's rendition of Christianity, or show interest in the relations between concept and symbol, on the one hand, and the relation between concept and meta-narrative, on the other. Given the philosophically licensed ambition to save the world, distinctions between Hegel and the reflective Christian tradition – should they be sustainable – would speak to differences that do not make a difference.

But if not the *dramatis personae* in the 1830s, about whom there is a learned literature, then who does grasp the meta-philosophical backdrop of Hegel's thought in the immediate wake of his death?[58] In the end, what announces this backdrop to be speculative in Hegel's basic concern, is the 'mirror' or *speculum* in and through which the whole rises to self-consciousness, in and through the thinking of an otherness that constitutes the self.[59] It is Kierkegaard also who, in the nineteenth century, rightly worries about the overall constitution of Hegel's thought as a philosophy of 'mediation' (*Vermittlung*), which insists on the prerogative of concept and explanation. It is naïve, Kierkegaard thinks, to assume that Hegel's double commitment will preserve the sense of any of Christianity's basic symbols, for example, creaturehood, sin or redemption wrought by Christ.[60] Speculative philosophy in a sense provides an instruction in complacency that is 'aesthetic' in the pejorative sense of being self-absorbed. Hegelianism is characterised by the divine point of view, the view from nowhere that frowns on partiality and perspective and that makes pre-emptive strikes against positions that would fundamentally challenge speculative philosophy's aspiration and performance of closure.

Yet Kierkegaard fails to engage the relation between logic and meta-narrative. In addition, the Trinity is not discussed at all – Kierkegaard seems to follow Kant (and on some accounts Schleiermacher) in making this symbol an *adiaphora*, that is, a construct marginal to Christian faith considered as grounded in a specific kind of experience. A number of important Hegelians and anti-Hegelians of some stature, however, did reflect comprehensively on both of these. I shall highlight Ferdinand Christian Baur (1772–1860), a Protestant, and Franz Anton Staudenmaier (1800–56), a Catholic. Both begin concerted reflection on Hegel in the 1830s and, in the case of Staudenmaier, never cease. What is interesting about both of these engagements is that whatever the final verdict – Baur's is overwhelmingly positive, Staudenmaier's negative – on Hegel's philosophy of religion, his holism is a feature that attracts both. For example, Staudenmaier's twenty-year engagement with Hegel gradually evolves into the most comprehensive critique of Hegelian thought of the nineteenth century and from a Catholic point of view,[61] although early in his career he lauds Hegel's idea of the organic whole and avails of it as leverage against Scholastic-style propositionalist theology.[62] At the same time he welcomes Hegel's view of the Trinity, which he regards as a synecdoche in the theological sphere of the principle of unity. Over time, these pluses turn into minuses in that Hegelian holism functions at the expense of the integrity of Christian symbols and Hegel's Trinitarianism bears no relation to the actual theological tradition, but is rather a developmental ontology with roots in neo-Platonism and Gnosticism. Staudenmaier belatedly comes to conclusions already arrived at by Baur in *Die christliche Gnosis* (1835), with the major difference being that Baur thinks that the differences between Hegel and the theological tradition are to Hegel's credit.[63] Baur in fact celebrates the association between Hegel and ancient esoteric traditions and opines that Hegel's philosophy of religion represents the return to prominence of these marginalised forms of thought after a questionable Catholic interregnum. One of the more conspicuous features of these ancient forms of thought is their meta-narrative structure (which admits of triadic schematisation). Neither Baur nor Staudenmaier are involved in eisegesis here. Hegel regularly recalls these discourses throughout *Lectures on the Philosophy of Religion* and lavishes praise on them in *Lectures on the History of Philosophy*.[64]

Neither Baur nor Staudenmaier moved beyond formal considerations of the relations between philosophy and Christianity and the complex relations between conceptual and symbolic formulation, on the one hand, and narrative formation, on the other. Neither questions Hegel's claim concerning the unsurpassability of Christianity as a religion; and in neither case are Hegel's reflections on the absolute status of art and its third place in a discursive hierarchy contested. Nor can one find any engagement with Hegel's view of the superiority of the linguistic arts and his reflection on genre.

Perhaps the only Christian thinker who has taken account of all of these Hegelian elements, including Hegel's reflections on the status of art, his reflection on the relations between art and both religion and philosophy, his articulation of literary genres and his valorisation of tragedy in general and Greek tragedy in particular is the great twentieth-century Catholic theologian Hans Urs von Balthasar. Of course, Balthasar is appreciative of Hegel's achievements, many of which he believes are theologically relevant. My aim here is merely to flag an engagement so comprehensive none greater than it can be thought. The crucial points to be made are that:

(1) Balthasar thinks that the constellation of elements in Hegel's thought that we have been considering are the truly central ones.
(2) Balthasar suspects that on all the important points, for example, discursive hierarchy, separation of art from Christianity, the nature of tragedy, the relation of philosophy to Christian symbols and narrative, Trinitarian articulation, Hegel is wrong in some fundamental respects.
(3) Balthasar privileges aesthetics in general as the epistemic ground for theology and thinks through the close relationship between art and Christianity.[65]

The limitations of Baur's and Staudenmaier's nineteenth-century engagement with Hegel are shown up then by comparison with the twentieth-century Balthasar. Particularly conspicuous is the sidelining of aesthetic considerations in both. This is true also of Ernst Troeltsch, whose theology takes on Hegel's holism, narrative frame and Trinitarian landscaping, but tries to modify its epistemic and ontological claims in order to deflate justification of the status quo and a theodicy that is secured by historical closure, which is also a semantic and alethic closure.[66] A number of theologians in the Protestant tradition have found Troeltsch's modification of Hegel theologically helpful. Peter Hodgson would be included among these.[67] It is no secret then that much of modern German theology is constituted by an engagement with Hegel. This is especially true of thinkers within the Protestant tradition. Wolfhart Pannenberg, Eberhard Jüngel and Jürgen Moltmann seriously engage Hegel. Whatever the level of critique in the appropriation, one is left in no doubt that Hegel is the theological German philosopher *par excellence*. None of the three branch out in the way that Balthasar does to engage Hegel's aesthetics, his theory of genres, his artistic judgements on the side, and his view of discourses of art, religion and philosophy and their relative authority. Of the three above-mentioned German theologians, perhaps it is only Jüngel, with his interest in metaphor and his anxiety regarding the possibility of its erasure, who has the negative capability of extending critique of Hegel in the way that Balthasar has done.

6.4 The impact of Hölderlin on theology

Hölderlin's reputation is as a great Romantic poet, or maybe even *the* greatest lyric poet in the German language. I would like to propose – counterintuitive though it may appear – that his influence on theology has been considerable, if indirect. I identify four tracks in twentieth-century religious thought in which Hölderlin plays an important role. The first is the role he plays in Heidegger's construction of an autochthonous form of religion that prefers, like many German Romantics and Idealists, Greek religion to confessional and philosophical forms of Christianity. Hölderlin, with Meister Eckhart, contributes to Heidegger's articulation of a way beyond modernity characterised by an exacerbation of subjectivity and a corresponding objectification and technicalisation of reality. Second, Hölderlin comes into theology via Walter Benjamin who elaborates a view of the whole subject to precisely that interruption that characterised Hölderlin's appropriation of Fichte.[68] And it is Benjamin who said of his thought that it is saturated with theology, and who yoked together, in much the way Hölderlin did, religious, artistic and philosophical considerations, and who saw that the issue was essentially the same in all three: that is, the clash between two different models of resolution, a kind of Hegelian model and one where the resolution remained in the order of promise.[69] Benjamin's considerations of the superiority of one form of resolution – resolution as non-resolution – is funnelled back into theology both directly, in that the very notion of 'interruption' is taken up in the theology of Johann Baptist Metz, and indirectly through the theological appropriation of critical theory, especially its view of negative dialectic and the distinction between the form of genuine art (which allows formlessness) and kitsch (which does not). Once again, if somewhat indirectly, Benjamin makes his way into postmodern discourses precisely as they make a religious turn, in the case of Derrida, in his essay on the apocalyptic tone and, in Agamben, in reflections on Saint Paul.[70] Again, both are decidedly anti-Hegelian, especially Derrida, and both grasp the correspondence between the semiotic mechanisms of the discourses of art, religion and philosophy. For theology to engage both of these postmodern discourses is also indirectly to engage Benjamin and, through him, Hölderlin.

I come now to the third and fourth tracks in theology where the appropriation of Hölderlin is evident. The German-speaking Catholic embrace of Hölderlin is not simply chauvinist cultural preference and nationalism. Romano Guardini, Erich Przywara and Hans Urs von Balthasar were all convinced that Hölderlin has something to contribute to theology.[71] Balthasar, who has the examples of the other two before him, is the most interesting.[72] For, like Henrich, Balthasar thinks that he belongs at least in part in the Idealist camp and that philosophical or pre-philosophical views continue to exercise influence in his poetry. He does not, however, take the stance that Heidegger's interpretation is totally without merit. As a theologian he is interested in how Christianity fares in Hölderlin's great poetry. Here, he senses that in Hölderlin there is both a marvellously close relation between Christianity and Greek religion and a relation of rivalry. On the most general level, however, for Balthasar, Hölderlin becomes a figure in the fight against Hegel's Idealism whose aesthetic holism is inimical to the irreducible particularity of Christ and the cross. The kind of aesthetic holism illustrated in Hölderlin is the right kind, what Balthasar subsumes under the rubric of 'theological aesthetics'. By contrast, the wrong kind of holism, the one that is based on full-scale speculative resolution, falls under the rubric of 'aesthetic theology' and is a counterfeit of the authentic mode of Christian resolution, which is never fully complete or apprehended.

The fourth and final appropriation of Hölderlin – once again a form of postmodern discourse – has as its background the Catholic theological engagement with the Hölderlin of Przywara and Balthasar, and as its provocation the Heideggerian appropriation of the great German lyric poet. Here, the interest is in rendering a Christian Hölderlin. Jean-Luc Marion fights this battle in his great essay on Hölderlin in 'Idol and distance' in which the German poet articulates a discourse announcing a situation of lack (*Fehl*), and attests to intimations of wholeness that are through and through relational and specifically involve the relation between fragile human being and the epiphanies of the sacred that are transformative.[73] While Marion recognises that gods such as Dionysus and Bacchus are emblems pointing to a mode of transcendence that does not leach the earth of value, so also, and even more, is Christ such an emblem (icon) in his relation to the Father and as inspired by the Spirit. Without intending to, Marion articulates a Biblically rooted, Johannine-inflected Trinitarianism of scrupulous modesty. This form of Trinitarianism does not necessarily displace the Christian doctrine of the Trinity, but it may deflate its conceptual pretensions. What Marion does not seem to notice – but a student like Jean-Yves Lacoste does – is that it also and even more deflates the Hegelian form of the Trinity, which throws mystery to the wind and thinks the Trinity not only to be explicable, but to be the very code of explanation.[74]

6.5 Conclusion

In this essay, following on the pioneering work of Dieter Henrich, I have argued that the works of G. W. F. Hegel and Friedrich Hölderlin spring from the same existential and discursive problematic about the relation of part and whole, multiplicity and unity, division and resolution, and initially articulates itself as a form of aesthetic Idealism. The basic lineaments of this aesthetic can be seen in the very earliest writings of both. One place where the overlap is especially evident is the fragment 'The oldest program towards a system in German Idealism' ['Ältestes Systemprogramm des deutschen Idealismus'] (1797), which, although written by Hegel, shows the trace of conversation with Schelling and Hölderlin.[75] What becomes obvious – at least retrospectively – is that aesthetic Idealism is essentially underdetermined and has the capacity for different emphases regarding how the paired terms relate. Aesthetic Idealism also permits different decisions regarding which of the three plenary discourses of art, religion and philosophy is in the best position to effect the correct kind of synthesis, as well as how they are to relate to each other. From the beginning, Hegel seems significantly more committed than Hölderlin to a form of resolution in which unity prevails. Furthermore, even if in his early years it is religion, whether Greek religion or a Greek-inflected form of Christianity that gets the nod, a couple of years into the nineteenth century, it is philosophy that is the supreme discourse: philosophy not only surpasses the other two discourses, but inspects and judges them. In addition, Christianity has emerged as 'consummate' religion, which has no rival. In contrast, in Hölderlin, poetry comes to play the role of plenary discourse, although Hölderlin finds it difficult to separate poetry from religion, on the one hand, and Greek religion from Christianity, on the other. To the extent to which Christianity is affirmed in Hölderlin, it is deeply experiential and figural, whereas in Hegel, as we have shown, although practices are important, beliefs matter and especially the Christian meta-narrative that admits of being elevated (*Erhebung*) to the level of the concept by way of triadic or Trinitarian synopsis. The overall aim of the third part of this essay was to indicate in a very broad way the history of effects of both thinkers in contemporary theology. In particular, I have shown that both Hegel and Hölderlin have exercised and continue to exercise considerable influence in theology, albeit of a somewhat indirect kind. In fact, it is hardly an exaggeration to suggest that these two forms of aesthetic Idealism are two of the most important contenders in the complex landscape of modern and postmodern theological thought.

Notes

1. On Spinoza see Jonathan I. Israel, *Radical Enlightenment: Philosophy and the Making of Modernity* (Oxford: Oxford University Press, 2001), esp. chs. 8, 13, 14, 16.
2. H. S. Harris, *Hegel's Development*, vol. II: *Night Thoughts* (Oxford: Clarendon, 1983), 144–88.
3. Dieter Henrich, *Between Kant and Hegel: Lectures on German Idealism* (Cambridge, MA: Harvard University Press, 2003), 216–30, esp. 227–9. See also *The Course of Remembrance and other Essays on Hölderlin*, Eckhart Förster (ed.) (Stanford, CA: Stanford University Press, 1997), 126–7, 135–6, also 97.
4. Henrich, *The Course of Remembrance*, 67–70, 104–8.
5. G. W. F. Hegel, *Phenomenology of Spirit*, trans. A. V. Miller (Oxford: Clarendon Press, 1977) [hereafter PS]; *Lectures on the Philosophy of Religion*, P. C. Hodgson (ed.), trans. R. F. Brown, P. C. Hodgson, J. M. Stewart, 3 vols. (Berkeley and Los Angeles: University of California Press, 1984–7); *Hegel's Philosophy of Mind: Being Part Three of the Encyclopaedia of the Philosophical Sciences* (1830), trans. W. Wallace (Oxford: Clarendon, 1977).
6. I cite Michael Hamburger's *Friedrich Hölderlin: Poems and Fragments* (Ann Arbor: University of Michigan Press, 1967), with occasional amendments.
7. Hans Küng, *The Incarnation of God: The Introduction to Hegel's Theological Thought as a Prolegomenon to a Future Christology*, trans. J. R. Stephenson (New York: Crossroad, 1987); Eberhard Jüngel, *God as the Mystery of the World: On the Foundation of the Theology of the Crucified One in the Dispute between Theism and Atheism*, trans. Darell L. Guder (Grand Rapids, MI: Eerdmans, 1983); on Balthasar, see my forthcoming *Anatomy of Misremembering*, vol. I: *Balthasar and the Specter of Hegel* (New York: Crossroad, 2013).
8. See Georg Lukács, *The Young Hegel*, trans. R. Livingston (London: Merlin Press, 1975).
9. Hegel, *Early Theological Writings*, trans. T. M. Knox (Philadelphia: University of Pennsylvania Press, 1948); Henrich, *Between Kant and Hegel*, 279–95, esp. 294–5; also *The Course of Remembrance*, 124–31.
10. See Henrich, *The Course of Remembrance*, 131.
11. For PS, see §19 of the preface, see also *Lectures on the Philosophy of Religion*, vol. III, 195.
12. On 'plasticity' see Catherine Malabou, *The Future of Hegel: Plasticity, Temporality, Dialectic*, trans. Lizabeth During (New York: Routledge, 2004).
13. See paragraphs 40–60 of *Hegel's Logic: Being Part 1 of the Encyclopaedia of Philosophical Sciences* (1830), trans. W. Wallace (Oxford: Clarendon Press, 1975), 65–94. On Spinoza, see *Lectures on the History of Philosophy*, vol. III: *Medieval and Modern Philosophy*, trans. E. S. Haldane and Frances H. Simson (Lincoln and London: University of Nebraska Press, 1995), 252–90.
14. See Hegel, *Vorlesungen über die Ästhetik 111* (Frankfurt a.M.: Suhrkamp, 1993), 318–574.

15. See F. Schiller, *On the Aesthetic Education of Man*, trans. E. M. Wilkinson and L. A. Willoughby (Oxford: Clarendon, 1967). On modern art, especially poetry and drama, see Schiller's 1795 essay *Über naïve und sentimentalische Dichtung* (Leipzig: Reclam, 2002).

16. See Steven Bungay, *Beauty and Truth: A Study of Hegel's Aesthetics* (Oxford: Oxford University Press, 1984), 147–87.

17. See PS, chapter 7.

18. See *Lectures on the Philosophy of Religion*, vol. II, 121–89 (1821), 455–97 (1924); 642–68 (1827) for Hegel's discussion of Greek religion as a religion of beauty.

19. See *Encyclopaedia*, vol. III, §§556ff.

20. For a discussion of Hegel's negative attitude towards Judaism, see Cyril O'Regan, 'Hegel and anti-Judaism: narrative and the inner circulation of the Kabbalah', in *The Owl of Minerva*, 28(20) (Spring) 1997, 141–82, esp. 142–56.

21. See PS, §§223–30; also *Lectures on the Philosophy of Religion*, vol. III, 238 (1824).

22. See Kant, *Religion within the Boundaries of Mere Reason and other Writings*, Allen Wood and George di Giovanni (eds.) (Cambridge: Cambridge University Press, 1998), 31–191, esp. 105–91.

23. See Hegel, *Lectures on the Philosophy of Religion*, vol. III, 341–42 (1927).

24. On *Sittlichkeit* see PS (§444–83); *Encyclopaedia*, vol. III (§§513–52), and especially *Hegel's Philosophy of Right*, trans. T. M. Knox (Oxford: Clarendon Press, 1967) (§§142–360).

25. See Hegel, *Lectures on the Philosophy of Religion*, vol. I, 123.

26. See Samuel M. Powell, *The Trinity in German Thought* (Cambridge: Cambridge University Press, 2001), 87–103.

27. Hegel, *Lectures on the Philosophy of Religion*, vol. III, 85–6, also 196–7, 289 (Valentinus), 84, 196, 287 (Philo), 289 (Böhme).

28. Hegel's departure from the Nicene standard is especially clear in the *Lectures on the Philosophy of Religion*, vol. III, 192–5 (1824); also 283–9 (1827). See my *The Heterodox Hegel* (New York: State University of New York Press, 1994) 126–40.

29. See O'Regan, *The Heterodox Hegel*, 238–40.

30. See Anicius Boethius, *De consolatione philosophiae. Opuscula theologica*, C. Moreschini (ed.) (Munich: K. G. Saur, 2000), 5.6, 9–11.

31. See Martin Heidegger, *Elucidations of Hölderlin's Poetry*, trans. Keith Hoeller (New York: Humanity Books, 2000).

32. Henrich, *The Course of Remembrance*, 104–8, also 97.

33. See Gérard Vallée, *The Spinoza Conversations between Lessing and Jacobi: Texts with Excerpts from the Ensuing Controversy* (Lanham, MD: University Press of America, 1988).

34. Henrich, *Between Kant and Hegel*, 279–95; *The Course of Remembrance*, 104–8.

35. See George Seidel, *Activity and Ground: Fichte, Schelling, and Hegel* (New York: George Olms Verlag, 1976), 96.

36. Henrich, *The Course of Remembrance*, 136.

37. On Fichte's finitism see Alexis Philoneko, *La liberté humaine dans la philosophie de Fichte* (Paris: Vrin, 1966).

38. Henrich, *Between Kant and Hegel*, 228–9; *The Course of Remembrance*, 136.

39. See Henrich 'Theories of imagination and longing and their impact on Schlegel, Novalis, and Hölderlin', in *Between Kant and Hegel*, 216–30; also *The Course of Remembrance*, 133–6.

40. This is a passage from a very late poem of Hölderlin, 'In lovely blueness' ('In Lieblicher Bläue'), much mined by Heidegger. See *Friedrich Hölderlin: Poems and Fragments*, 600–5, esp. 602–3. Heidegger comments on the Oedipus passage on a number of occasions. See for example, *Elucidations of Hölderlin's Poetry*, 64.

41. For this poem, see *Friedrich Hölderlin: Poems and Fragments*, 172–7, esp. 172.

42. For this poem, see *ibid.*, 392–9. 'Die Wanderung' is often translated as 'The migration'.

43. See PS, §736 (445–5); *Vorlesungen über die Ästhetik*, vol. III, 549–50.

44. Henrich, *The Course of Remembrance*, 131–3.

45. See Hans-Georg Gadamer, *Literature and Philosophy in Dialogue: Essays in German Literary Theory*, trans. Robert H. Paslick (New York: State University of New York Press, 1993), 67–86.

46. For 'Bread and Wine' ('Brot und Wein'), see *Friedrich Hölderlin: Poems and Fragments*, 242–53; for 'Patmos', see *ibid.*, 462–87 (2 versions).

47. *Ibid.*, 446–61 (2 versions).

48. *Ibid.*, 448–9.

49. See *Lectures on the Philosophy of Religion*, vol. III, 124–5 (1821 ms); also 325–36 (1827).

50. For 'Celebration of Peace' ('Friedensfeier') and 'To the Madonna' ('An die Madonna'), see *Friedrich Hölderlin: Poems and Fragments*, 432–45 and 518–29, respectively. I have refused Hamburger's translation of 'To the Virgin Mary' for 'An die Madonna'.

51. See Jean-Luc Marion, 'The withdrawal of the divine and the face of the father: Hölderlin', in *The Idol and the Distance: Five Studies*, trans. Thomas A. Carlson (New York: Fordham University Press, 2001), 81–136.

52. See Vallée, *The Spinoza Conversations*, 7–11, 22–7.

53. These are the last lines of 'Patmos'. I have made two alterations from Hamburger. I have translated *veste Buchstab* as 'fixed letter' and not as 'solid letter', which is not only non-idiomatic, but really does not make sense. Instead of translating *bestehendes* as 'existing' I have tried to capture the sense of perdurance of existence that is implied.

54. See Jacques Derrida, *Of Spirit: Heidegger and the Question*, trans. Geoffrey Bennington and Rachel Bowlby (Chicago: University of Chicago Press, 1989).

55. For the poem 'Der Ister', see *Friedrich Hölderlin: Poems and Fragments*, 492–7. For the apostrophe, see 492–3. Derrida speaks to this passage in *Of Spirit*, 81.

56. See Marion, *Idol and Distance*, 81–136.

57. See O'Regan, *The Heterodox Hegel*, 310–26.

58. See, for example, Lawrence S. Stepelevich (ed.), *The Young Hegelians* (Cambridge: Cambridge University Press, 1983); John Edward Toews, *Hegelianism: The Path towards Dialectical Humanism, 1805–1840* (Cambridge: Cambridge University Press, 1985). See also Jon Stewart, *Kierkegaard's Relation to Hegel Reconsidered* (Cambridge: Cambridge University Press, 2003).

59. See Rodolphe Gasché, *The Tain of the Mirror: Derrida and the Philosophy of Reflection* (Cambridge, MA: Harvard University Press, 1986), 13–105.

60. See Joel Rasmussen's essay in chapter 4 in this volume.

61. See especially, F. A. Staudenmaier, *Darstellung und Kritik des Hegelschen Systems. Aus dem Standpunkte der christlichen Philosophie* (Mainz: Kupferberg, 1844), reprinted (Frankfurt: Minerva, 1966).

62. See Staudenmaier, *Pragmatismus der Geistesgaben* (Tübingen: Laup, 1835).

63. F. C. Baur, *Die christliche Gnosis; oder die christliche Religionsphilosophie in ihrer geschichtlichen Entwicklung* (Tübingen: Osiander, 1835).

64. See the section on neo-Platonism in Hegel's *Lectures on the History of Philosophy*, vol. II, section 3, 374–453.

65. See my forthcoming *The Anatomy of Misremembering*, vol. I: *Balthasar and the Specter of Hegel* (New York: Crossroad, 2013).

66. See Ernst Troeltsch, *The Christian Faith*, Gertrud von le Fort (ed.), trans. Garrett E. Paul (Minneapolis: Fortress, 1991); *Religion in History*, trans. James Luther Adams and Walter F. Bense (Minneapolis: Fortress Press, 1991).

67. Peter C. Hodgson, *God in History: Shapes of Freedom* (Nashville: Abingdon Press, 1989).

68. For Benjamin's apocalyptic notion of 'interruption', see especially Benjamin's 'Theses on the philosophy of history', in Hannah Arendt (ed.), *Illuminations*, trans. Harry Zohn (New York: Schocken, 1969), 253–64. Benjamin constantly recurs to Hölderlin. In 1914–15 he writes on 'Dichtermut' and 'Blödigkeit', and Hölderlin is favourably mentioned in *Ursprung des deutschen Trauerspiels* (1928). For a good general account of Benjamin's relation to Hölderlin, see Philippe Lacoue-Labarthe, 'Poetry's courage', in *Walter Benjamin and Romanticism*, Beatrice Hanssen and Andrew Benjamin (eds.) (New York: Continuum, 2002), 163–79. For reflection on Benjamin's analysis of Hölderlin's poems, see Beatrice Hanssen, '"Dichtermut" and "Blödigkeit" – two poems by Friedrich Hölderlin, interpreted by Walter Benjamin', in *Walter Benjamin and Romanticism*, 139–62.

69. See especially Benjamin's elaboration of a theory of knowledge as a prologue to the Arcades project in *Benjamin: Philosophy, Aesthetics, History*, Gary Smith (ed.) (Chicago: University of Chicago Press, 1989), 48–83. For this particular statement, see 61.

70. See Derrida's 'On the newly arisen apocalyptic tone in philosophy', in *Raising the Tone of Philosophy: Late Essays by Immanuel Kant, Transformative Critique by Jacques Derrida*, Peter Fenves (ed.) (Baltimore: Johns Hopkins Press, 1998), 117–73. See also Giorgio Agamben, *The Time that Remains: A Commentary on the Letter to the Romans* (Stanford: Stanford University Press, 2008), 138–45.

71. See Romano Guardini, *Weltbild und Frömmigkeit* (Paderborn: Matthias-Grünewald/Schöningh, 1996). Originally published by Kösel Verlag in 1955; Erich Przywara, *Hölderlin: Eine Studie* (Nuremburg: Glock und Lutz, 1949).

72. See especially, *The Glory of the Lord. A Theological Aesthetics*. Vol. V: *The Realm of Metaphysics in the Modern Age*, trans. Oliver Davies, Andrew Louth, Brian McNeil, John Saward and Rowan Williams (San Francisco: Ignatius, 1991), 298–338.

73. Jean-Luc Marion, *The Idol and Distance: Five Studies* (New York: Fordham University Press, 2001), 81–136.

74. Jean-Yves Lacoste, *Experience and the Absolute: Disputed Questions on the Humanity of Man*, trans. Mark Raftery-Skehan (New York: Fordham University Press, 2001).

75. See Christoph Jamme and Helmut Schneider (eds.), *Mythologie der Vernunft: Hegels 'Ältestes Systemprogramm des deutschen Idealismus'* (Frankfurt a. M.: Suhrkamp, 1984), 36–9.

7

The autonomy of theology and the impact of Idealism: from Hegel to radical orthodoxy

JOHN WALKER

In this essay, I want to argue two theses. First, that the theological element in the impact of German Idealism has to be understood as *autonomous*. That is to say, there is a theological strand in the impact of German Idealism that must be understood as independent of its cultural, historical and philosophical reception. Second, understanding that autonomy means understanding the *context* of the theological thought of German Idealism in the whole discourse of the culture in which it originated and of the successive cultural worlds in which it has been received.

First, I will argue that the key to the trajectory of philosophical theology in German Idealism, and its subsequent legacy, is the work of Hegel. Hegel's central doctrine is a radically new idea of Revelation: a doctrine of theology and philosophy as different but related modes of self-conscious Spirit.[1] This idea entails not only the autonomy of theology but also – and for the same reasons – the autonomy of philosophy in relation to theology. This new idea of Revelation therefore implies a radical acknowledgement of the difference as well as the connection between the philosophical and theological modes of truth: it is the very opposite of the reduction of the life of faith to a secularised cultural narrative.

Second, I will argue that the theological reception of German Idealism after Hegel represents in large part the loss of this insight. The Idealist legacy in theology lost its credibility between Hegel and Karl Barth because the German Idealist mode in theology became detached from its philosophical roots and therefore part of the theologically impoverished and politically compromised narrative of *Kulturprotestantismus*. In the last three decades, however, there has been a renewed interest in German Idealism in theology. The theological current known as radical orthodoxy associated with John Milbank, Catherine Pickstock and Graham Ward has appropriated many of the insights of German Idealism in an effort to respond to the philosophical challenge of postmodernism and the renegotiation of boundaries between sacred and secular, which some elements of postmodernism have prompted.[2] However, such thinkers have characteristically been influenced less by the specifically philosophical elements of German Idealist theology than by the analogy between theology and narrative which they take that theology to imply. At the same time, the current known as 'religionless' or 'secular' Christianity associated with theologians like Don Cupitt and Mark Taylor has taken the theological legacy of German Idealism, especially the work of Hegel, to endorse the project of an entirely secularised Christianity that radical orthodoxy consistently rejects.[3]

In the concluding part of this essay I will argue that both these currents, despite acknowledging their debt to the Idealist legacy, misunderstand in some important ways the original context of that legacy and therefore its true contemporary relevance. The source of this misunderstanding is their failure to connect the autonomy of theology in the heritage of German Idealism to its origins in a sustained dialectic between the philosophical and theological modes of truth. The true impact of Idealism in theology is not the disconnection of theology from philosophical critique and so the reduction of theological truth to narrative. However, neither does the Idealist reinterpretation of Christian doctrine support the view that Christian theology can be recast in exclusively secular terms. The real modern meaning of Idealism for theology, I will suggest, is exactly the opposite of both kinds of reduction. Only by reconstructing the history of the Idealist tradition in theology can we understand its true meaning now.

First, I must sketch the emergence of Hegel's philosophical theology from the post-Kantian trajectory of German Idealism. In his early (pre-1804) theological writings, Hegel identifies himself explicitly as an heir of Kant and understands his task as bringing to fruition the whole movement of German Idealism that Kant's critical philosophy inaugurates. He associates Kant's idea of philosophy as critique – the self-reflective investigation of knowledge – with a shift in the central subject matter of philosophy from metaphysics to ethics, especially the philosophy of freedom and the reform of religion. In a text written in 1796 or 1797 and attributed to Hegel, known as 'The oldest programme for a system of German Idealism',[a] Hegel associates this project with the idea of art as Revelation and with the creation of a

---

a. 'Das älteste Systemprogramm des deutschen Idealismus'.

'mythology of reason',[b] in which philosophy will be embodied in narratives and images accessible to the people.[4]

These ambitions Hegel shares with his philosophical generation, especially his contemporaries Schelling and Hölderlin whom he meets whilst studying in the Tübingen Stift. However, the main burden of Hegel's early writings is not ethics or aesthetics, nor (at least after his early 'Fragments on popular religion and Christianity')[c] the creation of a new popular religion. It is a sustained analysis and critique of the philosophical and theological self-consciousness of German Protestantism in his age. His central concern is the apparently unbridgeable rift in the culture of Lutheran Germany between post-Kantian philosophical theology and the legacy of the Christian Revelation in positive faith and practice. In his essay on 'The positivity of the Christian religion'[d] Hegel diagnoses two kinds of dualism in the life of his age, which he believes are the consequences of this rift. First, a division has arisen in religious life itself. The Biblical narrative has become the dead object of philosophical theology. Its historicity is challenged by philological and historical scholarship. The interaction between scripture and doctrine is artificially constructed by critical theology; not realised in the life of the Christian community. This situation, he argues, has led to two equally destructive consequences: an arid rationalism, which reduces the articles of faith to moral maxims or merely analyses and chronicles their historical development, and an intense pietism, which eschews reflection altogether in favour of an empty because incommunicable intensity of feeling.[5] At the same time, a parallel division has arisen in the philosophical life of post-Kantian Germany. Post-Kantian ethics, Hegel argues, posits an absolute difference between the moral law and the contingent sources of desire and motivation. The enlightened post-Kantian philosopher therefore serves an ethical ideal as alien to his or her actual experience as an idol worshipped in ignorance.[6] Neither the philosophical nor the theological culture of Germany at the end of the eighteenth century, then, enables the living unity of experience and self-conscious reflection which Hegel will later call Spirit.

In his essay 'The spirit of Christianity and its fate'[e] Hegel moves some way towards such a conception, only to conclude that the historical fate of the primitive Christian Church no less than its modern protestant successors

b. 'Mythologie der Vernunft'.
c. 1793–94: 'Fragmente über Volksreligion und Christentum'.
d. 1796: 'Die Positivität der christlichen Religion'.
e. 1800: 'Der Geist des Christentums und sein Schicksal'.

is to remain in irreconcilable opposition to the secular world. For Hegel in 1800, the spirit received at Pentecost is not one of presence and comfort, but one that produces – precisely because it is also historically factual – a consciousness in the believer that is irrevocably alienated from the secular world:

> In all the forms of the Christian religion which have been developed in the advancing fate of the ages, there lies this fundamental characteristic of opposition in the divine which is supposed to be present in consciousness only, never in life . . . And it is its fate that Church and state, worship and life, piety and virtue, spiritual and worldly action, can never dissolve into one.[f,7]

The key word here is fate (*Schicksal*). For Hegel in 1800, Christianity has a fate, not a spiritual history. That is because, in Hegel's early understanding, the Spirit of Christianity is at once embodied in and divided against history. It is therefore condemned to a consciousness of infinite longing, in which the moment of incarnation embodied in the person of Christ is now suspended until the end of time. Hegel's early theology is therefore Christo-centric but clearly not Trinitarian. It interprets Ascension and Pentecost not as the assurance that the Spirit really is present in human history *because* it is human history, but as the sign that the one story in which spirit was really present is now over. The human spirit that now longs for the return of the incarnate word can and must therefore be *only* human.

Between this early essay of 1800 and his mature philosophy of religion written towards the end of his life, Hegel's understanding of Christianity changes radically. The key to this change is a development in Hegel's concept of Spirit that in turn implies a radical change in his understanding of the activity of philosophy itself.

This is already foreshadowed in Hegel's essay 'On the difference between Fichte's and Schelling's systems of philosophy'.[g] Here Hegel first advances the crucial thesis that the true task of philosophy is to mediate – that is, to enable intellectual communication – between the religious and the secular consciousness of his age. For Hegel now, the source of the need for

---

f. 'In allen Formen der christlichen Religion, die sich im fortgehenden Schicksale der Zeit entwickelt haben, ruht dieser Grundcharakter der Entgegensetzung in dem Göttlichen, das allein im Bewusstsein, nie im Leben vorhanden sein soll . . . es ist ihr Schicksal, daß Kirche und Staat, Gottesdienst und Leben, Frömmigkeit und Tugend, geistliches und weltliches Tun nie in Eins zusammen schmelzen können.' HW, I, 418.

g. 1801: 'Differenz des Fichteschen und Schellingschen Systems der Philosophie'.

philosophy is precisely this self-division[h] of consciousness itself.[8] True philosophy is neither one pole of the opposition, nor a neutral discourse that
describes and analyses the nature of the divorce. Philosophy is a mode of
consciousness that lives in and through both apparently opposed elements
and so, in that engagement, enacts their reconciliation. How can this happen?
The subtitle to *Faith and Knowledge*, an essay of 1802, provides a clue: 'The
reflective philosophy of subjectivity in its complete form in the philosophies
of Kant, Jacobi and Fichte'.[i] What is really new about this essay is that Hegel
is no longer chiefly concerned with the attitude of particular philosophers to
the problem of reason and revelation. He is concerned with the theological
significance of a particular *kind* of philosophy: the post-Kantian critical philosophy that he calls 'the reflective philosophy of subjectivity'. For Hegel in
this essay of 1802 (unlike in 'The spirit of Christianity and its fate' of 1800),
this kind of philosophy belongs to the spiritual formation of Protestantism:

> The great form of the world spirit that has come to cognizance of itself
> in these philosophies, is the principle of the North, and from the
> religious point of view, of Protestantism, this principle is subjectivity
> for which beauty and truth present themselves in feelings and
> persuasions, in love and intellect.[j,9]

What matters now is less what any of these particular philosophies *say*
about religious truth – whether, for example, it privileges rational criticism
over the life of piety or vice versa – but what the activity of philosophy,
conceived in this way, means as a mode of human experience. For Hegel, now,
the post-critical philosophy, in the totality of its forms and the antinomies
to which it gives rise, is not a discourse *about* Christianity. It is part of the life
of Christianity itself. That is because, in the consciousness of Hegel's time,
the old opposition between philosophy and faith has been transplanted into
philosophy itself:

> Civilisation has raised this latest era so far above the ancient antithesis
> of reason and faith, of philosophy and positive religion that the

---

h. 'Entzweiung'.
i. 1802: 'Glauben und Wissen oder die Reflexionsphilosophie der Subjektivität in der
   Vollständigkeit ihrer Formen als Kantische, Jacobische und Fichtesche Philosophie'.
j. 'Die große Form des Weltgeistes aber, welche sich in jenen Philosophien erkannt hat, ist das
   Prinzip des Nordens und, es religiös angesehen, des Protestantismus, – die Subjektivität, in
   welcher Schönheit und Wahrheit in Gefühlen und Gesinnungen, in Liebe und Verstand sich
   darstellt.' HW, II, 289.

opposition of faith and knowledge has acquired quite a different sense and has now been transferred into the field of philosophy itself.[k,10]

For Hegel, the post-Kantian philosophy of his age is essentially *Reflexionsphilosophie* or a philosophy of reflection. In other words, it is about the self-reflective interrogation of human consciousness. However, the self-consciousness of Hegel's age is unable to understand what religion is, because it believes that what Hegel calls the reflective philosophy of subjectivity is the only form of self-conscious knowledge. That philosophy therefore believes that it must oppose itself to the actual content of religion, which appears to it either as a body of historical doctrine or as a real but necessarily inarticulate form of experience. In this essay, Hegel claims that religion itself is intrinsically self-conscious. Not only the rationalist theology of the enlightenment, he argues, but also the pietism that reacts against it, involve mediation.[l,11] Philosophical rationalism opposes itself to a faith that it believes to be merely immediate, and thus in need of the reflective insight which only philosophy can provide. Faith rejects this kind of philosophy because it knows the mediation it offers to be inadequate to religious truth, because it is external to, or even at odds with, the actual life of the Spirit.

The Hegelian remedy is to show that both philosophy and religion as such – not just the reflective philosophy of Hegel's own post-Kantian age – are intrinsically self-conscious. Philosophy, for Hegel, is self-conscious in a way both necessarily related to and necessarily different from that of religion. Hegel's understanding of philosophy differs from that of his contemporaries because he believes that the particular kind of reflection and critique that philosophy offers is something more than a philosophical procedure brought to bear on the data of experience. He believes that self-consciousness belongs to human experience as such, and that both religion and philosophy are modes of experience in which self-consciousness becomes manifest. The task of philosophy as he understands it is to say how and why this is the case. Philosophy, for Hegel in 1802, is thus more than relevant to religion. *It has itself a religious purpose and meaning.* Its task is nothing less than to bring the religious and philosophical consciousness of modernity together by showing how each inheres in the other.

---

k. 'Über den alten Gegensatz der Vernunft und des Glaubens, von Philosophie und positiver Religion hat sich die Kultur der letzten Zeit so erhoben, daß diese Entgegensetzung von Glauben und Wissen einen ganz anderen Sinn gewonnen hat und nun innerhalb der Philosophie selbst verlegt worden ist.' HW, II, 287.
l. 'Vermittlung' HW, II, 299–301.

Hegel's *Faith and Knowledge* already foreshadows, although it does not fully express, what will become the major insight of his mature *Philosophy of Religion*. That is that the autonomy of theology in the Christian tradition also entails the autonomy of philosophy in relation to theology. In *Faith and Knowledge*, unlike 'The spirit of Christianity and its fate', he first posits the idea that philosophy can be an instrument of theological, indeed religious, reform.[12] Philosophy can be such an instrument because and not in spite of its character as radically self-conscious knowledge. For Hegel in 1802, the task of philosophy is to show the meaning of the divorce between the philosophical self-consciousness and the actual experience of protestant Christianity in his time. Philosophy can show that only because it has now become the reflective philosophy of subjectivity in its most fully developed form: precisely the consequence of the post-Kantian history of German Idealism that Hegel in *Faith and Knowledge* both criticises on its own terms and seeks to bring to fruition on the new ones that his argument proposes. Philosophy in the Hegelian mode can turn *Kritik* into a mode of experience only because it is itself the most radical form of *Kritik*: a critical consciousness which can be authentically true only if, and because, it also lives in and through the alienated consciousness which it constantly seeks to transcend.

Hegel expresses this insight at the end of the *Faith and Knowledge* essay in one of his most remarkable – and most easily misunderstood – formulations: the claim that philosophy can be the agent of a theological rebirth – what he calls a 'speculative Good Friday'[m] in the life of his age. What is most remarkable about this passage is that Hegel moves beyond a philosophical critique of the theological culture or *Bildung* of his age and into a doctrine of philosophy and theology as modes of experience that participate in the common experience of that age. Indeed he moves beyond the antithesis (though not the distinction) between philosophy and theology themselves, because both not only reflect critically, but are themselves part of, an emphatically Christian experience. That is, both the 'Death of God' which Hegel here identifies as a crucial moment of Christianity itself and – its corollary in the spiritual life of his time and culture – the death of an alienated subjectivity for which God can only be the opposite of the self-reflective mind. This is a speculative Good Friday but a Good Friday indeed. It is not the thesis or the object of philosophy but the very life that philosophy, *as* philosophy, must live:

---

m. 'Spekulativer Charfreytag'.

> But the pure concept or infinity as the abyss of nothingness in which
> all being is engulfed, must signify the infinite grief [of the finite] purely
> as a moment of the supreme Idea, and no more than a moment.
> Formerly the infinite grief only existed historically in the formative
> process of culture. It existed as the feeling that 'God himself is dead',
> upon which the religion of more recent times rests . . . By masking this
> feeling as a moment of the supreme Idea, the pure concept must give
> [it] philosophical existence . . . Thereby it must re-establish for
> philosophy the Idea of absolute freedom and along with it the absolute
> Passion, the speculative Good Friday in place of the historic Good
> Friday. Good Friday must be speculatively re-established in the whole
> Truth and harshness of its Godforsakenness . . . and [ascend] in all its
> earnestness and out of its deepest ground to the most serene freedom
> of its shape.[n],[13]

This is not the absent Spirit for which, Hegel had said in 1800, the disciples longed but of which they were deprived. It is the Spirit which is present and which the disciples, like their master and their present successors, must *suffer* to be present. Yet this suffering acceptance, at this point in Hegel's development, is still an event that is projected into the future and so expressed in the imperative mode (*muß*).

This essay is a key stage in Hegel's evolution of the idea of philosophy and religion as modes of absolute spirit that he first expounds in his *Lectures on the Philosophy of Religion*, which were first delivered in 1821 and revised several times before his death after the final sequence of lectures had been delivered in 1831.[14] What is new in Hegel's mature philosophy of religion is the doctrine that both philosophy and religion are modes in which the ultimate truth – absolute spirit or God – is revealed in human experience. They differ not in the truth that is their essential content, but in the mode in which they apprehend that truth. Philosophy grasps the truth of spirit in a presuppositionless and conceptually completely explicit form. It is therefore the form of discursive knowledge most appropriate to the modern consciousness, especially that informed by post-Kantian Idealism, for which truth can

n. 'Der reine Begriff aber oder die Unendlichkeit als der Abgrund des Nichts, worin alles Sein versinkt, muß den unendlichen Schmerz, der vorher nur in der Bildung geschichtlich und als Gefühl war, worauf die Religion der neuen Zeit beruht – das Gefühl: Gott selbst ist tot . . . eine philosophische Existenz geben und also der Philosophie die Idee der absoluten Freiheit und damit das absolute Leiden oder den spekulativen Karfreitag, der sonst historisch war, und ihn selbst in der ganzen Wahrheit und Härte seiner Gottlosigkeit wiederherstellen, aus welcher Härte allein . . . die höchste Totalität in ihrem ganzen Ernst und aus ihrem tiefsten Grunde, zugleich allumfassend und in die heiterste Freiheit ihrer Gestalt aufstehen kann und muß.' HW, II, 432–3.

only be the result of presuppositionless critique. Religion is the form of consciousness in which truth is apprehended in worship or prayer, for which the Spirit is not conceptualised by the self-conscious mind but represented (*vorgestellt*) in religious images and the imagination of our hearts. It is thus a mode in which God – the religious name for absolute spirit – is both acknowledged as absolutely other and yet experienced in a way more deeply inward than philosophy.[15] However, and most importantly, philosophy and religion are both intrinsically connected and can be made intelligible to each other because they are both modes of absolute spirit.

At the same time, Hegel advances another crucial thesis: that absolute spirit, in and of itself, is a religious reality. Absolute spirit is the philosophical name for God; and that name applies not only to the religious *mode* of absolute spirit, but to absolute spirit in and of itself. It follows that both the difference and the communication between religion and philosophy are part of the truth of God and therefore at the heart of the life of faith. Hegel's mature religious thought presents the incarnation of God in Christ as the paradigm of the most important task of philosophy: the mediation or *Vermittlung* of universal truth and particular experience. Of course, that mediation is not only theologically, but also culturally and historically relevant. However, for Hegel, the philosophical and theological mediation is the source of the cultural and historical one and not the other way around. Hegel's account of incarnation in the *Philosophy of Religion* is anything but aridly speculative, but neither is it historically or culturally reductive. Its focus is on the Death of Christ as a 'criminal'[o] without any trace of civic honour. At this point in Hegel's thought, at least, the idea of a Christianity of culture (*Kulturchristentum*) can only appear as a blasphemous absurdity. However, what is in question is more than the negation of the universal secular empire of Caesar by the universal spiritual one of Christ. It is the revelation and fullest possible expression of the universal itself – the ultimate truth of Spirit – in the life of a *particular* person *as* a particular person.[16] That is, one whose witness cannot be reduced to historical or cultural terms and therefore the one whom such terms must necessarily reject. For Hegel, as for Lessing, the universal truth of Christianity can never be proven by contingent truths of history, however they might be interpreted. For the purpose of Christianity is the redemption, by the transfiguration, of contingency itself. History – all of history – is the revelation of Spirit and of our response to it, for which and by which Christian history is made continuously real.[17]

---

o. 'Missethäter'. HW, XVII, 290.

In the *Philosophy of Religion* then, Hegel's reading of Pentecost is the exact opposite of his account in 'The spirit of Christianity and its fate'. The disciples no longer long for a spirit that is absent, but are possessed by a spirit that is present because they are its carriers:

> Therefore the conviction which they gained from the life [of Christ] was still not the full truth . . . it was the Spirit which gave them true insight, the Spirit which Christ says will lead them into the fullness of truth: 'The Spirit will lead you into all truth.'[p]

Hegel here understands Easter as the moment when Christianity negates, through the starkest sign of Roman legal judgement that is also Christianity's supreme symbol, the alienated and reified but still universal spirit of Rome. History is no longer the dead object of theological reflection, or a domain defined as contingent because theology is unable to grasp contingency as incarnation. It is the locus of Spirit and therefore of the self-consciousness of humanity. We can believe, and we can only *believe* that this is what history is, because the Spirit is already real in history in itself (*an sich*) and can become real in history for itself (*für sich*) – that is to say, for us (*für uns*) – when we make it so by grasping our historical experience as one of incarnation.

Two emphases emerge most clearly from Hegel's mature philosophical theology: the autonomy of the theological, a doctrine of absolute Spirit grounded in a theology of incarnation, and the autonomy of philosophy in relation to theology which that same doctrine also requires. Hegel, in other words, affirms both the connection and the difference between philosophical and theological discourse, and the relevance of both to the life of faith. He differs from his Idealist predecessors and contemporaries especially in that double affirmation. For Hegel, the problem of the relationship between philosophy and revelation must and can only be *philosophically* addressed. It cannot (as it could for Schelling) be transposed into the mode of art or mythology. But neither (as it could for Fichte) can the idea of revelation be deduced *a priori*: the dialectic between philosophy and revelation can only be understood as a moment of Christian history and tradition.

To be sure, that history and tradition are encountered in the *Philosophy of Religion* in the mode of narrative. However, Hegel never suggests that philosophical theology can or should be reinterpreted exclusively as a

---

p. 'Also diese Überzeugung, die sie aus seinem Leben haben könnten, war noch nicht die rechte Wahrheit, sondern erst der Geist . . . Den eigentlichen Aufschluß hat ihnen der Geist gegeben, von dem Christus sagt, daß er sie in alle Wahrheit leiten werde. "Das wird erst die Wahrheit sein, in die euch der Geist leiten wird."' HW, *ibid.*, 296.

cultural narrative, still less that the truth of his own philosophical theology depends on the future course which such a narrative might take. The logic of his argument suggests exactly the opposite. Hegel differs profoundly from Kant because the motivation for Hegel's philosophy of history is not ethical but theological.[18] Hegel's philosophy of history is predicated on his philosophical theology, not the other way around. There is nothing more alien to Hegel's thought than the analogical construction of history as if it can be read as the narrative of revelation which Kant attempted in 'Conjectural beginnings of the human race'[q] and 'Idea for a universal history from a cosmopolitan point of view'.[r] For that analogical perspective is the theological analogue of that alienated moral ideal – that *Sollen* or abstract moral commandment – which in his essay on *The Positivity of the Christian Religion* he had identified as the philosophical and Christian equivalent of worshipping an idol. Hegel at the end of his career offers not only a philosophical Good Friday but a theological Easter: a truth which is present but can be philosophically grasped only if it is experienced as real.

For Hegel, the truth of philosophy – indeed, especially the philosophy of Incarnation which he begins to write in the *Philosophy of Religion* – can neither be reduced to, nor negated by, the truth of cultural narrative by which philosophical truth, like every other kind, is actually transmitted. However, the truth of incarnation can be realised fully only in the continuing history of Christianity which it begins. It is clear from a passage that occurs only in the posthumously published 1831 version of his *Lectures on the Philosophy of Religion* that Hegel was acutely aware of the difference.[19]

Then Hegel writes of a disharmony (*Misston*), which he perceives as the inescapable consequence of the kind of philosophical reinterpretation of Christianity that he has just given. That interpretation, he insists, although it articulates a universally valid truth, is not generally accessible in the life of the Christian community (*Gemeinde*). The cultural situation of Hegel's age means that faith has now to be intellectually justified by the radically self-conscious mode of thought that is philosophy. But this intellectual synthesis is not yet a social and a cultural one. That is to say, it is linked only objectively and potentially (*an sich*), but not subjectively and actually (*für sich*) to the life of faith.

> When the time comes that the conceptual justification [of belief] is necessary, then in immediate consciousness and reality inward

---

q. 1796: 'Mutmaßlicher Anfang der Menschengeschichte'.
r. 1784: 'Idee zu einer allgemeinen Geschichte in weltbürgerlicher Absicht'.

consciousness and objective experience have become divorced so that there is no justification in immediate faith.[s]

This polarity is very much more than a theological or philosophical problem; it reflects a divorce at the heart of European Christendom itself:

> then the people, for whose ever solid reason truth can only be *represented*, cannot fulfil its own inner impulse. The people remain closest to the truth as infinite sorrow, but because their love has been misrepresented as a form of painless enjoyment, the people see themselves as deserted by their teachers. The latter have indeed been able to take comfort in reflection and have found satisfaction in finitude, in the virtuosity of subjectivity and so in what is most empty and vain. But the substantial kernel of the people cannot find its satisfaction there.[t]

In other words, the philosophical reinterpretation of Christianity – even that which Hegel has just offered his listeners in the lecture hall in Berlin – risks destroying the integrity of Christian life. That is because the philosophical synthesis has no correlation in the post-Enlightenment secular culture which Hegel's philosophical theology – and any that might succeed it in the same vein – claims to instruct. The point is that the philosophical interpretation or *Aufhebung* of Christianity enables us to see secular history as the history of Christendom: a secular domain articulated and expressed, even in its very difference, by the language of Christian theology. But this view of secular history can never command real theological assent – it will be nothing more than a plausible and possible perspective – unless it is rooted in the actual experience of the Christian community. That is to say, the philosophical synthesis will be hollow unless it actually articulates the experience of the *Gemeinde*: the Christian community that is involved equally in the secular world and the life of faith. This is the paradox that the late Gillian Rose recognised in her account of this passage in her early book *Hegel Contra*

---

s. 'Wenn die Zeit erfüllt ist, dass die Rechtfertigung durch den Begriff Bedürfnis ist, dann ist im unmittelbaren Bewußtseyn, in der Wirklichkeit die Einheit des Innen und Aussen nicht mehr vorhanden und ist im Glauben nicht gerechtfertigt.' HW, XVII, 343.

t. 'Dann weiß das Volk, für dessen gedrungen bleibende Vernunft die Wahrheit nur in der Vorstellung sein kann, dem Drange seines Innern nicht zu helfen. Es steht dem unendlichen Schmerze noch am nächsten . . . aber da die Liebe zu einer Liebe und zu einem Genuß ohne allen Schmerz verkehrt ist, so sieht es sich von seinen Lehrern verlassen; diese haben sich zwar durch Reflexion geholfen und in der Endlichkeit, in der Subjectivität und deren Virtuosität und eben damit im Eiteln ihre Befriedigung gefunden, aber darin kann jener substantielle Kern des Volks die seinige nicht finden.' *Ibid.*

Sociology. There she argues persuasively that Hegel's idea of history as the story of spirit necessarily implies a philosophical theology, because (as she writes) 'Hegel's philosophy has no social import if the absolute cannot be thought.'[20] But the converse is also true. Talk about absolute spirit is empty and vain if it is not concretely expressed in social and historical terms. Rose thus at least plausibly suggests that this concluding remark in his late *Philosophy of Religion* is a 'rare and revealing' moment in which 'Hegel does not disguise a *Sollen* as the rationality of the real, but simply despairs.'[21]

It is, I believe, a mistake to suppose that Hegel – here especially – gives up and simply despairs, or that we should do so as his theological heirs. Nevertheless, we must fully acknowledge the impact of one of Hegel's last and most crucial insights. What Hegel acknowledges here is one of the most important lessons of the history of German Idealism. That is that the emancipatory power of philosophy is real only insofar as it can be expressed in an actual cultural context. However – for the same reason – the truth of Idealism (in theology above all) cannot be reduced to the truth of the cultural narrative by which it is contingently and so possibly inadequately expressed. This double lesson, for Hegel, is as much a theological as a philosophical one, because the specifically philosophical insight into modernity that Idealism offers leads to a theological conclusion. The upshot of Hegel's philosophical grounding of Christian history is thus a radical acknowledgement that it is a history that cannot be grounded in philosophy alone. Just as the disciples after Pentecost have to *make* real, for their contemporaries and successors, what has been revealed to them as real in itself, so the post-Idealist Christian community must make real, in every age, the potential dialectic of philosophy and Christian experience which Hegel's argument outlines. What Hegel leaves us with – because and not in spite of the power of his synthesis – is a consciousness of the two poles as radically distant: a world in which the potential distance between what Christianity is and what it can say itself to be, is as great as ever before.

From this perspective, the apparent failure of the Idealist tradition as cultural narrative in nineteenth-century Germany can be seen as the strongest evidence for its theological truth. For we can understand that failure only in the terms that the theological legacy of Idealism, especially its culmination in the work of Hegel, suggests.

It was precisely the apparent philosophical success of the Hegelian synthesis, which had no objective correlation in either political or religious life, which led it to fall out of favour only a decade after Hegel's death. As

Schelling wrote in his later *Philosophy of Revelation*,[u] the immediate Hegelian aftermath was marked above all by a powerful reaction against philosophy from the side of secular life: 'Never has a so powerful reaction against philosophy arisen from the sphere of actual life as in this historical moment.'[v,22] But this is precisely because of the scope of the claim which philosophy in the Hegelian modes appears to make about secular life: 'This proves that philosophy has approached these vital questions on which it is not permitted, or even possible, to be indifferent.'[w]

In the decades between Hegel's death (1831) and the First World War, the Idealist tradition in theology was largely reduced to the terms of a particular cultural narrative. That is the story of German protestant culture in the nineteenth century, in which Neo-Hegelian conservative protestant theology, exemplified by the work of theologians like Philipp Marheineke and Ferdinand Christian Baur, became identified with an ethic of moral inwardness, closely allied to an uncritical acceptance of actual political power, by which that culture was defined. At the same time 'left' Hegelian thinkers like Bruno Bauer, D. F. Strauss and eventually Ludwig Feuerbach employed the Hegelian theological idiom as an instrument of social critique.[23] The obvious disjunction between that idiom and the actual condition of Germany in their time led them to conclude that, if the Idealist discourse has any meaning at all, it can only lie in the secularisation – that is, the reduction to cultural critique – of theology.

However, the theological failure of both these cultural narratives does not mean that Hegel's theological legacy – the most important means by which the impact of Idealism is made known in theology – is irrelevant to the subsequent course of German or indeed Christian theology. Quite the reverse. For Hegel, unlike most of his Protestant successors, the only narrative that really matters is that of incarnation: one which can be written by, only because it has also been given to, the self-consciousness of humanity. The capacity of a theology to provide a *culturally* successful narrative does not, therefore, prove its theological truth; neither is the opposite the case.

In the later decades of the nineteenth and the beginning of the twentieth centuries, the Idealist legacy was increasingly linked to the kind of

---

u. 1841: '*Philosophie der Offenbarung*'.
v. 'Noch nie hat sich gegen die Philosophie eine so mächtige Reaktion von Seiten des Lebens erhoben wie in diesem Augenblick.'
w. 'Dies beweißt, daß die Philosophie bis zu jenen Lebensfragen vorgedrungen ist, gegen die es keinem erlaubt, ja möglich ist gleichgültig zu sein.' *Ibid.*

Kulturprotestantismus exemplified by David Strauss' thoroughly Kantian rein-terpretation of protestant Christianity in *The Old and the New Faith*[x] in moral and aesthetic terms, Albrecht Ritschl's use of Christian theology to support a liberal philosophy of historical progress and Ernst Troeltsch's ill-fated attempt to construe Christianity as the absolute religion at the culmination of a supposedly Hegelian historical series. In the wake of the First World War, the whole project of philosophical theology in the Idealist mode, especially the idea of a theology of culture, was resoundingly rejected in Karl Barth's commentary on the 'Epistle to the Romans',[y] which acquired a growing European influence as the political temptations of German Protestantism became increasingly apparent over the next two decades.

In our own time, eighty years later, the theological strand in German Idealism, sometimes but not always in the Hegelian mode, is once again emphatically on the agenda. The theological re-appropriation of the Idealist tradition has been enormously fruitful, but I want to suggest that it risks a misunderstanding not dissimilar to that which led to the eclipse of Idealism in nineteenth-century German theology. The root of that misunderstanding lies in what we conceive the Idealist tradition to be and therefore in the terms we think appropriate to its reception.

In our own time, some of the most powerful evidence for the impact of Idealism has certainly come from theology, especially the reaffirmation of the autonomy of theology in the movement known as radical orthodoxy. This movement pleads persuasively for what Graham Ward has called 'the re-sacralisation of philosophy' based on a new kind of philosophical theology that owes much to a particular reading of German Idealism.[24] Central to that reading is an interpretation of the post-Kantian history of Idealism as a critique of *foundationalism*. That is the idea that philosophy, by a process of reflective critique, can provide a reliable basis for either theological or philosophical knowledge in abstraction from the actual engagement of philosophy, with the truth of human experience embodied in human history: in theological terms, the truth of incarnation. Ward, for example, sees Hegel as the key figure in the Idealist liberation of theology from a prior grounding in philosophical critique, and so as the source of a truly Trinitarian idea of both philosophical and theological truth.[25] This insight is indeed one of the most powerful legacies of German Idealism in theology, which makes it highly relevant to the radical orthodox project of a 'resacralisation' of both philosophy and social thought. However, the Idealist critique of foundationalism

---

x. 1873: *Der alte und der neue Glaube.*   y. 1918: 'Der Römerbrief'.

has also been linked – of course, in different ways and by different writers – to the different philosophical movement of post-modernism, especially its key thesis that truth finds its privileged – indeed, for some writers, its only – expression in the mode of narrative. The relevance of this position to the project of radical orthodoxy has been well captured by John Milbank, who argues as follows:

> In post-modernity there are infinitely many possible versions of truth, inseparable from particular narratives. Objects and subjects are, as they are narrated in a story. Outside a plot, which has its own unique, unfounded reasons, one cannot conceive how object and subject would be, nor even that they would be at all.[26]

On this view, theology is emancipated from the need to be philosophically grounded or expressed, because philosophy can no longer provide a foundational basis for human knowledge. There can be no single narrative of what modernity is and where it has come from. Equally, therefore, there can be no one compelling narrative of the place of philosophy and theology in modernity and their appropriate modern expression.

An adequate assessment of the impact of Idealism for theology now requires a radical distinction between these two positions. The message of German Idealism for theology is indeed that there can be no foundation for theology – neither in the philosophical critique of knowledge nor in the historical and philological critique of scripture – in abstraction from the life of the Christian community, whether philosophically educated or otherwise. However, this emphatically does not entail the thesis that theology is about narrative and representation and not about truth. John Milbank has claimed that:

> the priority given to structural relations allows theology to make a kind of half-turn back to pre-modernity . . . the things that can truly be spoken about are once again external – so the point is not to 'represent' this externality; not to know, but to intervene, originate.[27]

The relevance of the German Idealist tradition to contemporary theology is that it tells us exactly the opposite. As I have tried to show, the meaning of the post-Kantian history of German Idealism, especially its culmination in the work of Hegel, is precisely that there can be no 'half-turn back to pre-modernity', in which 'the things that can truly be spoken about are once again external'. The true import of Hegel's critique of the 'reflective philosophy of subjectivity' is that truth – especially, but not only, theological truth – can never be reified and so grasped as an *object* of the mind. The true end of *Kritik* is to overcome the standpoint of *Kritik* itself: to show that the critical philosophy, by its own immanent logic, moves towards a philosophy of spirit. Hegel of all thinkers shows us that this does not entail the sheer negation of the world of experience that is the concern of critique but its *Aufhebung* or sublation. That is to say, a transcendence that is real and actual because it does not leave the world of experience behind, but carries it with it: a consciousness which sees into the truth, but does not destroy what it sees.[28] To be sure, Hegel affirms that faith apprehends truth in the mode of representation (*Vorstellung*), not the philosophical concept (*Begriff*).[29] However, both modes of consciousness are unequivocally modes of *truth*, because they are both ways in which absolute spirit is revealed. For Hegel, philosophy is essentially the service of God,[z] and neither theology nor faith can do without philosophy if they seek a specifically conceptual expression. Of course, this does not entail the belief that such an expression is the only, let alone the only valid way in which faith can be expressed. On the contrary, it means that although religion can (sometimes) do without philosophy, philosophy cannot do without religion, because it encompasses religion.[aa] Philosophy encompasses religion because it is an activity which is both about, and part of, a reality which has to be given a religious as well as a philosophical name: absolute spirit. The autonomy of theology in German Idealism cannot be understood, historically or conceptually, except in terms of its indissoluble connection to the philosophical mode of truth.

The message of Idealism for theology is radically different from that of post-modernism. As Ward has written, one of the most potent reasons for the misunderstanding and therefore the marginalisation of religion in modernity is its commodification.[30] Commodification means the understanding or even self-understanding of religion as a particular interest or activity, separate from the rest of the secular world but ultimately to be articulated only in that world's terms. As we have seen, the history and legacy of German Idealism in theology does indeed offer a radical antidote to this kind of understanding. However, as Dietrich Bonhoeffer acutely showed, the apparent opposite of the cultural commodification of 'religion' – a faith which retreats into an inwardness incapable of any positive cultural embodiment – is in fact the reverse side of the same process.[31] The inwardness that eschews

---

z. 'Die Philosophie ist wesentlich Gottesdienst.' *Ibid.*, 28.
aa. 'Vielmehr liegt auch in dem Bisherigen, daß die Religion wohl ohne Philosophie, aber die Philosophie nicht ohne die Religion sein kann, sondern diese vielmehr in sich schließt.' HW, VIII, 24.

public conceptual articulation can, as much as its opposite, be a political and theological temptation if it is the product of cultural and psychological resentment. Hegel's critique of the German Protestantism of his time, especially its tendency to oscillate between the extremes of philosophical dialectic and pietistic expression, is as much a critique of this position – what Hegel calls 'the unhappy consciousness'[bb][32] – as it is of the opposite. The most important impact of German Idealism on theology now is that it shows a way beyond this sterile opposition, because it shows the antinomy itself to be unreal.

This message clearly has not been understood, although it has certainly been received, in some expressions of the radical orthodoxy movement. In *Radical Orthodoxy: A New Theology*, John Milbank and his colleagues describe their project as 'suspending the material': redefining what the words 'spiritual' and 'material' might mean in response to the secular narrative that they see Idealism as closing.[33] Once, as Milbank has argued, there was no secular, because what we call 'sacred' and 'secular' were one – in Christendom.[34] However, Milbank reads Hegel's philosophical theology as a false cultural narrative, which attempts to establish a counterfeit of the original unity by identifying the scope and idiom of the sacred with those of the modern protestant secular world.[35] For Milbank, therefore, the task of modern theology is the development of a new conception of theological reason that will, in a theological version of Marx's metaphor, stand Hegel on his head.[36] Theology must re-appropriate the central intellectual and cultural concerns of the secular world, by re-describing the secular sphere in terms of the catholic because universal whole which Hegel had tried to re-appropriate from the standpoint of its modern protestant outcome. To be sure, Milbank emphasises that the term *orthodox* is intended to transcend confessional boundaries. However, he makes the remarkable claim that Herder and Hamann have 'already in effect re-catholicised theology' and that Hegel's philosophical theology represents a regression from what their critique has already achieved.[37]

This is a profound misunderstanding of Hegel's philosophy and theology and of the history of German Idealism from which both emerge. In particular, it entirely misreads the kind of synthesis of philosophical and theological discourse that Hegel achieves in his mature philosophy of religion. As we have seen, that synthesis both acknowledges and discloses the meaning of the two poles by which the trajectory of German Idealist theology is defined.

bb. 'Das unglückliche Bewusstsein', HW, III, 163ff.

First, the emancipatory energy of post-Kantian critique, what Hegel calls 'the reflective philosophy of subjectivity', which defines itself as the source of human autonomy and which, Hegel shows, is also an energy immanent in the modern history of Christianity itself. Second, the need for that energy to be really present, really apprehended, in the lived history of the Christian community or *Gemeinde*. However, in that history, the distance between the two poles is neither bridged nor elided. On the contrary, Hegel's history of Christianity as the story of spirit is intended to reveal the full significance of the difference. We need to attend to both the modern origins of that history in the experience of his age and to the warnings he explicitly issues about its likely course in the future. However, this Milbank fails to do. For Milbank, like his interlocutor Slavoj Žižek in their recent dialogue, Hegel's thought is objectively atheistic.[38] Certainly there is nothing seriously at odds in Milbank's contribution, with the following judgement by Žižek:

> Spirit as a *virtual* entity in the sense that its status is that of a subjective presupposition: it exists only in so far as subjects act *as if* it exists. Its status is similar to an ideological cause like Communism or Nation.[39]

Such an interpretation is surely a travesty of Hegel's doctrine of spirit, especially his final account of the meaning of Easter. But it is a travesty that depends on a particular reading of the history of Idealism before Hegel and its impact after him. As we have seen, something very close to this was Hegel's own early understanding of the fate of the Christian community after the Ascension. The spirit of that community, Hegel said in 1800, yearned for what was absent because it could neither understand nor participate in what was present. The community, therefore, was left with a history that would always be a fate. For Hegel in 1831, that fate had become a history. The disciples could make the spirit real for themselves and for their successors because it was already real by God's own act. This idea is the exact opposite of the theological version of the Kantian regulative ideal which Žižek and Milbank falsely construct as a Hegelian Idealist cultural narrative, and of which they accurately foresee the political and cultural consequences.

Those consequences certainly became real in the century after Hegel's death. However, that is not the only impact of the Idealist tradition that matters for theology. What matters is how we appropriate that tradition now. The movement known as post-modernism presents both an opportunity and a temptation for contemporary theology. The opportunity consists in the liberation of theological discourse, often enabled by an approach to post-modernism via an appropriation of German Idealist theology, from the foundationalist view of the relationship between philosophy and theology: that is to say, the unwarranted belief that secular philosophy can or should establish the intellectual credentials for philosophical theology. This movement has inspired a plurality of self-grounding discourses in the humanities, in which a spectrum of epistemic and semantic modes – philosophical, literary, narrative, liturgical – articulate a plurality of interlocking modes of truth. However, that change in the cultural narrative – like all great moments of cultural change – represents also a radical temptation for theology. That is, for theology uncritically to adopt the narrative of the surrounding culture and therefore – the exact opposite of radical orthodoxy's theological intention – to assimilate itself to the dominant cultural agenda of the contemporary secular world.[40]

That temptation is shared, and for not dissimilar reasons, by an influential theological current ostensibly opposed to radical orthodoxy: the idea of 'religionless Christianity' associated with theologians like Don Cupitt in the United Kingdom and Mark Taylor in the United States.

In his most recent book, *The Meaning of the West* (2008), Cupitt offers a reading of Hegel's theology that differs in intention from that of Milbank but is similarly reductionist in effect. Cupitt differs from Milbank in that he fully endorses what he calls '[Hegel's] Christian atheist reading of Christianity' and uses it as one of the cornerstones of his project of a 'religionless Christianity'. For Cupitt, Hegel's account of incarnation as the beginning of a Christian history – that is to say, one which can only be written by a Christian philosophy – really can be reinterpreted to make the idea of 'Christian atheism' meaningful. He is completely explicit in his reading of Christianity as an objectively secular cultural narrative that underpins this idea. Thus he refers to the Christology of the Pauline letters as a 'Christological romance' and gives the following remarkable account of the Gospel narratives themselves:[41]

> Sometimes God rattles the scenery, as at Christ's death; but it is very noticeable that in the New Testament as a whole, which is supposedly God's final self-disclosure, God has almost totally disappeared and only Jesus Christ is seen. So the final Revelation of God is simply the Death of God which sets us free and the Christian atheist reading of Christianity, as developed in the Lutheran tradition by Hegel and others, is correct.[42]

How can it make sense to say 'God has almost totally disappeared and only Jesus Christ is seen' about Hegel's doctrine of incarnation, which is emphatically Trinitarian in kind? How can the statement 'the final Revelation of God is simply the Death of God which sets us free' make sense as a supposedly post-Idealist and post-Hegelian account of Christianity? The key to this misunderstanding surely lies in Cupitt's use of the word 'simply'.

'Simply' here really means 'only'. It signals Cupitt's thesis that the theological idea of *kenosis* – the process of divine self-emptying which is the meaning of incarnation – can be interpreted adequately by a secular philosophy which is itself conceived as independent of that process. This is surely to stand Hegel on his head. If Hegel's theology really were a secular reduction in this sense, then it would have ceased to develop at the position it had reached in 1800 with 'The spirit of Christianity and its fate'. Hegel's mature thought would be nothing more than the philosophical articulation of that spirit of alienated longing for an absent God, which, at that stage, Hegel had construed as the true spirit of Christianity. By the same token, his warning in the 1831 lectures against the conflation of the work of philosophy with that of the faith community would be redundant because – on Cupitt's reading – it is just such a conflation that Hegel's philosophy of religion recommends.[43] In such an interpretation of the Hegelian outcome of German Idealism, the history of German theology in the hundred years after Hegel's death would endorse and confirm, not radically confound, the logic of secular Christianity that became that of German Protestantism from 1831 until 1918. The projects of Christian atheism and the post-modern decoupling of theology from secular philosophy are both distinguished by a reductionist reading of the Idealist theological tradition. The first assumes that the history of German Idealism in theology, its culmination in the work of Hegel and its subsequent ossification as a cultural narrative really do justify the reinterpretation, indeed the reinvention, of the Christian tradition itself in wholly secular terms. The second takes the Idealist critique of foundationalism to warrant a theological discourse free not only of grounding or justification by secular philosophy, but of the need to be related to, and therefore appropriately expressed, in a language that the surrounding secular culture can also understand. The first negates the autonomy of theological reason, the second its context. The particular impact of Idealism in theology is to show us the need for both.

That connection is manifest not only in the Idealist tradition's greatest exponents, but also in its most consistent and principled critics. Karl Barth, for example, ultimately rejected the Idealist discourse in theology because of what he understood as its inescapable connection to a theology of culture and thus its denial of the supremacy of revelation. Yet no thinker was more aware of the power of that discourse and its emergence from the life of the Christian community. Assessing in 1947 the lasting impact of Hegel, Barth writes as follows: 'Ultimately theology rejected him merely for the same reasons which also made him unacceptable to modern cultural awareness. Who knows whether it was in fact the *genuinely* theological element in Hegel which made it shrink back.'[44] In view of the cultural legacy of Hegelian theology in the German-speaking world – which Hegel himself so acutely anticipates at the end of his 1831 *Lectures on the Philosophy of Religion* – this is surely an apt judgement. However, nothing was more alien to Barth than that pietistic rejection of the historically actual world which, as Barth himself so powerfully showed in his commentary on *The Epistle to the Romans*, can be the shadow side of a Christianity which is really the product of the spirit of its age.[45] Barth therefore warns equally insistently against the reduction of Christian truth to that of the secular world, and the equally unbiblical withdrawal from that world. He does not reject either extreme – the positions of Ludwig Feuerbach and Friedrich Schleiermacher – because objectively they are untrue.[46] Indeed, he acknowledges both as adequate responses to what Christendom (if not Christianity itself) has actually become in the cultural and historical aftermath of German Idealism. His judgement is precisely that both positions are true *only* objectively: that both have, in spite of their intention and idiom, become alienated from the actual life of the Christian community and so potentially inhibitive of that life. Such a judgement can be made only from within the life of the community in Barth's own time, which – as Barth manifestly recognises – is thoroughly informed by the inheritance of Idealism.

To sum up, the most important impact of the Idealist tradition in theology is a double insight. First, that the autonomy of theology can be understood and fully recognised only through the constant engagement of theology with secular philosophy and secular culture which the reception of German Idealism requires. That engagement presupposes now, as it did then, an acknowledgement of the autonomy of philosophy in relation to theology. Second, however, the Idealist tradition also teaches us that theology can be intellectually autonomous only if it is also part of a living religious tradition. Theology cannot recover the real unless it recognises that it is already *in* the real: the embodied tradition that is the precondition of its reflection.

These are peculiarly Idealist insights. To ignore them, and especially to ignore the link between them, is to obscure the real theological impact of Idealism by an artificial analogy between the original culture of German

Idealism and our own. Both cultures discovered, although in different ways, that philosophical theology can be written autonomously: that is to say, without being intellectually justified by, or reduced to, a separate and formally philosophical mode of truth. But to take this insight out of its cultural context in the history of German Idealism is to replace tradition, and therefore history, with narrative. The authentic message of Idealism is that narrative only makes sense within tradition, and tradition itself must be defined by the philosophical concept. Speaking of the Hegelian moment of that tradition, Cyril O'Regan explains this relationship as follows:

> For Hegel, ontotheological narrative perdures in the logical space of the concept. If it is true that perdurance is possible only because of the complete stripping away of narrative indices, it is also true that narrative not only is tolerated by logico-conceptual space but is intrinsic to it.[47]

Narrative, in other words, becomes essential to philosophy in the Idealist tradition only because it can accept the discipline that that tradition offers: what Hegel called 'the effort of the concept'.[cc] The narrative of spirit can never be arbitrarily, precisely because it must be freely, written. As Alasdair Macintyre reminds us, seeing ourselves as part of the narrative of a tradition means acknowledging that our freedom is always embodied. What we are is in large part what we inherit, and our freedom to become what we choose is real only because it is embedded in the narrative that we (also) write.[48] Macintyre aptly reminds us also that traditions die when they become Burkean: when they define and so close themselves on the terms that a particular moment of a tradition offers.[49]

How, then, can the Idealist tradition continue in theology? In the remarkable closing passage of his 1831 *Philosophy of Religion*, Hegel speaks of the 'infinite sorrow' of a people who 'see themselves as deserted by their teachers', and of theologians who 'have brought life to themselves by means of reflection (and) have found their satisfaction in finitude, in subjectivity and its virtuosity, and so in what is empty and vain.'[50] This most powerful passage also speaks of philosophers as 'an isolated order of priests, who must not mix with the world and whose work is to protect the possession of truth'. It is difficult to imagine a statement apparently more at odds with Hegel's own critique of both pietism and rationalism in the post-Kantian history of

---

cc. 'Die Anstrengung des Begriffs'. HW, III, 56.

German Idealism. However, his concluding judgement is both an objective analysis of the state of intellectual life at the time he is writing and, now more importantly, an acute diagnosis of the likely effect of the philosophical synthesis he has himself achieved. As Gillian Rose so perceptively showed, this seemingly most un-Hegelian of statements really means that philosophy must acknowledge not only its own inescapable connection to the life of faith, but also its own difference from that life. Philosophers are precisely *not* to act as Christian priests. As Rose writes, 'Hegel draws attention to the status of philosophy in order not to impose its concept.'[51] Of course, the point is not that philosophy should abandon the work of the concept. It is that philosophy must acknowledge that the notional scope of that work – the life of the Christian community – has not yet become the actual object of philosophical theology. Philosophy, like the community, has equally to work to make the connection real.

One of the most important lessons of Idealism for theology, now as much as it was in the classical age of German Idealism, is that cultural impact is not the same as truth. However, the Idealist tradition in theology does indeed have an impact that is especially relevant to our contemporary cultural situation, and a message that is equally important for theology, philosophy and the life of the community of faith. The relationship of that cultural impact to theological truth will depend on how contemporary theology responds. Above all, the legacy of Idealism warns us never to reduce that truth to either of the two dialectical poles by which Idealist theology is defined. The history of the Idealist tradition in theology does not teach (as many a German Idealist philosopher first thought) that philosophical theology can or should invent a new religion, let alone a *Volksreligion* or (Christian) mythology, for the people. Nor does it suggest that the great historical fact of Christianity – the history of incarnation to which, as Hegel especially showed, both modern philosophy and modern theology belong – can be reinterpreted as a secular philosophical narrative. The task of theology now is not to construct a new kind of Christianity, but once again, though in a new and different way, to comprehend the old one. There can never be two kinds of Christianity: one for philosophers and one for the people who would, in that case, be deserted by their teachers. We can avoid this destructive consequence only if we truly recognise not only the connection, but also the distance and difference between philosophical theology and the life of faith. For, as the German Idealist tradition, in particular, has taught us, the recognition of difference is the precondition for communication. 'Infinite sorrow' and its redemption belong to both the philosophers and the community. Idealism in theology still has an impact because it shows us why.

Notes

1. Hegel's term *Geist* is notoriously difficult to translate. It clearly includes the meanings of the English 'spirit' (sometimes in an explicitly theological sense) and 'mind': the objective meaning embodied in human social, ethical, and historical life. I have translated *Geist* as 'spirit' throughout, with capitalisation where an explicitly theological meaning is intended.
2. For representative statements of this position, see John Milbank and Simon Oliver (eds.), *The Radical Orthodoxy Reader* (London and New York: Routledge, 2009); and John Milbank, Catherine Pickstock and Graham Ward (eds.), *Radical Orthodoxy: A New Theology* (London and New York: Routledge, 1999).
3. See especially Don Cupitt, *The Meaning of the West: An Apologia for Secular Christianity* (London: SCM Press, 2008), and Mark C. Taylor, *After God* (Chicago and London: The University of Chicago Press, 2007).
4. See G. W. F. Hegel, *Das älteste Systemprogramm des deutschen Idealismus*, in Eva Moldenhauer and Karl Markus Michel (eds.), *Hegels Werke in zwanzig Bänden*, 20 vols. [hereafter HW] (Frankfurt a.M.: Suhrkamp, 1969-71) I, 234-6.
5. See Hegel, 'The positivity of the Christian religion', in Richard Kroner (ed.), *Early Theological Writings*, trans. T. M. Knox (Chicago: University of Chicago Press, 1948), 140-2; cf. 'Die Positivität der christlichen Religion', in HW, I, 184-6.
6. HW, I, 188f.
7. Hegel, *Early Theological Writings*, 301.
8. HW, II, 20. On this point see also Raymond Plant, *Hegel. An Introduction*, 2nd edn (Oxford: Blackwell, 1983), 79ff.
9. Hegel, *Faith and Knowledge*, trans. Walter Cerf and H. S. Harris (Albany: State University of New York Press, 1977), 57.
10. Hegel, *Faith and Knowledge*, 55.
11. *Ibid.*, 65-7.
12. That Hegel conceived of philosophy as an instrument of *religious* reform is very persuasively argued by Andrew Shanks in *Hegel's Political Theology* (Cambridge: Cambridge University Press, 1991), 71-102 (Chapter 2: 'Philosophy and dogmatics').
13. Hegel, *Faith and Knowledge*, 190-1.
14. The difference in content between the several sequences of Hegel's *Lectures on the Philosophy of Religion*, delivered in 1821, 1824, 1827 and 1831, is a notorious problem for Hegel scholarship, not least because Hegel's own manuscript is supplemented in most editions by the *Hefte* or written records provided by several of Hegel's students. The following exposition is based on HW, XVI and XVII. This edition contains elements from all four lecture-sequences, but crucially contains material from the final 1831 lecture sequence, on which the following argument is based. However, the text of this edition does not correspond to the most recent English edition which is *Lectures on the Philosophy of Religion, One-Volume Edition*, Peter C. Hodgson (ed.) (Berkeley, CA: University of California Press,

1988). The following translations from Hegel's *Vorlesungen über die Philosophie der Religion* are therefore my own.

15. On the relationship between religious and philosophical diction in Hegel, see John McCumber, *The Company of Words. Hegel, Language, and Systematic Philosophy* (Evanston, IL: Northwestern University Press, 1993), 54–6.

16. HW, XVII, 292ff.

17. On this point see Nicholas Boyle's acute analysis in *Sacred and Secular Scriptures: A Catholic Approach to Literature* (Notre Dame: University of Notre Dame Press, 2004), 51: 'Hegel, in short, has shown that the original claim that God can be known by reason needs to be made more precise: we can know by reason that only by faith can we know the God who has revealed himself and that if he has revealed himself he has done so as the one who reveals himself to faith.'

18. cf. Emil C. Fackenheim, *The God Within. Kant, Schelling and Historicity*, John Burbidge (ed.) (Toronto: University of Toronto Press, 1996), 34–49 ('Kant's concept of history').

19. HW, XVII, 342–4ff.

20. Gillian Rose, *Hegel Contra Sociology* (London: Athlone Press, 1981), 92.

21. *Ibid.*, 119.

22. F. W. J. Schelling, *Erste Vorlesung in Berlin*, 15. November 1841, in Manfred Schröter (ed.), *Schellings Werke*, 13 vols. (München: C. H. Beck, 1959); (first published 1927), VI, 755.

23. On the dispute between the so-called 'left' and 'right' Hegelians on the religious significance of Hegel's philosophy, see Jon Stewart, 'Hegel's philosophy of religion and the question of "right" and "left" Hegelianism', in Douglas Moggach (ed.), *Politics, Religion and Art. Hegelian Debates* (Evanston, IL: Northwestern University Press, 2011), 66–97.

24. Milbank *et al.*, *Radical Orthodoxy*, 1.

25. Graham Ward, *True Religion* (Oxford: Blackwell, 2003), 98ff.

26. John Milbank, 'Postmodern critical Augustinianism. A short summa in forty-two responses to unasked questions', in John Milbank and Simon Oliver (eds.), *The Radical Orthodoxy Reader* (London: Routledge, 2009), 49–50ff.

27. *Ibid.*

28. See e.g. HW, IV, 36: 'Die kraftlose Schönheit haßt den Verstand, weil er ihr dies zumutet, was sie nicht vermag. Aber nicht das Leben, das sich vor dem Tode scheut und von der Verwüstung rein bewahrt, sondern das ihn erträgt und in ihm sich erhält, ist das Leben des Geistes. Er gewinnt seine Wahrheit nur, indem er in der absoluten Zerrissenheit sich selbst findet.' [Beauty without intellectual power hates the understanding, because it attributes to the understanding a power which it does not possess. But the life of the Spirit does not shrink back from death and seek to preserve itself from devastation, but confronts death and sustains itself precisely in that confrontation. The Spirit finds its truth only when it finds itself in utter self-diremption.]

29. See HW, XVI, 138ff.

30. Ward, *True Religion*, viii, 115ff.

31. Dietrich Bonhoeffer, *Letters and Papers from Prison: The Enlarged Edition*, E. Bethge (ed.) (London: SCM Press, 1971), 287, 344–5.

32. For Hegel's explicit treatment of this theme, see HW, III, 163ff.

33. See Milbank *et al.*, *Radical Orthodoxy*, 1–20 ('Suspending the material: the turn of radical orthodoxy').
34. Milbank, *Theology and Social Theory: Beyond Secular Reason* (Oxford: Blackwell, 1990), 9.
35. *Ibid.*, 147–76 (Chapter 6: 'For and against Hegel').
36. cf. Karl Marx and Friedrich Engels, *The German Ideology*, Parts 1 and 2, trans. Roy Pascal (London: Lawrence and Wishart, 1940), 14; cf. *Die deutsche Ideologie, Marx-Engels, Werke*, 42 vols. (Berlin: Dietz Verlag, 1960–83), III, 26.
37. See also Milbank, 'The theological critique of philosophy in Hamann and Jacobi', in Milbank *et al.*, *Radical Orthodoxy*, 21–37.
38. John Milbank, 'Slavoj Žižek and John Milbank', in Creston Davis (ed.), *The Monstrosity of Christ: Paradox or Dialectic?* (Cambridge, MA: MIT Press, 2009), 372.
39. Creston Davis (ed.), John Milbank and Slavoj Žižek, *The Monstrosity of Christ*, 60.
40. This is exactly the temptation against which John Milbank and Graham Ward have recently warned. See John Milbank and Graham Ward, 'The radical orthodoxy ten years on – the return of metaphysics', in Michael Hoelzl and Graham Ward (eds.), *The New Visibility of Religion: Studies in Religion and Cultural Hermeneutics* (London and New York: Continuum, 2008), 151–69, especially 162ff.
41. Don Cupitt, *The Meaning of the West: An Apologia for Secular Christianity* (London: SCM Press, 2008), 23.
42. *Ibid*, 9.
43. See also Mark Taylor's similar reading in *After God*, 154–64 ('Self-embodiment of God').
44. Karl Barth, *Protestant Theology in the Nineteenth Century: Its Background and History*, Colin Gunton (ed.), trans. Brian Cozens and John Bowden (London: SCM Press, 2001) (first published 1947), 407.
45. See Karl Barth, *The Epistle to the Romans*, trans. (from the 6th edn) Edwyn C. Hoskyns (London: Oxford University Press, 1968) (first published 1918), 275–80.
46. Barth, *Protestant Theology*, 456, 459, 522ff.
47. Cyril O'Regan, *The Heterodox Hegel* (Albany: State University of New York Press, 1994), 363.
48. Alasdair Macintyre, *After Virtue: A Study in Moral Theory* (3rd edn with prologue) (London: Duckworth, 2007), 213–18.
49. *Ibid.*, 221–2.
50. *Lectures on the Philosophy of Religion, One-Volume Edition*, Peter C. Hodgson (ed.) (Berkeley, CA: University of California Press, 1988).
51. Rose, *Hegel contra Sociology*, 92.

8

Faith and reason

NICHOLAS ADAMS

This essay has as its focus Hegel's contribution to our contemporary thinking about the relation between theology and philosophy, through an engagement with two of his most fascinating discussions. The first is his account of 'The Enlightenment struggle against superstition' in the *Phenomenology of Spirit*; the second is his retrieval of Anselm's ontological argument in the *Lectures on the Philosophy of Religion*. This discussion exhibits in some ways a curious *lack of impact* of Idealism in contemporary thinking, in an area where Hegel has a distinctive and compelling – yet unfulfilled – contribution to make.

Discussions of 'faith' and 'reason' have two principal and rival ways of arranging their material: either historically or taxonomically. An historical account, looking at the Christian tradition, might discuss the relation between faith and reason in Augustine, Thomas, Descartes, Leibniz, Kant and Hegel, and then show how modern (especially Protestant) theological traditions take up these conceptions of the relation between faith and reason, including Luther, Calvin, Schleiermacher, Barth, 'theology after Wittgenstein', reformed epistemology, radical orthodoxy and so on. A taxonomical account might divide approaches into those that treat faith and reason as opposed, as hierarchically related, as complementary or as identical; it might look at topics such as proofs for the existence of God, philosophical defences of doctrinal claims, conceptions of the university disciplines of theology and of philosophy. Whether one takes the historical or the taxonomical route some account will be needed of how terms such as fides, ratio, intellectio, Glaube, Vernunft, Verstand, faith, reason, understanding are handled in the various thinkers, texts or forms of thinking under consideration.

I propose to take a different approach. This is because Hegel makes a radical departure from the prior tradition, which does not fit neatly into an historical narrative, and because he offers radical proposals that cannot be readily accommodated to the familiar taxonomies. Hegel is self-conscious about his relation to the prior tradition and is explicit in his critique of then-contemporary ways of thinking about the relation of faith and reason. I shall explore two facets of this in section 8.1 (Modern problems) and section 8.2 (Medieval solutions). The first, 'The Enlightenment struggle against superstition', is his account of how certain accounts of faith and certain accounts of reason *produce*, and not merely encounter, their rivals. In the course of this discussion Hegel develops a system of classification in which classes overlap. The second, his account of Anselm's ontological proof, displays Hegel's unusual approach to the relation between philosophy and theology, in particular his attempt to tease out certain philosophical lessons from the early tradition's theological exploration. In this case Hegel develops a logic of distinction-in-inseparable-relation, which he offers as an alternative to more common logics of opposition.

8.1 Modern problems

Hegel's discussion of 'The Enlightenment struggle against superstition'[a] comes about two thirds of the way through the *Phenomenology of Spirit*, in the middle of the chapter on 'Reason', in a sub-section entitled 'Spirit'. It is not the discussion that attracts the most theological interest. That interest, where it exists at all, is often focused on the figure of '*das unglückliche Bewußtsein*', which comes much earlier in the book, and which completes the chapter on 'Self-consciousness'. The reasons for this focus are doubtlessly many, but two suggest themselves immediately: it is the first substantial discussion of a 'religious' topic in the *Phenomenology*; and it comes immediately after the famous '*Herrschaft und Knechtschaft*' discussion that is so dramatically brought centre-stage at the start of Kojève's influential interpretation of Hegel's thought.[1] This section is indeed more intimately referred to by its interpreters as '*Herr und Knecht*', subtly changing the title to that of its principal *dramatis personae*, in order to bring out more fully the drama of this extraordinary account of the origins of self-consciousness. Those theologically minded readers who do not want to read the whole of the *Phenomenology* know that they must at least get this far: the drama of the master and the slave and the discussion of the unhappy consciousness that follows it. It is often taken as an account of medieval Christianity, and thus

a. 'Der Kampf der Aufklärung mit dem Aberglauben'.

has a peculiar resonance for those who seek to recover the significance of medieval theology for modern thought.[2]

The focus here is on a later section that concerns the Enlightenment. It displays two qualities that might motivate continued interest in it. The first is the surprisingly contemporary feel of the discussion in the light of current writing by the so-called 'new atheists', led by Richard Dawkins, together with a variety of religious responses that often accept the terms of debate offered by their opponents. We shall see that Hegel's account is far subtler. The second is Hegel's presentation of two competing ways of thinking and his diagnosis of a deficient system of classification that characterises both positions: in this case it is the Enlightenment critique of religion and religious rejections of the Enlightenment. Hegel sides neither with 'Enlightenment' nor with 'faith', but seeks to identify what he characteristically and gnomically terms 'the truth' that is to be discerned when one overcomes the false oppositions that both forms of thinking display.

'The Enlightenment struggle against superstition' comes in the discussion of 'Spirit' and is best interpreted as a contribution to the wider elaboration of what spirit is. Despite the religious connotations of the term there is consensus among commentators on the *Phenomenology* that Hegel discusses peculiarly *human* agency in his various discussions of spirit. (When Hegel speaks of the Holy Spirit in the *Phenomenology*, as he does in this section, he explicitly names it at §553 '*heiliger Geist*'.) Spirit is glossed early on in the work as 'I that is we, and we that is I' (§177).[3] It represents Hegel's approach to overcoming a familiar false opposition in modern philosophy between the individual and the community. It locates what one might call the significant sphere of subjectivity neither in the solitary agent nor in the collective social group; instead it introduces a pair of terms (in this case 'I' and 'we') and refuses either to separate them or to fuse them: they remain distinct, but are handled in relation to each other.

Within the wider frame in which the false opposition of 'I' and 'We' is overcome, a further set of false oppositions is considered in this section of the *Phenomenology*: between 'insight' and 'faith', 'form' and 'content', 'self-consciousness' and 'naïve consciousness'. In each case Hegel will show that the Enlightenment falsely takes the terms in these pairs to be opposed to each other and he draws attention to the one-sidedness that arises as a consequence. Such a system of classification, in which terms are opposed, has the curious effect of producing the very phenomena that are taken to be the problem. In this case the Enlightenment sets up a false opposition between 'insight' and 'faith'; it gives a falsely opposed characterisation of each; it identifies itself with 'insight'; it loads the term 'faith' with a heavy freight of negative characteristics; it then launches an attack on the faith that its system of classification has produced. Hegel thus says, in a typically obscure formulation, that the Enlightenment is actually struggling against itself. What he means is that the Enlightenment's system of classification is deficient and produces a set of self-defeating battles that have real historical and social consequences. He also argues that religious thinking of a particular kind likewise displays a certain fatal one-sidedness, especially when it mounts a defence of itself in the terms prescribed by the Enlightenment. Hegel's resolution of these various false oppositions is the development of an alternative system of classification in which classes are not falsely opposed, but in fact overlap. Hegel thus does not seek to reject the Enlightenment in favour of faith, or faith in favour of the Enlightenment, but to identify what he calls 'the truth' of the Enlightenment that the Enlightenment itself cannot articulate. This truth will be one in which the classes 'insight' and 'faith' overlap.

'The Enlightenment struggle against superstition' will be taken here to be divided broadly into two parts: §§541–5 offer a narrative of the Enlightenment's rejection of religious faith; §§546–75 pursue a philosophical analysis of this narrative and situate that analysis within the wider aims of the *Phenomenology*. For reasons of space our focus will be the first part.

The first part as a whole takes as its starting point the apparent opposition of 'Enlightenment' on the one side and 'religious faith' on the other. Commentary on this part often displays a tendency either to focus on the fate of 'religious faith', and to treat the Enlightenment as an episode in the adventures of religious faith in the modern period, or to focus on the fate of 'The Enlightenment' and to treat religious faith as a peculiar moment in the outworking of the Enlightenment's self-understanding.[4] I assume there is no such choice to be made: the history of religious faith in Europe includes the Enlightenment and there can be no useful account of that faith that is not simultaneously an account of the Enlightenment; and the Enlightenment is primarily a development within the post-Reformation Christian tradition. Hegel's genius is to see – in such recent events – that neither 'Enlightenment' nor 'faith' can be adequately conceived independently of each other. My focus will be on Hegel's differentiation of systems of classification.

The first part (§§541–5) rehearses the story of the Enlightenment's rejection of religious faith. A broad paraphrased summary of each section is offered here.

§541:   'Pure insight' (*reine Einsicht*) is a general term that includes various forms of consciousness that orient themselves negatively to their

objects; it spread out over Europe as 'the Enlightenment'. Its principal agent is the self, and the 'purity' in question is a defining character
of its way of thinking. It is not *what* it thinks about that marks it but
how it thinks: it undermines its objects, whatever they happen to be,
and ceaselessly calls them into question. Chief among these objects
is religious faith which, by contrast, is wholly defined by its content and by its object (rather than by the self). Faith has a kind of
motionless solidity, whereas insight is constantly in motion.

§542:   Insight is oppositional. It sees faith as opposed to it, and thus opposed
to reason and truth. It takes faith as a tissue of superstitions, prejudices and errors. Insight discerns two kinds of further deficiency
in faith, which come into view when insight describes the kind of
thinking that faith displays. On the one hand faith is marked by
immediacy, naïveté and a general lack of reflection. On the other
hand faith is marked by a highly reflective evil intention, conceit and
deception, above all displayed in the priesthood. The masses display
'bad insight' and the priests display 'bad intention'. Despotic rulers
ruthlessly exploit both in pursuit of their own power, control and
pleasure but, at the same time, share with their subjects the same
superstitions.

§543:   Insight distinguishes between irrational thinking, which just needs
to become rational, and oppressive thinking, which is the mark of
the priesthood and the despot. Insight advocates rationality far more
than it attempts directly to oppose oppression. It aims to change how
the masses think rather than how the corrupt leaders act.

§544:   There are two sides to this advocacy. On the one hand it shares with
faith its truth-oriented subjectivity; on the other hand it repudiates
faith's God-oriented objectivity. It is not faith's orientation that is
rejected but the false object to which it takes itself to be oriented.
When insight makes the 'purity' or 'honesty' of faith explicit, it
actually identifies something about itself too.

§545:   Insight and faith share a concern with this purity. This is why, in
the end, insight's purity proves irresistible to faith itself. Purity is
'in the air'. Faith becomes gradually accustomed to this atmosphere.
But what it breathes in is a kind of infection: it is a simplicity in
which everything is dissolved, forgotten, unprejudiced. *Everything*.
By the time faith notices this corrosive effect it is too late: faith itself
has become utterly colonised by this way of thinking and even its
attempts to rid itself of the infection are guided by the very ways

of thinking against whose conclusions it struggles. Such defensive attempts display two tendencies: they reinforce the corrosive rationalism and they often, in fact, betray the very faith they seek to shore up. Diderot dramatised the process whereby the new music comes to supplant the old. It happens gradually, people appreciate its beauty, they get used to it. It is just how the Jesuits converted non-believers in China and India. The strange god is humbly placed next to the traditional idol. Gradually it gets stronger until 'one morning it shoves its comrade with its elbow and – crash! bang! – the idol is on the floor'. What new music does for the old, and what the Jesuits did for indigenous Chinese and Indian religions, the Enlightenment does for traditional faith. It's a bloodless coup. In a parody of John's Gospel (John 3: 14–15), a new serpent is raised up, and it has painlessly shed its old skin.

This then is Hegel's compelling account of how the Enlightenment comes to transform religious faith. From the Enlightenment's point of view, this is pretty much the end of the story. From the point of view of the 'new atheists' it is a kind of fairytale ending that should have been the end of the matter around 1800. For some reason (actually the same reason Hegel identified: corrupt institutions shoring up their dishonest power) religious superstition persists in an unholy afterlife, and a rather bloodier battle remains to be fought in the Shires, some time after Sauron's might has been overcome without weapons in Mordor.

Yet Hegel does not end his account here. He has barely begun. This account of the apparent supersession of faith by insight is barely five paragraphs in length. Hegel's analysis, which does not at all mirror the Enlightenment's self-perception, is nearly six times as long. Hegel's interest is not so much in the supersession, which he regards as wholly illusory, as in the relation of one class, insight, to another: faith. Hegel's account of 'faith and reason' is in any case entirely subservient to the dominant narrative of 'thinking and being' in the *Phenomenology*. The apparent conflict between 'scientific truth' and 'religious superstition' is a display of much deeper tectonic movement, which will turn out to be an entirely different way of handling the relation of subject to object, thinking to being. In fact, it will turn out that the Enlightenment *fails* to embrace this alternative way of thinking just as much as the faith it rejects. Indeed, faith in Hegel's account *succeeds* in anticipating such an alternative in a surprising way, which is why the penultimate chapter of the 'Reason' section of the *Phenomenology* is called 'Religion' rather than 'Science' or 'Rationalism': for Hegel it is religion that paves the way for an adequate modern *Wissenschaft*, not Enlightenment philosophy or the natural sciences. In other words, Hegel's account in §§541–5 might be thought to echo the rhetoric of the new atheism; but the account, in fact, utterly undermines it. This is remarkable and thus needs to be examined.

Some commentators read the first narrative section as an historical narrative about the Enlightenment, just as they read the 'unhappy consciousness' as an historical narrative about medieval Catholicism. However, the temptation is probably best resisted: Hegel's vagueness and his tendency to use terms such as 'pure insight' and 'naïve consciousness' are not best viewed as inexact history but as an attempt more precisely to identify the philosophical shifts that Hegel wishes to analyse. One of Hegel's more unusual intellectual traits is his tendency to de-historicise the narrative and to present certain forms of thoughts as developments of rival and problematic systems of classification and logics.

How then does Hegel upset the Enlightenment supersessionist narrative, a story in which superstitious faith is overcome by rational thought? It begins further back in the *Phenomenology* when Hegel discusses faith around §496. This is 'the world of self-alienated spirit', in which faith is described as a movement of flight from the sensual world into a realm of 'pure consciousness': it is a retreat into the subject. One can guess at the historical movements being gestured at: Jürgen Stolzenberg, for example, sees various late seventeenth-century movements such as German pietism (he names August Hermann Francke as its representative) and French Jansenism and pietism, as well as later developments such as Methodism in England.[5] But again, Hegel's focus is more clearly discerned if one does not resist his de-historicised account. The faith that interests Hegel is one whose distinguishing mark is a bid for purity, an emphatic anti-institutionalism and an embrace of subjectivity. When one encounters the 'pure consciousness' of 'pure insight' in §541, therefore, one sees that it is not original to the Enlightenment at all; it is a further development of certain kinds of independent religious movement from a century before. *The possibility of the Enlightenment lies in the very faith it rejects.* This is why Hegel insists on a certain shared identity: 'faith and insight are the same pure consciousness' (§541); 'pure insight is *in itself* one and the same as the naïve consciousness' (§544); 'both are essentially the same' (§545).[b] (We can set aside for the moment Hegel's equal emphasis on what distinguishes them.)

b. 'Glauben und Einsicht dasselbe reine Bewußtsein . . . sind . . . sie [die reine Einsicht] *an sich* das selbe mit ihm [das unbefangene Bewußtsein] ist . . . beide wesentlich dasselbe sind.' Hegel, *Gesammelte Werke*, Kritische Ausgabe, ed. Deutsche Forschungsgemeinschaft in Verbindung mit

We can thus see the first way in which the Enlightenment supersessionist narrative is disturbed by Hegel: it is accomplished by refusing to accept its terms of reference. It must strike most readers of 'the Enlightenment struggle against superstition' as odd that the whole section has very little to say about 'the Enlightenment' or about 'superstition': the words hardly crop up at all. With remarkable discipline Hegel refers instead to 'pure insight' and 'faith'. Given that 'pure insight' is in fact a product of faith's 'pure consciousness', a certain counter-narrative starts to emerge, a counter-narrative in which Hegel largely refuses the terms of debate offered by the Enlightenment.

Faith retreats from the sensuous world into subjectivity; faith produces a form of 'pure consciousness'; this turn to the subject (emphatically in the late seventeenth century, but already present in the Lutheran doctrine of *sola fide*) forks in the eighteenth century and is displayed in 'faith' and in 'insight', which both reject institutional authority as a source of truth. The 'diffusion' (*Verbreitung*, the same word that Hegel later uses of the toxic air that faith comes to breathe) of insight comes to be known as 'the Enlightenment'. But pure insight does not see itself as a child of faith's pure consciousness. Instead, it produces an account in which faith is opposed to reason and its account of faith is two-sided: it is simultaneously naïveté and deception. This produces two corresponding, and quite different, tasks. One is oriented to the subject, the other to the object. Insight seeks to cure subjectivity of its naïveté; and it seeks to excise the deceptive object. It thus separates 'bad insight' (*schlechte Einsicht*) (§542), which is nonetheless 'honest' (*ehrlich*) (§543), from 'bad intention' (*schlechte Absicht*) (§542), which practises 'deceit' (*Betrug*) (§543). Insight takes itself to be engaged in a fight and so it generates its enemy. It identifies naïve subjectivity as a property of ordinary folk, whom it honours, and the deceptive object as a confection of the scheming priests, whom it denounces. The process Hegel diagnoses is one of progressive emphatic bifurcation. The readers of the *Phenomenology* are encouraged to notice how there is a splitting of 'insight' and 'faith', and there is then a further splitting within faith of 'bad insight' and 'bad intention'. This splitting is 'essential' from the point of view of insight. The contrast of 'Enlightenment' and 'superstition' (to use its own terms) is absolute. Similarly, the contrast between 'priests' and 'people' is total. Hegel takes a quite different view. Where the Enlightenment sees 'essential' differences, Hegel sees 'historical' developments. The emphatic contrast between 'insight' and 'faith' is illusory: they both stem from a 'religious'

der Rheinisch-Westfälischen Akademie der Wissenschaften (Hamburg: Meiner, 1968ff.) [hereafter GW], ix, 293, 294–5, 295.

anti-institutional turn to the subject. (The contrast between 'priests' and 'people' is not one that Hegel explicitly undermines.)

Hegel's historical turn is remarkable enough. But philosophically we see something even more extraordinary. The Enlightenment's system of classification is binary. It makes either/or judgements: 'superstition' or 'enlightenment', 'priests' or 'people', 'naïveté' or 'insight', 'honesty' or 'deception' and so forth.[c] Within such a system of classification the classes are exclusive. The task of judgement is correspondingly one of determining how phenomena are to be assigned. Acts of prayer, for example, can be assigned in only one way and thus become classified as 'superstition' or as 'naïveté'.

Hegel's system of classification is non-binary. It makes both-and judgements: pure faith *includes* pure insight; pure insight is 'the same as' pure faith. Within this quite different system of classification the classes overlap. The task of analysis is thus to discern the kinds of overlapping class that are in play. 'Pure consciousness' is a tool that permits the philosopher to see how the classes 'insight' and 'faith' overlap. The 'naïveté' of faith overlaps with the 'purity' of insight. The rationality of the 'outbreaks' of religious rebellion against the Enlightenment overlaps with the rationality of the Enlightenment itself. Indeed the metaphors of the 'compliant atmosphere' or of the 'pervading infection' are dramatic images for what philosophically are overlapping classes.[d] Because insight has its roots in a certain kind of Protestant faith, and because faith, in turn, becomes utterly colonised by insight, any system of classification that seeks to do justice to them must operate with overlapping classes. The Enlightenment fails to do this, and thus produces a false narrative that is an effect of its deficient system of classification.

There is a further interesting feature of Hegel's analysis. One of the aspects of the 'simplicity' of pure consciousness that is toxic to religious life is its tendency to forget. Its unremitting negativity undermines whatever it considers in such a way that its contents are forgotten. Once this has taken place, it becomes possible to remember the past, but in an utterly changed form: 'the infection has permeated every organ of spiritual life. Only then does memory alone still preserve the dead mode of spirit's previous shape as a vanished history'.[e] The *Phenomenology* is itself a record of such memories; it is in part a scrapbook of shapes of spirit. The Enlightenment forgets; the

---

c. 'Aberglaube/Aufklärung; Priester/Volk; unbefangen/Einsicht; ehrlich/Betrug'. GW ix, 294–6.
d. 'widerstandslose Atmosphäre... durchdringende Ansteckung', §545.
e. 'Die Ansteckung alle Organe des geistigen Lebens durchdrungen hat; nur das Gedächtnis bewahrt dann noch als eine... vergangene Geschichte die tote Weise der vorigen Gestalt des Geistes auf.' GW ix, 296.

Phenomenology remembers. But the death of a shape of spirit is not thereby reversed. There is neither manic retrieval nor depressive nostalgia. There is instead the owl of Minerva who takes flight only when dusk falls. Memory thus takes on an ambiguous character in Hegel's intellectual account. The purpose of remembering the 'dead mode' (*die tote Weise*) is not to quicken the dead but to enable one to develop a system of overlapping classes.

The false opposition of 'pure consciousness' and 'superstitious content' is only overcome when one shows how the classes overlap. The attempt by insight to diagnose the error of faith itself errs. The 'error of faith', from the point of view of insight, is that it treats something given from outside as true; it assigns truth to the pronouncements of an external authority. But, says Hegel, this is not what one sees in (Protestant) faith at all. The anti-institutional turn to the subject in the sixteenth and seventeenth centuries does quite the opposite: to echo Psalm 51, it assigns truth in the inward parts. Both faith and insight are anti-institutional in their refusal to receive external pronouncements as true. To be 'in error', as the Enlightenment says faith is, is to receive a falsehood. But faith (even according to insight) is a form of self-consciousness. It is thus not 'received' at all. It is produced. Where one is dealing with a form of consciousness that displays the subject possessing itself in some way, it makes no sense to speak of externally oriented delusion.

And so the Enlightenment gets hopelessly confused. It tells the faithful that (a) they themselves invent their object of devotion and (b) they receive their object of devotion from deceptive priests. Which is it? It cannot be both. The actual error of the Enlightenment is much deeper and more serious than the supposed error of superstition. The Enlightenment sunders subject (who invents God) and object (the received God). This is an instance of a much broader problem in modern philosophy of which the Enlightenment is one of many symptoms, from Descartes to Fichte: subject and object are falsely opposed. It is not altogether in error, however. Spirit is a matter of overcoming the false opposition of individual and collective, or 'I' and 'we'. In both insight and faith, so-called Enlightenment and so-called superstition, we can discern aspects of spirit in a promising but unsatisfactory way. Insight expresses the 'form' of spirit, in its insistence on 'thinking' and in its incipient turn to 'the concept'. Faith expresses the 'content' of spirit, in its focus on the object, on God. Insight finds itself in an 'emptied' world that it cannot inhabit and it envies the meat-and-potatoes world of faith. Faith inhabits a rich world of meanings that it cannot 'think', and it falls short of the conceptual promise held out by insight. When faith tries to think, it compromises what it inhabits, because it permits the corrosive atmosphere of the Enlightenment to undermine the contents of its traditions.

Faith and insight are both alienated from spirit, and for the same reason: they are marked by a turn to 'pure consciousness'. The problem is the purity. Insight is determined *not* to inhabit; faith is determined to inhabit *at any cost*. They are each inconsistent in different ways. Insight pursues a remorseless refusal of content but in such a way that it invents the very faith it attacks.

What is needed is a shape of thinking where the 'form' of thinking, with its emphasis on subjectivity, is appropriately matched to the 'content' of what is thought, with its emphasis on objectivity. Insight displays an emphasis on form; faith displays an emphasis on content. Insight rehearses a turn to the subject (which it learned in any case from anti-institutional faith); faith performs a concern with the object (from which it constantly becomes alienated whenever it internalises insight's critique). Such a reconciled shape of thinking, where subject and object receive their due, will be found neither in Enlightenment nor in those forms of faith that either exhibit 'pure consciousness' or that hang on in a bloody-minded way to the 'external' object. It will be found in religion, where the community performs the overcoming of the false opposition of 'I' and 'We', and thus genuinely exhibits 'spirit', but most of all it will be found in absolute knowing, where spirit is grasped in a way that overcomes a further false opposition that persists in religion: the false opposition of subject and object.

We can now consider the upshot for us of Hegel's account of faith and reason. There are two principal lessons that Hegel offers. The first is an historical one: the emphatic notion of 'reason' advocated by the Enlightenment *philosophes* was itself a development of an anti-institutional form of 'faith' articulated first by Luther and then refined in forms of pietism, Jansenism, Quietism and Methodism. It has been a mistake to think that faith and reason are essentially opposed to each other; they are historically entwined. The second is a philosophical one: the false opposition of faith and reason is itself an expression of a deeper deficient system of classification in which classes are falsely opposed. Hegel offers a rival system of classification in which classes overlap.

In relation to the new atheism Hegel offers a radical critique in advance. The new atheist critique of religion is a rehash of the Enlightenment struggle against superstition and is just as contradictory. Religious beliefs are 'make-believe' on the one hand; and they are the product of 'damaging education' on the other. They are simultaneously 'bad insight' and 'bad intent'. They are displays of 'naïveté' and of 'deception'. The problems with the new atheism are partly historical and partly philosophical. On the historical side there is a lack of appreciation of the ways in which the natural sciences are themselves a product of shifts in theology. Likewise, there is a failure to grasp that the forms of fundamentalist, creationist and intelligent-design arguments that they reject are themselves the products of a Christian imagination which struggles against an internalised toxic Enlightenment discourse and which displays an explicit antagonism to the natural sciences that are falsely believed to undermine Christian teaching. On the philosophical side, the 'scientific' thinking of the new atheists operates with a system of classification in which classes are mutually exclusive and in which false oppositions govern a wide range of judgements. It can only be cured through a system of classification in which classes overlap. This therapy is required for atheism and fundamentalism alike. So long as it is refused, Hegel's account of the Enlightenment struggle against superstition will remain an eccentric text whose possibilities remain perpetually available but unused.

8.2 Medieval solutions

Section 8.1 has rehearsed Hegel's development of a system of classification in which classes overlap, an approach that is distinct from what one might call a 'scientific' system of classification in which classes tend to be mutually exclusive: fish or fowl, chalk or cheese. Scientific systems of classification are appropriate when dealing with 'nature', but they tend to fail to do justice to phenomena that have to do with human self-understanding. These phenomena are not so easily pigeonholed and they call for a rather different form of classification such as the kind Hegel offers. We now turn to the development of an alternative logic that guides the use of this system of classification. Instead of a logic in which terms are either opposed or equated, it handles terms in such a way that their distinctions are preserved but where neither term can be adequately considered independently of the other. I use the inelegant hyphenated form distinction-in-inseparable-relation for this alternative logic.

Hegel's remarkable system of classification has no name in the *Phenomenology*. It is instead signalled by counter-intuitive and seemingly baffling claims, such as the idea that insight and faith are 'the same'. This is not sameness in the sense of being identical. It is obviously not the case that there is no difference between insight and faith. It is, rather, a claim that the classes overlap. Hegel's alternative logic does have a name, however: Hegel calls it simply 'the concept'. It comes into play whenever two terms that are falsely opposed in much modern philosophy are handled in such a way that they are distinct but in inseparable relation. Such pairs typically include, for Hegel, subject and object, individual and community, thinking and being. We are no longer dealing with classes of objects, but logical terms whose relation is in question.

The system of classification concerns phenomena in the world: such social forms as 'insight' and 'faith' for example. The logic does not deal in phenomena but in metaphysical terms like 'substance and accident' (to use an Aristotelian pair) or 'subject and object' (to use a Kantian pair). It is striking that in Hegel's philosophy the systems of classification and the logic have a similar character: they refuse falsely equating or falsely opposing the categories in which they deal.

Some preliminary remarks are in order before considering Hegel's treatment of Anselm's ontological argument for the existence of God. Kant's criticism of the ontological argument is often taken to be a defining moment in the tradition of ontological arguments. His double insistence that (1) one can refuse subject and predicate together without contradiction and (2) being is not a real predicate, are generally what attract the interest of philosophers who wish either to defend or to refute the ontological argument. Hegel's interest in the ontological argument generally goes unremarked except by specialists in Hegel's thought or historians of ideas.

There are two reasons to think Hegel's account is worthy of investigation. First, Hegel believes that Anselm's argument merits several pages of analysis: we should try to find out why that is. Second, Hegel claims that Anselm's argument stands in need of critique but that Kant's critique is the wrong one: we might be curious to know what a more adequate critique looks like. The principal reason why Hegel is not much read or widely discussed is probably the obvious one. Hegel's discussions are cast in his typical categories and style and unless one already knows what Hegel means by 'concept' or 'representation' it is difficult to see what the point of his argument is: the plain sense of Hegel's prose is obscure unless one is already familiar with the language of the *Phenomenology* and the *Science of Logic*.

For reasons of space, a paraphrase of Hegel's argument will be given and I shall concentrate on Hegel's first lecture series of 1821. The discussions of Anselm in the later lecture series in 1824, 1827 and 1831 are more thoroughly worked out, but they also streamline the argument in a way that smoothes over some of the more arresting claims Hegel makes. For that reason I have chosen the rougher 1821 account. I shall assume that readers are familiar with Anselm's argument in the *Proslogion* and will not rehearse it independently of Hegel's analysis.

In the 1821 lecture manuscript, the discussion of Anselm comes in the third part on 'The Consummate Religion', which is a discussion of Christianity. This third part is itself divided into three sections: 'abstract concept', 'concrete representation' and 'community, cultus'. Anselm appears in the middle of the first 'abstract concept' section. Before we arrive at the particular discussion of Anselm, Hegel has clarified at least two things:

(1)   If one focuses on metaphysical Christian speech about God, this takes the form 'God is spirit, God has reality, and exists through his concept; the proof of God's being [*Dasein*] is from his concept'.[f] (By 'metaphysical', Hegel presumably has in mind a broadly Aristotelian shape of discussion.) Hegel notes that previously he had charted the ascent from finitude to infinitude in discussions of God. In metaphysical speech we see it the other way round: the progress is from concept to being (*Sein*).

(2)   God's 'determination' (*Bestimmung*) is that God is 'the *absolute* idea, which is absolutely, that is, that he is *spirit*.[g,6] Hegel here takes up the categories of the *Science of Logic*, which closes with a chapter on 'the absolute idea'. There are two claims here. First, God is the *absolute* idea and this idea 'is' absolutely; second, saying that God is 'spirit' is a way of talking about the idea being 'absolutely'. The meaning of 'absolute' and 'absolutely' as adjective and adverb merits a longer discussion of the final chapter of the *Science of Logic* than can be offered here.[7] Briefly stated, Hegel means to invoke a form of thinking in which one considers the structure of thinking independently of any content it might have. Here, the idea seems to be that before we get to any particular predication of God, which will be treated in the second section on 'concrete representation', we have an unqualified 'absolute' idea whose absoluteness can be glossed as 'spirit'.

'Absolute idea' and 'spirit' are obviously Hegel's words and not the words of the medieval tradition. Hegel is clarifying for his lecture audience that his interpretation of Christian metaphysics is offered in terms from his own philosophy, namely 'absolute idea' and 'spirit'. Hegel takes it for granted that his audience already knows the kinds of term found in Christian metaphysical

---

f. 'Gott ist Geist, Gott hat Realität, existiert durch seinen Begriff; Beweis vom Dasein Gottes aus seinem Begriff.' Volumes 29–31 of the critical edition (indicated by GW in this volume) are in preparation. The citation here is from the best currently available edition: G. W. F. Hegel, *Vorlesungen über die Philosophie der Religion: Die vollendete Religion*, ed. W Jaeschke (Hamburg: Felix Meiner, 1995), 5.

g. 'Er die *absolute* Idee ist, die absolute, d.i. daß er der *Geist* ist.' Hegel, *Vorlesungen über die Philosophie der Religion*, ed. Jaeschke, 5.

speculation. These would include Greek Aristotelian terms like 'ousia' (sub-stance) or Latin scholastic terms like 'intellectus' (understanding). Hegel's habit is to re-author the Greek and Latin categories in German. His audience is taken to be familiar with that project, and Hegel's purpose is to identify the primary categories in play when considering Christian metaphysical speech about God. Hegel goes on to clarify that the point of the language of the 'absolute idea' is to signal the unity of concept and reality in Christian meta-physical speech. Likewise, whereas the 'absolute concept' names the divine nature, we see in Christian metaphysical speech a unity of divine and human nature, which Hegel says is what he means by 'spirit'.

Before we get to the discussion of Anselm, then, Hegel has already sig-nalled what interests him about certain features of Christian metaphysical thinking. *Christian metaphysical speech about God deals in 'unity': both a unity of concept and reality and a unity of divine and human nature.* The discussion of Anselm is best interpreted, in my view, as part of that wider metaphysical interest.

We can see in advance the great obstacle to the general reader who wishes to engage with Hegel's account of Anselm. The reader, like Hegel's audience, already has to know what is signalled by Hegel's terms 'concept', 'absolute idea', 'spirit'. Worse, Hegel equivocates in the meaning of 'concept' (*Begriff*) in this discussion. Sometimes he means his own distinctive account of the concept familiar from the *Phenomenology* but sometimes he means concept in a more straightforward sense, as when he talks of 'the Christian concept of God'. The reader is expected to be flexible enough to know what is going on. Most philosophers of religion today are trained in the analytical tradition and that training is not adequate for grasping the plain sense of Hegel's claims. Thus either hundreds of philosophers of religion can be retrained or Hegel can be ignored.

We can now turn to Anselm.[8] Hegel has clarified that Christian speech deals in a unity of concept and being, and that the ontological proof seeks to exploit that unity in order to prove God's existence. Hegel finds this interesting because it enables one to discern two contrary tendencies in Christian thinking. The first is to unify concept and being. The second is to separate them. To try to prove the existence of God from the concept of God is to take 'existence' as in some way independent of the 'concept'. Hegel wants to see how this works in Anselm's ontological proof.

Anselm's system of classification, in Hegel's rendering, is one in which various terms are in play. These include concept (*Begriff*), being (*Sein*), real-ity (*Realität*), perfection/imperfection (*vollkommen/unvollkommen*), content

(*Inhalt*). Not only are these terms in play: they are arranged hierarchically. God as content is God as the most perfect being. The mere concept (*der bloße Begriff*) is imperfect. Hegel refers to this hierarchy as the abasement of the concept: by refusing the idea that God is 'only' concept, it takes the concept to be deficient in some way. Hegel zeroes in on this move.

God's perfection in the medieval tradition is the unity of concept and being, or concept and reality (Hegel uses both terms, being and reality; they seem more or less convertible in this account). If one has concept without being, or concept without reality, then one has a certain imperfection. Hegel points out that in the modern way of thinking, humanity is a '*concrete identity*' – a unity of concept and being. When modern thinkers consider what humanity is, they assign to it a unity of concept and being, whereas God is treated only as a concept. (Hegel is clearly thinking of Kant here, although he is not named.) Thus when modern thinkers confront Anselm's claim that to treat God *only* as a concept is to introduce imperfection into one's account of God, this causes a problem. Modern thinkers want to hold on to the perfection of God *and* treat God only as a concept. But Anselm says that to hold on to the perfection of God is to insist on the unity of concept *and* being.

Hegel's point is thus not primarily about Anselm's formulation. It is about how modern thinkers react to it. In the modern point of view to be affirmatively and truly real (*die affirmative wahrhafte Realität*) is to exhibit an empirical unity of thinking and being. The truly real is the physical person right there in front of you. But for Anselm the representation of perfection is a thought: the thought of the most universal. When a modern thinker says something is 'real' he is talking about something you can touch. When a medieval thinker says something is 'perfect' he is talking about something you can conceive. All sorts of trouble is in store when modern thinkers try to get their heads around the relation of 'perfection' to 'reality' and the role that conceiving plays vis-à-vis physicality.

Anselm's proof has three moves, Hegel says. (1) The concept of God is (a) a possible concept, (b) the most entirely real being, (c) merely or abstractly positive. (2) Being is reality. Therefore, (3) the concept is subsumed under such realities. Interestingly, Hegel does not gloss this further at this stage. His form of words is not immediately clear, however, so I shall risk offering an alternative form of Anselm's proof, as Hegel presents it: (1) The concept of God is of what is most real; (2) being is real; therefore (3) the concept includes being.

Hegel has been alluding obliquely to Kant in his talk of 'modern thinkers' and in his formulation of the most entirely real being (*das allerrealste Wesen*), which is his German rendering of *ens realissimum*. (One of the most interesting features of Hegel's philosophy is his utter commitment to rendering Greek and Latin terms in German on the grounds that only then are they truly being thought about rather than merely cited. It is the doom of his translator, or the translator who wants to stay as close as possible to the German, merely to cite and not to think.) He now brings Kant explicitly into the frame.

Kant, in Hegel's account, has a two-fold objection against this proof. (1) Being cannot be plucked out of the concept, because being is something other than the concept. (2) Being is not a reality or a predicate: it adds nothing to the object's content; it is merely form. (These days we would expect to note that Kant is dealing with Descartes' version of the ontological argument. Hegel does not note this and proceeds as if Kant is offering a critique of Anselm.)

At this point, one aspect of Anselm's proof is unpacked: God should be what is *most perfect*; if God were merely a representation he would not be most perfect because perfection includes being and not only representation. Anselm asserts that perfection includes representation and being. 'Quite right', Hegel says. In general, talk about truth has to do with representation or the concept; Anselm insists that the opposite determination, being, must be included. 'Quite right', Hegel says again. Hegel insists moreover that all people, including all philosophers, are fundamentally committed to the idea that perfection is such a unity. Now, concept and being are indeed different. 'Quite right', he says once more. But in their mere difference they are finite and untrue. It is the task of reason, and indeed of ordinary, everyday thinking, not to treat things that are finite and untrue as if they were absolute. Thinking is a matter of universality, of the concept. Hegel then parodies Kant's famous formula regarding the relation of concepts and intuitions with a quite different intent. 'The concept without entire objectivity is an empty representation, opinion; being without concept is disintegrating externality and appearance.' Modern metaphysical analysis has imposed an alien formalism on Anselm's way of thinking in such a way that its meaning and content is lost.

Hegel does not say who is responsible for this formalism: his approach typically is to reconstruct shapes and patterns in a way that traces their principal lines rather than to provide a lifelike image, more Beethoven's late string quartets than Haydn's picturesque *Creation*. The shapes he alludes to here are reminiscent of modern systematic developments of scholastic Aristotelian terms, developments which undermine what those scholastic arguments originally attempted to express. Hegel now reconstructs what Anselm sought to express.

The first Anselmian insight is that the concept of God expresses the 'most real', and that this content is affirmed abstractly. This is not a system of classification in which there are various concepts of which the concept of God is one; the concept of God is not part of a system of classification at all, but is '*the* concept', it is 'the *absolute reality*'.[h]

The second insight is that God is 'all reality' and this implies that being is contained in the concept. Hegel affirms the correctness of this formulation and qualifies this being as 'a moment of the concept'. Terms like 'moment' are clearly not native to Anselm, but are Hegel's own. We can paraphrase it. From the side of thinking, as one surveys the concept of God, various aspects come successively to light, one of which is being. One of the modern developments that Hegel embraces emphatically is the turn to the subject. He observes that when one treats concepts within such a framework, concepts are 'subjective' in the sense that subjects judge according to concepts. Thus there is a marked differentiation from being, which of course is not something that proceeds from subjectivity. The whole point of talking about being in a framework that makes subjectivity central is precisely to evoke that which is not subjective.

Our (modern) interest in Anselm lies partly in the attempt to remove subjectivity from the concept, Hegel suggests. This is an extraordinary approach that goes to the heart of Hegel's refusal of Kant's account of concepts. For a frame of thinking in which concepts are inherently subjective, the attempt to remove subjectivity from the concept poses something of a challenge. What it offers is a quite different way of handling the concept. We already know what this different way is: being is contained in it. In order to interpret Anselm, one needs to be attentive to two rival ways of treating the concept. In modern philosophy, with its focus on subjectivity, concepts are opposed to reality. Not only do they not include being: the whole point of talking about concepts is to exclude being. By contrast, in Anselm's ontological argument, the concept 'negates' its subjective quality. Hegel here offers another idiosyncratic description: not only is this subjective quality negated of the concept; the concept includes within itself this negation. Negation is not best rendered as an external operation brought to bear on the concept; it is better discerned as something proper to the concept itself. One cannot see

---

h. 'Gott ist nicht ein Begriff, sondern der Begriff; dies die *absolute Realität*.' Hegel, *Vorlesungen über die Philosophie der Religion*, ed. Jaeschke, 10.

this unless one affirms, as Anselm does, that to speak of 'perfection' or 'the true' is to affirm the unity of concept with reality.

Hegel playfully suggests that when Kant says that 'being' adds nothing to the concept, there is a sense in which he is right even from an Anselmian point of view. If the concept already includes being, then one does not need to 'add' being to it. Of course Kant does not mean this. Kant's concept is a 'subjective' concept. One can imagine an object without such an object needing to 'be'. The content of such a concept is the same, whether the object 'is' or 'is not'. Kant is right to distinguish between the content of the concept and the being of the object. In the realm of finite objects this is right. But the framework for Anselm's argument is not this finite realm: it concerns God. When one talks of God, the content is concept and being together. That is all there is to Anselm's metaphysics; when Anselm invokes 'perfection' it is this unity that he affirms. Now, Anselm presupposes that God is the most perfect being and in modern philosophy such a presupposition can without contradiction be called into question. Hegel concedes and indeed affirms this, but makes another strong claim: to talk of 'perfection' or of 'absolute truth' is to talk of the unity of concept and being, quite independently of what one has to say about God. Anselm may just presuppose that God is perfect. In a more modern idiom one needs a demonstration, and for Hegel this will not primarily be about God; it will instead be a demonstration that the 'pure concept' overcomes a separation of thought and existence. That is not a demonstration that Anselm undertakes: it is a modern project that is stimulated by Anselm's argument.

Anselm's view is that to say 'God' is to affirm the unity of thought and existence. His modern successors introduce a range of technical terms like 'possibility' and other concepts whose frame is the modern turn to the subject. Hegel's critique of these successors is that their primary allegiance is to maintaining the integrity of these technical terms, whereas for Hegel the 'interest of reason' is to sublate (*aufheben*) them. Hegel means by this what he generally means by sublate: where there are false oppositions in play, the task of philosophy is to overcome them and offer a better account of the relation between terms. In this case, the terms are 'thinking' and 'being' or 'thought' and 'existence' or 'concept' and 'reality'.

Hegel's final criticism of certain forms of modern thinking is brief and somewhat reminiscent of insights displayed by Hamann. Modern thinkers are quite happy to affirm a union of reason and sensibility when they inquire into humanity; but when they inquire into God they affirm that here we have *only* a concept and insist that one cannot go beyond this. Hegel points out that if one expresses arbitrary prejudices like this then there is no hope of doing justice to forms of thinking such as those exhibited by Anselm.

We should take stock. What does Hegel's subtle discussion of Anselm's ontological argument tell us about his understanding of the relation of faith and reason? Hegel teaches twelve lessons.

(1) To talk of perfection or truth is to talk of a unity of pairs of terms: 'thinking' and 'being', 'thought' and 'existence' or 'concept' and 'reality'.

(2) Anselm's proof is an exploitation of this unity: an affirmation of 'thinking' God will lead to an affirmation of God's 'being'.

(3) Thinking and being are indeed different; the question is how they are related to each other.

(4) For Anselm 'perfection' means a relation where these two different terms are united.

(5) For modern philosophy these two different terms must always be separate.

(6) At least they are separate when one considers God; when one considers humanity there is in fact a willingness to acknowledge and an insistence upon a unity of reason and sensibility.

(7) The tendency of modern philosophy to separate these different terms is errant; it confines itself to the world of ordinary, everyday objects in which such separation has its place; but making this separation absolute – insisting that it *always* applies – is to set up a false opposition.

(8) The remedy for this tendency is to develop forms of thinking in which different terms are, in certain cases, related in unity; this will be a concern with an all-encompassing notion of truth and not just the realm of finite things; such a way of thinking will overcome the false opposition of these different terms.

(9) The tendency of modern philosophy to privilege the integrity of its technical distinctions over the pursuit of an all-encompassing notion of truth is also errant; it treats its own historically developed tools as if they are timeless truths.

(10) The remedy for this tendency is to notice different ways in which different terms can be related, for example as a 'unity' (as for Anselm) and as 'opposed' (as for Kant); the false sense that they must *always* or *essentially* be opposed is mitigated by such historical attentiveness.

(11) To attend to Anselm is to recover a form of thinking in which thinking and being are different but united.

(12)   Anselm 'simply' inherits this account of the unity of thinking and being. For modern philosophy, by contrast, the articulation of this unity is a strenuous task that involves overcoming the false opposition between thinking and being inaugurated by Descartes.

In *The Conflict of the Faculties* Kant famously insisted that the task of theology is to transmit received truths, whereas the task of philosophy is to submit all claims (even theological ones) to criticism. Hegel offers a different model of their relation. Theology displays certain shapes of reasoning. The example of Anselm offers such a shape of reasoning in which there is a unity of thinking and being. The task of philosophy is to attend to these shapes and to investigate the systems of classification and the patterns of logic that guide their use. This is a particularly fruitful task when it facilitates remedying errant forms of reasoning in modern philosophy. The example of Kant offers such an errant form of reasoning in which there is a false opposition of thinking and being, for example. Attending to Anselm's theology thus provides resources for a philosophy that seeks to overcome its own errant tendencies.

In this model of the relation between faith and reason the terms are curiously intertwined. They are not identical: Anselm's 'faith' exhibits a certain shape of 'reason', in his case a shape in which thinking and being are related in a unity. Such faith could (and has) exhibited quite different shapes of reason. There is no inevitability to this particular shape. But faith always exhibits *some* shape of reason or other, and whatever shape it exhibits can be investigated in an ordered way. The relation of theology to philosophy is thus a relation in which theology *exhibits* shapes of reason and philosophy *investigates* them. This is not primarily a differentiation in which theology *asserts* and philosophy *criticises*. It is a division of labour in which theology *performs* and philosophy *reflects*. This way of putting things means that these two disciplines are different but related. There can be no reflection without a prior performance on which to reflect, and it is quite likely that many forms of performance will have moments of reflection.

One of the marks of modern theology is that these moments of reflection obtrude more and more insistently. For Hegel, this is not a threat to the integrity of faith. Reflection does not undermine performance: it presents opportunities for the kind of philosophical investigation of the tradition that Hegel offers in his account of Anselm. It makes possible a sophisticated retrieval of apparently long-dead insights. Kant is often taken to have annihilated the ontological argument, whether it is that of Anselm, Descartes or Leibniz. Hegel's account of Anselm shows that this is far from the case.

Kant pitted a modern demand for a separation of thinking and being against a medieval tendency to imagine a unity of thinking and being. In Hegel's account Kant is the loser.

Anselm is not held up as a model for modern philosophy, as if somehow we might return in an ecstasy of nostalgia to the undisturbed certainties of the eleventh century. Rather, his shapes of reasoning are investigated in order to discern resources for overcoming the false oppositions of modern philosophy. Such overcoming is a distinctly *modern* task. That Hegel sees this is displayed in his choice of vocabulary: 'concept', 'spirit', 'absolute idea'. These are not medieval terms: they are Hegel's technical modern vocabulary for addressing modern philosophical problems. Hegel does not produce a medieval solution, after all, but a modern solution that is made possible by the investigation of Anselm's shapes of thinking. This also brings into view what Hegel thinks is the most salient criticism of Anselm's argument: it presupposes the perfection of God, whereas the task is to demonstrate the unity of concept and existence.

What is striking in our own further examination of Hegel's investigation into Anselm is how contemporary it is. False oppositions persist into our own time: subject and object, thinking and being, individual and community, science and history, myth and truth, academic and confessional ... and many others. Hegel offers a fascinating and generative model for our own attempts to overcome these false oppositions. His account of Anselm is a good place to see this model in action.

Most importantly, however, Hegel develops two philosophical approaches with far-reaching significance beyond the narrow sphere of faith and reason. The first is a system of classification in which classes overlap, as we saw in his account of the classes 'insight' and 'faith' in 'The Enlightenment struggle against superstition'. The second is a logic in which terms are different but in unity or, in an alternative formulation, distinct-in-inseparable-relation. In the face of forms of thinking in which the dominant systems of classification are those in which classes are mutually exclusive and in which the dominant logics are logics of opposition, Hegel offers extraordinary possibilities for re-imagining and re-thinking our own patterns of reasoning, and perhaps the forms of 'faith', whatever they may be, in which those patterns are performed.

8.3 The impact of Idealism

Hegel's patterns of thinking about faith and reason have been highly influential in the history of ideas in certain respects and almost completely ignored in others. His account of the Enlightenment struggle against superstition has been replayed in more recent historical work. Amos Funkenstein's *Theology and the Scientific Imagination* is a virtuosic rehearsal of the ways in which developments in 'scientific' thinking are elaborations of moves already made in earlier modern theology.[9] Michael Buckley's *At the Origins of Modern Atheism* traces the ways in which theological developments generate cultural movements that reject theology itself.[10] Stephen Toulmin's *Cosmopolis* describes the genesis of modern philosophy as an expression of internal contradictions produced by Reformation and counter-Reformation theology.[11] John Milbank's *Theology and Social Theory* presents modern sociology as an expression of innovations internal to theology.[12] These four texts have become classics and each, in its different way, is a repetition of Hegel's account of the Enlightenment struggle against superstition. They are narratives of forms of thought that set themselves up against, or gradually become opposed to, theology, but whose own development is part of the internal development of theology itself. Hegel is the first philosopher to argue that theology produces (and does not merely confront) its own rivals and the more recent contributions to the history of ideas are repetitions, with fascinating variation, of Hegel's original theme.

At the same time, Hegel is rarely acknowledged explicitly by his later students. 'The Enlightenment struggle against superstition' is the model, but it is generally not cited as the source. This is not because of some undetected plagiarism in contemporary scholarship: it is probably because Hegel has so utterly shaped aspects of the modern historical imagination that the impact of the *Phenomenology* is in many quarters no longer noticed. Funkenstein, Buckley, Toulmin and Milbank pay Hegel the highest compliment in imitating the shape of his historical reconstruction.

If Hegel's account of the Enlightenment is so familiar as to be invisible, his account of Anselm is utterly unfamiliar. Philosophers of religion are generally able without a second thought to rehearse Kant's criticism of the ontological argument, but if one asks whether Hegel's criticism of Kant and his defence of Anselm is persuasive, this often provokes genuine curiosity: it is not widely known that Hegel has anything worthwhile to say about the ontological argument. Karl Barth wrote an entire book on Anselm's ontological argument: Hegel's interpretation does not appear in it at all.[13] Likewise, in the more recent *Cambridge Companion to Anselm*, in the chapter by Brian Davies on the ontological argument, both Kant and Barth are discussed, but not Hegel.[14] Hegel offers one of the most fascinating retrievals of the ontological argument: it is an account that attempts a radical remedy for the tendency of modern philosophy falsely to oppose thinking and being. It passes largely unnoticed. Discussions of Hegel rarely engage in detail with his account of the ontological argument; discussions of the ontological argument rarely engage in detail with Hegel's critique of Kant.

It is for this reason that this essay has rehearsed Hegel's arguments in some detail, rather than alluding to them in passing. This is somewhat preliminary work and it will fall to future scholars to recover those aspects of the impact of Idealism where it has become so familiar that we no longer notice it and, on the other side (as in the case of the ontological argument), to enable Idealism to have the impact that it deserves.

Notes

1. Alexandre Kojève, *Introduction to the Reading of Hegel*, R. Queneau and Allan Bloom (eds.), trans. J Nichols (New York: Cornell University Press, 1980), 3–30.
2. John Burbidge offers a typically nuanced account of the way in which Hegel's account of the 'unhappy consciousness' might or might not be taken as a discussion of medieval religious life: 'Unhappy consciousness in Hegel: an analysis of medieval Catholicism?' in *Hegel on Logic and Religion: The Reasonableness of Christianity* (Albany: State University of New York Press, 1992), 105–18. Burbidge offers a persuasive argument that Hegel is not best understood as offering a critique of medieval Christian thought.
3. All references are to Terry Pinkard's unpublished translation of the *Phenomenology*, which preserves the paragraph numbers assigned by A. V. Miller in his 1977 translation. The relevant passages in the German critical edition are G. W. F. Hegel, *Gesammelte Werke*, ed. W. Bonsiepen and R. Heede (Hamburg: Felix Meiner, 1980) [hereafter GW], IX, 293–6.
4. Hyppolite's classic commentary *Genesis and Structure of Hegel's Phenomenology of Spirit* tends to take the fate of religious faith as the primary focus; more recently, Jürgen Stolzenberg has offered an interpretation in which the fate of the Enlightenment is the primary focus. Neither interpretation denies the importance of the other, but their emphases make important differences to the kind of shape that Hegel's discussions have taken.
5. Jürgen Stolzenberg, 'Hegel's critique of the Enlightenment', in Kenneth Westphal (ed.), *The Blackwell Guide to Hegel's Phenomenology of Spirit* (Oxford: Wiley-Blackwell, 2009), 197.
6. Translations are my own. Hegel is difficult to interpret in the translation by Peter Hodgson because the note-like quality of the manuscript is mitigated and rounded out into complete sentences. Hodgson here has 'the definition of God [is] that he is the *absolute idea* – i.e. that he is *spirit*'. This makes it look as though Hegel is clarifying the term 'absolute idea' through the term 'spirit'. This is manifestly not so.
7. See Nicholas Adams, 'The absolute idea', in *The Eclipse of Grace: Divine and Human Action in Hegel* (Oxford: Blackwell-Wiley, 2013), 117–65.
8. Hegel, *Vorlesungen*, vol. III, 8ff. (74bff. in the critical edition; 69ff. in Hodgson's translation).

9. Amos Funkenstein, *Theology and the Scientific Imagination* (Chicago: University of Chicago Press, 1986).

10. Michael Buckley, *At the Origins of Modern Atheism* (New Haven: Yale University Press, 1987).

11. Stephen Toulmin, *Cosmopolis: The Hidden Agenda of Modernity* (Chicago: University of Chicago Press, 1990).

12. John Milbank, *Theology and Social Theory* (Oxford: Blackwell, 1990).

13. Barth's *Anselm: fides quaerens intellectum* was completed in 1931. The Lasson edition of the *Lectures* was published by Felix Meiner between 1927 and 1930, with the material on 'Die absolute Religion' and the proofs of the existence of God published in 1929 and 1930; the *Jubiläumsausgabe* of the *Lectures* was published by Frommann around the same time, in 1928. It would seem that Barth had not seen either of these when he wrote *Anselm*. Its second edition, in 1958, was merely a re-publication and included no new material.

14. Karl Barth, *Anselm: fides quaerens intellectum*, trans. I. Robertson (London: SCM, 1960); Brian Davies, 'Anselm and the ontological argument', in B. Davies and B. Leftow (eds.), *The Cambridge Companion to Anselm* (Cambridge: Cambridge University Press, 2004), 157–78.

9

Rabbinic Idealism and Kabbalistic realism: Jewish dimensions of Idealism and Idealist dimensions of Judaism

PAUL FRANKS

For over two centuries, Jewish philosophy and post-Kantian Idealism have been intertwined. Habermas has rightly noted 'the German Idealism of the Jewish philosophers', asking how, given the Christian or post-Christian character of Idealism, this intimacy is possible.[1] In what follows, I offer an answer. First, however, I will deepen the puzzle. For what is internal to Idealism is not only Christianity or post-Christianity, but specifically the claim that Christianity or post-Christianity has superseded Judaism. Accordingly, Idealism constitutes a challenge to Judaism, which must justify its continued existence in the modern world. This makes it more puzzling that Idealism has attracted so many Jewish philosophers. To solve this puzzle, it is necessary to show that both Kantian and post-Kantian Idealism have what I will call Jewish dimensions – namely, rabbinic Idealism and Kabbalistic realism.[2] By articulating these dimensions, Jewish philosophy has contributed to the inner development of Idealism. Moreover, by re-appropriating these dimensions as *Jewish*, Jewish philosophers have found within Idealism the resources to respond to the Idealist challenge, by demonstrating that Judaism has not been superseded.

The seeds of all these developments lie in works by Salomon Maimon, published between 1790 and 1793.[3] In a sadly illuminating illustration of Idealism's complex relationship to Judaism and Jewishness, Kant said of Maimon, 'none of my critics understood me or the main questions so well.'[4] He also complained about Maimon's proposed 'improvement' of the critical response to these questions that, 'Jews always like . . . to gain an air of importance for themselves at someone else's expense'.[5] The anti-Judaic trope is all too familiar. Anxiety concerning Christianity's derivativeness from Judaism and Judaism's capacity for vitality under adverse conditions gives rise to the prejudice that Jews cannot be original and that, since Jewish promotion is always undeserved, it must always involve some non-Jew's unfair demotion. Maimon was interested only in contributing to philosophy. His successors were also interested in showing that Judaism deserved to survive in the modern world.

9.1 The Idealist challenge to Judaism

Karl Leonhard Reinhold, the first German Idealist, made Kant's philosophy famous by presenting it as 'the Gospel of pure reason' that would resolve, once and for all, the conflict between reason and faith.[6] Whether the various forms of Kantian and post-Kantian Idealism are Christian or post-Christian need not be decided here. Driven by their distinctive interest in the rationality of history and the history of reason, these philosophies inherit Christianity's need to negotiate its relationship with its precursor: with Judaism, or whatever serves as its structural analogue.

At one extreme lies Marcionism: the view that Christianity is the antagonist of Judaism, to which it owes exactly nothing. At the opposite extreme lie views that ascribe continuing roles to both Christianity and Judaism. Various views lie in between, including the supersessionist view that Judaism should not only acknowledge Christianity as its fulfilment, but should cease to exist once Christianity has arrived.[7] The presupposition of Idealist discussions of Judaism is that Torah is, above all, law. Two millennia earlier, the Septuagint had translated 'Torah' as 'nomos'. However, what was once the law of nature, or the law that imitated nature, had become, in Spinoza's hands, a political arrangement, a vestige of a vanished state.[8]

Kant saw one aspect of the law – the prohibition of the representation of God – as sublime.[9] But in the rest of the Mosaic law he saw no sublimity. Given by a deity external to reason, the Torah was surely heteronomous. Indeed, since religion consisted of the faith and hope required for morality, and since morality was autonomous, Judaism was not religion but politics. Yet, precisely because of Judaism's sublime idea of an unrepresentable God, it was especially dangerous. Unlike the demands of desire, Judaism could be mistaken for morality. The purification of religion would require 'the euthanasia of Judaism' – from Christianity as well as from Judaism itself.[10] Kant was so insistent that Jesus 'appeared as though descended from heaven', taking nothing from Judaism, that Fichte's neo-Marcionism becomes intelligible.[11] He regarded Judaism as misanthropic and retained only the Gospel of John.

Hegel and Schelling, however, were supersessionists. Indeed, Christianity's supersession of Judaism was a principal model for their versions of sublation. On the one hand, supersession is an abstraction, an idealisation of ancient history. On the other, Idealist sublation finds in concrete, actual Judaism one of its principal applications. Hegel and Schelling inherited Kant's idea that Judaism was especially dangerous because it represented the stage immediately prior to salvation, where consciousness could easily become paralysed, as if mesmerised by slavery in the guise of freedom.[12] But they did not share Kant's formal conception of freedom as autonomy. What Judaism lacked, in Hegel's view, was a collective identification with the Lord that would give human action as such an essential role in God's recognition of God-self in the other, which alone could reconcile infinity with finitude. This lack explained why Judaism had remained frozen for millennia: parochially particular and excluded from history's march towards the universality of the absolute religion, which was at last in view.

A major debate of the time was whether, a thousand years after their civil rights were removed by the Christianised Roman Empire, Jews should become citizens of the modern European states that were superseding Christendom. That Jews should, as humans and as residents, become citizens, was agreed by Kant, Fichte, Schelling and Hegel. Disagreement focused on whether Jews should shed their Judaism as a *pre-condition* of emancipation or as its *consequence*.[13] That Judaism should be dispensed with was beyond question. Within Idealism's modern world, Jews *as humans* would be welcome. But Jews *as Jews* would find no place. This was the new, Idealist version of the Christian challenge that Jewish philosophy would have to face after Kant.

9.2 Kant, Plato and Rabbinic Idealism

Kant's critical philosophy has an explicitly Platonic dimension. After the Aristotelian emphasis of the 'Analytic' of the *Critique of Pure Reason* on cognition's need for both intelligible form and sensible matter, it is striking that, in the 'Dialectic', Kant insists on the necessity for *ideas*, too: rational forms that wholly transcend the senses and that are incapable of instantiation by sensible matter. These ideas play an essential role in setting the ends of cognition and also in the transition from theoretical to practical philosophy, where they provide the structure of rational faith. It is in this context that Kant claims to understand Plato better than Plato understood himself.[14]

Aristobulus, the first known Jewish philosopher, is said to have claimed that Plato knew the laws of Moses.[15] To be sure, the high point of medieval Jewish philosophy is often said to occur with Maimonides, who did not admire his more Platonic predecessors, and who affirmed as true every Aristotelian statement about the sublunar realm.[16] But, like other Arabic-speaking 'Aristotelians', there was more Platonism and neo-Platonism in Maimonides' view than he could have known, thanks to texts such as the *Theology of Aristotle*, actually an epitome of Plotinus' *Enneads*. Moreover, precisely because of Maimonides' self-professed Aristotelianism, Plato was favoured by those who opposed Maimonides' radical rationalism in the name of 'Kabbalah' or tradition received from an authoritative source.

The association with Platonism was reinforced during the Renaissance by Pico della Mirandola, who had an entire library of Kabbalistic texts translated from Hebrew and Aramaic, just as Marcilio Ficino had translated previously unknown Platonic texts. Both Kabbalah and Platonism were presented as *prisca theologia*, anticipating Christianity. Simultaneously, open practitioners of Judaism were expelled from the Iberian peninsula, revitalising Kabbalistic thought in Renaissance Italy, and the idea of an accord between Kabbalah and Platonism became more important to Kabbalistically inclined Jewish writers. Thus, Isaac Abarbanel, a distinguished Iberian Jew taking refuge in Italy, wrote that Jeremiah was Plato's teacher and it became commonplace to compare Platonic ideas to the Kabbalistic *sefirot*: the ten numbers or divine attributes mediating between the infinite and the created, finite world.[17] Even when new and less Platonic waves of Kabbalistic thinking spread from the Galilee throughout the Jewish world in the seventeenth century, they appeared initially in a neo-Platonic guise, both in the Jewish community beyond the land of Israel, and among the Christians who gained access to Kabbalistic works only in the late-seventeenth century, with the massive translation project of the *Kabbala Denudata*.[18] In the words of Abraham Herrera, author of one of the translated works, 'we follow our ḥakhamim or wise men sages and the Platonic philosophers who, being more divine [than the Peripatetics], are more in agreement with them.'[19]

It should hardly be surprising, then, that a Kantianism emphasising the transcendence of the senses in the name of the idea of the good has attracted Jewish philosophers, especially since Kant identifies the idea of the good with the idea of the law. Salomon Maimon and Hermann Cohen, two major Jewish philosophers who developed the Platonic aspect of Kantianism, were both admirers of Maimonides, but also both emphasised what they took to be the Platonic aspect of Maimonideanism, an aspect seen as consonant with the best of rabbinic thinking. I will characterise their principal contributions to Idealism before turning to the responses enabled by these developments to the Kantian challenge to Judaism.

For both Maimon and Cohen, the sticking point in Kant's philosophy was the innovative notion of space and time as *a priori* forms of sensible intuition. This played a central role in Kant's response to the problem of the heterogeneity between what is given to sense perception and what is intelligible to reason, a problem that must be overcome if we are to understand how modern natural science can apply mathematics in order to make what is given to sense perception intelligible. Early modern philosophers, seeking to ground a post-Copernican version of natural science in which mathematical theorising may override the immediate evidence of the senses, rejected the Aristotelian view that metaphysical structures, such as the relationship between substantial form and accidental quality, are latent within the content of sense perception, so that mere abstraction may render these structures available for cognition. Instead, in the early modern view, what is given to sense perception consists solely of sensible qualities, whose instantiations may be located within a spatio–temporal field characterisable by means of mathematics. However, a sensible world bereft of metaphysical structure also lacks any distinction between explanans and explanandum. Even if we could give a complete mathematical description of the universe as it alters over time, this would not suffice to yield a distinction between qualitative and substantial changes, or an account of the causal relations among alterations. Kant's solution to the problem of heterogeneity was to introduce an additional level of form. What is given to sense perception, in this view, is not mere cognitive matter, but rather matter informed by the *a priori* forms of human sensible intuition, and this additional level of spatio–temporal form provides the basis for the application of mathematics in a way that enables the development, not only of static geometry, but of dynamics and of physical theories that yield explanations exploiting metaphysical structure.

This is highly innovative. The form of sensible intuition is supposed to render matter intelligible, yet it does not meet all the traditional conditions of form. Spatio–temporal form has arbitrary features – space's three-dimensionality and Euclidean character, time's uni-directionality – that Kant explained as expressions of human finitude. But this satisfied neither Maimon nor Cohen. Maimon thought that Kant's account was closely tied to the geometric proof-method of construction in intuition. But, in contrast to conceptual methods, such proofs could show only *that* such-and-such is the case but not *why*. Geometry needed better methods and the application of geometry and calculus to what is given in sense perception depended on useful fictions. For Cohen, the notion of a form of sensible intuition – the intermediate level in what he takes to be Kant's three-fold account of the *a priori* – was all too susceptible to misinterpretation as a merely psychological feature of the human mind, a construal that would lead to an utter failure to address the problem of knowledge with which Kant is properly concerned.[20] Rudolf Hermann Lotze, a key figure in the period between Maimon's time and Cohen's, argued against what came to be called psychologism, although cognition requires psychic processes for its realisation and the psychological study of these processes is entirely valid, and that it is nevertheless a category mistake either to identify cognition with these processes or to explain the former in terms of the latter. Lotze urged a return to the seed of truth in Plato's theory of ideas.[21] Independently of Jewish philosophical tradition, there were reasons to renew Kantianism's Platonic side.

Maimon and Cohen differed in two main respects. First, Maimon was pessimistic as to whether the problem of the application of mathematics to what is given in sense perception could be solved, whereas Cohen, writing nearly a century later, thought that it *had* been solved. Second, Cohen rejected any use of the idea of God that threatened to undermine divine transcendence and the unbridgeable gap between divinity and humanity. Yet Maimon's solution, as we shall see, did just that. Notably, however, Maimon and Cohen both appealed to Maimonides' *Guide*. That is, each appealed to an aspect of the *Guide* often considered to contradict the aspect appealed to by the other.

In his *Essay on Transcendental Philosophy*, which deeply influenced the early development of German Idealism, Maimon drew a structural analogy between the major questions of Kant's transcendental deduction, of Cartesianism, and of Maimonides' encounter with Aristotelianism:

> If we want to consider the matter more carefully, we will find that the question *quid juris* [i.e., the question of the legitimacy of applying the forms of the understanding to what is sensibly given] is one and the same as the important question that has been treated by all previous philosophers, namely the explanation of the community between soul and body, or even as the explanation of the origination of the world (with respect to its matter) from an intelligence.[a,22]

Since all three questions ultimately concerned the heterogeneity of form and matter, and since he thought the Kantian solution by way of *a priori* forms

---

a. 'Wollen wir die Sache genauer betrachten, so werden wir finden, daß die Frage quid juris? mit der wichtigen Frage die alle Philosophen von jeher beschäftigt hat, nämlich die Erklärung der Gemeinschaft zwischen Seele und Körper, oder auch mit dieser, die Erklärung von Entstehung der Welt (ihrer Materie nach) von einer Intelligenz; einerlei ist.' Maimon, *Versuch*, 62–3.

of the matter of sense perception a failure, Maimon was free to attempt a solution modelled on Maimonides.

To be sure, the first step of Maimon's solution could hardly have been less Maimonidean. It was an attempt to explain the basic concept of calculus, the differential, by introducing *ideas of understanding*. Whereas Kant's ideas of reason are limit-concepts of the *identity* of a manifold of instances of the same concept, Maimon's ideas of understanding are limit-concepts of the difference between instantiating a quality and not instantiating it. But how are we to make sense of these differentials, which are no more given to sense perception than are instances of ideas of reason? We may treat differentials as grounds for the application of calculus, according to Maimon, only insofar as

> We assume an infinite understanding (at least as idea), for which the forms are at the same time objects of thought, or that produces out of itself all possible kinds of connections and relations of things (the ideas). Our understanding is just the same, only in a limited way.[b,23]

This idea of the infinite understanding emerges from what Maimon takes to be the three-fold unity of Kant's ideas of reason:

> We have here (if I may be permitted to use the expression) a trinity: God, the world, and the human soul. That is to say, if by world, we mean simply the intellectual world, i.e. the sum total of all possible objects that can be produced from all possible relations thought by an understanding; and if by soul, we mean an understanding (faculty of thinking) that relates itself to this world, so that all these possible relations can be thought by it; and if by God, we mean an understanding that actually thinks all these relations (I don't know what else I should think by *ens realissimum*), then these three things are the very same thing.[c,24]

b. 'Wir nehmen an (zum wenigsten als Idee) einen unendlichen Verstand, bei dem die Formen zugleich selbst Objekte des Denkens sind; oder der aus sich alle mögliche Arten, von Beziehungen und Verhältnissen der Dinge (der Ideen) hervorbringt. Unser Verstand ist eben derselbe, nur auf eine eingeschränkte Art.' *Ibid.*, 64–5.

c. 'Wir haben hier, (wenn mir der Ausdruck erlaubt ist) eine Dreieinigkeit: Gott, die Welt und die menschliche Seele, nämlich verstehen wir unter Welt bloß die intellektuelle Welt, d.h. den Inbegrif aller möglichen Objekte, die durch alle mögliche, von einem Verstande gedachten Verhältnisse hervorgebracht werden können, und unter Seele, ein Verstand, (Denkungsvermögen) daß sich darauf bezieht, so daß alle diese mögliche Verhältnisse von ihm gedacht werden können, unter Gott aber einen Verstand, der alle diese Verhältnisse wirklich denkt, (denn sonst weiß ich nicht, was ich unter *Ens realissimum* denken soll), so sind diese drei ein und eben dasselbe Ding.' *Ibid.*, 206.

Maimon clarified this idea in his commentary on what Maimonides called 'the dictum of the philosophers': '[God] is the intellect as well as the intellectually cognising subject and the intellectually cognized object, and . . . those three notions form in Him, may He be exalted, one single notion in which there is no multiplicity.'[25] This formula, according to Maimonides, applies to the human intellect when it is active. Maimon interpreted the formula in light of Kant's account of the *constitutive* role of the categories of the understanding: the categories are at once both concepts of the mind and features of reality insofar as the mind constitutes reality. Elsewhere Maimon stated that,

> *Creatio ex nihilo* is not altogether foreign to our concepts. We find this concept within ourselves, for the human mind can think *a priori* objects by means of the understanding, and give them *a priori* matter or present them as objects through the faculty of the pure imagination; it is only incapable of giving them *a posteriori* matter.[d]

Now, Maimon believed that the problem of the heterogeneity of sensibility and understanding – which Maimon calls the *questio quid juris* – could be solved only by means of the idea of an infinite, constitutive intellect of which the human intellect is a finite version. However, there was a further problem – the *questio quid facti* – concerning whether and to what extent such a solution is *applicable*. Taking a Platonic view, Maimon said that, 'We are godlike [in mathematics]', because the human intellect is constitutive in *pure* mathematics.[e] But in applied mathematics and physics, the idea of the constitutive intellect is a regulative goal which we can only approximate. Thus Maimon was a 'rational dogmatist' in his response to scepticism and in his application of this response to pure mathematics. But he was an 'empirical sceptic' in his rejection of the solution's application to natural science. Maimon summarised his position thus:

> Our talmudists (who, from time to time, have certainly produced thoughts worthy of a Plato) say, 'The students of wisdom find no rest, neither in this life nor yet in the life to come,' to which they relate, in

---

d. 'Das Erschaffen aus Nichts liegt nicht gänzlich ausser unsern Begriffen. Wir nehmen diesen Begriff aus uns selbst her, indem die menschliche Seele durch den Verstand Objekte *a priori*, d.h. die Form (aus sich selbst, welches, in Beziehung aufs Object, aus nichts heisst) denken, und durch die reine Einbildungskraft denselben *a priori* Materie geben, oder dieselben also Objekte darstellen kann; nur dass sie nicht im Stande ist, ihnen den Stoff *a posteriori* zu geben.' Maimon, *Philosophisches Wörterbuch* (Berlin: Unger, 1792), 31 [my translation].

e. 'Wir sind hierin Gott ähnlich.' Maimon, *Streifereien im Gebiete der Philosophie* (Berlin: Vieweg, 1793), 20 [my translation].

their own way, the words of the Psalmists, 'They go from power to power, appear before the Lord in Zion'.[f,26]

Almost a century later, Cohen arrived independently at a somewhat similar view: an adequate solution of the *questio quid juris* concerning the justification of human knowledge would require the overcoming of Kant's notion of the *a priori* forms of sensibility and the development of a more Platonic interpretation of calculus as the transcendence of sensibility. However, Cohen believed that the mathematical work of Augustin Cournot had now enabled this interpretation.[27] At the same time, only an adequately scientific Idealism could enable a proper understanding of the idea of the differential or of the infinitesimal, regarded – in the way that Cohen thought every proper idea should be regarded – as an *hypothesis* or ground-laying, and as a *method*.[28]

Ultimately, Cohen characterised the method at work in calculus and in modern natural science at its best in terms of what he calls *the principle of origin*: '*Only thought itself can produce what can count as being*'.[29] The principle rules out any contribution from an independent faculty of sensibility. Positively, it emphasises the methodological role of infinite judgements, in which thought gives itself a direction for the determination of something by delimitation, by negating some privation in a way that situates thought's subject matter without yet fully determining it. This is not *creatio ex nihilo*, but it is perhaps *creatio ab nihilo*.[30] Pure, methodological thought starts from some particular nothing – from some particular puzzle, raised perhaps with respect to some particular set of sense perceptions, and it determines its further direction by asking, not in the first place 'what is it?', but rather 'what is it not?'[31] Only by means of delimitation can thought find its way towards a positive determination. The infinitesimal method of modern natural science exemplifies the principle by asking after the infinitesimal difference between what is and what is not – in other words, by asking 'What is not what "it" is?' in a mathematical way that sets thought on the path to the application of mathematics to the 'it' in question.

The most important difference between them is the fact that Cohen would have rejected Maimon's appeal to the three-fold unity of intellect, intellectually cognising subject and intellectually cognised object. In

f. 'Unsere Talmudisten (die gewiß zuweilen Gedanken geäussert haben, die eines Plato würdig sind) sagen: "Die Schüler der Weisheit finden keine Ruhe, weder in diesem noch in dem künftigen Leben"; worauf sie nach ihrer Weise die Worte des Psalmisten (84,8) beziehen: "sie wallen von Kraft zur Kraft, erscheinen vor der Allmacht in Zion".' Maimon, *Versuch*, 444, citing TB Berakhot, 64a/Moed Katan, 29a and Ps.84:8.

an essay on Maimonides' ethics, interpreted as more Platonic than Aristotelian, Cohen said of the dictum of the philosophers, 'this equation proves meaningful not only with reference to God: pantheism applies it to human reasoning.'[g,32] The positive characterisation of God as three-fold intellectual unity appeared to conflict with Maimonides' argument that we may appropriately ascribe to God only negations of privations – in Cohen's terms, we may make only infinite judgements – and that we may make no positive judgements about God, with the sole exception of judgements ascribing attributes of action, whose purpose is not the determination of the divine essence, but rather the determination of human action. To identify the human intellect with the divine intellect, even in part, and to identify the ground of the intelligible with theoretical intellect, would undermine reason's role in the determination of what ought to be and to be done, and it would undermine God's role in underwriting reason. Since Cohen regarded Maimonides as the principal exponent of Jewish monotheism, which was opposed not only to polytheism but also to the pantheism into which it may be tempted to slip, Cohen presumably followed those commentators who think that Maimonides merely cites the dictum in order to apply it to the human intellect *in actu*, not to endorse its application to God.

In Cohen's view, monotheism involved commitment to the uniqueness and incomparability of God. While this commitment is in no sense an exclusive possession of the Jewish people, Judaism is historically the site of the origination of this commitment and the history of Judaism, more than of any other religious tradition, is the history of steadfast loyalty to it. Only monotheism – preserved in its purity by Judaism at its best – can save Idealism and can thereby enable a genuinely scientific philosophy. If polytheism is incompatible with the systematic unity demanded by reason, then pantheism – and, for that matter, panentheism – is incompatible with the very possibility of ethics, another necessity of reason. For there can be no ethics without the distinction between being and what ought to be, and this distinction is best grounded in the distinction between everything that is and God.

Maimon accepted Spinoza's and Kant's view that Judaism is essentially a legal system that somehow survived the state's destruction. Consequently, Maimon saw no reason why, just as he could opt to leave one state for another, he should not be permitted to leave the Jewish virtual state for a

---

g. 'Diese Identität hat nicht nur für Gott eigentlichen Sinn; und der Pantheismus macht sie auf die menschliche Vernunft anwendbar.' Cohen, *Charakteristik des Ethik Maimunis*, 118.

different one. Alas, no state would give him civil rights. In effect, however, Maimon abandoned Judaism for the republic of letters. Lazarus Bendavid, friend of Maimon and student of Kant, proposed instead that, in exchange for civil rights, Jews should give up the 'ceremonial law', while retaining Jewish monotheism and its prophetic articulation.[33] Kant misunderstood this as a call for Jews to publicly adopt the religion of Jesus, if not of Christ, but it was actually an early expression of Reform Judaism.[34] One of early Reform's central ideas was the identity of prophetic ethics with Kant's ethics of autonomy.

Hermann Cohen is perhaps the movement's most intellectually significant representative. But his version of Kantian Judaism was more sensitive to Jewish tradition than most. Cohen had at first been attracted to a cruder view. Notwithstanding his traditional training for the rabbinate, he had secured his appointment as the first Jewish philosophy professor in Germany by assuring Friedrich Albert Lange that, 'what you call Christianity I call prophetic Judaism'.[35] He had proposed radical changes in Jewish practice and called for 'the dissolution of religion into ethics'.[h] Cohen's mature view, however, granted religion, if not full independence, then at least its own 'peculiarity' [*Eigenart*] as a dimension of ethical life, and his account of Judaism as pure monotheism distinguished it sharply from Christianity, since incarnationism was a way-station on the road from the Philonic logos to Spinozistic and Hegelian pantheism. He also found a more rational grounding for traditional Jewish observance, to which he claimed always having been emotionally attached.

Cohen sharply criticised Moritz Lazarus' *Ethics of Judaism*, an apologetic work that identifies the rabbinic preference for the performance of divine commandments for their own sake (*lishmah*) with the ethics of autonomy. Lazarus responded to Eduard von Hartmann's assertion that any theistic ethics must be incompatible with autonomy:[36]

> The moral principle is, indeed, not above and not beside the Divine Being; it is in itself. Precisely for that reason it is at the same time God – in God inasmuch as he is the prototype of morality. To repeat: not because the principle is in God is it the moral principle, but because it is the moral principle, in itself and absolutely, therefore it is necessarily in God.[i,37]

---

h. 'Auflösung in die Ethik'. Cohen, *Der Begriff der Religion im System der Philosophie* (Giessen: Töppelman, 1915), 42 [my translation].
i. 'Nein, nicht über und nicht neben dem göttlichen Wesen ist das Moralprincip; es ist in sich selbst, aber eben deshalb ist es zugleich in Gott, in Gott, weil und in wie fern er das Urbild aller

Cohen, however, regarded this formulation – along with Lazarus' general manner – as both philosophically sloppy and insensitive to the distinctive features of Judaism. For Lazarus, morality was in 'the ethical man' just as it was in God, except that God was the archetype. But this is analogous to the position of those who say that active intellect is in the human just as it is in God, except that it is in God without limit. It is analogous, in short, to Maimon's position. Christians may speak of God as the archetype but this is because they think of Christ as the archetype of the moral disposition that has taken human form. Cohen did not regard this as a possible Jewish view and he thought that Lazarus had failed to explain the notion of autonomy.

For Cohen, the notion of autonomy was primarily methodological: like any region of life in which reason has a share, ethics must be established in its own terms, and it must have a pure origin. Thus, ethical norms could have no extra-ethical source, whether sensuous or divine, in the same way that cognitive norms could have no extra-cognitive source. But this did not mean that the idea of God had no role to play. As we have seen, Cohen thought that divine immanence – and, indeed, any mediation of divine transcendence – undermined ethics. But divine transcendence was also a threat: if the idea of the good wholly transcended the sensible world, then how could we reasonably hope to realise it? To solve this problem, Cohen corrected Kantian ethics in two ways, both drawing upon Judaism.

First, Cohen was dissatisfied by Kant's appeal to 'the fact of reason' in order to demonstrate the actuality of our capacity to act ethically. Cohen objected to the very idea of appeal to a feature of the subject, whether an innate capacity or an actual demonstration. Just as a scientific critique of cognition must take its cue from objective scientific cognition, in other words, from pure natural science, so a scientific critique of ethics must take its cue from the pure aspect of some objective ethical science. Thus, in his *Ethics of the Pure Will*, Cohen replaced the fact of reason by the pure science of jurisprudence. Finally, law – valorised by rabbinic Judaism and denigrated by Paul – would receive its philosophical due.

Second, the proper role of the idea of God is to orient ethics towards the goal of a society governed in accordance with the ideal legal system and to ground faith in progress towards that goal. With Maimonides, we may

Sittlichkeit ist; und ich muss noch einmal wiederholen: Nicht weil das Princip in Gott ist, deshalb ist es das Moralprincip, sondern weil es das Moralprincip auch an sich und ganz absolut ist, deshalb ist es nothwendig in Gott.' Lazarus, *Ethik*, 101.

negate any privation with respect to God, and we may take this to mean that God is the pure origin of the pertinent positive attribute, the guarantor of its realisability. The relationship between the human and the divine is best expressed, neither as transcendence nor as immanence, but rather as *correlation*. Guarantor of the distinction between what is and what ought to be, and underwriter of faith in the coming of what ought to be, the divine will must remain both distinct from and yet in intimate relation to the human.[38] Creation, revelation and redemption are explained in terms of correlation. Redemption is the correlation between the divine and human wills, in which the commandment to become holy – to realise the divine will in the present – implicates human agency in the realisation of the messianic age. This age should be understood, not as a moment that will at some point come to be present, but rather as a futural reality – in rabbinic terminology, the world to come (*olam ha-ba*) – that is correlated with each present moment. When, and only when, a just society no longer needed the Jewish people as witness, Jewish particularity would have served its purpose. Meanwhile, the Jewish notion of correlation is an essential safeguard against the threat to reason posed by the identification or mediation of the divine and the human.

In Cohen's wake, scions of two rabbinic dynasties developed neo-Kantian versions of orthodox Judaism. Isaac Breuer, pioneer of the Agudat Yisrael movement and grandson of Samson Raphael Hirsch who founded German–Jewish separatist orthodoxy, explored the necessary conditions for the possibility of jurisprudential science and argued that the Kantian idea of the moral law was the highest ethical norm intelligible to unaided human reason. Yet that idea was empty. Only a substantive law given by the creator of nature as the founding norm of a nation, thereby empowered to articulate and implement that law, could fill the void.[39] Joseph Dov Soloveitchik, leader of American modern orthodoxy and grandson of Ḥayyim Soloveitchik who founded the dominant school of Talmudic analysis, set out to write his dissertation on Maimonides' Platonism but instead produced one on Cohen's philosophy of science. Soloveitchik said, glossing Maimonides, that 'every cognitive act is an infinitesimal participation in the Deity's infinite understanding'.[40] In a Copernican turn indebted to Cohen, however, the exemplary object of this cognition is not the real structure of the physical world, but the ideal, normative structure of the world of practice studied by Talmudists. This Platonic domain is significant because of what Breuer calls 'cosmonomy': the lawgiver is also the creator, who delegates ethical creativity to humans.

9.3 Jacobi, Luria and Kabbalistic realism

A Kabbalist pioneered the Kantian defence of traditional Judaism. *The Book of the Covenant*, by the otherwise obscure Pinchas Eliyahu Horowitz, includes a Kabbalistic anthropology, along with information about contemporaneous science, and a virulent attack on medieval Jewish philosophy. After rebutting arguments that Jews are obligated to justify their faith philosophically, the author introduced an unprecedented blow against the philosophers. Kant had shown that human beings are incapable of metaphysical knowledge and that, for any proof of a metaphysical thesis, an equally compelling proof of a counter-thesis can be given. Maimon's attempt to save Leibniz' doctrine of monads from Kant's critique of metaphysics in his commentary to Maimonides' *Guide*, was rebutted.[41]

Unable to read Maimon's German-language *Essay*, Horowitz did not understand that Maimon conceived infinitesimals as ideas of the understanding that could be justified transcendentally insofar as they enabled the application of mathematics to that which is given to the senses. Horowitz composed a grateful prayer for Kant's *Critique of Pure Reason*:

> When this book and its subject matter became known to me, I lifted up my hands to God the Most High and I said, 'Blessed be the All-encompassing, blessed be He, that the time and the season has arrived to remove the ways of reflection from the land, and the proofs of the philosophers will be entirely cut off even among the nations, and truth will spring forth from the land and righteousness from the heavens, to repair the world in faith and in knowledge of God from received traditions [*ha-mekubalot*] and from what has been transmitted from fathers to the hearts of their children'.[42]

Probably thanks to Horowitz, Kant's antinomies were mentioned in *Life of Man*, Abraham Danzig's summation of Jewish law, which rejected Maimonides' view that Jews are obliged to *know* that God exists and is one *by means of demonstrative proof*. Since Kant had shown that metaphysics is antinomic, demonstrative proof was useless, and faith should be based on traditions (*mekubalot*).[43]

So far, 'Kabbalah' meant Jewish tradition in general and it was defended by appeal to Kant's critique of rational metaphysics. A philosophically richer sense of Kabbalah and its relation to Idealism is found in the Spinozism controversy instigated in 1785 by Friedrich Heinrich Jacobi in his *Letters to Herr Moses Mendelssohn concerning the Doctrine of Spinoza*, which was – along with

Kant's *Critique* – one of the principal sources of post-Kantian Idealism.[44] Jacobi claimed first-hand knowledge of the scandalous fact that Lessing, Mendelssohn's friend, was a self-confessed Spinozist. If Jacobi hinted in his book at a Spinozistic reading of Kant, he also sought in correspondence to recruit Kant as an ally against the moderate rationalism of Mendelssohn, which Jacobi thought could only lead – if articulated consistently and honestly – to the horrors of Spinozism.[45] In other words, Mendelssohn and others who claimed to reconcile rationalism with theism were either fools or liars. It was in this context that Kant acquired widespread fame, when Reinhold presented Kantian rational faith as resolving the dispute between Jacobi and Mendelssohn. Reinhold's attempt to reconstruct the foundations of Kantian faith in a way that would meet the Spinozistic demand for a rigorous system produced the pioneering version of German Idealism.

In the reported conversation with Lessing, Jacobi presented three positions: two positions between which Lessing vacillated – both equally harmful to religion, ethics and, in general, rational agency – and Jacobi's radical alternative. Remarkably, *Jacobi presented each of the three positions in Kabbalistic terms.* To understand why, we must recall that, in the course of the seventeenth and early-eighteenth centuries, European Jewry had been transformed by Kabbalistic thought and practice, which were no longer the esoteric possession of an elite. Moreover, a central aspect of the Renaissance had been the emergence of Christian interest in Kabbalah, which was thought to contain the same *prisca theologia* as the Platonic texts imported from Byzantium. In the sixteenth century major Kabbalistic developments were associated with Moses Cordovero and Isaac Luria and their circles in Safed and in the seventeenth century these new ideas swept European Jewry. By the early eighteenth century, the rationalist tradition of Maimonides and his successors had become marginal. So-called Lurianic Kabbalah was in effect Judaism's official theology. These two trends – the Kabbalisation and Lurianisation of Judaism, and the development of Christian Kabbalism – met in *Kabbala Denudata*, a library of Zoharic and Lurianic texts translated into Latin by Christian Knorr von Rosenroth and published with texts by Henry More and Franciscus Mercurius van Helmont. Thus, a century before the Spinozism controversy, Lurianic Kabbalah had become the vital source of Jewish ideas and was well known to European intellectuals. This was the context in which Spinoza's philosophy had been received and Jacobi could assume that Lessing and others would share the idea that Spinoza was in some sense a Kabbalist.[46]

As it first became known to Christian scholars such as Pico della Miran-dola during the Renaissance, Kabbalah was a Platonic – or, rather, neo-Platonic – tradition. Lurianic Kabbalah was also initially published within a broadly neo-Platonic framework, thanks to the influential but obscure Israel Sarug. His student, Abraham Herrera, a former *converso* educated in Christian philosophy and theology, wrote *Gates of Heaven*, the most extensive and sophisticated neo-Platonic exposition of Lurianic Kabbalah, which was translated in *Kabbala Denudata*. However, Lurianic Kabbalah could not fit within a neo-Platonic framework without distortion.

The mythic, Lurianic narrative, which focused to an unprecedented extent on what precedes creation, involved the following elements, all of which left their mark on German Idealism. First, the divinity in itself or the infinite (*eyn sof*) was understood as overwhelming force not only to create but also to destroy.[47] Second, there could be no creation of a finite other and no revelation to a finite other without the self-negation of divine negativity – without withdrawal, contraction or veiling (*tsimtsum*). Lurianic Kabbalists continued to speak of emanation (*atsilut*), but their understanding differed from the neo-Platonic conception of creation and revelation as overflow from the overwhelmingly positive One. Third, the immediate consequence of the divine will to reveal itself was the form to which human beings should aspire. In neo-Platonism, this form was perfect wisdom. However, in Lurianic thought, it is the supernal human (*adam elyon*) who is, in its immediate version, incapable of stably embodying divine negativity. Thus, the breaking of the vessels (*shevirat ha-kelim*) was a primordial 'event' manifesting this incapacity and provided the basis for the origin of evil within the world.[48] Fourth, moreover, human beings had a central role: it was up to humans, not only to perfect themselves and the world they inhabit but also to perfect the supernal human form in an act of reparation (*tikkun*) through which alone divinity could fully realise itself. Accordingly, human history acquired an importance entirely missing from the neo-Platonic picture. Our current, materially embodied existence was not merely a degradation from which we must seek to return to our true, spiritual essence. Rather, it was the arena within which divine revelation must occur, and this revelation required human beings to develop adequate relations of reciprocal recognition, not only within human society but also between aspects of the divine structure – the visages or configurations (*partsufim*) – that alone could constitute the stable embodiment of divine negativity knowing itself by means of its other.

This background illuminates the three Kabbalistic positions sketched by Jacobi. The first is the demythologised position that Jacobi associated with

Spinoza. It resembles neo-Platonism insofar as the infinite one (Spinoza's substance) gives rise immediately to infinite form (the infinitely many infinite attributes) of which the many finite things, understood *sub specie aeternitatis*, are derivative. However, unlike the neo-Platonists, Spinoza – as Jacobi (mis)understood him – conceived the infinite one as indeterminate and the finite many as determinate only in virtue of negation, hence as *non-entia*.[49] The specification of infinite attributes and the determination of particular modes of these attributes were understood as delimitations of infinite substance, hence as manifestations of a *tsimtsum* that was no event.

The second, naturalistic position deploys *tsimtsum* in order to view the universe as a single. The concept is used to overcome a tension involving divine infinity and finitude: say, the possibility of God dwelling in a particular sanctuary, or the possibility of anything finite co-existing with the infinite. The divine capacity for self-limiting – for contracting into or out of a space – without compromising infinity is supposed to resolve the tension. In Lessing's naturalistic version, the world is the organic body of the world-soul, which must periodically contract and expand.[50] The focus is on the cycle of what Kabbalists call *histalkut* (withdrawal) and *hitpashtut* (expansion), not on *tsimtsum* as its primordial ground.[51]

Jacobi also characterised the third position, which was his alternative to the first two, in Kabbalistic terms. He reported advocating to Lessing

> the Kibbel, or the kabbalah in the *strict sense* – that is, *taking as starting point the view* that it is impossible, in and for itself, to derive the infinite from a given finite, or to define the transition from the one to the other, or their proportion, through any formula whatever. Hence, if anyone wants to say anything on the subject, one must speak on the basis of revelation.[j,52]

Through an entirely mundane revelation,

> we know that we have a body, and that there are other bodies and other thinking beings outside us . . . we become aware of *other actual things*, and, of that with the very same certainty with which we become aware of ourselves, for without the *You*, the *I* is impossible.[k,53]

j. 'Ich nahm daher Gelegenheit für das Kibbel, oder die Cabbalam *im eigenlichsten Sinne, aus dem Gesichtspunkte* zu reden: dass es an und für sich selbst unmöglich sey, das Unendliche aus dem Endlichen zu entwickeln, und den Übergang des einen zu dem andern, oder ihre Proportion, durch irgend eine Formel heraus zu bringen; folglich, wenn man etwas darüber sagen wollte, so müsste man aus Offenbarung reden.' Jacobi, *Über die Lehre*, 34.

k. 'Wissen wir, dass wir einen Körper haben, und dass ausser uns andre Körper und andre denkende Wesen vorhanden sind . . . werden wir . . . andre *würkliche Dinge* gewahr, und zwar mit

This anticipates theistic revelation, which also essentially involves Kabbalah in the specific sense of *being the recipient of a second person address*. Here, *tsimtsum* is the self-restraint required both to communicate and to receive communication.

Each of the Kabbalistic positions sketched by Jacobi contributed to German Idealism. In a clear allusion to Jacobi's thesis that 'the philosophy of the kabbalah is...undeveloped or newly confused Spinozism',[l,54] Maimon wrote that,

> In fact, the kabbalah is nothing but expanded Spinozism, in which not only is the origin of the world explained by the limitation of the divine being, but also the origin of every kind of being, and its relation to the rest, is derived from a separate attribute of God. God as the ultimate subject and the ultimate cause of all beings, is called *Ensoph* (the Infinite, of which, considered in itself, nothing can be predicated). But in relation to the infinite number of beings, positive attributes are ascribed to him; these are reduced by the Kabbalists to ten, which are called the ten *Sefirot*.[m,55]

Maimon explained *tsimtsum*, not as a primordial event, but as the limitation of the divine being whereby the world originates from its infinite ground. In Hegel, we may perhaps find a similarly demythologised version of *tsimtsum* as the negation of the negation that enables determinacy in the realm of logic, which consists of 'God as he is in his eternal essence before the creation of nature and of a finite spirit'.[n,56] However, Hegel also developed a version of the Lurianic *shevirat ha-kelim*: the dialectical instability of the immediate, which is the origin of a reparative history that is no mere return to an initial state.

eben der Gewissheit, mit der wir uns selbst gewahr werden; denn ohne *Du*, ist das *Ich* unmöglich.' *Ibid.*, 162–3.

l. 'Die Cabalistische Philosophie, so viel davon der Untersuchung offen lieft, und nach ihren besten Commentatoren, von Helmont dem Jüngeren und Wachter, ist, *als Philosophie*, nichts anders, als unentwickelter, oder neu verworrener Spinozismus.' *Ibid.*, 171.

m. 'In der Tat ist die Kabbala nichts anderes als erweiterter Spinozismus, worin nicht nur die Entstehung der Welt aus der Einschränkung des göttlichen Wesens überhaupt erklärt, sondern auch die Entstehung einer jeden Art von Wesen und ihr Verhältnis zu allen übrigen aus einer besonderen Eigenschaft Gottes hergeleitet wird. Gott als das letzte Subjekt und die letzte Ursache aller Wesen heißt En-ßof (das Unendliche, wovon an sich betrachtet nichts prädiziert werden kann). In Beziehung auf die unendlichen Wesen aber werden ihm positive Eigenschaften beigelegt, diese werden von den Kabbalisten auf zehn reduziert, welche die zehn Sephirot genannt werden.' Maimon, *Lebensgeschichte*, I, 141.

n. 'Die Darstellung Gottes...wie er in seinem ewigen Wesen, vor dem Erschaffen der Natur und eines endlichen Geistes ist.' Hegel, *WdL*, HW, XXI, 34.

In his philosophy of nature, Schelling developed Lessing's naturalistic position. He explicitly cited Jacobi's report when he said in 1797 that, 'it is only the freedom of our volition that supports the entire system of our representations, and the world itself consists only of this expansion and contraction of the spirit'.[o,57] His argument began with the Jacobian rejection of any transition between the finite and the infinite. It proceeded to the Fichtean notion that spirit is at once both infinite and finite, or is rather the reciprocal relation of infinite or limit-transgressing and self-limiting activities. And it concluded with a conception of everything natural as the manifestation of the reciprocity of these two activities, striving towards self-organisation and, ultimately, self-consciousness.

According to the third Kabbalistic position, revelation is the touchstone of the *realism* that Idealism is supposed to enable. One crucial example must suffice. In letters to Jacobi accompanying his *Foundations of Natural Right*, Fichte claimed to have finally attained complete agreement with Jacobi's realism.[58] In Fichte's transcendental idiom, Jacobi's requirement to speak of the infinite only on the basis of revelation became the thesis that *a summons by another* is a necessary condition for coming-to-be a rational agent.

Fichte's argument exhibits the structure of *tsimtsum*. The infinity of the I can co-exist with its finitude, as divine infinity can co-exist with finitude, only through self-limitation. However, unlike the divinity that gives birth to itself, I can come into being as self-limiting only insofar as I find myself addressed in the second person by another who self-limits by foregoing the use of force in order to enter the realm of communication. Regardless of the content of any particular summons, what is given in the event of the summons is the unavoidability of responsiveness, on which is grounded both the legitimacy of law and the freedom of the individual will.[59]

When he broke with Fichte, Schelling moved in a recognisably Lurianic direction. Seeking to explain what creation must be if the freedom to do evil is to be possible, Schelling resolved the Jacobian problem differently in 1804: 'In a word, there is no continuous transition from the Absolute to the actual; the origin of the phenomenal world is conceivable only as a complete falling-away from absoluteness by means of a leap'.[p,60] Thus the fall of the human is an image of the fall that is creation itself, which is an exile

o. 'Nur die Freiheit unseres Wollens ist es, was das ganze System unserer Vorstellungen trägt, und die Welt selbst besteht nur in dieser Expansion und Contraktion des Geistes.' Schelling, SSW, I, 396.
p. 'Mit Einem Wort, vom Absoluten zum Wirklichen gibt es keinen stetigen Uebergang, der Ursprung der Sinnenwelt ist nur als ein vollkommenes Abbrechen von der Absolutheit, durch einen Sprung, denkbar.' Schelling, SSW, VI, 38.

of divinity from the world, demanding reparation. Schelling took a further step in 1809, when he considered divinity *prior* to creation. If the freedom to do evil is to be possible, then there must be a dark ground that is in the One but that is not (yet) the One: the yearning of the One to give birth to itself, to reveal itself, to become God.[61] *Ground* must be distinguished from *existence* and freedom originates in the tension between them. All creatures, insofar as they exhibit this tension, contain both the will to unity and the possibility of an alienation of this will from its proper end, an alienation that amounts to disease when the life of the part no longer serves the life of the whole. Only the human being is the image of God whereby revelation is accomplished and in the human being alone is this tension capable of giving rise to evil: an individual will that perversely opposes the proper end of the whole. Schelling then argued that creation, insofar as it arises from the One's yearning to give birth to itself, can only be thought as a 'contraction' or 'self-restriction' of divinity.[62] In various versions of the *Philosophy of the World-Ages*, Schelling sought an adequate narrative form for an account of this primordial event – from which the natural cycles of contraction and expansion are derivative.

In light of Kabbalah's impact on Idealism, it is not surprising that Jewish philosophers, especially those with Kabbalistic backgrounds, recognised in Idealism a kindred spirit. At the beginning, Maimon served as a mediator. Thus Naḥman Krochmal responded to a request for help in understanding the Kantian categories by recommending Maimon's commentary on the unity of the intellect with its activity and its objects.[63] Although he officially endorsed the pre-Kabbalistic philosophy of Abraham ibn Ezra, Krochmal drew both on Idealism and on traditional Jewish sources. He ascribed to ibn Ezra the Idealist distinction between sensuous representation, reflection and concepts or ideas, which he designated with names of sefirot: *da'at*, *binah* and *hokhmah*.[64] He also ascribed to him belief in creation by *tsimtsum*, which he distinguished from *creatio ex nihilo*, as well as a distinction between essence (*etsem*) and form (*tsurah*) resembling Schelling's distinction between ground and existence.[65]

For Krochmal, the perplexity of the age was historicism: if every civilisation was eventually superseded, how could Judaism survive as anything other than a curiosity? Drawing on Hegel as well as the tradition that each of the nations had been assigned a guardian angel that it could mistake for a god, Krochmal argued that all nations were revelations of spirit, and all were subject to the law of rise and decline governing organisms. Through the Jewish people alone, thanks to their pure monotheism, was *absolute* spirit revealed, and it alone could survive successive cycles without ever succumbing. Krochmal declared Judaism – not Christianity or post-Christian modernity – the absolute religion, which should be universal.

Fifty years later, Elijah Benamozegh employed Idealist resources to defend Kabbalah's most decisive departure from Platonism: its contention that human activity can repair not only the world (*tikkun olam*) but also divinity itself (*yiḥud ha-Shem*, unification of the Name). Benamozegh cited Fichte's argument that the infinite will legislating the moral law also constitutes a supernatural world, and that within this world finite wills are bound by a universal law – equivalent to the law of gravity in the natural world – according to which each act that conforms to duty has immediate consequences for every other finite will.[66] He emended Fichte's view in one respect: human beings not only 'give strength to God' when they act well; they also weaken divine power when they act badly.[67] Benamozegh also argued that Judaism already had a universal dimension: the seven laws of the Noachide covenant. Jews needed additional laws because of their special mission to humanity. But universal religion comprised the Noachide laws, interpreted Kabbalistically.

Jacobi's third position – 'Kabbalah in the strict sense' of second-personal interaction – was developed in the dialogical philosophies of Buber and Rosenzweig. Buber began his account of the dialogical principle's history with an early letter in which Jacobi passed from the existence of the external world to immediate encounter with a finite second person as a 'source of life' and thence to immediate encounter with the divine. Here Jacobi articulated the divine need for the finite other in terms that must have resonated with Buber's Hasidic background: 'If You were One without number, You would be without life, without love, without power and seeds.'[q,68] Buber characterised Hasidic tales as folk embodiments of Kabbalah: 'the myth of I and You, of the caller and the called, the finite which enters into the infinite and the infinite which has need of the finite'.[r,69] He clarified later that every I–You encounter involved *tsimtsum*.

Rosenzweig was the first to draw explicitly the connection between Idealism and Kabbalah. In the 1917 letter containing the 'germ-cell' of his *Star of Redemption*,[70] he noted the affinity between Schelling's 'dark ground' and Lurianic *tsimtsum*, and later called the *Star* an attempt to fulfil Schelling's

---

q. 'Wenn Du Eins wärest ohne Zahl, so wärest Du ohne Leben, ohne Liebe, ohne Macht und Saamen.' Jacobi, *Auserlesener Briefwechsel*, Friedrich Roth (ed.) (Leipzig: Fleischer, 1825), I, 331 [my translation].

r. 'Die Legende ist der Mythos des Ich und Du, des Berufenen und des Berufenden, des Endlichen, der ins Unendliche eingeht, und des Unendlichen, der des Endlichen bedarf.' Martin Buber, *Die Legende des Baalschem* (Frankfurt a.M.: Rütten and Loening, 1908), vi–vii.

prophecy of a 'narrative philosophy'.[71] However, in its aspiration to systematicity, the *Star* was deeply responsive to Hegel. Like his teacher, Cohen, Rosenzweig believed that the encounter with Idealism could solicit from Judaism a fruitful justification of its role in modernity. But he also believed that Judaism, alongside Christianity with which it has a complex and dynamic relationship, could complete Idealism's response to Jacobi, by developing a rigorous system that avoids pantheism and enables freedom. According to Rosenzweig, such a system will be achieved only insofar as God the creator lovingly reveals God-self to the human being, who responds, not only as an individual, but also by recognising other individuals in neighbourly love, and insofar as all individuals collectively recognise God.[72] Philosophy can articulate this system but it can be realised only in the redemptive fulfilment of prophetic promise. Only then will it be resolved whether this fulfilment takes the form expected by Christians or that expected by Jews. Until then, Jews and Christians should play their equally necessary roles in the economy of revelation, separated by an unavoidable 'enmity', yet intimately linked in ways that could be as fruitful as Rosenzweig's relationships with his Christian interlocutors.

In an influential exchange, Rosenzweig acknowledged Buber's achievement: by insisting that Torah is not only law but – and, indeed, more literally – 'teaching' and by showing in the case of Hasidism that Jewish teaching is spiritually vibrant, Buber had liberated modern Judaism from the embarrassment of having to justify itself on Kant's terms by showing that, despite appearances, it is an expression of individual autonomy.[73] Yet Buber retained one Kantian prejudice of nineteenth-century Reform Judaism: he could not admit that traditional Jewish observance was also capable of spiritual vitality. For Buber, the regularisation of practice ossified past I–You encounters and blocked new ones. Rosenzweig, however, argued that the challenge of Jewish observance is to transform law (*Gesetz*) into command (*Gebot*, *mitsvah*), which has an I–You structure. He compared the regularised covenantal relationship to marriage. Both have an I–You interior that is invisible from a third-person perspective, and both challenge their participants to sanctify the everyday in the name of love. This has reversed Reform Judaism's original hostility to traditional practice.

Rosenzweig's *Star* is present in Lévinas' *Totality and Infinity* 'too often to be cited'.[74] Instead of seeking systematicity, however, Lévinas sought to de-privilege metaphysics, including its Idealist versions. He insisted on the primacy of an ethics of the other inspired by Rosenzweig and articulated Kabbalistically. Like Cohen, he saw in the Platonic idea of the good beyond being 'the most profound teaching, the definitive teaching, not of theology, but of philosophy'.[75] However, separation should not be regarded neo-Platonically, as degradation. Rather, infinity contracts to leave room for separation; separate beings, turned towards the infinite, form a society; and thus 'Man redeems creation'. De-ontologising Kabbalistic terms, Lévinas sought to develop an ethics modelled on Judaism, but valid for theists *and atheists*, hence truly universal.

9.4 Conclusion

Jewish philosophers have drawn upon Idealism to defend Judaism against the Idealist challenge. To the charge that Judaism is an enslavement deceptively resembling genuine freedom, Platonically inclined Jewish post-Kantians (e.g., Cohen, Breuer and Soloveitchik) have argued that the Mosaic law expresses a monotheism that alone can save the distinction, essential to reason, between 'is' and 'ought'. Kabbalistically inclined Jewish philosophers (e.g., Krochmal, Benamozegh, Rosenzweig) have contended that the Hegelian conception of freedom as collective participation in divine liberation applies at least as well to Judaism as to Christianity or to modernity. To the accusation that Judaism is overly particular, some (e.g., Krochmal) have responded that, in the messianic age, it will be universal, and others (e.g., Cohen) that it will be transcended. Others (e.g. Benamozegh) have argued that Judaism already has a universal, Noachide dimension or (e.g., Rosenzweig) that Judaism can already acknowledge Christianity's special mission. Thanks to Buber and Rosenzweig, the dialogical commandment has displaced the ancient idea of Torah as law. These responses have been possible insofar as Jewish philosophy has enriched Idealism, by supplying or helping to develop some of its central ideas. Refined in Idealism's crucible, these ideas could then be re-appropriated for Judaism's defence against supersession by modernity. Judaism's continuing contributions to Idealism are arguably the best demonstrations of its continued vitality.[76]

Notes

1. Jürgen Habermas, 'Der deutsche Idealismus der jüdischen Philosophen', in *Philosophisch-Politische Profile* (Frankfurt a.M.: Suhrkamp, 1981), 39–64; English translation: *Philosophical–Political Profiles*, trans Frederick G. Lawrence (Cambridge, MA: MIT, 1985), 21–43.

2. My argument develops and supplements Habermas' answer, which focuses on the Kabbalistic aspect alone. See Habermas, 'Der deutsche Idealismus', 39–40: 'Weil schon in den Idealismus selber kabbalistisches Erbe eingeströmt und von ihm aufgesogen ist, scheint sich dessen Licht im Spektrum eines Geistes um so reicher zu brechen, indem etwas vom Geist der jüdischen Mystik, wie immer sich selbst auch verborgen, noch fortlebt'; trans. in 'German Idealism', 37–59: [Because the legacy of the Kabbalah already flowed into and was absorbed by Idealism, its light seemed to refract all the more richly in the spectrum of a spirit in which something of the spirit of Jewish mysticism lives on, in however hidden a way.] For discussion, see P. Franks, 'Inner anti-Semitism or Kabbalistic legacy? German Idealism's relationship to Judaism', in *International Yearbook of German Idealism*, VII (2010), 254–79.

3. Salomon Maimon, *Versuch über die Transcendentalphilosophie* (Berlin: Voß und Sohn, 1790); *Gibeath Hamore* in *More Nebuchim*, Isaac Euchel (ed.) (Berlin: Officina Scholae Liberae Judaicae, 1791); *Salomon Maimons Lebensgeschichte*, 2 vols. (Berlin: Vieweg, 1792–3).

4. GS, XI, 50.

5. *Ibid.*, XI, 495.

6. Karl Leonhard Reinhold, 'Briefe über die Kantische Philosophie', Dritter Brief, in *Der Teutsche Merkur*, 1787, I, 39.

7. On supersessionism, see R. Kendall Soulen, *The God of Israel and Christian Theology* (Minneapolis, MN: Fortress, 1996).

8. See P. Franks, 'Sinai since Spinoza: reflections on revelation in modern Jewish thought', in *The Significance of Sinai: Traditions about Sinai and Divine Revelation in Judaism and Christianity*, George Brooke, Loren Stuckenbruck and Hindy Najman (eds.) (Leiden: Brill, 2008), 331–52.

9. GS, V, 274.

10. *Ibid.*, VII, 53.

11. FSW, I/8, 269–72.

12. Hegel, *PhdG*, GW, IX, 257 (§340); Friedrich Wilhelm Josef von Schelling, *Schellings sämmtliche Werke*, Karl Friedrich August Schelling (ed.), 14 vols. (Stuttgart: Cotta: 1856–61), XIV, n 146–7 [hereafter SSW].

13. GS, VII, 53; Fichte, Immanuel Herman (ed.), *Johann Gottlieb Fichtes sämtliche Werke*, 8 vols. (Berlin: Veit and Co., 1845–6). Reprinted as vols. I–VIII, *Fichtes Werke*, 11 vols. (Berlin: de Gruyter, 1971), VI, 149–51 [hereafter FSW]; HW, VII, §209, §270; Werner J. Cahnman, 'Friedrich Wilhelm Schelling über die Judenemanzipation', in *Zeitschrift für Bayerische Landesgeschichte*, 37:2 (1974), 614–25.

14. Kant, *KrV*, A314/B370.

15. Aristobulus, 'Fragment 3', in *The Old Testament Pseudepigrapha*, James H. Charlesworth (ed.) (Garden City, NY: Doubleday, 1985), II, 839.

16. Moses Maimonides, *Guide of the Perplexed*, trans. Shlomo Pines (Chicago, IL: University of Chicago Press, 1965), II, chapter 24, 326.

17. I. Abarbanel, *Perush 'al Nevi'im Aharonim* (Jerusalem: Bnei Arbel, 1960), 205. Augustine ascribed this claim to Ambrose but eventually rejected it. Also see Moshe Idel, 'Jewish Kabbalah and Platonism in the Middle Ages and the Renaissance', in Lenn E. Goodman (ed.), *Neo-Platonism and Jewish Thought* (Albany, NY: State University of New York Press,

1992), 319–51; *Kabbalah in Italy 1280–1510* (New Haven, CT: Yale University Press, 2011), Chapter 13.

18. *Kabbala Denudata*, 2 vols., Christian Knorr von Rosenroth (ed. and trans.) (Sulzbach, 1677 and Frankfurt a.M., 1684).

19. A. Herrera, *Gate of Heaven*, trans. Kenneth Krabbenhoft (Leiden: Brill, 2002), Book 8, chapter 14, 370.

20. Disentangling the Kantian *a priori* from psychology is a principal aim of Cohen in *Kants Theorie der Erfahrung* (Berlin: Dümmler, 1871; 2nd edn, 1885; 3rd edition, Berlin: Cassirer, 1918).

21. R. H. Lotze, *Logik* (Leipzig: Hirzel, 1874), I, 493–511; trans. in Lotze, *Logic* (Oxford: Clarendon Press, 1888), II, 200–22.

22. S. Maimon, *Essay on Transcendental Philosophy*, trans. Nick Midgley, Henry Somers-Hall, Alistair Welchman and Merten Reglitz (New York: Continuum, 2010), 37.

23. *Ibid.*, 38.

24. *Ibid.*, 78.

25. Maimonides, *Guide*, I, chapter 68, 163.

26. *Essay*, 227.

27. See H. Cohen, *Das Prinzip der Infinitesimal-Methode und seine Geschichte* (Berlin: Dümmler, 1883).

28. See H. Cohen, *Platons Ideenlehre und die Mathematik* (Marburg: Elwertsche, 1878).

29. H. Cohen, *Logik der reinen Erkenntniss* (Berlin: Cassirer, 1902), 81.

30. *Ibid.*, 70.

31. *Ibid.*, 73.

32. *Ethics of Maimonides*, trans. Almut Bruckstein (Madison, WI: University of Wisconsin Press, 2004), 130.

33. Lazarus Bendavid, *Etwas zur Charakteristik der Juden* (Leipzig: Stabel, 1793).

34. See also S. Ascher, *Leviathan oder über Religion in Rücksicht des Judentums* (Berlin: in der Frankeschen Buchhandlung, 1792).

35. F. Rosenzweig, 'Einleitung', in H. Cohen, *Jüdische Schriften*, Bruno Strauss (ed.) (Berlin: Schwetschke, 1924), I, xxiv.

36. Eduard von Hartmann, *Die Selbstzersetzung des Christentums und die Religion der Zukunft* (Berlin: Duncker, 1874), 29; trans. Henrietta Szold in Moritz Lazarus, *The Ethics of Judaism* (Philadelphia, PA: Jewish Publication Society, 1900), 126–7.

37. *Ethics*, 131.

38. See H. Cohen, *Religion der Vernunft aus den Quellen des Judentums* (Leipzig: Fock, 1919), English: *Religion of Reason out of the Sources of Judaism*, trans. Simon Kaplan (Oxford: Oxford University Press, 2000).

39. I. Breuer, *Die Neue Kusari* (Frankfurt a.M.: Rabbiner Hirsch Gesellschaft, 1934), 357–9; trans. Jacob Levinger in *Concepts of Judaism* (Jerusalem: Israel Universities Press, 1974), 276–9.

40. Joseph B. Soloveitchik, *U-vikashtem mi-sham*, Ha-Darom LXVII (1979), 44; trans. Naomi Goldblum in *And From There You Shall Seek* (Jersey City, NJ: Ktav, 2008), 97.

41. Pinchas Eliyahu Horowitz, *Sefer ha-Brit* (Brünn: Josef Karl Neumann, 1797), 118–19.

42. *Ibid.*, 119.

43. Abraham Danzig, *Ḥayyei Adam* (Vilna: Kschandz Lubansky, 1810), 1. Reference to Kant was removed from later editions, reflecting an increasingly anti-philosophical attitude among the Lithuanian rabbinic elite.

44. See P. Franks, *All or Nothing: Systematicity, Transcendental Arguments, and Skepticism in German Idealism* (Cambridge, MA: Harvard University Press, 2005).

45. *Ibid.*, 85–93.

46. See P. Franks, 'Nothing comes from nothing: Judaism, the Orient, and the Kabbalah in Hegel's reception of Spinoza', in Michael della Rocca (ed.), *The Oxford Handbook of Spinoza*, (Oxford: Oxford University Press, forthcoming).

47. See P. Franks, 'Inner anti-Semitism or Kabbalistic legacy?', 271–3.

48. This doctrine is rooted in the Zoharic exposition of the seven kings of Edom who died without leaving a successor (Genesis 36:31–9).

49. F. H. Jacobi, *Über die Lehre des Spinoza in Briefen an den Herrn Moses Mendelssohn* (Breslau: Löwe, 1785), 113; trans. George di Giovanni in *Main Philosophical Writings* (Montreal, QC and Kingston, ON: McGill-Queen's University Press, 1994), 219–20. See also *All or Nothing*, 170 and 'Nothing comes from nothing'.

50. See F. H. Jacobi, *Über die Lehre*, 34–5; trans. in *Main Philosophical Writings*, 196.

51. A Lurianic gloss on Zohar I, 15b.

52. Jacobi, *Main Philosophical Writings*, 195–6.

53. *Ibid.*, 231.

54. *Ibid.*, 233–4.

55. F. H. Jacobi, *Autobiography*, trans. John Clark Murray (Champaign, IL: University of Illinois Press, 1888), 105.

56. Hegel, *The Science of Logic*, trans. George di Giovanni (Cambridge, Cambridge University Press, 2010), 29.

57. Thomas Pfau (trans. and ed.), *Idealism and the Endgame of Theory: Three Essays by F. W. J. Schelling* (Albany: State University of New York Press, 1994) [hereafter IET], 99.

58. See FSW, III/1, letter 335; trans. Daniel Breazeale in *Early Philosophical Writings* (Ithaca, NY: Cornell University Press, 1993), 413–14.

59. See Franks, 'Inner anti-Semitism or Kabbalistic legacy?', 273–4.

60. Schelling, *Philosophy and Religion*, trans. Klaus Ottmann (Putnam, CT: Spring, 2010), 26.

61. Schelling, *Philosophische Untersuchungen über das Wesen der menschlichen Freiheit*, SSW, VI, 358; trans. Jeff Love and Johannes Schmidt in *Philosophical Investigations of the Essence of Human Freedom* (Albany, NY: State University of New York Press, 2006), 28.

62. See Schelling, *Stuttgarter Privatvorlesungen*, SSW, VII, 421–84; English: *Stuttgart Seminars* in IET, 195–268. The Christian Kabbalist Friedrich Christoph Oetinger is probably Schelling's source. Schelling borrowed primary Kabbalistic texts from the library, not for himself, but for Franz Josef Molitor, the nineteenth-century's pre-eminent Christian Kabbalist. See Molitor, *Philosophie der Geschichte oder über die Tradition*, 4 vols. (Frankfurt a.M.: Hermannsche Buchhandlung, 1827; Münster: Theissingsche Buchhandlung, 1834, 1839, 1853).

63. N. Krochmal, *Kitvei Rabi Naḥman Krokhmal*, Simon Rawidowicz (ed.) (Berlin: Ajanoth, 1924), 420–2.

64. *Ibid.*, 317.

65. *Ibid.*, 302–13.

66. E. Benamozegh, *Israël et l'humanité* (Paris: Leroux, 1914), 362; trans. Maxwell Luria in *Israel and Humanity* (Mahwah, NJ: Paulist Press, 1995), 96; citing Fichte, *Die Bestimmung des Menschen*, FSW, II, 282, 296, 298; trans. Peter Preuss as *The Vocation of Man* (Indianapolis, IN: Hackett), 94, 105, 106.

67. Psalm 68.35 as interpreted in Zohar, II, 32b.

68. Also see M. Buber, *Das Dialogische Prinzip* (Gütersloh: Gütersloher Verlagshaus, 2006), 299–320; trans. Maurice Friedman as 'On the history of the dialogical principle' in *Between Man and Man* (London: Routledge, 1947), 249–64.

69. Martin Buber, *The Legend of the Baal Shem*, trans. Maurice Friedman (London: Routledge, 2002), xii–xiii.

70. F. Rosenzweig *Dev Stern der Erlösung* (Frankfurt a.M.: Kaufmann, 1921); translated as *The Star of Redemption*, trans. Barbara Galli (Madison, WI: University of Wisconsin Press, 2005).

71. See F. Rosenzweig, *Philosophical and Theological Writings*, trans. Paul Franks and Michael Morgan (Indianapolis, IN: Hackett, 2000), 57, 121.

72. See B. Pollock, *Franz Rosenzweig and the Systematic Task of Philosophy* (Cambridge: Cambridge University Press, 2009), 224–5.

73. Martin Buber, 'Offenbarung und Gesetz. Aus Briefen an Franz Rosenzweig', *Almanach des Schocken Verlags auf das Jahr 5697* (Berlin: Schocken, 1936–7), 147–54; trans. Nahum Glatzer as 'Revelation and law (Martin Buber and Franz Rosenzweig)', in Franz Rosenzweig, *On Jewish Learning* (Madison, WI: University of Wisconsin Press, 1955), 109–18.

74. E. Lévinas, *Totalité et Infini* (The Hague: Nijhoff, 1961), 14; *Totality and Infinity*, trans. Alphonso Lingis (The Hague: Nijhoff, 1979), 28.

75. *Ibid.*, 104–5.

76. I thank Tyson Gofton, Hindy Najman, Michael Morgan and Benjamin Pollock for helpful conversations.

10

'In the arms of gods': Schelling, Hegel and the problem of mythology

G EORGE S. W ILLIAMSON

Im Arme der Götter wuchs ich groß. Hölderlin[1]

The dream of ancient Hellas and its gods shaped the intellectual projects of Schelling, Hölderlin and Hegel from the very beginning. As students in Tübingen, they came to see Greece as a second homeland, whose language, culture and geography were as familiar as those of Germany but infinitely more attractive. To express their sense of the fundamental unity of the world, they adopted the slogan "Ἐν καὶ Πᾶν' [one and all]. And when they sought to realise their hopes for a new union of poetry, philosophy and religion they called for a 'new mythology', with the Greek gods serving as model and inspiration. Even after Schelling and Hegel distanced themselves from such youthful utopianism, Greek mythology remained a crucial reference point for their philosophies. In their mature systems, it would serve as a rich source of metaphors and narratives, as a tool for critiquing and reconstructing Christian theology and (for Schelling) as a key to explicating the subterranean forces at work in the human psyche across the ages.

In turn, Idealism's rich legacy of speculation on myth would leave a last-ing impact on the 'science' of mythology.[2] To be sure, Vico and Herder had already identified myth as the storehouse of a people's earliest ideas about nature, religion, morality and law. Yet it was Idealist philosophy, partic-ularly that of Schelling, that systematised these insights while suggesting that mythology could provide an intuition of the absolute itself. By linking mythology to the highest aspirations of religion and metaphysics, Schelling helped create a template that would be followed by many generations of scholars, whether philologists, theologians or anthropologists. Indeed, one can find echoes of the Romantic–Idealist approach to myth in the work of F. Max Müller, Franz Rosenzweig, Martin Heidegger and Mircea Eliade, among others. At the same time, however, the elevation of myth to a central category of cultural analysis gave new power to the project of demythologisation. The 'negative' concept of myth – as a form of illusion, distortion, or under-developed knowledge – became a tool for undermining not just particular stories or legends but entire religions, worldviews and social structures.

This essay will provide a survey of the Idealist engagement with mythology, focusing on the writings of Schelling, Hegel and D. F. Strauss. After discussing Schelling's early forays into the study of myth in Section 10.1, Sections 10.2 and 10.3 consider the origins and implications of the Romantic–Idealist project of a 'new mythology' and its significance for Schelling's early philosophy. I then investigate Hegelian approaches to myth, Section 10.4 focusing on Hegel's *Phenomenology of Spirit* and Section 10.5 on Strauss' *Life of Jesus*. Section 10.6 deals with Schelling's late lectures on the philosophy of mythology, including his 'tautegorical' interpretation of myth. Section 10.7 concludes, with some comments on the legacy of Idealism for myth scholarship in the late nineteenth and early twentieth centuries.

10.1 Myth as *Philosopheme*: Schelling and the *Aufklärung* debate on myth

In 1793, at the age of 18, Friedrich Schelling published his first journal article. 'On myths, historical legends, and philosophemes of the Ancient World' appeared in *Memorabilien*, which was the organ of the *Aufklärer* and arch-rationalist H. E. G. Paulus.[3] That Schelling's essay should appear in this journal is not surprising, since it built on the enlightened debate over myth as it had developed up to this point. Earlier in the eighteenth century, the tendency among European scholars had been to see myth as either a distorted form of history or the product of priestly fraud.[4] According to Jaucourt's article on 'fable' in the *Encyclopédie*, mythology was 'a confused mixture of the fancies of the imagination, the dreams of philosophy, and the debris of earliest history' whose 'analysis is impossible'. Still, Jaucourt recommended the study of mythology to artists, for whom it served as a source of 'interesting subjects' and 'allegories'.[5] By the time Jaucourt's article was published, however, countervailing approaches to myth could already be detected. In particular, travel accounts of West Africans and American Indians led a number of writers to conclude that the religious beliefs and practices of these peoples were typical of humanity in its childhood and thus explained the origins of the ancient myths. In *Du culte des dieux fétiches* (1760), for example, Charles de Brosses argued that the religious ideas of primitive peoples were the result of fear and ignorance, which had led them to deify animals and inanimate objects.[6] Such fetishes, Brosses maintained, lay behind the animal gods of the ancient Egyptians and the more anthropomorphic deities of the Greeks.

A similar anthropological impulse informed the writings of Johann Gottfried Herder and the philologist Christian Gottlob Heyne on ancient mythology, though with a crucial shift in tone and emphasis. While de Brosses stressed stupidity and fear, these authors saw awe and wonder as the emotions driving mythopoesis. In his account of the origins of Homeric mythology, Heyne cited the ancients' 'poverty of speech' and their tendency to transpose abstract thoughts into stories as factors that led them to present their ideas about nature and the cosmos in the form of myth. At the same time, however, Heyne described the moment of myth-creation in mystical, almost ecstatic terms: at these times, the ancients were seized by a 'holy enthusiasm' that allowed them to represent the objects of their thoughts directly to their listeners.[7] An even more emphatic reversal of the encyclopaedists' stance could be found in Herder, who praised the spirit of freedom and reverence that animated the mythologies of the 'savage' peoples and contrasted them favourably with their modern descendants.

In 'On myths', Schelling drew on these influences while articulating an argument on behalf of what he called 'mythical philosophy'. Following Heyne, he described ancient myth as originating in an oral culture that relied heavily on gesture, bodily movement and other appeals to the senses. This helped to explain the childlike naïveté and taste for the miraculous that was characteristic of myth. At the same time, however, myth performed an important social function, as its stories were passed down from fathers to sons, celebrated in festivals and songs and commemorated on monuments. Myth, according to Schelling, 'brought harmony and unity to uneducated hordes of men and became a gentle bond through which the society of a single family was joined to a single doctrine, a single belief, and a single activity'.[a] What undermined myth was the emergence of writing, which gradually eclipsed the oral culture that had nurtured the old stories and allowed them to fall into the hands of artists. Yet as soon as they were consciously manipulated, treated as allegories or used to arouse or entice audiences, these stories lost their unique charm and power.

---

a. 'Brachte in ungebildete Menschenhorden Harmonie und Einheit, und ward ein sanftes Band, durch welches die Gesellschaft zu Einer Familie zu Einer Lehre, zu Einem Glauben, zu Einer Thätig keit verbunden wurde.' SSW, I, i, 63.

Even as Schelling drew a firm line between myth and art, he sought to elaborate the links between myth and philosophy. Since the Renaissance, numerous scholars had attempted to treat the ancient Greek myths as distortions or misunderstandings of an original philosophical or theological doctrine. Schelling, however, insisted that ancient philosophy took the form of myth from the very beginning. Steeped in a world of sensuality, even the wisest of the ancients were compelled to express their intimations of the truth in the form of narrative and imagery. In general, this argument paralleled Heyne's, yet one can detect a new note in Schelling's suggestion that the mythical *philosophemes* penetrated more deeply into the secrets of nature and the psyche than later theories built out of 'dead concepts'. These included the Greek myths of Prometheus and Pandora, as well as the Biblical tale of Adam and Eve, which provided a striking account of the psychological state in which humanity found itself after the first use of its freedom.[8] For the young Schelling, therefore, the ancient myths were not merely illustrations of philosophical ideas: rather, they constituted a form of philosophy in themselves.

Schelling can be seen arguing along several fronts in 'On myths'. On the one hand, he was continuing the project, initiated in his dissertation, of identifying certain narratives of the Bible as mythical.[9] Indeed, one can detect in this article an almost point by point refutation of Johann Jakob Hess' 'Determination of the boundary of what in the Bible is myth and what is true history' (1792), in which Hess argued against using the term 'myth' to describe even the first chapters of Genesis on the rather tenuous grounds that myth was essentially pagan and thus never intended as real history, while the Bible as true religion was intended as real history.[10] Yet Schelling wanted not only to tear down the crumbling wall between revelation and mythology but also to vindicate the philosophical and theological content of the Greek myths themselves. In this regard, he fed into a broader current of German Philhellenism that had its roots in the aesthetic writings of Johann Jacob Winckelmann and that by the 1790s had become the basis for a wide-ranging critique of modern civilisation and Christianity itself, which was derided as 'Oriental' and unfree. As will be seen, this critique of 'Christian modernity' would form a crucial context for Hegel and Schelling's speculations on mythology.

10.2 The new mythology

In his dialogue 'Iduna, or the apple of rejuvenation' (1796) Johann Gottfried Herder staged a conversation between 'Alfred' and 'Frey' in which the former lamented the lack of a home-grown mythology in Germany. According to

Alfred, a mythical poetry based in the German language and mindset would capture the imagination of children and adults far more powerfully than the foreign myths of the Greeks, creating the conditions for an efflorescence of literature. Unfortunately, the closest thing to a German mythology was the Icelandic *Edda*, which Frey rejected as too 'north polar' despite Alfred's entreaties on its behalf.[b,11] In general, Schelling, Hegel and the Jena Romantics shared Frey's scepticism toward Nordic mythology, which they saw as far inferior to that of the Greeks. At the same time, however, they came to embrace the idea of a 'new mythology' that would bring about not just a renewal of literature, but also a new philosophy, religion and politics.

The appeal of 'the new mythology' for Schelling, Hegel and their generation reflected the confluence of several historical trajectories. Foremost among them was the descent of the French Revolution into terror in 1793–4, a development that led philosophically minded intellectuals not only to rethink their positions on the revolution but to do so in the form of a critique of subjective, i.e., Kantian and Fichtean, forms of Idealism. In his *Letters on the Aesthetic Education of Mankind* (1795), Friedrich Schiller argued famously that if 'man is ever to solve the problem of politics in practice he will have to do so through the problem of the aesthetic, because it is only through beauty that man makes his way to freedom.'[c,12] Rejecting the Kantian notion of duty as an insufficient spur to morality, Schiller maintained that art alone had the ability to elevate the masses to the standpoint of practical reason. In developing this argument, he gestured back to the ancient Greek polis, whose union of freedom, harmony and beauty stood in stark contrast with the divided 'machine-state' of the modern era. A similar set of concerns animated the thinking of Hölderlin, which he articulated in the form of a critique of Fichte. First, he maintained that the absolute did not reside in self-consciousness, as Fichte had maintained, but rather in a pre-conscious Being. At the same time, he distanced himself from Fichte's pro-Jacobin politics, arguing instead that a union with Being could only be approached through the aesthetic. As he wrote in the draft preface to his novel *Hyperion* (1796), 'a new empire awaits us where beauty is queen.'[d,13] For Schiller and Hölderlin, therefore, aesthetics offered the only path to a unified polity.

b. 'Nordpolarisch'. Johann Gottfried Herder, *Sämmtliche Werke*, ed. B. Suphan, 33 vols. (Berlin: Weidmann, 1877–1913), XVIII, 491.

c. 'Man, um jenes politische Problem in der Erfahrung zu lösen, durch das ästhetische den Weg nehmen muß.' Friedrich Schiller, *Sämtliche Werke*, ed. Wolfgang Riedel, 5 vols. (Munich: Carl Hanser, 2004), IV, 573.

d. '[E]s wartet, um mit Hyperion zu reden, ein neues Reich auf uns, wo die Schönheit Königin ist.' Hölderlin, *Werke in einem Band*, ed. Hans-Jürgen Balmes (Munich: Hanser, 1996), 313.

It was this intellectual context that helped produce the so-called 'Oldest System Programme of German Idealism', an unsigned document written in Hegel's hand that probably dates from 1796 or 1797. After describing the need for a new ethics and a new physics, the document turned to a critique of the state, which treated free individuals as 'cogs in a machine' and thus deserved to wither away. The author also called for the overthrow of superstition, the prosecution of the priesthood and the abandonment of traditional doctrines of God and immortality. The idea that would unite everything was beauty, taken in its 'Platonic' sense as the pinnacle of philosophy. In this way, 'poetry... would become in the end what it was in the beginning – the teacher of mankind, because there is no more philosophy and no more history: poetry alone will outlive all the other sciences and arts.'[e,14]

The question, of course, was how this ideal could be realised. Here the author proposed a new, sensual religion – a new mythology:

> I will speak here of an idea that, as far as I know, has occurred to no one – we must have a new mythology, but this mythology must stand in the service of ideas. It must become a mythology of *reason*. Until we make the ideas aesthetic, i.e., mythological, they have no interest for the *people* and, conversely, until mythology is rational a philosopher must be ashamed of it. So the enlightened and the unenlightened must finally reach out their hands to each other, mythology must become philosophical and the people reasonable, and philosophy must become mythological in order to make the philosophers sensual. Then eternal unity will reign among us. No longer the contemptuous look, no longer the blind trembling of the people before its wise men and priests. Only then can we expect an *equal* development of *all* powers, of the individual as well as of all individuals. No power will be suppressed and universal liberty and equality of spirits will reign! – A higher spirit, sent from heaven, must establish this new religion among us. It will be the last and greatest work of mankind.[f,15]

e. 'Die Poesie... wird am Ende wieder, was sie am Anfang war – *Lehrerin der Menschheit*; denn es gibt keine Philosophie, keine Geschichte mehr, die Dichtkunst allein wird alle übrigen Wissenschaften und Künste überleben.' Eva Moldenhauer and Karl Markus Michel (eds.), *Hegels Werke in zwanzig Bänden*. 20 vols. (Frankfurt a.M.: Suhrkamp, 1969–71), I, 235.

f. 'Zuerst werde ich hier von einer Idee sprechen, die, soviel ich weiß, noch in keines Menschen Sinn gekommen ist – wir müssen eine neue Mythologie haben, diese Mythologie aber muß im Dienste der Ideen stehen, sie muß eine Mythologie der *Vernunft* werden. Ehe wir die Ideen ästhetisch, d.h. mythologisch machen, haben sie für das *Volk* kein Interesse; und umgekehrt, ehe die Mythologie vernünftig ist, muß sich der Philosoph ihrer schämen. So müssen endlich Aufgeklärte und Unaufgeklärte sich die Hand reichen, die Mythologie muß philosophisch werden und das Volk vernünftig, und die Philosophie muß mythologisch werden, um die

As this passage shows, the 'System programme' marked a considerable radicalisation of the programme laid out in Schiller's *Letters on Aesthetic Education*. While Schiller appeared to subordinate art to the tasks of morality, the 'System programme' sought to ground absolute freedom in beauty itself. And while the *Letters* emphasised the need to raise up the masses in order to integrate them into an ethical state, the 'System programme' called for levelling the state in the name of equality. Finally, while Schiller seemed daunted at times by the imponderables of aesthetic politics, notably the difficulty of realising such a project in the context of Christian modernity, the 'System programme' called outright for the overthrow of Christianity and its replacement with a 'mythology of reason'.

On discovering this document in the State Library in Berlin, Franz Rosenzweig concluded that it was based on a manuscript by Schelling. Yet further research suggests that it was written by Hegel after all.[16] Hegel's unpublished writings from 1793 to 1796 demonstrate his interest in the possibility of a civic religion, his extreme doubts about the usefulness of Christianity for this task and his fascination with Herder's ideas on myth. In addition, Hegel was in correspondence with Hölderlin and likely had access to drafts of *Hyperion*, whose ideas appear to infuse the 'System programme'. It has even been suggested that the 'System programme' be seen as an act of one-upmanship on the part of Hegel, as if he were trying to surpass the radicalism of Hölderlin's empire of beauty with the even more audacious notion of a new mythology.[17] In the end, however, the standpoint presented in the 'System programme' would be short-lived. By the end of 1797, Hegel had revalidated Christianity as a religion of love and begun to move toward the position of *The Phenomenology of Spirit*.

Was Schelling familiar with the contents of the 'System programme'? Although there can be no definitive answer to this question, it appears that he took his own path to the 'new mythology'. In the three years after his departure from Tübingen in 1795, Schelling established himself as a philosopher of the first rank due to his studies of Fichte's philosophy and his creation of a *Naturphilosophie* that presented nature as 'unconscious spirit'. During this time, he did not completely abandon the theological questions that had animated his earliest writings. In 'On revelation and popular instruction' (1798),

Philosophen sinnlich zu machen. Dann herrscht ewige Einheit unter uns. Nimmer der verachtende Blick, nimmer das blinde Zittern des Volks vor seinen Weisen und Priestern. Dann erst erwartet uns *gleiche* Ausbildung *aller* Kräfte, des Einzelnen sowohl als aller Individuen. Keine Kraft wird mehr unterdrückt werden. Dann herrscht allgemeine Freiheit und Gleichheit der Geister! – Ein höherer Geist, von Himmel gesandt, muß diese neue Religion unter uns stiften, sie wird das letzte größte Werk der Menschheit sein.' HW, I, 236.

for example, Schelling criticised those theologians who tried to prop up the tottering concept of revelation by identifying it as a postulate of practical reason. Sounding a populist note, he accused those who wielded revelation as a tool of authority of perpetrating a 'fraud' against the people.[18] Still, there was no mention in this essay of aesthetics or mythology as solutions to the problem of popular education. That would come about only after Schelling's arrival in Jena in 1798. It was there that he encountered Goethe, Schiller and the Romantic circle that had formed around August Wilhelm Schlegel, Friedrich Schlegel and Novalis. Friedrich Schlegel and Novalis, in particular, were well attuned to the aesthetic questions arising out of post-Fichtean Idealism, including the possibilities of a new mythology.

Schelling first mentioned the 'new mythology' in the closing pages of his *System of Transcendental Idealism* (1800). Here Schelling narrated the progressive education of the self until the absolute became objective for it in the work of art. In art, the ground of harmony between infinite and finite, unconscious and conscious, that was formerly available only to the philosopher in the moment of intellectual intuition, became available to ordinary consciousness in the moment of aesthetic intuition. For this reason, it was the

> only true and eternal organon and document of philosophy, which ever and again continues to speak to us of what philosophy cannot depict in external form, namely the unconscious element in acting and producing, and its original identity with the conscious.[g,19]

For Schelling, the resolution of philosophy in art marked not only the completion of his system but also a return to its origins in ancient Greece. Philosophy, and the sciences that emerged from it, had first grown out of poetry. With philosophy and the sciences having reached completion, one could expect them to return 'like so many streams back into the ocean of poetry from which they took their source'.[h,20] The model for such a synthesis already existed in Greek mythology, which contained within it an infinite array of meanings and symbols all united in a single comprehensive whole.

g. 'Das einzige wahre und ewige Organon zugleich und Document der Philosophie sey, welches immer und fortwährend aufs neue beurkundet, was die Philosophie äußerlich nicht darstellen kann, nämlich das Bewußtlose im Handeln und Produciren und seine ursprüngliche Identität mit dem Bewußten.' SSW, III, 627–8.

h. 'Als ebenso viel einzelne Ströme in den allgemeinen Ocean der Poesie zurückfließen, von welchem sie ausgegangen waren.' SSW, III, 629.

> But how a new mythology is itself to arise, which shall be the creation, not of some individual author, but of a new race, personifying, as it were, one single poet – that is a problem whose solution can be looked for only in the future destinies of the world, and in the course of history to come.[i,21]

This entire passage bears a striking resemblance to the 'System programme'. In particular, both texts presented philosophy as giving way to a higher work of poesy, which would take the form of a new mythology. At the same time, however, Schelling's *System* lacked the incendiary rhetoric of the 'System programme'. The issues of religion and politics, while implied, were not addressed directly, and there was certainly no talk of an egalitarian levelling of the distinction between philosopher and people. Indeed, for much of the *System of Transcendental Idealism*, Schelling seemed intent on reinforcing distinctions: between the philosopher (for whom intellectual intuition was possible) and the non-philosopher (for whom it was not), and between the genius (the only individual capable of creating true art) and the non-genius (or hack). In general, what was presented in the 'System programme' as an urgent, revolutionary task now appeared as a long-term cultural project. Such gradualism reflected not only Schelling's growing political conservatism, but also a conception of Greek myth that broke decisively with the standpoint of his earlier writings on this topic.

10.3 Mythology as absolute poesy: Schelling's *Philosophy of Art*

This new conception of myth came to the fore in Schelling's lectures on the philosophy of art (1802–3), which contain some of his most extensive ruminations on ancient and modern mythologies.[22] By the time he delivered these lectures, Schelling had reconceived the absolute (which he now referred to as God or the universe) as the total identity of ideal and real, infinite and finite, universal and particular. This absolute contained all the particular forms of the universe, each of which was divine in and of itself. Viewed from the perspective of the ideal, these were the Platonic ideas, but viewed from the perspective of the real, they were the gods. And, according to Schelling, it was this standpoint that defined the ancient Greeks' 'belief' in their gods.

---

i. 'Wie aber eine neue Mythologie, welche nicht Erfindung des einzelnen Dichters, sondern eines neuen, nur Einen Dichter gleichsam vorstellenden Geschlechts seyn kann, selbst entstehen könne, dieß ist ein Problem, dessen Auflösung allein von den künftigen Schicksalen der Welt und dem weiteren Verlauf der Geschichte zu erwarten ist.' SSW, III, 629.

> The Greeks did not at all take the gods to be real in the sense, for example, that common understanding believes in the reality of physical objects; from that perspective the Greeks considered the gods to be neither real nor unreal. In the higher sense they were more real for the Greeks than every other reality.[j,23]

In other words, Greek religion suggested an alternative to faith in unseen objects, pointing out a path beyond both the Christian God and the Kantian thing-in-itself.

This conception of the gods represented a decisive rejection of the allegorical interpretation, according to which the gods 'meant' something other than what they were. Instead, Schelling offered a 'symbolic' interpretation, according to which the Homeric gods contained an absolute indifference of the ideal and the real. Here he drew heavily from Karl Philipp Moritz's *Götterlehre* (1791), which had presented ancient mythology as a 'language of imagination' in which 'Jupiter' simply meant 'Jupiter', 'Mars' meant 'Mars', etc.[24] Schelling, however, sought to go beyond Moritz by demonstrating the actual necessity of the symbolic interpretation, grounding it in the principles of his identity philosophy. In the process, he rejected Heyne's approach as just another variant of the allegorical interpretation. Allegory and *philosopheme*, Schelling now declared, were the product of a later, republican era, which coincided with the mystery religions and the rise of philosophy. On this view, the Homeric gods were the creation of neither an individual nor a race but of a collective *acting* as an individual. In this sense, the origin of mythology was identical with the origin of 'Homer'.

The law of the gods, according to Schelling, was pure limitation on the one hand and absoluteness on the other. Each god received a particular characteristic – wisdom, love, strength – yet was also a divinity. The gods acted completely in accord with their own natures and thus experienced no disjunction between freedom and necessity. For that reason one could not speak of the morality or immorality of the gods but only of their blessedness and naïveté. This helped to explain the sometimes cruel humour of the gods, such as their endless ridicule of the lame Vulcan. Together, however, the gods formed a totality that was bound together through procreation ('theogony') and that included every possible relationship and embroilment within it.

---

j. 'In dem Sinn, wie etwa ein gemeiner Verstand an die Wirklichkeit der sinnlichen Dinge glaubt, haben *jene* Menschen die Götter überhaupt nicht genommen und weder für wirklich noch für nicht wirklich gehalten. In dem höheren Sinne waren sie den Griechen reeller als jedes andere Reelle.' SSW, V, 391.

As a result it was the absolute poesy from which every possible artistic form was able to emerge.

If Greek religion was based on a realistic mythology, Christianity was characterised by an Idealistic mythology. In this regard, it was typical of the 'Oriental' religions, which symbolised the finite through the infinite (rather than the infinite through the finite, as was the case in Greek mythology). In Schelling's view, the victory of this Oriental principle could not be explained by reference to the Christian religion alone. Well before the rise of Christianity, antiquity had become detached from nature and had come to feel a sense of homelessness. This manifested itself in ancient Rome in a widespread sense of saturation and boredom, a fascination with superstitions and mystery religions and a general orientation toward the Orient. As the old gods lost their power and as Rome was visited with catastrophe upon catastrophe, the people threw themselves 'into the arms of providence' and took up the cross.[k,25]

Christianity for Schelling represented a fundamental inversion of Greek mythology. 'In the latter', he wrote, 'the universe is intuited as nature, in the former as a moral world.'[l,26] Thus while Greek mythology was based on a unity of finite and infinite, Christianity was based on an opposition between infinite and finite accompanied by the (moral) demand that this opposition be reconciled through action. This subordination of the finite to the infinite, of nature to God, explained why in Christianity the absolute could only be represented allegorically. It also explained Christianity's fundamentally historical nature. 'Every particular moment of time is a revelation of a particular side of God, and in each he is absolute. What Greek religion possessed as simultaneity, Christianity possesses as succession.'[m,27] With this new sense of history, Christianity marked the onset of the modern world.

The opposition between finite and infinite principles underlying Christianity was already evident in the Biblical accounts of the life of Jesus. The bulk of the Gospel narratives were constructed from fables based on Old Testament prophecies. In this sense, Jesus was a 'historical person whose biography was largely determined before he was born.'[n,28] Yet Christ's

---

k. 'In die Arme der Vorsehung.' SSW, V, 429.

l. 'In dieser wird das Universum angeschaut als Natur, in jener aber als moralische Welt.' SSW, V, 430.

m. 'Jeder besondere Moment der Zeit ist Offenbarung einer besonderen Seite Gottes, in deren jeder er absolut ist; was die griechische Religion als ein Zumal hatte, hat das Christenthum als ein Nacheinander.' SSW, V, 288.

n. 'Eine historische Person, deren Biographie schon vor ihrer Geburt verzeichnet gewesen.' SSW, V, 426.

world-historical importance derived primarily from the undeniable fact of his death and resurrection. This 'fact' highlighted the essential difference between Christianity and paganism: unlike the pagan gods, Christ entered the finite world not to elevate it but to nullify it through his suffering and death.

> It is as if Christ, as the infinite that has entered finitude and sacrificed it to God *in* his human form, constituted the conclusion of the era of *antiquity*. He is there merely to draw the boundary – the last god.[o,29]

As a god who suffered voluntarily, Christ could never be an adequate object for art, which explained why painters preferred to depict him as an infant, rather than as an adult.

Because Christianity had no true symbols, only symbolic *acts*, its mythology could draw from one of two sources. On the one hand, it could base its mythology on the liturgical acts of baptism, Eucharist and so forth. Or it could draw its mythology from the stories of the apostles, saints and other heroes of the Church. In general, however, modernity was a time of individuals rather than collectives and of change and transformation rather than stability and permanence. Thus it was usually left to the truly original poets to sum up the historical experience of their particular era, to give it universality and transform it into a (temporary) mythology. This was the achievement of Shakespeare, Dante and Goethe's *Faust*.

While such individual mythologies were grounded in particular experiences of history, the *Naturphilosophie* developed by Schelling and others promised an intuition of the infinite in the finite similar to that found in Greek mythology. In his *Discourse on Poesy* (1800), Friedrich Schlegel had floated the idea that the new physics might be a source of a new mythology.[30] In his philosophy of art, Schelling endorsed this notion but cautioned that symbols could not simply be invented out of whole cloth but instead had to come to life as independent beings on their own. This would require Christian culture to somehow go beyond itself and re-implant its historical, Idealistic deities back into nature (just as the Greeks had transformed nature into history). 'It is not we who want to give the Idealist culture its gods through *physics*. We rather await its gods, gods for which we are holding the

---

o. 'Es ist, als ob Christus als das in die Endlichkeit gekommene und sie in seiner menschlichen Gestalt Gott opfernde Unendliche den Schluß der *alten* Zeit machte; er ist bloß da, um die Grenze zu machen – der letzte Gott.' SSW, V, 432.

symbols ready perhaps even before they have developed independently from physics.'[p,31] For Schelling, the prospect of such an event seemed distant. Yet the moment when history returned to nature and succession became simultaneity would be 'the unadulterated Homeros', the beginning of a new era of art and culture.[q,32]

Taken as a whole, Schelling's lectures on the philosophy of art offered a sustained critique of Christian modernity based on the absence of myth within it. On the one hand, Schelling echoed Schiller's earlier complaints about the lack of community and the disjunction between man and nature caused by the collapse of the Homeric universe. On the other hand, he built on his earlier criticisms of the Christian revelation as antithetical not just to philosophy but to the project of human freedom. The attraction of a new mythology, for Schelling and for Romantics like Novalis and Schlegel, was that it promised to ground the project of cultural and political reconciliation in an artwork that was at once universal and yet a product of modernity itself. As we shall see, however, this privileging of mythology – as concept and as project – would be challenged by Hegel, starting with the *Phenomenology of Spirit*.

10.4 Mythology as representation: Hegel's *Phenomenology of Spirit*

Because he taught in Jena from 1801 until 1806, Hegel would have been well aware of Schelling's lectures on the philosophy of art. And given their close partnership for much of this period, it is not surprising that Hegel's account of human consciousness paralleled certain aspects of Schelling's *System of Transcendental Idealism*. At the same time, however, Hegel came to reject Schelling's notion of the Absolute as the point of identity in favour of a more dynamic and processual notion of the Absolute that was both subject *and* substance, that engaged in a constant movement of self-differentiation and reconciliation, and that could only be grasped through philosophy. As a result, Hegel also rejected Schelling's notion of intellectual intuition and his privileging of art and mythology as a means for intuiting the absolute. Indeed, Hegel avoided the words 'myth' and 'mythology' altogether and instead used the term 'representation' (*Vorstellung*) to refer to any type of

---

p. 'Nicht wir wollen der idealistischen Bildung ihre Götter durch die *Physik* geben. Wir erwarten vielmehr ihre Götter, für die wir, vielleicht noch ehe sie in *jener* ganz unabhängig von dieser sich gebildet haben, die Symbole schon in Bereitschaft haben.' SSW, V, 449.

q. 'Der reine Homeros.' SSW, V, 449.

metaphorical, imagistic or sensible thinking. It was only through Strauss'
Life of Jesus that the concept of myth came to be associated with Hegelianism.
Yet while Hegel avoided the language of myth, he can be seen as engaging in
a form of demythologisation that allowed him to move beyond the pictorial
representations of religion while preserving their contents for the project of
scholarship and philosophy.[33]

The stark contrasts between Schelling's and Hegel's approaches to
Greek paganism and Christianity are evident in the section on 'Religion'
in the *Phenomenology of Spirit* (1807). The *Phenomenology* leads the reader on
a philosophical–historical journey of consciousness that begins with basic
problems of epistemology and concludes at the standpoint of absolute knowing. 'Religion' marked a crucial stage because it was only here that spirit came
to be conceived as a self-conscious subject that embraced the totality of the
world. What separated religion from the absolute standpoint was that in religion this self-consciousness was still represented as fundamentally divided
from human consciousness. In other words, the gods or God were seen as
existing in a 'beyond' that was distinct from and purer than the secular world.
In religion, the symbolic 'garment' in which self-conscious spirit appeared
was taken as its essential truth, disguising the fact that the object of consciousness in religion was actually the self-consciousness of spirit as a whole.
As Thomas Lewis notes, this amounted to a projection theory of religion, in
which human self-consciousness was thrust on to imaginary divine entities.[34]
Hegel's task in this section of the *Phenomenology* was not only to transform
these representations into concepts but, in so doing, explain the dynamic
interactions between these representations and the human communities in
which they emerged.

Hegel presented the history of religion according to a three-fold scheme
that began with the 'natural religion' of the Orient, moved to the Greek
'religion of art', and culminated in the 'manifest religion' of Christianity.
Thus, for Hegel, nature was associated not so much with Greek paganism as
with the Persian, Indian and Egyptian religions, which represented the divine
in the shape of light, plants and animals, and half-human statues. Religion
only acquired the shape of consciousness in the anthropomorphic gods of
Greece, who were recognised by the Hellenes as the embodiment of their
own essence and the work of their own hands. In this regard, Greek religion
exhibited the ethical spirit of a free nation that was fundamentally different
from the despotisms of Persia, India and Egypt. Yet this religion of art was
inherently unstable and ultimately collapsed, not because of the intrusion
of an alien 'Oriental' worldview, but due to its own internal contradictions,

which gave rise to an individualism that could no longer be satisfied with the limited ethical world of the gods.

This dialectic played itself out through the various stages of Greek religion. The first moment centred around the statues of the Olympian gods, whose human form was a triumph over the nature gods of India and Egypt. Nonetheless, the production of these statues created a divide between the artist and the work of art as he realised that he had not really created a being like himself. Whether the statue was worshipped or the artist's craft was acclaimed, there was nothing in the blessed existence of the god that reflected the actual work involved in constructing the statue. 'Since his work comes back to him simply as joyfulness, he does not find therein the painful labour of making himself into an artist, and of creation, nor the strain and effort of his work.'[r,35] This sense of alienation between artist and the object of his own labour (a formulation used later by Karl Marx) inspired an opposite approach. Rather than embody the god in an external thing with no self-consciousness, the divine was evoked in hymns, which poured out of the artist's self-consciousness through the medium of language. The problem, however, was that these hymns lacked objective existence. For Hegel, the objectivity of the statue and the subjectivity of the hymn would only find their reconciliation in the cult, where participants sacrificed their possessions to the god and purified themselves in the process. But even the cult failed to provide an adequate representation of self-consciousness:

> Yet it is still not the self that has descended into its depths and knows itself as evil; but it is something that only *immediately* is, a soul that cleanses its exterior by washing it, and puts on white robes, while its inward being traverses the imaginatively conceived path of works, punishments, and rewards, the path of spiritual training in general, i.e. of ridding itself of its particularity, as a result of which it reaches the dwellings and the community of the blest.[s,36]

For Hegel, the Greek cult elided the problem of human evil by offering the participant a relatively pain-free path into the ranks of the blessed (but not fully human) gods.

---

r. 'Indem es ihm als Freudigkeit überhaupt zurückkommt, findet er darin nicht den Schmerz seiner Bildung und Zeugung, nicht die Anstrengung seiner Arbeit.' HW, III, 518.

s. '[D]och ist sie noch nicht das Selbst, das in seine Tiefen hinabgestiegen sich als das Böse weiß, sondern es ist ein *Seiendes*, eine Seele, welche ihre Äußerlichkeit mit Waschen reinigt, sie mit weißen Kleidern antut und ihre Innerlichkeit den vorgestellten Weg der Arbeiten, Strafen und Belohnungen, den Weg der die Besonderheit entäußernden Bildung überhaupt [hin]durchführt, durch welchen sie in die Wohnungen und die Gemeinschaft der Seligkeit gelangt.' HW, III, 522.

In Hegel's account of Greek religion, the cultic mysteries, as well as more public rituals like the Olympic games and the Bacchic rites, were steps toward the truly 'spiritual' forms of art, which included epic and tragedy. In the Homeric epic, one could see the various tribes assembled into a common nation, which was represented as a pantheon that embraced both nature and the ethical world. The minstrel's song brought forth this world as a recollection of a bygone age of heroes and gods. Like the cult, the epic was primarily concerned with presenting the relationship of the divine and the human. Yet here, too, there was a fundamental incoherence of representation, as the commingling of gods and heroes in the epic ended up dividing the action and undermining the seriousness of the whole. On the one hand, the heroes could be seen as mere playthings of the gods. On the other hand, the gods seemed dependent on human tribute even as they avoided any real engagement with the world of mortals. Indeed, it was only in tragedy that human individuality acquired a kind of universality and pathos.

> The [tragic] hero is himself the speaker, and the performance displays to the audience – who are also spectators – *self-conscious* human beings who know their rights and purposes, the power and the will of their specific nature and know how to assert them.[t,37]

The problem, however, was that tragedy also brought forth a growing split in Greek religion between the increasingly self-confident individual and the traditional ethical order, a divide thematised in the *Oresteia* and *Antigone*. As a consequence, the gods and the ethical order they embodied were no longer seen as trustworthy or honourable, to the point that, in the comedies of Aristophanes, the gods were presented as mere masks of the human. For Hegel, one might say, Greek religion contained a demythologising process within itself.

The increasing self-assertion of the individual and his legal rights was carried forth in Roman culture, leading to an emptying of the older ethical order and its gods.

> The statues are now only stones from which the living soul has flown, just as the hymns are words from which belief has gone. The tables of the gods provide no spiritual food and drink, and in his games and

t. 'Der Held ist selbst der Sprechende, und die Vorstellung zeigt dem Zuhörer, der zugleich Zuschauer ist, *selbstbewußte* Menschen, die ihr Recht und ihren Zweck, die Macht und den Willen ihrer Bestimmtheit *wissen* und zu *sagen* wissen.' HW, III, 534.

festivals man no longer recovers the joyful consciousness of his unity with the divine.[u],[38]

Yet the death of the gods, and the 'unhappy consciousness' that accompanied it, prepared the ground for the manifest or revealed religion: Christianity. The passion of Christ was not the 'nullification' of the finite, as Schelling had argued, but rather the moment in which humanity finally recognised its own suffering mirrored in the divine, just as the divine found its own completion in fully adopting mortal form. This truth was not immediately present in the Gospel account of Christ's death and resurrection, however. Instead, it was only revealed when the Holy Spirit appeared to the Christian community or, in Hegel's language, became incarnate *in* the Christian community. At that point, the Absolute was almost entirely freed from pictorial language or revelation. Or to put it another way, the end of demythologisation marked the completion of 'revelation' (understood in Hegel's terms, of course). From here it would just be one more step to Absolute Knowing, when the pictorial language of 'God' and 'man' was abandoned and the path of human consciousness recollected just as Homer once recalled the feats of gods and men.

10.5 The Gospels as myth: D. F. Strauss' *Life of Jesus*

Hegel continued to develop his views on paganism and Christianity, expanding and subtly modifying his position in his Berlin lectures on the philosophy of religion. Against conservative critics of his religious philosophy, he insisted that his position was consistent with Lutheran orthodoxy.[39] Yet his attitude toward many traditional tenets of Protestantism was ambiguous at best, particularly when it came to the historical truth of the Gospel narratives. In the Berlin lectures, Hegel subtly elided this question by including the Homeric myths, the life of Jesus, and national histories under the broad rubric of representation, arguing that each possessed both a sensible outward form and an inner spiritual meaning.[40] According to Hegel, the truth of the Christian revelation was only apparent once the visible Christ had given way to the invisible Spirit. For this reason, he argued, the life of Jesus could not and should not be a subject for investigation by the Christian churches.[41]

While Hegel was able to sidestep the life of Jesus problem during his lifetime, a number of factors brought it to a head after his death in 1831.

---

u. 'Die Bildsäulen sind nun Leichname, denen die belebende Seele, so wie die Hymne Worte, deren Glauben entflohen ist, die Tische der Götter ohne geistige Speise und Trank, und aus seinen Spielen und Festen kommt dem Bewußtsein nicht die freudige Einheit seiner mit dem Wesen zurück.' HW, III, 547.

First, a belief in the literal truth of the Bible had become increasingly central to the Pietist 'Awakening', which came to dominate conservative religious circles in Prussia. At the same time, the life of Jesus had emerged as a key issue for rationalist and liberal theologians, who were concerned to separate the historical kernel from the supernatural chaff of the Gospels, typically by eliminating the miracle stories and downplaying the Resurrection. By the 1830s, however, a backlash against this type of theological rationalism was in full swing, which led a number of Hegel's followers to insist that his philosophy confirmed not only the broad truths of Christianity but also its specific dogmatic and historical content.[42] It was in this contentious context that D. F. Strauss published *The Life of Jesus* (1835), which argued that the Gospel narrative of Jesus was composed almost entirely of myths.

The notion that the Bible contained myth was not new, of course.[43] Schelling was willing, as early as 1792, to apply Heyne's theory of myth to the Garden of Eden narrative, an interpretation that was developed more fully by the theologian Johann Philipp Gabler. Nor was the mythical approach confined to Genesis. In an 1802 study, for example, Georg Lorenz Bauer dismissed numerous elements of the Old and New Testaments as mythical in an effort to highlight what he saw as the Bible's historical core. But it was not until W. M. L. de Wette's *Contributions to the Introduction to the Old Testament* (1806–7) that the term 'myth' was applied not just to individual stories but entire books of the Bible, including those that had the 'feel' of history. Influenced by Herder and Schelling's emphasis on the intimate link between myth and ancient national life, de Wette argued that the Pentateuch constituted a Hebrew national epic, which was written well after the events it described in order to justify religious practices that had emerged only in the wake of the Babylonian captivity.

Although Strauss could draw on de Wette's approach, there were obvious objections to interpreting the Gospel life of Jesus as the mythical creation of a group or community. Most significantly, it was hard to imagine how a set of myths and legends could have sprung up around the person of Jesus Christ in the short interval between his death and the composition of the Gospels.[44] Strauss resolved this issue by arguing that these narratives were not invented out of whole cloth but instead reflected long-standing expectations among the Jewish people concerning the person of the messiah. The effectiveness of this approach can be seen in Strauss' handling of the Transfiguration, when Jesus appeared to his disciples surrounded by light and standing next to Moses and Elijah. According to the 'supernaturalist' interpretation, this episode was a dramatic confirmation of Jesus' messianic mission and a genuinely miraculous event. According to the 'naturalist' interpretation, the miraculous aspects of this narrative were a result of an overactive Oriental imagination or perhaps the blinding effects of the sun. For Strauss, however, this story was a product of the long-standing expectation that the Messiah would commune with other great religious figures of the Hebrew tradition, thus it had no historical basis whatsoever. This approach to the Gospels was not entirely novel: Schelling had suggested it in an almost offhand way in his philosophy of art and in his *Lectures on the Method of Academic Study* (1803).[45] The difference was that Strauss applied this interpretation to almost the entirety of the Gospel history, so that by the end of his book, Jesus had been reduced to a shadowy, almost unknowable figure.

Even as he debunked the Gospel Jesus, Strauss tried to save the figure of Christ for the Hegelian project. In a concluding essay, he argued that Christ was best seen as a representation of the idea of the 'godman', the union of infinite and finite. But,

> if the idea of the unity of divine and human nature is granted reality, does this mean that it must have become reality in one individual, but not before and afterwards? That is not the way that the idea realises itself, to pour out its contents into a single example and to be miserly toward all the rest. Instead, it likes to distribute its riches in a multitude of exemplars that mutually complete themselves.[v,46]

Not one man, but rather all of human history constituted the true union of human and divine, the true source of miracles, and the true redemption from sin. Having laid out this speculative Christology, however, Strauss was confronted by a dilemma, one that had troubled Hegel and Schelling before him: how, as a pastor or an intellectual, could one communicate these speculative insights to those still caught in the grips of 'representation'? Should one try to raise them up to the speculative standpoint and risk alienating them? Or should one speak in their language and risk being unmasked as a liar? In the end, Strauss found no way out of this dilemma. Instead, he could only offer the weak sentiment that 'time would tell' whether humanity

---

v. 'Wenn der Idee der Einheit von göttlicher und menschlicher Natur Realität zugeschrieben wird, heißt dieß soviel, daß sie einmal in einem Individuum, wie vorher und hernach nicht mehr, wirklich geworden sein müsse? Das ist ja gar nicht die Art, wie die Idee sich realisiert, in Ein Exemplar ihre ganze Fülle auszuschütten, und gegen alle andern zu geizen, sondern in einer Manchfaltigkeit von Exemplaren, die sich gegenseitig ergänzen, ... liebt sie ihren Reichtum auszubreiten.' Strauss, *Leben Jesu* vol. II, 734.

would be better served through enforced silence or open speculation on these questions.[w,47]

10.6 Mythology as religious consciousness: Schelling's lectures on the philosophy of mythology

Schelling's late philosophy of mythology can be seen as a response not only to Hegel's philosophy of religion, but to the Hegelian philosophy as a whole.[48] While Hegel published and lectured on aesthetics, law, nature and the philosophy of history, Schelling compressed his insights into history, politics and natural history into a massive series of lectures on mythology and revelation which he first delivered in 1828 and then repeated, reworked and expanded over the course of the 1830s and 1840s. Rather than accept the Hegelian notion of 'representation', he doubled down on his previous commitment to 'mythology', to which he now assigned an almost unprecedented explanatory power. At the same time, he redeemed the previously suspect term 'revelation', which became a central concept for his late, 'positive' philosophy.

Even before the publication of Hegel's *Phenomenology of Spirit*, Schelling had begun to distance himself from the assumptions that had undergirded his identity philosophy. Like many of his fellow Romantics, he was deeply troubled by the destruction and disorder wrought by the Napoleonic Wars. While Hegel stressed the harmony between reason and reality, Schelling came to emphasise the fallenness of the world and the distance between God and his creation. In his view, no purely rational understanding of consciousness could account for the human capacity for good and evil. Thus in his analysis of human freedom he found it necessary to posit an unruly or irrational principle at the ground of human consciousness. When humanity was in union with God, this principle existed as a subordinate power, but when humanity rebelled against God, this power came to the fore, resulting in a sort of madness. Yet this 'madness' was precisely the condition for human freedom and autonomy.

In making this argument about human freedom, Schelling was also making an argument about the freedom of God, whom he conceived as a distinct personality rather than an impersonal Absolute. For God to be truly free, however, he could not be defined as purely rational. Instead, Schelling argued, the same unruly principle that was present in human will was also present in God's will and came to the fore when he created the world. It was

w. 'Die Zeit wird lehren.' *Ibid.*, 744.

this unruly power in God (that in God which was 'not God') that explained the possibility of a truly autonomous world and its eventual rebellion against God. The presence of this power also explained why God had to intervene once more – in the form of revelation – in order to restore the original harmony with creation and within himself. It was in order to describe the moments of the divine will that Schelling developed a system of three potencies: A1 (the material potency that, when it rebelled, became the 'B' potency), A2 (the ideal potency) and A3 (the spiritual potency that brought the ideal and material potencies into harmony). These potencies formed the basis for not only God's will but also the natural world and the human psyche.

Schelling's theory of potencies provided the philosophical basis for his famous 'tautegorical' interpretation of myth. 'Mythology is not *allegorical*, it is *tautegorical*. To mythology the gods are actually existing entities, that are not something *else*, do not *mean* something else, but rather *mean* only what they are.'[x,49] This was so because mythology, which Schelling defined as *Götterlehre* or the doctrine of the gods, was nothing other than the play of the potencies. The stories of rising and falling deities reflected not only the power of these potencies over the human psyche but the actual participation of God in the 'theogonic' process. In Schelling's view, no other interpretation could account for the truly horrific aspects of ancient religion, such as the practice of burning children alive. These types of practices could only be explained by reference to a supernatural power that 'was able to impose silence on the natural feeling that was opposed to such monstrous demands.'[y,50] In addition, the notion of a theogonic process helped to explain the parallels between the world's mythologies and the evolution of those mythologies from the most primitive nature worship to the universal mythology of the Greeks.

In Schelling's view, humanity had originally existed in a single undifferentiated mass under the restrictive reign of one god, the material potency (A1/B). What launched the theogonic process was the dawning into consciousness of the ideal potency (A2), which was experienced as the coming of a new god whose existence challenged the power of the first. This moment generated a crisis, later commemorated in the Biblical myth of the Fall and the Greek myth of the Rape of Persephone, that resulted in the scattering

---

x. 'Die Mythologie ist nicht allegorisch, sie ist *tautegorisch*. Die Götter sind ihr wirklich existierende Wesen, die nicht etwas anderes *sind*, etwas anderes *bedeuten*, sondern *nur* das bedeuten, was sie sind.' SSW, XI, 195–6.

y. 'Dem natürlichen Gefühl, das so unnatürlichen Forderungen sich entgegensetzte, konnte nur eine *übernatürliche* Thatsache Stillschweigen gebieten.' SSW, XI, 82–3.

of the peoples across the earth and the formation of its religions. In the first mythologies, however, humanity remained under the sway of the earliest god, whose consciousness of his weakness made him jealous and demanding. This type of religion, which included the Hebrew religion, was not a true monotheism, since it was based on the knowledge of only a single potency. Instead, it was merely a 'relative monotheism'.[51] Schelling thus saw the move from monotheism to polytheism, where the ideal god A2 held sway, as a sign of progress and a step toward the liberation of humankind. Whereas the first god was restrictive and repressive, the second god (who in Greece took the form of Dionysus) was largely benevolent, suffering and absorbing the blows of the jealous first god while teaching humanity the elements of agriculture and political order. Indeed, it was only through polytheism that 'nations' proper came into being.

While there were three true polytheistic systems (in Egypt, India and Greece), the highest of these was Greek mythology since it alone was able to mediate between the material god B and the ideal god A2. The relative harmony among these potencies allowed the Greeks to adopt a free relationship to their mythology, which was the condition of their art and philosophy. Thus for Schelling's late philosophy, the rise of Homer marked both the beginning of poetry and the end of true mythology. Likewise, it was only at the end of mythology that Hesiod could compose his *Theogony*, which shed light not only on the Greek gods but on the theogonic process as a whole. Meanwhile, the Greeks were granted an intimation of the coming Christian revelation in the Eleusinian mysteries, which foretold the arrival of Dionysus Iakchos, who was portrayed as an infant in the arms of the virgin Persephone. Iakchos was the third, spiritual potency, which would harmonise the first two potencies and restore the original Trinitarian monotheism at the level of consciousness and freedom. This was as far as the mythological process could go, however, because the actual revelation of God would come only in the person of Jesus Christ, the real existing A2.

What is striking in all of this is the systematic displacement of the Christian salvation narrative from the Bible into pagan mythology. Judaism, in Schelling's view, was simply the outward medium in which the saviour appeared. Aside from that, it had no inward connection to Christianity or its revelation.

> In a certain sense Christ was more for the pagans than for the Jews. The Jews felt this as well. They saw him as only a modification of the pagan principle. The Jews, however, were only something as the

bearers of the future. That medium would become useless, blown away like the shell from the kernel.[z,52]

For Schelling, Christ's ethical teachings were neither unique nor particularly important for Christianity. The crucial fact was Christology (again the tautegorical interpretation) and the pre-existence of the Son and his sufferings for all peoples, not just the Jews.

Schelling's conception of the pre-existence of Christ and his primarily pagan mission was a significant reversal of Strauss' 'mythical approach'. Indeed, in the 1841–2 lectures on the philosophy of revelation, Schelling addressed Strauss directly when he criticised those who granted the historicity of Jesus but maintained that the events of his life were myths composed by his followers. Schelling described this as an 'escape route' for those who did not want to accept the Christian revelation. In Strauss' case, however, it was exacerbated by the fact that he had ignored Schelling's later philosophy in developing his speculative Christology. In any case, Schelling argued, Christ's significance was independent of the 'completely accidental tales' that were told about him.[aa]

Although Schelling's lectures on the philosophy of mythology and revelation had a rather muted impact in his lifetime (they were published only posthumously), they would exercise a considerable influence on German thought once they were rediscovered in the first decades of the twentieth century. For one thing, the 'tautegorical' interpretation provided a way of taking mythology seriously as a phenomenon in its own right, with the power to shape the psyches of those in its thrall. In addition, Schelling's emphasis on rising and falling gods, on the multiple layers of mythological consciousness, and on the ways these factors were expressed in religious liturgy (or, on a Freudian reading, the 'symptom') broke through the rationalism and historicism that governed most readings of mythology in his day. In the process, however, Schelling developed an alternative to the Hegelian reading of politics and history. For Schelling, it was religion – in the form of mythology – that formed the basis of a nation and its laws. Political order was not something that was created through planning or statecraft; instead it was a product of the theogonic process itself. Indeed, Schelling condemned

---

z. 'Allerdings war Christus in gewissem Sinne mehr für die Heiden als für die Juden. Das empfanden auch die Juden; sie sahen ihn als eine Modifikation des heidnischen Prinzips an. Die Juden waren aber nur Etwas als die Träger der Zukunft, und das Mittel ward zwecklos, wie die Hülle vom Kerne hinweggeweht.' Schelling, *Philosophie der Offenbarung 1841/42*, Manfred Frank (ed.) (Frankfurt a.M.: Suhrkamp, 1977), 285.

aa. 'Ganz zufälligen Erzählungen.' Schelling, *Philosophie der Offenbarung*, 310.

as 'fanaticism' all attempts to devise a perfect state.[bb] Instead, he placed his hopes in a 'philosophical religion' – not a religion of reason but a religion able to grasp the entirety of religious history, overcome the divisions between Protestants, Catholics, and Orthodox, and, so he hoped, provide the condition for lasting peace in the years to come.

10.7 Legacies

What was the legacy of Idealist speculation on myth? Only a glimpse of an answer can be provided here. First, however, it must be remembered that the concept of myth operative in much of early Idealism was part of a longer and broader current of Romantic and proto-Romantic speculation on the role of myth. According to this concept, myths were narratives of gods, heroes or other supernatural beings that provided the cultural substrate and binding power for ancient cultures. What Idealism, particularly the philosophy of Schelling, added to this was a system of thought that elevated myth from a conditional, culturally bound artefact to a phenomenon that offered a direct intuition of God or the Absolute and that was powerful enough to overcome history itself ('the last and greatest work of mankind').

    This Romantic–Idealist conception of myth would not have gained traction in nineteenth-century culture without a further assumption, which was that modernity was, by its very definition, the time without myth.[53] In many ways, this notion was a carry-over from the Enlightenment, insofar as the *philosophes* conceived myth as a tissue of distortions, lies and superstitions that would be done away by the spread of reason. In the writings of Herder and Schelling, however, the absence of myth came to be identified as the source of all that was problematic in modern culture. In particular, the perceived absence of myth became a means of critiquing what was perceived as an atomistic, divided and overly privatised modern society, dominated by a 'machine-state' and lacking any sense of public culture.[54] Paralleling this cultural critique, however, was a theological–political critique of the Biblical revelation, which was dismissed because it produced heteronomy and because it was the product of a foreign, 'Oriental' culture. The appeal of a 'new mythology' lay in the possibility of recreating the lost religious, social and political unity by means of a cultural phenomenon that flowed freely from (German–Greek) humanity itself.

---

bb. 'Schwärmerei.' SSW, XI, 552.

The Romantic–Idealist concept of myth lay at the basis of the attempts to reconstruct national mythologies not only in Germany, but also in England, Ireland, Finland and elsewhere. Yet it could also serve as the basis for a hermeneutics of suspicion, as was the case in Strauss' *Life of Jesus*. By identifying the Gospel history as the mythical creation of a specific historical community, Strauss undermined the cultural authority of the Bible and traditional theology as a whole. In the end, however, Strauss' procedure more closely resembled that of Nietzsche than that of Hegel, who by avoiding the powerful but dangerous language of myth attempted to preserve the content of the Christian revelation even as he moved beyond it.

These 'positive' and 'negative' valencies within the discourse on myth would shape German and European discussions well into the twentieth century. Indeed, quite a few intellectual rivalries were defined by opposing attitudes towards myth. Consider, for example, the contrasting attitudes of Richard Wagner and Nietzsche (after 1878), Carl Jung and Sigmund Freud, and especially Martin Heidegger and Ernst Cassirer, whose long-running debate over the value of myth shaped philosophical discourse into the 1940s.[55] In many of these cases, the contest between myth and anti-myth carried a subtheme of 'paganism' vs. 'Hebraism', which testifies to the ease with which the longing for myth could lock hands with anti-Semitism. On the other hand, there were also a number of attempts to recapture a specifically Jewish mythology, such as in the early writings of Martin Buber.

Aside from its many ramifications through European culture, the Idealists' engagement with mythology also has a bearing on our understanding of Idealism as a philosophical movement and a historical moment. In particular, it highlights not only the many differences between Schelling and Hegel, but also the degree to which they moved in the same intellectual universe, which was defined by a deep seriousness concerning matters of religion, a belief in the meaningfulness of history, and a sense that ancient Greece and its gods remained crucial to the understanding of both.

Notes

1. 'I grew up in the arms of gods.' Friedrich Hölderlin, *Werke in einem Band*, ed. Hans Jürgen Balmes (Munich and Vienna: Carl Hanser, 1990), 70.
2. Cf. Friedrich Max Müller, *Contributions to the Science of Mythology* (London: Longmans, Green, and Company, 1897).

3. Friedrich Schelling, 'Ueber Mythen, historische Sagen und Philosopheme der ältesten Welt', SSW, I.1, 43–83.

4. Christoph Jamme, *Einführung in die Philosophie des Mythos: Neuzeit und Gegenwart* (Darmstadt: Wissenschaftliche Buchgesellschaft, 1991), 18–19.

5. Louis, chevalier de Jaucourt, 'Mythologie', *The Encyclopedia of Diderot and d'Alembert Collaborative Translation Project*, trans. Nelly S. Hoyt and Thomas Cassirer (Ann Arbor: MPublishing, University of Michigan Library, 2003). Trans. of 'Mythologie', *Encyclopédie ou Dictionnaire raisonné des sciences, des arts et des métiers*, vol. X. Paris, 1765.

6. Charles de Brosses, *Du culte des dieux fétiches, ou Parallèle de l'ancienne Religion de l'Egypte avec la Religion actuelle de Nigritie* (N.p.: n.p., 1760).

7. Christian Gottlob Heyne, 'Ueber den Ursprung und die Veranlassung der Homerischen Fabeln', *Neue Bibliothek der schönen Wissenschaften und der freyen Künste* 23:1 (1779), 1–53, here 13.

8. SSW, I:1, 74–6.

9. 'Antiquissimi de prima malorum humanorum origine philosophematis Genes. III explicandi tentamen criticum et philosophicum' [1792], SSW, I, 1–40.

10. Johann Jakob Hess, 'Grenzenbestimmung dessen, was in der Bibel Mythos und was wahre Geschichte ist', *Bibliothek der heiligen Geschichte*, vol. II (1792), 153–254.

11. All translations are my own unless otherwise noted.

12. Friedrich Schiller, *Letters on the Aesthetic Education of Man*, trans. Elizabeth M. Wilkinson and L. A. Willougby, in *Essays*, Walter Hinderer and Daniel O. Dahlstrom (eds.) (New York: Continuum, 1995), 90.

13. Translation, GSW. This discussion of Hölderlin draws from the succinct analysis in the editors' introduction to Christoph Jamme and Helmut Schneider (eds.), *Mythologie der Vernunft: Hegels 'ältestes Systemprogramm' des deutschen Idealismus* (Frankfurt a.M.: Suhrkamp, 1984), 19–76 and esp. 45–53.

14. *Ibid.*

15. *Ibid.*

16. See esp. Otto Pöggeler, 'Hegel, der Verfasser des ältesten Systemprogramms des deutschen Idealismus', in Jamme and Schneider (eds.), *Mythologie der Vernunft*, 126–43.

17. Jamme and Schneider, editorial introduction, *Mythologie der Vernunft*, 57–8.

18. Schelling, 'Über Offenbarung und Volksunterricht', SSW, I, 474–82, here 479.

19. Schelling, *System of Transcendental Idealism (1800)*, trans. Peter Heath (Charlottesville, VA: University Press of Virginia, 1978) [hereafter STI], 231.

20. STI, 232.

21. *Ibid.*

22. The following discussion is based on the text of the 1804–5 Würzburg lectures, which were first published in SSW, V, 353–736.

23. Friedrich Schelling, *Philosophy of Art*, trans. Douglas Stott (Minneapolis: University of Minnesota Press, 1989), 35 [hereafter PA].

24. Karl Philipp Moritz, *Götterlehre, oder mythologische Dichtungen der Alten*, Horst Günther (ed.) (Frankfurt a.M. and Leipzig: Insel, 1999), 9–10.

25. PA, 61.

26. *Ibid.*, 61.

27. *Ibid.*, 63.

28. *Ibid.*, 59.

29. *Ibid.*, 64.

30. Friedrich Schlegel, *Kritische Friedrich-Schlegel-Ausgabe*, Ernst Behler (ed.) I (Munich: Ferdinand Schöningh, 1967), 284–351, esp. 319.

31. PA, 76.

32. *Ibid.*, 77.

33. This reading is derived in part from Thomas A. Lewis, 'Religion and demythologization in Hegel's *Phenomenology of Spirit*', in Dean Moyar and Michael Quante (eds.), *Hegel's Phenomenology of Spirit: A Critical Guide* (Cambridge: Cambridge University Press, 2011), 192–209. Also useful in this context has been Peter Kalkavage, *The Logic of Desire: an Introduction to Hegel's 'Phenomenology of Spirit'* (Philadelphia: Paul Dry, 2007).

34. Lewis, 'Religion and demythologization', 195.

35. G. W. F. Hegel, *Phenomenology of Spirit*, trans. A. V. Miller (Oxford: Clarendon Press, 1977), 429.

36. *Ibid.*, 433.

37. *Ibid.*, 444.

38. *Ibid.*, 455.

39. On the context of Hegel's lectures on the philosophy of religion, see esp. Laurence Dickey, 'Hegel on religion and philosophy', in Frederick C. Beiser (ed.), *The Cambridge Companion to Hegel* (Cambridge: Cambridge University Press, 1993), 301–47.

40. Hegel, *Lectures on the Philosophy of Religion*, 147–8; cf. HW, XVI, 142–3.

41. HW, XVI, n 468.

42. On this, see John Toews, *Hegelianism: The Path to Dialectical Humanism, 1805–1841* (Cambridge: Cambridge University Press, 1982).

43. On this history, see Christian Hartlich and Walter Sachs, *Der Ursprung des Mythosbegriffes in der modernen Bibelwissenschaft* (Tübingen: Mohr, 1952).

44. Strauss, *Das Leben Jesu, kritisch bearbeitet*, 1st edn, 2 vols. (Tübingen: Osiander, 1835), I, 66–75.

45. SSW, V, 302.

46. Trans. GSW.

47. Strauss, *Leben Jesu*, II, 734.

48. On Schelling's late philosophy of mythology, see Edward Allen Beach, *The Potencies of God(s): Schelling's Philosophy of Mythology* (Albany: State University of New York Press, 1994).

49. Friedrich Schelling, *Historical-Critical Introduction to the Philosophy of Mythology*, trans. Mason Richey and Markus Zisselberger (Albany, NY: State University of New York Press, 2007), 136. Trans. modified.

50. *Ibid.*, 61.

51. On the links between Schelling's notion of relative monotheism and F. Max Müller's theory of henotheism, see George S. Williamson, *The Longing for Myth in Germany: Religion and Aesthetic Culture from Romanticism to Nietzsche* (Chicago: University of Chicago Press, 2004), 217–25.

52. Trans. GSW.

53. On this, see Jean-Luc Nancy, 'Myth interrupted', in *The Inoperative Community*, Peter Connor (ed.) (Minneapolis: University of Minnesota Press, 1991), 43–70.

54. This is the emphasis of Manfred Frank's *Der kommende Gott* (Frankfurt a.M.: Suhrkamp, 1982).

55. On Heidegger and Cassirer in this context, see Peter Eli Gordon, *Continental Divide: Heidegger, Cassirer, Davos* (Cambridge, MA: Harvard University Press, 2010).

11

Dialectic and analogy: a theological legacy

ROWAN WILLIAMS

In his splendidly magisterial and opinionated lectures on *Protestant Theology in the Nineteenth Century*,[1] Karl Barth picks up a throwaway parenthesis by Novalis on the concept of God:

Gott ist bald $1 \times \infty$ – bald $1/\infty$ – bald 0.[2]

This gnomic formula is then used by Barth as the springboard for an eloquent reflection on the essence of the Romantic dilemma about the sacred: to say that God is the infinite multiplication or the infinite division of a 'given quality of the ego or of life' is to posit a divinity that is ultimately defined as a function of some pre-existing constant – infinite, we might say, but not finally different; but the characteristically Romantic sensibility constantly moves in the direction of an other not determined by the ego, an other that is the condition of possibility for the union of subject and object. So the divine may be figured as the 'infinitisation' of the ego's play, the ego's dance, the indefinite variety of the constant ego's relations to infinity; but this cannot be all. What then might it mean to say that God is 'sometimes nought'? For Barth this is where we see a recognition of the irruption of an incalculable otherness into what had been merely a world of the immediate constant and a background indefiniteness – a recognition of the inescapable death of the ego. 'For 0 is certainly not merely a harmless little point which is passed through between $+1$ and -1':[3] the God who is 'sometimes 0' is irreducibly opposed to the given life or ego presupposed in the first part of the formulation: this is a God who makes the entire dance of the ego either possible or impossible. And so the God who is an infinitising of something given and the God who both negates and affirms the entire system cannot be 'God' in the same sense.[4] From the theologian's point of view, either you affirm the dance of Romantic dialectic or you look to the 'positive non-determinate' of which nothing can

274

be said until it has itself in some sense allowed the saying. Barth continues with a long discussion of some of Novalis' devotional poetry to push the question of whether Novalis had actually understood what he appeared to be saying with his mathematical axiom – concluding that the jury must remain out, to the extent that, while Novalis undoubtedly uses phraseology that suggests he is ultimately affirming no more than a symbolist humanism religiously clothed, he nonetheless leaves enough of the language of death and night in proximity to what he says about Christ and the apprehension of Christ to make us give him the benefit of the doubt.[5]

It is a vintage piece of Barthian deconstructive reading. Novalis' tantalising note in fact points in a rather different direction from what Barth makes of it. It is clear from the full text of this fragment that Novalis is trying out ways of expressing what it might mean to think of 'proofs' of God's existence in the framework of radical limit concepts in mathematics, like infinity and nought, so as to capture the 'hybrid' character of a concept of God as that which is revealed, in an essentially 'moral' revelatory encounter, both as the point in which the capacities of the finite soul are unified and as the unity of all that draws or attracts the ego from beyond itself; thus imagined, the divine remains decisively beyond our knowing.[6] But it is not an accident that Barth's impassioned and partisan reading comes immediately before his chapter on Hegel in *Protestant Theology*, in the course of which he observes in passing that Hegel is 'unquestionably most akin to Novalis' of all the thinkers he is examining.[7] His reading of Novalis is a prolegomenon to the reading of Hegel, a reading no less remarkable than what he has to say about the poet. It is both an uncompromising rejection of Hegel and a summons to theologians to take him seriously. Hegel, Barth argues, is the philosopher who gives Romanticism its ultimate rationale, who recognises and 'sublates' the dilemma expressed in Novalis' formulation (the claims made for the possibility of an indefinite expansion of the subject and, in tension with this, the unsettling intuition of a confrontation with what is radically other, which alone makes the subject's ecstasy possible); yet 'his own received him not'. By the middle of the nineteenth century, says Barth, Hegel had become a philosophical embarrassment, and all serious philosophical movements after this period essentially go back behind him to an Enlightenment that has not yet been 'overcome' by the speculative moment. We need to understand what is going on in this refusal of Hegel: the modern ego is, in Hegel's work, offered a supreme mirror in which to regard its own nature, its aspiration to universality and self-transparency, its 'immediacy' in creative capacity, its final and decisive capture, both narrative and conceptual, of the human past. So why does modernity not simply embrace this system, why does it not recognise in Hegel the voice of its deepest aspirations?[8] Part of the answer, according to Barth, is to be found precisely – and ironically – in Hegel's *theological* confidence. Hegel sweeps away any notion that faith and reason are at odds, and has no time for a Wolffian concordat between proximate but separate spheres for theology and philosophy; and he makes human epistemological self-confidence inseparable from confidence in God: only in relation to God can we actually think, and think what thinking is. In Barth's account, it is largely this theological agenda that makes the mid- and late nineteenth-century Protestant mind retreat in panic to Kant and/or Schleiermacher, to secure once again a place for the finite, uncertain subjectivity for which God is always a problematic and distant object.

What theology has to take seriously in Hegel is the identification of truth with God; without this identification, theology will be damagingly dependent on other discourses at every point.[9] Theology also needs to reckon with the way in which Hegel sees this truth as 'event', as something that cannot be apprehended without the conforming of the knowing subject to what truth is at that moment 'doing'.[10] Most fundamentally, perhaps, theology, in the light of Hegel, ought to be able to liberate itself from anything claiming to be a 'science of the spirit', any claim that theology deals with a specific set of experiences with a demarcated territory on the map of the human condition. The theologian needs to share Hegel's ambition – but in a paradoxical way. There is indeed a synthesis to be sought and spoken of, but it is 'the incomprehensible synthesis of God', a phrase unfortunately not explicated by Barth in this context, though we shall see some of what it might mean when we turn to Barth's own constructive work.[11] This is both the most important point of contact with and the most radical point of departure from Hegel for the theologian: Barth's challenge to Hegel is whether there is finally any room for an *encounter* between the human and the divine; or is the Hegelian picture only a fantastically deferred and re-routed vision of a human form of mental life reconciled with its own unlimited possibilities? Is there any sense in which the God of Hegel's conceiving can be said to be *free?*[12]

This discussion adumbrates very clearly the governing principles of particularly the early volumes of Barth's *Church Dogmatics*; the first volume was in process of publication at the time Barth was giving the lectures that became *Protestant Theology*. Although the whole of this latter work is in various ways a clearing of the ground for the *Dogmatics*, these final pages of the chapter on Hegel have some of Barth's clearest and most suggestive points for theological method. Of these we might summarise the most important as the principle that *truth is not passive*. To know the truth is to be identified with a process or activity that is not generated by the finite subject, whether in terms of ideas or 'experiences'. The truth is not known either by the initiating of exploration or by the analysis of a particular sensibility. There is no distance to be traversed so as to arrive at a truth removed from the knowing subject, nor is there a protected area of human subjectivity in which we may be safely encouraged to find the presence of the divine. God is the 'original subject', the active truth who alone establishes the possibility of knowledge of his – or any – truth.[13] As Barth expounds his version of Trinitarian doctrine, knowledge of God becomes possible because God eternally 'repeats' who or what he is in the eternal Word, the Son, in whom what is primordially unknowable becomes manifest: God posits himself as knowable, as 'repeatable'; he establishes his own image of his own divinity.[14] Finally in the work of the Holy Spirit, he creates the possibility of our receiving and (in a complex sense that does not allow us to think of 'owning' what we know) appropriating the divinity that has been made knowable in the Word.[15] This is to summarise a vastly sophisticated argument very inadequately indeed; but the point is to underline the continuity of the method here with what is sketched in Barth's discussion of Hegel. It is his attempt to answer his own challenge to theologians to take Hegel seriously; and taking Hegel seriously means to recast the knowledge of God as a being-activated-by the self-repeating action of God as this is opened up to self-reflection in and by the Spirit. In harmony with the Hegel chapter's agenda, this entails a dissolution of any dualism between sacred and secular as well as any suggestion of a fusion or co-operation between finite act and infinite. We know God not because we initiate any act of our own but because we are caused to receive the self-repeating action of God.

Barth's closing questions to Hegel anticipate a very different but in some ways comparable set of challenges articulated by Conor Cunningham when he discusses Hegel in *Genealogy of Nihilism* – a chapter tellingly entitled 'Hegel's consummate philosophy: the univocity of *Geist*': Cunningham's intriguing and sometimes convoluted argument is essentially that Hegel's dissolution of all dualisms leaves him with a basically empty notion of *Geist*.[16] Spirit in Hegel is always, and can only be, an unconditional and exhaustive cancellation of any non-provisional place to stand, so that any apparent determination can be *nothing but* its opposite. Thus nothing is constantly appearing as something and so there is an ultimate equivalence of something and nothing. There is no 'here' and 'there', even, or especially, in regard to finitude and infinity. Thinking itself becomes the thinking of nothing and so collapses into a void.[17] We are left with a 'univocity of non-being';[18] and thus, most significantly, with a programmatic prohibition of anything we could call *relation*. Cunningham also observes that, if being and non-being are assumed into a single univocal *Geist*, there is no way of characterising nothingness as *loss*.[19] Like Barth, Cunningham reads Hegel as dissolving any possible content for the notion of encounter. He hints, at one or two points, that Hegel's 'nihilism', the 'univocity of non-being', may, like a variety of postmodern nihilisms, prove to be the philosophical key to a recovered doctrine of creation, opening our eyes to the recognition that 'nothing existing as something' is indeed the condition of where we are but is so in virtue of a primordial reality of excess or gift which grounds the endlessness of desire.[20] But his analysis of Hegel actually leaves little room for such a retrieval: because every position is dissolved or disallowed, everything must collapse not simply into sameness but into a sameness of vacuity.

One way of understanding these arguments is to see Barth and Cunningham as, in their different ways, reading Hegel as ruling out any doctrine of *analogy*.[21] Barth's attitude to this question is notorious and we shall be returning to his treatment of it in a little while. Cunningham's interpretation is connected with the wider argument of his monograph, which sees the nemesis of western philosophy as rooted in the refusal of a proper metaphysics of participation that would allow us to speak both of distance and of continuity within finite being and in regard to the relation between finite and infinite being. For Cunningham, Hegel leaves us with the unacceptable alternatives of finite and infinite spirit confronting one another as simply each other's other, versions of the same absolute subject in different logical spaces (and therefore finally univocally related), or the collapse of finite and infinite spirit alike into an ultimate monism in which the finite is instrumental to the infinite's realisation.[22] This is a controversial reading, as I hope may become evident; but the point about analogy is one worth spending time on. Hegel famously asserts that all thinking is the thinking of what is *necessary*: 'the aim of philosophy is to banish indifference and to ascertain the necessity of things'.[23] Objects of thought cannot be present to the mind as – so to speak – casually plural; they are invariably mutually implicated and mutually defining. As soon as an object is properly *thought*, you cannot say of it that it might have been otherwise: to *think* it is to locate it as the specific other to some determinate (already thought) other. By the unique alchemy of the dialectic, this is at the same time to say that an object when thought in these terms is thought as supremely self-related, at one with itself and dependent on no other: the casual plurality of imperfectly thought elements is dissolved and recovered in the internal mutuality of an actually realised state of affairs. And every such state of affairs, object, situation, particular subjectivity, is itself only imperfectly thought until its character is uncovered as implicated in its 'other'; *ad infinitum*, or rather *ad consummatum*.

One of the implicit questions pressed by those critics of Hegel whom we have been considering is to do with what sense we can then make of the fluidity of an object-world where the identity of an object does indeed require it to be thought in terms of what it is not – but not in terms of the exclusive or exhaustive *binary* contradiction presupposed by Hegel. If a strictly Hegelian account of language and knowledge has to deal with the phenomenon of an otherness that is not and cannot be specified in exclusively binary terms, it has to deal with an 'excess' in objects of thought, the dimension that escapes being simply 'the other of its other', whether we call it a 'residue' or a 'redundancy', in the medieval sense of an overflow beyond pure self-identity, or simply a capacity for underdetermined differentness from itself. It is this that opens up discussion of the philosophical role of metaphor, as in Ricoeur's groundbreaking studies of the subject. Ricoeur quite defensibly insists on the separation of analogy and metaphor, but he also recognises what he calls the 'intersection' of the two in the different ways in which they work with this 'overflow' or extension of meaning.[24]

But before exploring this more fully, we must return to Barth for a while. Barth's celebrated dismissal of the *analogia entis* as 'the invention of the Antichrist' is often invoked.[25] During the same years that he was working on the first volume of the *Church Dogmatics* and refining the lectures on *Protestant Theology*, he was involved in debate with the Jesuit philosopher Erich Przywara, whose most important and original work on analogy was published in the same year as the first volume of the *Dogmatics*. As we shall see, Przywara's essay offers a very distinctive response to Hegel, which is indeed radically different from Barth's yet no less challenging; and we shall see also how this debate helped to shape one of the most significant theological enterprises of the twentieth century. Initially Barth takes up what is agreed to be the very untraditional phrase, *analogia entis*, and effectively interprets it in the light of that 'religious *a priori*' to which he is so resolutely opposed.[26] To affirm an 'analogy of being' between finite and infinite is precisely to retreat from the challenge to theology that he sees in Hegel: it is to search the territory of human activity and experience for something reminiscent of or 'open to' the infinite act of God, and as such it is to deny the identity of God with truth itself, the non-passivity of truth and the event-character of knowledge of God. It is to include God and creation within one conceptual map, as in Novalis' $1 \times \infty$ and $1/\infty$, and to refuse the death of the ego in the face of the God who is 0, who puts to death the self-identical subject. It entails 'applying the secular "There is" to God';[27] it canonises 'an onlooker's standpoint'.[28] Thus, in addition to being totally repugnant to the essential Reformed affirmation of the unconditional priority of divine act and freedom, the *analogia entis*, in Barth's eyes permits us to ignore the most serious philosophical challenge of modernity, the Hegelian system. Barth makes relatively little of this Hegel-related background in *explicit* terms in the first volume of the *Dogmatics*, but the connection is manifest. And his quite lengthy and detailed rebuttal of early nineteenth-century Catholic 'Romantic' theology, especially the Tübingen theologians such as Drey and Möhler, reflects a clear sense that Catholic theology in this era was heavily dominated by a process of domesticating the 'neo-Protestantism of Hegel and Schleiermacher' (an odd turn of phrase). More fundamentally, though, he argues that this process is one in which Idealist theology is itself brought back home to its ultimate roots in a Catholic – and essentially un-Christian – identification of revelation with the Church.[29] Ironically, Hegelian Idealism is in this perspective a resurgence of medieval Catholicism in its most subtle and seductive shape, and its theological challenge is essentially that of the Thomist synthesis (as Barth understands that synthesis). Yet at the same time, this is a Hegelianism that has itself failed to tackle the most fundamental challenge of Hegel's thought, which is a challenge to analogy as usually understood.

Barth's own response to the challenge tacitly agrees that Hegel is himself an implicit enemy to analogical thinking (which is why he is theologically interesting for Barth as later Romantic sub-Hegelian thinkers are not), and that a post-Hegelian theology must share this enmity. His early doctrine of the Word of God, as we have seen, is in some central respects a theological transcription of Hegel's rejection of a finite–infinite dualism. But the difficulty that surfaces in this theology is that Barth, by reading Hegel as an ally in the campaign against analogy as he understands it, seems to leave himself with a stark dilemma as to the relation of God to creation. The language of the first volumes of the *Dogmatics* at its most rhetorically intense could be understood to imply a picture of divine and finite action as simply mutually exclusive – which is a picture that entails a univocal understanding of finite and infinite being, two modes of action that are in competition for one logical space. Yet creation exists and is affirmed by God in his decision to be the God of *this* world, *this* history; there is no possibility in Barth of 'absorbing' the created into the uncreated. He cannot countenance anything resembling ontological monism, but the question remains of how he is to avoid univocal dualism, with all the difficulties that a commentator like Cunningham identifies. Barth's God cannot simply be 'the other of his (created) other', but the early repudiations of analogy leave us with the problem of how precisely to avoid such an implication.

The later parts of the *Dogmatics* – as recent scholarship has made more and more clear – go far towards addressing this, most constructively and effectively in connection with the doctrine of election:[30] God both truly and freely wills his other, as the one to whom he speaks, the one who is made in order to be called into a covenant relationship.[31] And because this entails belief in a God who is, so to speak, 'oriented towards covenant' in his own eternal action, we can, with appropriate caution, think in terms of an *analogia relationis*: the eternal relation of Father and Son establishes the prototype for God's relation with the finite.[32] Connecting this to the context of thought in Barth's earlier discussions, we could say that there really *is* a sense in which God as a covenanting God is the other of his created other, but only because it is presupposed that God has so chosen and freely acted. What is said in *Dogmatics* III.1 about the dependent actuality of creation is wholly clear about creation's ontological solidity; but this solidity is conceived strictly in terms of creation's own orientation towards encounter with the creator in covenant. There is nothing created that is outside this or irrelevant to it; it is a transcription into Reformed theological language of the principle that Barth had identified in Hegel, that all thinking of the finite–infinite relation must be as a matter of direct engagement with the infinite action. Once again, there is no 'spectator's' position to be found.

In the course of his discussion in this volume of the *Dogmatics*, Barth lets fall a telling observation. He is obviously a little uncomfortable even with the language of *analogia relationis*, lest it be heard as reinstating some theory of univocal likeness between finite and infinite: thus, he says: 'Analogy, even the analogy of relation, does not entail likeness but the correspondence [*Entsprechung*] of the unlike'.[33] It is as though 'correspondence' has a less malign resonance than 'likeness', as though 'likeness' inevitably carried the suggestion of univocity; and the distinction between the terms would bear further examination. Since he goes on to define his version of analogy in terms of the 'repetition' of the infinite self-relatedness of God in the finite realm, recalling the importance in the earlier volumes of this idea of repetition, we may assume that the use of *Entsprechung* carries the idea of a *derivative* similarity established by the *Sprache* of God, which would make sense in the context of relating the analogy of relation to God's 'internal' act of self-repeating. What is of focal importance is the implied insistence on *language*, on free self-communication, as the ground of analogical relation, language being something that always already carries with it some notion of a change freely initiated by a subject and establishing the parameters for response. We are brought back to Barth's most serious gravamen against Hegel, that he allows no sense to any idea of divine freedom, so that the 'reconciliation' he promises can only be a reconciliation of the ego with its possibilities (Novalis' first formulation once more, God as $1 \times \infty$). From Barth's point of view, Hegel's God is bound to be silent.

Taking stock of our discussion thus far, we have seen that Barth's treatment of Hegel can be seen as centring upon two basic insights. Positively, Hegel can be invoked by the theologian as the philosopher who, above all others, blocks off any discourse that countenances a continuity between finite and infinite, and thus blocks off any version of analogy that envisages qualities possessed or instantiated in different degrees by different subjects on a single scale of being. Any such continuity installs a vicious dualism at the heart of theology, which amounts to idolatry because it posits a God who is a member of the same class as the knowing subject; and the related dualism of subject and object, with its assumption of a privileged and distanciated position for the knower, is likewise disallowed, pointing inexorably to the priority of knowledge as the event of involvement and encounter, never susceptible to a simply third-person rendering. Yet negatively, Hegel, in dissolving the various dualisms that theology has to avoid, also dissolves the very *idea* of a genuine encounter: God as the other of the finite, never God without that otherness, is incapable of what theology understands by revelation. In Barthian terminology, a Hegelian God cannot repeat himself: he can only be present in the stages of the single dialectical story of spirit's self-emancipation. Hegelian freedom of spirit is thus for Barth antithetical to the freedom of God as witnessed to in Christian speech and belief; and – reverting to Cunningham's critique of Hegel – a freedom of 'Spirit' without divine freedom becomes vacuous, a dissolution of the human.[34] Behind some of the specifics of the arguments lies the complex issue of how otherness itself is to be thought about and whether Hegel ends up committing us to a binary logic of opposition that unduly tightens up the way our language and our habits of reference actually work.

As I have hinted, the Barthian problematic, with its roots in Barth's positive and negative responses to Hegel, is of immense importance to the theology of the last three quarters of a century. European Protestant theology especially in the post-war period had another of its reversions to Kantian anxieties, in the shape of Bultmann's anti-supernaturalism (for all its Heideggerian vocabulary, it still reads – as Barth rejoiced to observe – as another flight back behind Hegel). Barth's own attempts to follow his understanding of what Hegel allows and disallows for theology, including his uncompromising rejection of what he understood as analogical thinking, were too radical for most and this rejection of 'natural theology' generated two sorts of reaction. Some, from Brunner to Pannenberg, sought to rein-state a theology in which human reasoning about the finite world had at least a confirmatory role in theology. Others, like Bultmann and his heirs, were content to agree that natural theology and analogical thinking had had their day, but declined to accept the Barthian ontology of divine self-repetition in favour of a highly individualised ethic of self-definition in response to the address of the wholly alien Word of judgement, a Word quite as indepen-dent of any history as of any miracle or sacrament. Meanwhile, European Catholic theology became increasingly entangled in a different but paral-lel set of concerns about the 'supernatural': does the transcendent liberty of God require us to believe (as neo-scholastic theology was interpreted as claiming) that there is such a thing as 'natural' human fulfilment indepen-dently of divine grace? If not, how can we speak of a human potential for grace without introducing a covert notion of God or grace as, once again, 'the other of its other', simply the complement of a created capacity? The recovery of an older and more subtle theology of grace by scholars like Henri de Lubac forced a reconsideration of how the nature–supernature relation should be framed. The debates between Hans Urs von Balthasar and Karl Rahner as to the theological legitimacy of supposing human beings to be equipped with an innate *Vorgriff* of transcendent or illimitable being pro-vided a Catholic parallel to discussions and anxieties elsewhere about the religious *a priori*.[35] A generation or so on from this, issues about the indepen-dence of God from the world surfaced again in 'Process theology', shaped (unfortunately) by the later Whitehead rather than by Hegel. A Schelling-influenced Trinitarian theology – in Moltmann and his followers – attempted to re-inscribe both radical difference and even a kind of tension in the divine life and a mutuality of defining relation between God and world. And a persistent strand of 'non-realist' theological writing, shaped by a variety of postmodern schemata, has strongly resisted any discourse of transcendence in the usual sense, embracing just the ontological collapse into unthematised desire that Cunningham's monograph traces through the history of western philosophy.[36] In one way or another, a great deal of this theological history is, under the surface, about whether there is a thinking of analogy that does not lead us into an idolatrous univocity or an implicit monism. In what is left of this essay, I propose to look briefly at Barth's interlocutor Przywara in the light of this question, examining his own appropriation and critique of Hegel as charting a possible trajectory for theology that might avoid the increasingly sterile legacies of some of the twentieth-century debates just sketched. Przywara has begun to re-emerge as a serious subject of study in the English-speaking world over the last few years – it has been belatedly recognised that someone acknowledged as a major intellectual influence by Barth, Rahner and von Balthasar deserves more than a footnote or two – but we have yet to see a full-length treatment of how he engages with Hegel.[37] What follows is not that treatment, but an opening of the subject that will, I hope, suggest that in mapping the theological impact of German Idealism, Przywara may be a very significant point of orientation.

Before turning to his work, it may be helpful to add one or two further observations about the readings of Hegel we have had in view, if only to avoid leaving any misleading impression of what Hegel actually says. As Cunningham comes close to admitting, his nihilistic reading could itself be taken as doing exactly what Hegel himself prohibits – attempting to stand at a distance from the activity of thinking so as to talk about the impossible subject of how discourse relates to reality. The monistic understanding, which takes away the specificity of the given, can only be advanced as a reading of Hegel by ignoring what it means for Hegel to say that the final unity of the free self-awareness in and with spirit as such is only intelligible as unity-with-the-other;[38] or by sidestepping the necessary *simultaneity* of infinite freedom with the moment of actual thought in the specific apprehension of the object; or by minimising the emphasis (paradoxically complementary to this last point) on the impossibility of arresting thought in this or that specific moment and translating its content into a distanced analysis of 'reality' as such. In the *Philosophy of Nature* (§247), Hegel can write of the 'objectifying' perception of the particular natural phenomenon as 'the divine Idea . . . held fast for a moment outside the divine love'. And the restoration of the idea to the context of love is what thinking aims at: a dissolution of the particular *as conceived in isolation from its capacity to be thought/united with*. This is not at all the same as saying that the particular is 'absorbed' into anything, or even that particularity is a stage on the way to an undifferentiated reality. Those are distortions that can only arise when we try to think thinking outside the thinking of what is actually there to be thought here and now. To use Hegel's own terminology, these problems arise when we try to *represent* thinking outside its own activity, which means – as a number of creative modern Hegelians, including notably Gillian Rose and Andrew Shanks have argued – that Hegel's own representation of his philosophy needs the solvent of his own relativising of representation.[39] Shanks, in his most recent essay on Hegelian interpretation, observes that to accuse Hegel of refusing 'transcendence' (as does William Desmond in a sustained polemic against Hegel's schema) is to misconceive what he is doing, at least in his most distinctive writing: Hegel is criticising a highly specific form of thinking about transcendence, that form which envisages God as the other of the unreconciled consciousness (what Shanks calls the 'unatoned state of mind').[40] How if at all we find words for a recognition by the 'atoned' mind of a divine being not exhausted by being the other of any other is, Shanks argues, an open question for a sympathetic reader of Hegel.

I think he is probably right about this. But the very fact that it remains so acute a matter of debate, indeed that it so shapes the response of a Barth as well as a Cunningham or a Desmond, suggests that the issue is not by any means clear in Hegel's corpus. Part of the interest and importance of Przywara lies in his willingness to reframe this and other questions; though the intimidating density of his style continues to deter even well-disposed readers. In effect, however, he offers a structurally fairly straightforward scheme into which aspects of the Heglian problematic can be slotted in a way that allows them to be thought through freshly and outlines a model of analogy which, so far from being the idolatrous construction Barth imagines, in fact settles most of Barth's own concerns within the framework of a theologically informed ontology not at all alien to what Barth himself sketches in CD, III.1.

The scheme (as outlined in almost impossibly compressed form in his *Analogia entis*) is roughly as follows. We begin from the irreducible duality in our apprehension between the act of knowing and the object of knowing; we cannot say anything interesting or coherent about either without the other. Metaphysics is therefore – to use Przywara's own terminology – both a meta-noetics and a meta-ontics; it obliges us to analyse both the act and the object of knowing, in a way that from the very start puts in question a 'pure' Idealist construction of the subject and the would-be robust but essentially crude realism of, for example, some neo-scholastic discussions. There is an inescapable '*zu einander*' in metaphysical language, a 'balance of tension' to be recognised in what is being thought, which in turn involves us in the recognition of a temporal or process-related dimension in our knowing (there are no timeless subjects or objects), and a capacity to distinguish between the 'being-there' and the 'being-thus' (*Dasein* and *Sosein*, though not simply with their Heideggerian associations) of what is known. There can be no thinking of the concept without reference to the *Da*, the givenness of a certain process of becoming; no engagement with the historical givenness without recognising the continuity-in-change of the *So*. All of this is the essence of what Przywara calls a 'creaturely' metaphysic, a metaphysic that focuses on the tension of a being-thus which is 'in and above' the being-there. If truth is to do with the right identification of the being-thus and history is the right following through of the being-there, we can equally well say that the metaphysical problem is that of 'truth in-and-above history', in dealing with which we establish the 'foundation, goal and meaning' of what we think/engage with.[41] The next step is to show how this strictly formal account of the metaphysical agenda opens up on to a theological dimension: a world in which it is possible to think 'foundation, goal and meaning' is a world in which we can think in and through time or process and thus one in which we apprehend the indwelling of form in a fluid and finite medium.[42] Articulating this is a matter of very delicate philosophical judgement and we are constantly liable to unbalance what we say in the direction of privileging either the form or the medium. Hence the risks of absorbing form into process or process into form (these are my terms rather than Przywara's), and only a properly theological metaphysic can preserve the balance by positing a relation between God and creation that is formally comparable to that between form and process – the 'in-and-above' relation that we have seen to characterise the finite object of thought. Upset the *theological* balance here, and you are left with the alternatives of a God who is no more than an aspect of the process or a God who is the sole true agent or object. Significantly, Przywara identifies the latter as the specific risk of Reformed theology, and asserts that such a theology is liable to tumble over into being no more than another variety of immanentist philosophy, as well as giving encouragement to other philosophies that are in effect 'de-theologised theologies'.[43] It is pretty clear that he has both Barth and Heidegger in his sights here. And the first section of the book ends with a declaration that the structure outlined so far is one that is consciously meant to confront Hegel. The 'in-and-above' model is one which presupposes that 'concept' is born in 'mystery' – that is, that the formative agency of God in the process of finite reality is the inexhaustible hinterland of what is given to us to know: we are 'seized' by the concept in its God-derived particularity so that we may be 'integrated' into the unfathomable priority of God's act. The point in regard to Hegel is, of course, that it is not possible even in principle to arrive at an identification with infinite spirit in any sense that makes representation redundant, and that the final realisation of the concept in thinking is inseparable from a confrontation with the positive formlessness of God (echoes of the 'positive non-determinate' that Barth looks for in Novalis). There remains a gap between the rhythm of divine life and that of our thinking and, for Przywara, this means that the life of the finite creature has in it a deeper level of freedom. Hegel, says Przywara, reads the universal fact of 'being-over-against', the mutual exclusions of plural existence solely in terms of contradiction – and thus also is bound to see the life of the eternal Logos as less a self-communication than an unbroken cycle of contradiction and dialectical self-recovery.[44]

The relation of this to the question of analogy is explored in the second part of Przywara's essay, and it is here that we see him engaging more directly with Hegel. He proposes what is in effect an alternative three-fold structure to that of Hegel, in terms developed from Aristotle, though going far beyond what classical thought envisaged: *logizesthai*, *dialogizesthai* and *analogizesthai* designate the stages of a thinking that can do justice to the presence of the 'positive non-determinate'.[45] The first is 'pure logic', an immediacy of perception of things in their abiding truth. Inaccessible to finite minds, it acts as a kind of regulative idea, not in the abstract Kantian sense but as a shorthand for the knowledge of things that is based in God's self-knowledge (a good Thomist and Augustinian principle) and thus grounds their fundamental continuity as substances or subjects. 'Dialogical' thinking is the outcome of the impossibility of 'pure logic', the deconstruction of the apparently given so as to penetrate it more deeply. The sharpness of the negative serves to uncover a more unconditional understanding of the unity of what is thought (it is, we might say, a 'testing to destruction') and articulates the *tension* to which Przywara has already drawn our consideration. But in this passage to a unity-in-tension, thinking moves to the analogical plane. We become able to articulate a unity that is not identical with any moment of our perception, which is both 'critical' in the sense of being distanced from any one such moment and united with the mysterious inner life of what is thought. Our knowing is thus neither absorbed in what is known nor paralysed by the contradictions of actual engagement with the objects of thought. Analogy is what moves us on from a dialectic that threatens to collapse into an ultimate self-identity: if the basic principle remains that everything is simply 'the other of its other', there is no residue in the relation. And this obviously is significant not only for what we say about the life of this or that moment or object of thought but for the relation between God and creation: God is never exhaustively the other of creation. God is God, the identity of essence and existence, of *Da* and *So*, in a mode of being radically inaccessible to finite conceptuality, defined by the internal differentiation of the Trinity. His being is thus outside any process of measurement or proportion; by the sheer gift simultaneously of existence and intelligible form to the finite, God establishes a world in which tension is inbuilt in our apprehension and thus 'analogical' thinking becomes of central importance. It is both a connecting mode of thought and one that connects to the infinite source, tracing the critical reality of unity in difference between finite things and between all finitude and God.[46]

A fuller discussion, particularly of the way in which all this is spelled out in the later sections of Przywara's essay in relation to specific texts of Aquinas, and of the consistently Christological way in which the whole scheme is theologically developed, is beyond the scope of this essay; the point of the preceding summary is simply to bring into focus a notably original response not only to Hegel but to Barth's identification of what is theologically challenging in Hegel.[47] The interest of Przywara's scheme is that it unambiguously denies any possibility of understanding God and creation univocally, or of Barth's bugbear, the attempt to speak of God and creation from a third-person standpoint, while equally unambiguously refusing any suggestion of a monism of divine action such as the early Barth might be read to imply. Against Hegel (as he understands him), Przywara affirms what might be called a non-rivalrous difference: not all difference must essentially be rendered in binary terms, with the one moment of thought being understood only as its other's other. There remains always the bare fact of givenness – strictly understood as the free bestowal of being and meaning – and thus the dimension of the strictly unsayable, of mystery, within the tensive (I use the term with conscious indebtedness to Ricoeur's vocabulary) thinking of all finite objects. Against Barth (as he understands him, and I think he identifies accurately a serious problem in the early Barth, though his critique does not apply so easily to the Barth of volumes III and IV of the *Dogmatics*), he affirms not a continuity of being between finite and infinite but a model of divine being-in-the-other that allows full scope for the tension between the conditioned and the unconditioned and thus allows us to see grace – and incarnation – as the proper crowning of creation and created action, without compromising divine liberty. Balthasar's metaphysics of gratuity and dramatic/temporal differentiation represents, as Ben Quash has admirably shown, a sustained engagement with Hegel.[48] But it would be an engagement far less effective and searching without Przywara's reshaping of the questions about analogy generated by Hegel and by Barth's particular theological reading of Hegel.

Does Przywara understand Hegel and Barth correctly? As I have hinted, I believe we have no alternative but to recognise in Hegel the duality of register that Andrew Shanks underlines in his study, the duality of an urge to intellectual/systematic closure and a passion for the unfinished or unexhausted pursuit of a truth that is never yet spoken as it might be.[49] This latter Hegel is one with whom Przywara could pursue a deeply fruitful conversation. As for Barth, it is uncomfortably clear that he had read little or nothing of Przywara's monograph on analogy and continues to speak of the *analogia entis* in complete disregard of the way in which it is explained by Przywara and others; and it is hard not to see some justice in the Jesuit's strong implied criticism of what I earlier called a monism of divine action.[50] But whether or not Barth adequately digested Przywara's argument, or even the critique to which he responds briefly in CD, I.1 of the *Dogmatics*, Przywara's own theological integrity and intelligence led him to a position not at all radically different from the argument that the *Dogmatics* developed. Przywara would not, I suspect, have used the language of 'covenant' as does Barth to reintroduce an analogical principle; but insofar as this notion carries with it just the sense of a radical, *ex nihilo* bestowal of relationship that Przywara insists upon, there are connections to be traced.

Both ultimately direct us to a Christological account of analogical language, and there is some irony in the fact that Hegel would undoubtedly have approved. There are many ways of approaching the immense theological legacy of Hegel and his epigones; but to trace it in terms of the tensions between the dialectical and the analogical has the advantage of connecting it closely, as I have tried to indicate, with some of the most far-reaching theological debates of the last century, debates which are very far from defunct today. For the metaphysically inclined Christian theologian, the convergence of Christology and ontology remains an inescapable direction of travel. Hegel, Barth and Przywara alike are still necessary companions on that intellectual journey.

Notes

1. Karl Barth, *Protestant Theology in the Nineteenth Century: Its Background and History*, Colin Gunton (ed.), trans. Brian Cozens and John Bowden (London: SCM Press, 2001) (first published 1947) [henceforth PT]; the German original is *Die Protestantische Theologie im 19. Jahrhundert* (Zurich: Zollikon, 1947).

2. No.125 in *Das Allgemeine Brouillon* from 1798–9 in *Novalis Werke*, ed. and with commentary by Gerhard Schulz (Munich: C. H. Beck, 4th edn, 2001), 493.

3. PT, 365.

4. *Ibid.*, 366.

5. *Ibid.*, 371–82.

6. See the note on the Novalis text on pp.795–6 of Schulz's edition, especially the quotation from Manfred Dick's criticism of Barth's reading: there is no 'infinitising' of the ego; 'Das Ich ist bestimmt durch diese gesuchte und doch nie zu erreichende unendliche Grösse.'

7. PT, 392.

8. *Ibid.*, 384–91 on the reception of Hegel and whether the age of Hegel is past or yet to come; it is worth noting the remarkable statement that nineteenth-century German intellectuals 'In making Hegelianism the subject of irony... were making themselves the subject of irony.'

9. *Ibid.*, 415.

10. *Ibid.*, 415–16.

11. *Ibid.*, 416–17.

12. *Ibid.*, 417–21, esp. 420 on the way in which Hegel can appear to make God subject to necessity.

13. Barth, *Church Dogmatics*, vol. I.1, G. W. Bromiley and T. F. Torrance (eds.) (Edinburgh: T. and T. Clark, 2nd edn, 1975) [henceforth CD, I.1], 247.

14. E.g. *ibid.*, 316: 'It is not impossible nor is it too petty a thing for [God] to be His own *alter ego* in His revelation.'

15. E.g. *ibid.*, 462: 'This being of ours is thus enclosed in the act of God... To have the Holy Spirit is to let God rather than our having God be our confidence.'

16. Conor Cunningham, *Genealogy of Nihilism: Philosophies of Nothing and the Difference of Theology* (London and New York: Routledge, 2002), 100–30.

17. E.g. *ibid.*, 112–13.

18. *Ibid.*, 111, 124.

19. *Ibid.*, 116: 'We now no longer think that Being has lost something in losing itself to nothingness. For the determination which arises from negation is transformed by essence into the basis of identity.'

20. *Ibid.*, 105, 125, elaborated in chapters 9 and 10.

21. Cf. the throwaway remark of F. C. Copleston, *A History of Philosophy*, vol.VII. *Modern Philosophy, Part 1: Fichte to Hegel* (New York: Image Books, 1965), 41: 'in the absence of any clear idea of the analogy of being the notion of a finite being which is ontologically distinct from the infinite cannot stand.' This leads Copleston into a discussion of what he calls the 'anthropomorphic' temptations of post-Kantian Idealism – effectively a charge of univocity, the assumption that what is true of the finite consciousness is true of infinite consciousness.

22. Cunningham, *Genealogy of Nihilism*, 104–5.

23. *Hegel's Logic (Part one of the Encyclopaedia of the Philosophical Sciences, 1830)*, trans. William Wallace (Oxford: Clarendon Press, 1975, 3rd edn), 174; cf., for example, 208ff. It is this question of the definition of necessity that most puzzles Richard Bernstein in his generally sympathetic essay 'Why Hegel now?', reprinted in his *Philosophical Profiles* (Cambridge: Polity Press, 1986), 141–75. See 165–7 on this issue: Bernstein is critical of Taylor's

1975 study of Hegel for not providing an adequate analysis of the concept, but does not himself tackle the way the *Logic* addresses necessity as whatever it is in the order of things that prohibits an *atomistic* account of plural phenomena.

24. Ricoeur, *The Rule of Metaphor: Multi-Disciplinary Studies of the Creation of Meaning in Language*, trans. Robert Czerny with Kathleen McLaughlin and John Costello, SJ (London: Routledge and Kegan Paul, 1978), especially chapter 8 and 278–80.

25. CD, I.1, 13.

26. E.g. *ibid.*, 187–98.

27. *Ibid.*, 41.

28. *Ibid.*, 239.

29. *Church Dogmatics*, vol. I.2, G. W. Bromiley and T. F. Torrance (eds.), trans. G. T. Thomson and Harold Knight (Edinburgh: T. and T. Clark, 1956), 559–72.

30. See, for example, the excellent discussion by Bruce McCormack, 'Karl Barth's version of an "analogy of being": a dialectical No and Yes to Roman Catholicism', in Thomas Joseph White (ed.), *The Analogy of Being: Invention of the Antichrist or the Wisdom of God?* (Grand Rapids and Cambridge: Eerdmans, 2011), 88–144 – building on his earlier and groundbreaking study of Barth's theological evolution, *Karl Barth's Critically Realistic Dialectical Theology: Its Genesis and Development, 1909–36* (Oxford and New York: Oxford University Press, 1995).

31. McCormack, 'Karl Barth's version', 136. See Karl Barth, *Church Dogmatics*, vol. III. *The Doctrine of Creation, Part 1*, trans. J. W. Edwards, O. Bussey and Harold Knight, G. W. Bromiley and T. F. Torrance (eds.) (Edinburgh: T. and T. Clark, 1958) [henceforth CD III.1], §41 ('Creation as benefit'), passim and §42.2 ('Creation as actualisation'), especially pp. 363–4.

32. *Ibid.*, 191–206; see McCormack, 'Karl Barth's version', 135–9.

33. *Ibid.*, 196 (220 in the German original (Zurich: Evangelischer Verlag Zollikon, 1940)).

34. *Genealogy of Nihilism*, 123–4.

35. See John Milbank, *The Suspended Middle: Henri de Lubac and the Debate Concerning the Supernatural* (Grand Rapids: Eerdmans, 2005); and, on Balthasar and Rahner, Rowan Williams, 'Balthasar, Rahner and the apprehension of being', in Rowan Williams, *Wrestling with Angels. Conversations in Modern Theology*, Mike Higton (ed.) (London: SCM Press and Grand Rapids: Eerdmans, 2007), 86–105. For a different reading of the problem, critical of the present writer's interpretation, see Karen Kilby, 'Balthasar and Karl Rahner', in *The Cambridge Companion to Hans Urs von Balthasar* (Cambridge: Cambridge University Press, 2004), 256–68.

36. In addition to Cunningham, see Jeffrey L. Kosky, 'The birth of the modern philosophy of religion and the death of transcendence', in Regina Schwartz (ed.), *Transcendence. Philosophy, Literature, and Theology Approach the Beyond* (New York and London: Routledge, 2004), 13–30.

37. The first serious study in English is Thomas O'Meara, *Erich Przywara, S. J.: His Theology and his World* (Notre Dame, IN: University of Notre Dame Press, 2002); but for a thorough exploration of Przywara's hinterland, see the exceptionally interesting two-part essay (the length of a short book, in fact) by John R. Betz, 'Beyond the sublime: the aesthetics of the analogy of being', *Modern Theology* 21.3 (2005), 367–411 and 22.1, 1–50. The discussion continues in *The Analogy of Being* (see note 30, above).

38. The *locus classicus* is the opening twenty pages or so of the *Phenomenology*.

39. Gillian Rose, *Hegel Contra Sociology* (London: Athlone Press, 1981), especially ch.7; Andrew Shanks, *Hegel and Religious Faith: Divided Brain, Atoning Spirit* (London: T. and T. Clark International, 2011), especially ch. 2 on what he calls 'Hegel 1', the philosopher who exemplifies 'perfect openness' in the search for an unqualified human solidarity.

40. *Ibid.*, 57–8.

41. Erich Przywara, *Analogia Entis. Ur-Struktur und All-Rhythmus* (Einsiedeln: Johannes Verlag, 1962) (this edition incorporates both Przywara's original 1932 text, slightly revised, and a number of essays mostly from later in his career on related subjects), 60: 'Wahrheit in-über Geschichte'.

42. *Ibid.*, 'Philosophische und theologische Metaphysik', 60–97.

43. 'Ent-theologisierte Theologien', *ibid.*, 70.

44. *Ibid.*, 89–91, contrasting 'Gegensatz', the natural and given over-against-ness of objects for thought, with 'Widerspruch'.

45. *Ibid.*, 99–104.

46. *Ibid.*, 121–4: 'Mithin ist das Verhältnis zwischen innergeschöpflicher und zwischen-gott-geschöpflicher Analogie selber Analogie' (124).

47. See part 2 of Betz's essay (see footnote 37), and his contribution to Thomas White's collection (see footnote 30), 'After Barth: a new introduction to Erich Przywara's *Analogia entis*', 35–87, especially 82–6; also the essay in the same volume by Kenneth Oakes, 'The cross and the *analogia entis* in Erich Przywara', 147–71.

48. Ben Quash, *Theology and the Drama of History* (Cambridge: Cambridge University Press, 2005); see also his essay, 'Drama and the ends of modernity' in Lucy Gardner, David Moss, Ben Quash and Graham Ward (eds.), *Balthasar at the End of Modernity* (Edinburgh: T. and T. Clark, 1999), 139–71, especially 145–54 on Balthasar and Hegel.

49. See Shanks, *Hegel and Religious Faith*.

50. Betz, 'After Barth', 70–82, summarises Barth's criticisms and Przywara's responses over many years; see also Eberhard Mechels, *Analogie bei Erich Przywara und Karl Barth. Das Verhältnis von Offenbarungstheologie und Metaphysik* (Neukirchen: Neukirchener Verlag, 1974), and Keith Johnson, *Karl Barth and the Analogia Entis* (London: T. and T. Clark International, 2010). Eberhard Jüngel explores the implications of Barth's cautious move towards a theological acceptance of analogy in some sense and his reflections on the Barth-Przywara debate can be found in his *Gott als Geheimnis der Welt. Zur Begründung der Theologie des Gekreuzigten im Streit zwischen Theismus und Atheismus* (Tübingen: Mohr/Siebeck, 1977) (356–8 and 385–9 are of particular interest on Przywara, touching also on his influence on Rahner). Several of the essays collected in his *Barth-Studien* (Gütersloh: Benziger, 1982), examine the stages in Barth's move 'from dialectic to analogy'. The title of Jüngel's book is an echo, surely not accidental, of Przywara's 1923 work, *Gottgeheimnis in der Welt* (Munich: Theatiner Verlag). It is not clear whether Barth ever actually *read* Przywara's *Analogia entis*, however familiar he may have been or thought himself to be with Przywara's thought.

Bibliography

A. Primary literature – German Idealism

Collected Works: Standard Editions

Fichte, J. G., *Fichtes Werke*, 11 vols. Berlin: de Gruyter, 1971. Reprint of *Johann Gottlieb Fichte's sämmtliche Werke*, ed. Immanuel Hermann Fichte, 8 vols. Berlin: Veit & Co., 1845–6 [FSW], and *Johann Gottlieb Fichte's nachgelassene Werke*, ed. Immanuel Hermann Fichte, 3 vols. Bonn: Marcus, 1854–5 [Nachlass].

J.G. Fichte-Gesamtausgabe der Bayerischen Akademie der Wissenschaften, ed. R. Lauth *et al.* 41 vols. planned. Stuttgart-Bad Cannstatt: Frommann-Holzboog, 1964– .

Hegel, G. W. F., *Gesammelte Werke. Kritische Ausgabe*, ed. Deutsche Forschungsgemeinschaft in Verbindung mit der Rheinisch-Westfälischen Akademie der Wissenschaften, 32 vols. planned. Hamburg: Meiner, 1968– [GW].

Werke in zwanzig Bänden, ed. Eva Moldenhauer and Karl Markus Michel, 20 vols. Frankfurt am Main: Suhrkamp, 1969–71 [HW].

Kant, I., *Kant's gesammelte Schriften*. Ausgabe der königlich preussischen Akademie der Wissenschaften. Berlin: Reimer [now W. de Gruyter], 1902– [GS].

Werke in sechs Bänden, ed. Wilhelm Weischedel. Wiesbaden: Insel Verlag, 1956–62 [KW].

Schelling, Friedrich Wilhelm Joseph von, *Historisch-kritische Ausgabe*, ed. Jörg Jantzen *et al.* 40 vols. planned. Stuttgart-Bad Cannstatt: Frommann-Holzboog, 1976– [HKA].

Schellings sämmtliche Werke, ed. Karl Friedrich August Schelling, 14 vols. Stuttgart: Cotta, 1856–61 [SSW].

Other texts

Fichte, Johann Gottlieb, *Early Philosophical Writings*, trans. Daniel Breazeale, Ithaca, NY: Cornell University Press, 1993.

Grundlage der gesamten Wissenschaftslehre, in J. G. Fichte, *Gesamtausgabe der Bayerischen Akademie der Wissenschaften*, vols. I–II: *Werke 1793–1795*, ed. Reinhard Lauth and Hans Jacob, Stuttgart: F. Frommann, 1965.

Science of Knowledge, ed. and trans. Peter Heath and John Lachs, Cambridge: Cambridge University Press, 1982.

The Vocation of Man, trans. Peter Preuss, Indianapolis, IN: Hackett, 1987.

Hegel, G. W. F., 'Das älteste Systemprogramm des deutschen Idealismus', HW, I, 234–6.

'Die Positivität der Christlichen Religion', HW, I, 184–6.

Early Theological Writings, trans. T. M. Knox, Philadelphia: University of Pennsylvania Press, 1948.

Elements of the Philosophy of Right, ed. Allen W. Wood, trans. H. B. Nisbet, Cambridge: Cambridge University Press, 1991.

Enzyklopädie der philosophischen Wissenschaften im Grundrisse (1830), ed. W. Bonsiepen and H.-C. Lucas, Hamburg: Felix Meiner, 1992.

Faith and Knowledge, trans. Walter Cerf and H. S. Harris, Albany: State University of New York Press, 1977.

Hegel's Aesthetics: Lectures on Fine Art, trans. T. M. Knox, 2 vols., Oxford: Clarendon Press, 1975.

Hegel's Logic: Being Part One of the Encyclopaedia of the Philosophical Sciences (1830), trans. William Wallace, 3rd edn, Oxford: Clarendon, 1975.

Hegel's Philosophy of Mind: Being Part Three of the Encyclopaedia of the Philosophical Sciences (1830), trans. W. Wallace, Oxford: Clarendon Press, 1977.

Hegel's Philosophy of Right, trans. T. M. Knox, Oxford: Oxford Clarendon Press, 1967.

Lectures on the History of Philosophy, vol. III: *Medieval and Modern Philosophy*, trans. E. S. Haldane and Frances H. Simson, Lincoln and London: University of Nebraska Press, 1995.

Lectures on the Philosophy of Religion, ed. P. C. Hodgson, trans. R. F. Brown, P. C. Hodgson and J. M. Stewart, 3 vols., Berkeley and Los Angeles: University of California Press, 1984–7.

Phänomenologie des Geistes, ed. Wolfgang Bonsiepen and Reinhard Heede, Hamburg: Felix Meiner, 1980.

'Phenomenology', trans. Terry Pinkard [unpublished translation].

Phenomenology of Spirit, trans. A. V. Miller, Oxford: Clarendon Press, 1977.

'The positivity of the Christian religion', in *Early Theological Writings*, ed. Richard Kroner, trans. T. M. Knox, Chicago: University of Chicago Press, 1948, 140–2.

The Science of Logic, ed. and trans. George di Giovanni, Cambridge: Cambridge University Press, 2010.

Vorlesungen: Ausgewählte Nachschriften und Manuskripte, ed. Walter Jaeschke, vol. V: *Vorlesungen über die Philosophie der Religion*, part 3, Hamburg: Felix Meiner, 1984.

Vorlesungen über die Ästhetik, vol. III, Frankfurt am Main: Suhrkamp, 1993.

Vorlesungen über die Philosophie der Religion. Teil 3: Die vollendete Religion, ed. Walter Jaeschke, Hamburg: Felix Meiner, 1995.

Wissenschaft der Logik. Zweiter Band. Die subjektive Logik (1816), ed. Friedrich Hogemann and Walter Jaeschke, Hamburg: Felix Meiner, 1981.

Kant, Immanuel, *Religion within the Boundaries of Mere Reason and other Writings*, ed. Allen Wood and George di Giovanni, Cambridge: Cambridge University Press, 1998.

Schelling, Friedrich Wilhelm Josef von, *Erste Vorlesung in Berlin*, 15 November 1841, in
    Manfred Schröter (ed.), *Schellings Werke*, 13 vols., Munich: C. H. Beck, 1959 (first
    published 1927), VI.
Historical-critical Introduction to the Philosophy of Mythology, trans. Mason Richey and
    Markus Zisselberger, Albany: State University of New York Press, 2007.
Idealism and the Endgame of Theory: three essays by F. W. J. Schelling, ed. and trans.
    Thomas Pfau, Albany: State University of New York Press, 1994.
Philosophical Inquiries into the Nature of Human Freedom, trans. James Gutman, La Salle:
    Open Court Classics, 1992.
Philosophical Investigations of the Essence of Human Freedom, trans. Jeff Love and
    Johannes Schmidt, Albany: State University of New York Press, 2006.
Philosophie der Offenbarung 1841/42, ed. Manfred Frank, Frankfurt am Main:
    Suhrkamp, 1977 [1993].
Philosophie der Weltalter (1813), SSW, XIII, 109–84.
Philosophie der Weltalter (1815), SSW, XIII, 199–384.
Philosophy and Religion, trans. Klaus Ottmann, Putnam, CT: Spring, 2010.
Philosophy of Art, trans. Douglas Stott, Minneapolis: University of Minnesota Press,
    1989.
Philosophy of the World-Ages, trans. Frederick de Wolfe Bolman Jr, New York:
    Columbia University Press, 1942.
System of Transcendental Idealism, trans. Peter Heath, Charlottesville: University Press
    of Virginia, 1978.
The Abyss of Freedom/Ages of the World, trans. Judith Norman, Ann Arbor: University of
    Michigan Press, 1997.
The Ages of the World, trans. Jason M. Wirth, Albany: State University of New York
    Press, 2000.
Urfassung der Philosophie der Offenbarung. Teilband 2, ed. Walter E. Ehrhardt
    (Philosophische Bibliothek, vol. 445b), Hamburg: Felix Meiner, 1992.

B. Other primary literature

Abarbanel, Isaac, *Perush 'al Nevi'im Aharonim*, Jerusalem: Bnei Arbel, 1960.
Aristobulus, 'Fragments', trans. Adela Yarbro Collins, in James H. Charlesworth (ed.),
    The Old Testament Pseudepigrapha, Garden City, NY: Doubleday, 1985, II, 831–42.
Ascher, Saul, *Leviathan oder über Religion im Rücksicht des Judentums*, Berlin: in der
    Frankeschen Buchhandlung, 1792.
Balthasar, Hans Urs von, *The Glory of the Lord. A Theological Aesthetics*, vol. V: *The Realm of
    Metaphysics in the Modern Age*, trans. Oliver Davies, Andrew Louth, Brian McNeil,
    John Saward and Rowan Williams, San Francisco: Ignatius, 1991.
Barth, Karl, *Anselm: fides quaerens intellectum*, trans. I. Robertson, London: SCM, 1960.
Church Dogmatics, vol. I.1, ed. and trans. G. W. Bromiley and T. F. Torrance 2nd edn,
    Edinburgh: T. and T. Clark, 1975.
Church Dogmatics, vol. I.2, ed. G. W. Bromiley and T. F. Torrance, trans. G. T.
    Thomson and Harold Knight, Edinburgh: T. and T. Clark, 1956.

Church Dogmatics, vol. III.1, ed. G. W. Bromiley and T. F. Torrance, trans. J. W. Edwards, O. Bussey and Harold Knight, Edinburgh: T. and T. Clark, 1958.

Der Römerbrief, 2nd edn, Munich: Christian Kaiser, 1922.

Die Protestantische Theologie im 19. Jahrhundert, Zurich: Zollikon, 1947.

Die Protestantische Theologie im 19. Jahrhundert: ihre Vorgeschichte und ihre Geschichte, 6th edn, Zürich: EVZ, 1994.

Protestant Theology in the Nineteenth Century: Its Background and History, ed. Colin Gunton, trans. Brian Cozens and John Bowden, London: SCM Press, 2001 (first published 1947).

The Epistle to the Romans, trans. Edwyn C. Hoskyns (from 6th edn), London: Oxford University Press, 1968.

Baur, Ferdinand Christian, *Das Christenthum und die christliche Kirche der ersten drei Jahrhunderte*, Tübingen: Fues 1853.

Die christliche Gnosis; oder die christliche Religionsphilosophie in ihrer geschichtlichen Entwicklung, Tübingen: Osiander, 1835.

Die Epochen der kirchlichen Geschichtsschreibung, Tübingen: Fues, 1852.

Symbolik und Mythologie oder die Naturreligionen des Althertums, Stuttgart: Metzler, 1824.

Benamozegh, Elijah, *Israel and Humanity*, trans. Maxwell Luria, Mahwah, NJ: Paulist Press, 1995.

Israël et l'humanité. Étude sur le problème de la religion universelle et sa solution, Paris: Leroux, 1914.

Bendavid, Lazarus, *Etwas zur Charakteristik der Juden*, Leipzig: Stabel, 1793.

Benjamin, Walter, 'Theses on the philosophy of history', in *Illuminations*, ed. Hannah Arendt, trans. Harry Zohn, New York: Schocken, 1969.

Blumenberg, Hans, *Work on Myth*, trans. Robert M. Wallace, Cambridge, MA: MIT Press, 1988.

Boethius, *De consolatione philosophiae. Opuscula theologica*, ed. C. Moreschini, Munich: K. G. Saur, 2000.

Bonhoeffer, Dietrich, *Letters and Papers from Prison: The Enlarged Edition*, ed. E. Bethge, London: SCM Press, 1971.

Brosses, Charles de, *Du culte des dieux fétiches, ou Parallèle de l'ancienne Religion de l'Egypte avec la Religion actuelle de Nigritie* (1760).

Buber, Martin, *Die Legende des Baalschem*, Frankfurt am Main: Rütten & Loening, 1908.

'Offenbarung und Gesetz. Aus Briefen an Franz Rosenzweig', *Almanach des Schocken Verlags auf das Jahr 5697*, Berlin: Schocken, 1936–7, 147–54.

'Revelation and law (Martin Buber and Franz Rosenzweig)', in Franz Rosenzweig, *On Jewish Learning*, trans. Nahum Glatzer, Madison: University of Wisconsin Press, 1955, 109–18.

'The history of the dialogical principle', in *Between Man and Man*, trans. Maurice Friedman, London: Routledge, 1947, 249–64.

The Legend of the Baal Shem, trans. Maurice Friedman, London: Routledge, 2002.

'Zur Geschichte des dialogischen Prinzips', in *Das Dialogische Prinzip*, Gütersloh: Gütersloher Verlagshaus, 2006, 299–320.

Calvin, Jean, *Institution de la religion chrétienne*, Geneva: Labor et Fides, 1967.

Cohen, Hermann, *Charakteristik der Ethik Maimunis* in Wilhelm Bacher, Markus Brann, David Simonsen and Jakob Guttman (eds.), *Moses ben Maimon*, Leipzig: Fock, 1908, 63–134 [reprinted in Cohen, *Jüdische Schriften*, ed. Bruno Strauss, 3 vols., Berlin: Schwetschke, 1924, III, 221–89].

Das Prinzip der Infinitesimal – Methode und seine Geschichte, Berlin: Dümmler, 1883.

'Das Problem der Jüdischen Sittenlehre: Eine Kritik von Lazarus' Ethik des Judenthums', *Monatsschrift für Geschichte und Wissenschaft des Judentums* [reprinted in Cohen, *Jüdische Schriften*, III, 1–35].

Der Begriff der Religion im System der Philosophie, Giessen: Töppelman, 1915.

Ethics of Maimonides, trans. Almut Bruckstein, Madison: University of Wisconsin Press, 2004.

Kants Theorie der Erfahrung, Berlin: Dümmler, 1871; 2nd edn, 1885; 3rd edn, Berlin: Cassirer, 1918.

Platons Ideenlehre und die Mathematik, Marburg: Elwertsche, 1878.

Religion der Vernunft aus den Quellen des Judentums, Leipzig: Fock, 1919.

Religion of Reason out of the Sources of Judaism, trans. Simon Kaplan, Oxford: Oxford University Press, 2000.

Danzig, Abraham, *Ḥayyei Adam*, Vilna: Kschandz Lubansky, 1810.

Dorner, Isaak, *A System of Christian Doctrine*, trans. Alfred Cave and J. S. Banks, Edinburgh: T. & T. Clark, 1888–91 (vol. I, 1888).

Empson, William, *Collected Poems*, London: Chatto, 1977.

Feuerbach, Ludwig, *Das Wesen des Christentums*, Leipzig: Wigand, 1841.

Das Wesen des Christentums: Text nach der dritten Auflage Leipzig 1849, Leipzig: Reclam, 1969.

Essence of Christianity, trans. M. Evans, New York: Blanchard, 1855.

Gadamer, Hans-Georg, *Literature and Philosophy in Dialogue: Essays in German Literary Theory*, trans. Robert H. Paslick, New York: State University of New York Press, 1993.

Wahrheit und Methode. Grundzüge einer philosophischen Hermeneutik, 4th edn, Tübingen: Mohr, 1975.

Hartmann, Eduard von, *Die Selbstzersetzung des Christentums und die Religion der Zukunft*, Berlin: Duncker, 1874.

Heidegger, Martin, *Elucidations of Hölderlin's Poetry*, trans. Keith Hoeller, New York: Humanity Books, 2000.

Herder, Johann Gottfried, *Auch eine Philosophie der Geschichte zur Bildung der Menschheit*, in *Schriften zu Philosophie, Kunst und Altertum 1774–1787*, ed. Jürgen Brummack and Martin Bollacher (Bibliothek deutscher Klassiker, 105), Frankfurt: Deutscher Klassiker Verlag, 1994.

Ideen zur Philosophie der Geschichte der Menschheit, *Text*, in *Werke*, ed. Wolfgang Pross, III. i, Munich: Hanser, 2003.

Sämmtliche Werke, ed. B. Suphan, 33 vols., Berlin: Weidmann, 1877–1913.

Über den Ursprung der Sprache, in *Frühe Schriften 1764–1772*, ed. Ulrich Gaier (Bibliothek deutscher Klassiker, 1), Frankfurt: Deutscher Klassiker Verlag, 1985.

Vom Geist der ebräischen Poesie, in *Schriften zum Alten Testament*, ed. Rudolf Smend (Bibliothek deutscher Klassiker, 93), Frankfurt: Deutscher Klassiker Verlag, 1993.

Herrera, Abraham Cohen de, *Gate of Heaven*, trans. Kenneth Krabbenhoft, Leiden: Brill, 2002.

Puerto del cielo, ed. Kenneth Krabbenhoft (ed.), Madrid: Fundación Universitaria Española, 1987.

Hess, Johann Jakob, 'Grenzenbestimmung dessen, was in der Bibel Mythos und was wahre Geschichte ist', *Bibliothek der heiligen Geschichte*, vol. II (1792), 153–254.

Heyne, Christian Gottlob, 'Ueber den Ursprung und die Veranlassung der Homerischen Fabeln', *Neue Bibliothek der schönen Wissenschaften und der freyen Künste* 23, 1 (1779), 1–53.

Hölderlin, Friedrich, *Poems and Fragments*, trans. Michael Hamburger, Ann Arbor: University of Michigan Press, 1967.

Horowitz, Pinchas Eliyahu, *Sefer ha-Brit*, Brünn: Josef Karl Neumann, 1797.

Jacobi, Friedrich Heinrich, *Auserlesener Briefwechsel*, ed. Friedrich Roth, Leipzig: Fleischer, 1825.

Main Philosophical Writings, trans. George di Giovanni, Montreal, QC, and Kingston, ON: McGill-Queen's University Press, 1994.

Über die Lehre des Spinoza in Briefen an den Herrn Moses Mendelssohn, Breslau: Löwe, 1785.

Jaucourt, Louis, chevalier de, 'Mythologie', in *The Encyclopedia of Diderot & d'Alembert Collaborative Translation Project*, trans. Nelly S. Hoyt and Thomas Cassirer, Ann Arbor: MPublishing, University of Michigan Library, 2003.

Kierkegaard, S., *Concluding Unscientific Postscript*, ed. and trans. Howard V. Hong and Edna H. Hong, Princeton: Princeton University Press, 1992.

Either/Or, ed. and trans. Howard V. Hong and Edna H. Hong, 2 vols., Princeton: Princeton University Press, 1987.

Fear and Trembling, ed. and trans. Howard V. Hong and Edna H. Hong, Princeton: Princeton University Press, 1983.

Kierkegaard's Journals and Notebooks, ed. and trans. Niels Jørgen Cappelørn *et al.*, 11 vols., Princeton: Princeton University Press, 2007– .

Philosophical Fragments, ed. and trans. Howard V. Hong and Edna H. Hong, Princeton: Princeton University Press, 1985.

Practice in Christianity, ed. and trans. Howard V. Hong and Edna H. Hong, Princeton: Princeton University Press, 1991.

Søren Kierkegaard's Journals and Papers, ed. and trans. Howard V. Hong and Edna H. Hong, 7 vols., Bloomington: Indiana University Press, 1967–8.

Søren Kierkegaards Skrifter, ed. Niels Jørgen Cappelørn *et al.*, 55 vols., Copenhagen: Gad, 1997– .

The Concept of Irony, ed. and trans. Howard V. Hong and Edna H. Hong, Princeton: Princeton University Press, 1989.

The Point of View, ed. and trans. Howard V. Hong and Edna H. Hong, Princeton: Princeton University Press, 1998.

The Sickness unto Death, ed. and trans. Howard V. Hong and Edna H. Hong, Princeton: Princeton University Press, 1980.

Krochmal, Naḥman, *Moreh Nevukhei ha-Zeman*, in *Kitvei Rabi Naḥman Krokhmal*, ed. Simon Rawidowicz, Berlin: Ajanoth, 1924.

Lazarus, Moritz, *Die Ethik des Judentums*, 2 vols., Frankfurt am Main: Kaufmann, 1901.
  The Ethics of Judaism, trans. Henrietta Szold, 2 vols., Philadelphia, PA: Jewish
    Publication Society, 1900.
Lévinas, Emmanuel, *Totalité et Infini*, La Haye: Nijhoff, 1961.
  Totality and Infinity, trans. Alphonso Lingis, The Hague: Nijhoff, 1979.
Lotze, Rudolf Hermann, *Logic*, trans. Bernard Bosanquet, 2 vols., Oxford: Clarendon
    Press, 1888.
  Logik, 3 vols., Leipzig: Hirzel, 1874.
Maimon, Salomon, *Essay on Transcendental Philosophy*, trans. Nick Midgley, Henry
    Somers-Hall, Alistair Welchman and Merten Reglitz, New York: Continuum,
    2010.
  Gibeath Hamore in More Nebuchim, ed. Isaac Euchel, Berlin: Officina Scholae Liberae
    Judaicae, 1791.
  Philosophisches Wörterbuch, Berlin: Unger, 1792.
  Salomon Maimons Lebensgeschichte, 2 vols., Berlin: Vieweg, 1792–3; partially translated
    as *Autobiography* by John Clark Murray, London: Alexander Gardner, 1888
    [reprinted Champaign: University of Illinois Press, 2001].
  Streifereien im Gebiete der Philosophie, Berlin: Vieweg, 1793.
  Versuch über die Transcendentalphilosophie, Berlin: Voß und Sohn, 1790.
Maimonides, Moses, *Guide of the Perplexed*, trans. Shlomo Pines, 2 vols., Chicago, IL:
    University of Chicago Press, 1965.
Marheineke, Philipp Konrad, *Die Grundlehren der christlichen Dogmatik als Wissenschaft*,
    Berlin: Duncker und Humblot, 1827.
Martensen, Hans Lassen, *Af Mit Levnet*, 3 vols., Copenhagen: Gyldendal, 1882–3.
Marx, Karl and Engels, Friedrich, *Die deutsche Ideologie*, in *Werke*, 42 vols., Berlin: Dietz
    Verlag, 1960–83, III.
  The German Ideology, parts 1 and 3, trans. Roy Pascal, London: Lawrence and Wishart,
    1940.
Molitor, Franz Josef, *Philosophie der Geschichte oder über die Tradition*, 4 vols., Frankfurt
    am Main: Hermannsche Buchhandlung, 1827; Münster: in der Theissingschen
    Buchhandlung, 1834, 1839, 1853.
Møller, Poul Martin, 'Om Begrebet Ironie', in *Efterladte Skrifter*, 2nd edn, 3 vols.,
    Copenhagen: Reitzel, 1848, III, 152–8.
  *Tanker over Mueligheden af Beviser for Menneskets Udødelighed, med Hensyn til den nyeste
    derhen hørende Literatur*, in *Efterladte Skrifter*, 3 vols., Copenhagen: Reitzel, 1842, II,
    158–272.
Moritz, Karl Philipp, *Götterlehre, oder mythologische Dichtungen der Alten*, ed. Horst
    Günther, Frankfurt am Main and Leipzig: Insel, 1999.
Müller, Friedrich Max, *Contributions to the Science of Mythology*, London: Longmans,
    Green, and Company, 1897.
Müller, J. T. (ed.), *Die symbolischen Bücher der evangelisch-lutherischen Kirche, deutsch und
    lateinisch*, Gütersloh: Bertelsmann, 1900.
Novalis, *Werke*, ed. Gerhard Schulz, 4th edn, Munich: Verlag C. H. Beck, 2001.
Przywara, Erich, *Analogia entis. Ur-Struktur und All-Rhythmus*, Einsiedeln: Johannes
    Verlag, 1962.

Gottgeheimnis in der Welt, Munich: Theatiner Verlag, 1923.

Hölderlin: Eine Studie, Nuremburg: Glock und Lutz, 1949.

Rahner, Karl, *Foundations of Christian Faith: An Introduction to the Idea of Christianity*, trans. William V. Dych, New York: Crossroad, 1978–87.

'On the theology of the incarnation', in *Theological Investigations*, trans. Kevin Smyth, vol. IV, New York: Crossroad, 1982, 105–20.

'The theology of the symbol' in *Theological Investigations*, trans. Kevin Smyth, vol. IV, London: Darton, Longman & Todd, 1966, 221–52.

The Trinity, trans. Joseph Donceel, London: Burns and Oates, 1970.

'Trinity, divine; trinity in theology', in *Sacramentum Mundi*, ed. Karl Rahner *et al.*, vol. VI, New York: Herder, 1970, 295–308.

Reinhold, Karl Leonhard, 'Briefe über die Kantische Philosophie', 4 instalments, *Der Teutsche Merkur*, Weimar: Verlag der Gesellschaft, 1786–7 [reprinted in expanded form, 2 vols., Leipzig: Göschen, 1790–2].

Letters on the Kantian Philosophy, trans. James Hebbeler, Cambridge: Cambridge University Press, 2005.

Ricoeur, Paul, 'Doing philosophy after Kierkegaard', in Joseph H. Smith (ed.), *Kierkegaard's Truth: The Disclosure of the Self*, New Haven: Yale University Press, 1981, 325–42.

'Kierkegaard and evil', in *Kierkegaard's Truth: The Disclosure of the Self*, ed. Joseph H. Smith, New Haven: Yale University Press, 1981, 313–25.

'Kierkegaard et le mal', *Revue de théologie et de philosophie* 4 (1963), 292–302.

'Philosopher après Kierkegaard', *Revue de théologie et de philosophie* 4 (1963), 303–16.

'Toward a hermeneutic of the idea of revelation', trans. David Pellauer, *Harvard Theological Review* 70,1–2 (January–April 1977), 1–37.

The Rule of Metaphor: Multi-Disciplinary Studies of the Creation of Meaning in Language, trans. Robert Czerny with Kathleen McLaughlin and John Costello SJ, London: Routledge and Kegan Paul, 1978.

Rosenkranz, Karl, *Der christliche Glaube*, in *Jahrbücher für wissenschaftliche Kritik* (1830), Berlin: de Gruyter, 2003.

Rosenroth, Christian Knorr von *et al.*, *Kabbala Denudata*, 2 vols., Sulzbach, 1677 and Frankfurt am Main, 1684.

Rosenzweig, Franz, 'Einleitung', in Hermann Cohen, *Jüdische Schriften*, ed. Bruno Strauss, Berlin: Schwetschke, 1924.

Philosophical and Theological Writings, trans. Paul Franks and Michael Morgan, Indianapolis, IN: Hackett, 2000.

Der Stern der Erlösung, Frankfurt am Main: Kaufmann, 1921.

The Star of Redemption, trans. Barbara Galli, Madison: University of Wisconsin Press, 2005.

Schiller, Friedrich, *Essays*, ed. Walter Hinderer and Daniel O. Dahlstrom, New York: Continuum, 1995.

On the Aesthetic Education of Man, trans. E. M. Wilkinson and L. A. Willoughby, Oxford: Clarendon Press, 1967.

Sämtliche Werke, ed. Wolfgang Riedel, 5 vols., Munich: Carl Hanser, 2004.

Über naïve und sentimentalische Dichtung, Leipzig: Reclam, 2002.

Schlegel, Friedrich, *Kritische Friedrich-Schlegel-Ausgabe*, ed. Ernst Behler, Munich: Ferdinand Schöningh, 1967– .

Schleiermacher, F. D. E., *Der christliche Glaube nach den Grundsätzen der evangelischen Kirche*, Berlin: Reimer, 1822.

   Hermeneutik und Kritik, ed. Manfred Frank, Frankfurt a.M.: Suhrkamp, 1977.

   Über die Religion. Reden an die Gebildeten unter ihren Verächtern, ed. H.-J. Rothert (Philosophische Bibliothek, 255). Hamburg: Felix Meiner, 1970.

Staudenmaier, F. A., *Darstellung und Kritik des Hegelschen Systems. Aus dem Standpunkt der christlichen Philosophie*, Mainz: Kupferberg, 1844; Frankfurt: Minerva, 1966.

   Pragmatismus der Geistesgaben, Tübingen: Laup, 1835.

Strauss, David Friedrich, *Das Leben Jesu kritisch bearbeitet*, 1st edn, 2 vols., Tübingen: Osiander, 1835.

   Die christliche Glaubenslehre in ihrer geschichtlichen Entwicklung und im Kampfe mit der modernen Wissenschaft, vol. I, Darmstadt: WBG, 2009.

   The Life of Jesus Critically Examined, trans. M. Evans, London: Chapman Brothers, 1846.

Tillich, P., 'Schelling und die Anfänge des existentialistischen Protestes (1955)', in *Paul Tillich: Gesammelte Werke IV: Philosophie und Schicksal*, ed. Renate Albrecht, Stuttgart: Evangelisches Verlagswerk, 1961, 133–44.

   Systematische Theologie I/II, Berlin and New York: de Gruyter, 1987.

   'Systematische Theologie von 1913', in *Paul Tillich: Gesammelte Werke. Ergänzungs- und Nachlassbände*, vol. IX, ed. Doris Hummel and Gerd Lax, Berlin and New York: de Gruyter, 2009, 273–434.

Tindal, Matthew, *Christianity as Old as the Creation: or, The Gospel, a Republication of the Religion of Nature*, London: [s.n.], 1730.

Toland, John, *Christianity not Mysterious Or, A Treatise shewing, that there is Nothing in the Gospel Contrary to Reason, Nor above it: And that no Christian Doctrine can be Properly call'd a Mystery*, London: [s.n.], 1702 (1st edition 1696).

Troeltsch, Ernst, 'Die Krise des Historismus', *Neue Rundschau* 33,1 (1922).

   Religion in History, trans. James Luther Adams and Walter F. Bense, Minneapolis: Fortress Press, 1991.

   The Christian Faith, ed., Gertrud von le Fort, trans. Garrett E. Paul, Minneapolis: Fortress, 1991.

Vallée, Gérard, *The Spinoza Conversations between Lessing and Jacobi: Texts with Excerpts from the Ensuing Controversy*, Lanham, MD: University Press of America, 1988.

C. Secondary literature

Adams, Nicholas, 'Eschatology sacred and profane: the effects of philosophy on theology in Pannenberg, Rahner and Moltmann', *International Journal of Systematic Theology* 2 (2000), 283–306.

   'The Bible', in Nicholas Adams, George Pattison, Graham Ward (eds.), *The Oxford Handbook of Theology and Modern European Thought*, Oxford: Oxford University Press, 2013, 545–66.

   The Eclipse of Grace: Divine and Human Action in Hegel, Oxford: Blackwell-Wiley, 2013.

Agamben, Giorgio, *The Time that Remains: A Commentary on the Letter to the Romans*, Stanford, CA: Stanford University Press, 2008.

Axt-Piscalar, C., *Der Grund des Glaubens. Eine theologiegeschichtliche Untersuchung zum Verhältnis von Glaube und Trinität in der Theologie Isaak August Dorners*, Tübingen: Mohr Siebeck, 1990.

Barth, Ulrich, *Die Christologie Emanuel Hirschs: eine systematische und problemgeschichtliche Darstellung ihrer geschichtsmethodologischen, erkenntniskritischen und subjektivitätstheoretischen Grundlagen*, Berlin and New York: de Gruyter, 1992.

Beach, Edward Allen, *The Potencies of God(s): Schelling's Philosophy of Mythology*, Albany: State University of New York Press, 1994.

Bernstein, Richard, *Philosophical Profiles*, Cambridge: Polity Press, 1986.

Betz, John R., 'Beyond the sublime: the aesthetics of the analogy of being', *Modern Theology* 21,3 (2005), 367–411 and 22,1, 1–50.

Bowie, Andrew, 'Introduction', in Friedrich Schleiermacher, *Hermeneutics and Criticism*, trans. Andrew Bowie, Cambridge: Cambridge University Press, 1998, vii–xxxi.

'The philosophical significance of Schleiermacher's hermeneutics', in Jacqueline Mariña (ed.), *The Cambridge Companion to Friedrich Schleiermacher*, Cambridge: Cambridge University Press, 2005, 73–90.

Boyle, Nicholas, 'Lessing, Biblical criticism and the origins of German classical culture', *German Life and Letters* 34 (1981), 196–213.

Sacred and Secular Scriptures: A Catholic Approach to Literature, London: Darton, Longman and Todd, 2004; Notre Dame: University of Notre Dame Press, 2005.

Breuer, Isaac, *Die Neue Kusari*, Frankfurt am Main: Rabbiner Hirsch Gesellschaft, 1934 [partially translated in *Concepts of Judaism*, trans. Jacob Levinger, Jerusalem: Israel Universities Press, 1974].

Buckley, Michael, *At the Origins of Modern Atheism*, New Haven: Yale University Press, 1987.

Bungay, Steven, *Beauty and Truth: A Study of Hegel's Aesthetics*, Oxford: Oxford University Press, 1984.

Burbidge, John, 'Unhappy consciousness in Hegel: an analysis of medieval Catholicism?' in *Hegel on Logic and Religion: The Reasonableness of Christianity*, Albany: State University of New York Press, 1992, 105–18.

Cahnman, Werner J., 'Friedrich Wilhelm Schelling über die Judenemanzipation', in *Zeitschrift für Bayerische Landesgeschichte* 37,2 (1974), 614–25.

'Schelling and the new thinking of Judaism', *Proceedings of the American Academy for Jewish Research* 48 (1981), 1–56.

Copleston, F. C., *A History of Philosophy*, vol. VII: *Modern Philosophy, Part 1: Fichte to Hegel*, New York: Image Books, 1965.

Corduan, Winfried, 'Elements of the philosophy of G. W. F. Hegel in the transcendental method of Karl Rahner', Ph.D. dissertation, Rice University, 1977.

'Hegelian themes in contemporary theology', *Journal of the Evangelical Theological Society* 22 (1979), 351–61.

Crockett, C. and Davis, C. (eds.), *Hegel and the Infinite*, New York and Chichester: Columbia University Press, 2011.

Cunningham, Conor, *Genealogy of Nihilism: Philosophies of Nothing and the Difference of Theology*, London and New York: Routledge, 2002.

Cupitt, Don, *After God: The Future of Religion*, London: Phoenix, 1998.

The Meaning of the West: An Apologia for Secular Christianity, London: SCM Press, 2008.

Davies, Brian, 'Anselm and the ontological argument', in Brian Davies and B. Leftow (eds.), *The Cambridge Companion to Anselm*, Cambridge: Cambridge University Press, 2004, 157–78.

Davis, Creston (ed.), Slavoj Žižek and John Milbank, in *The Monstrosity of Christ: Paradox or Dialectic?*, Cambridge, MA: MIT Press, 2009.

Derrida, Jacques, *Of Spirit: Heidegger and the Question*, trans. Geoffrey Bennington and Rachel Bowlby, Chicago: University of Chicago Press, 1989.

'On the newly arisen apocalyptic tone in philosophy', in Peter Fenves (ed.), *Raising the Tone of Philosophy: Late Essays by Immanuel Kant, Transformative Critique by Jacques Derrida*, Baltimore, MD: Johns Hopkins University Press, 1998.

Deuser, Hermann, 'Religious dialectics and Christology', in Alastair Hannay and Gordon Marino (eds.), *The Cambridge Companion to Kierkegaard*, Cambridge: Cambridge University Press, 1998, 376–96.

Søren Kierkegaard: Die paradoxe Dialektik des politischen Christen. Voraussetzungen bei Hegel. Die Reden von 1847/48 im Verhältnis von Politik und Ästhetik, Munich: Matthias-Grünewald-Verlag, 1974.

Dews, Peter, *The Idea of Evil*, Oxford: Blackwell, 2007.

Dickey, Laurence, 'Hegel on religion and philosophy', in Frederick C. Beiser (ed.), *The Cambridge Companion to Hegel*, Cambridge: Cambridge University Press, 1993, 301–47.

Dostal, Robert J. (ed.), *The Cambridge Companion to Gadamer*, Cambridge: Cambridge University Press, 2002.

Eagleton, Terry, *Reason, Faith and Revolution*, New Haven, CT: Yale University Press, 2010.

Emery, Gilles, OP and Levering, Matthew (eds.), *The Oxford Handbook of the Trinity*, Oxford: Oxford University Press, 2011.

Evans, C. Stephen, *Kierkegaard on Faith and the Self: Collected Essays*, Waco: Baylor University Press, 2006.

Fackenheim, Emil, *The God Within: Kant, Schelling and Historicity*, ed. John Burbidge, Toronto: University of Toronto Press, 1996.

The Religious Dimension in Hegel's Thought, Bloomington and London: Indiana University Press, 1967.

Feldman, Burton and Richardson, Robert D. Jr, *The Rise of Modern Mythology, 1680–1860*, Bloomington: Indiana University Press, 1972.

Fischer, H., 'Die Christologie als Mitte des Systems', in Hermann Fischer (ed.), *Paul Tillich: Studien zu einer Theologie der Moderne*, Frankfurt am Main: Athenäum, 1989, 207–29.

Förster, Eckhart (ed.), *The Course of Remembrance and other Essays on Hölderlin*, Stanford, CA: Stanford University Press, 1997.

Frank, Manfred, *Vorlesungen über die neue Mythologie*, vol. I: *Der kommende Gott*, Frankfurt am Main: Suhrkamp, 1982, vol. II: *Gott im Exil*, Frankfurt am Main: Suhrkamp, 1988.

Franks, Paul, *All or Nothing: Systematicity, Transcendental Arguments, and Skepticism in German Idealism*, Cambridge, MA: Harvard University Press, 2005.

'Inner anti-Semitism or Kabbalistic legacy? German Idealism's relationship to Judaism' *International Yearbook of German Idealism* 7 (2010), 254–79.

'Nothing comes from nothing: Judaism, the Orient, and the Kabbalah in Hegel's reception of Spinoza', in Michael della Rocca (ed.), *The Oxford Handbook of Spinoza*, Oxford: Oxford University Press, forthcoming.

'Sinai since Spinoza: reflections on revelation in modern Jewish thought', in George Brooke, Loren Stuckenbruck and Hindy Najman (eds.), *The Significance of Sinai: Traditions about Sinai and Divine Revelation in Judaism and Christianity*, Leiden: Brill, 2008, 331–52.

Franz, Michael (ed.), *'An der Galeere der Theologie': Hölderlins, Hegels und Schellings Theologiestudium an der Universität Tübingen*, Tübingen: Hölderlin-Gesellschaft; Eggingen: Edition Isele, 2007.

Frei, Hans W., *The Eclipse of Biblical Narrative: A Study in Eighteenth and Nineteenth Century Hermeneutics*, New Haven and London: Yale University Press, 1974.

Fulda, Ludwig, *Aufruf an die Kulturwelt* in *Manifest der 93*, text available online at www.nernst.de/kulturwelt.htm.

Funkenstein, Amos, *Theology and the Scientific Imagination*, Chicago: University of Chicago Press, 1986.

Gabriel, Markus, *Der Mensch im Mythos. Untersuchungen über Ontotheologie, Anthropologie und Selbstbewußtseinsgeschichte in Schellings 'Philosophie der Mythologie'*, Berlin and New York: de Gruyter, 2006.

Gasché, Rodolphe, *The Tain of the Mirror: Derrida and the Philosophy of Reflection*, Cambridge, MA: Harvard University Press, 1986.

Geiger, Wolfgang, *Spekulation und Kritik: die Geschichtstheologie Ferdinand Christian Baurs*, Munich: Kaiser, 1964.

Gerber, Uwe, *Christologische Entwürfe*, vol. I: *Von der Reformation bis zur Dialektischen Theologie*, Zürich: EVZ, 1970.

Gibbs, Robert, *Correlations in Rosenzweig and Levinas*, Princeton, NJ: Princeton University Press, 1992.

Gockel, Heinz, *Mythos und Poesie. Zum Mythosbegriff in Aufklärung und Frühromantik*, Frankfurt am Main: Klostermann, 1981.

Gordon, Peter Eli, *Continental Divide: Heidegger, Cassirer, Davos*, Cambridge, MA: Harvard University Press, 2010.

Graevenitz, Gerhart von, *Mythos. Zur Geschichte einer Denkgewohnheit*, Stuttgart: Metzler, 1987.

Graf, Friedrich W., *Kritik und Pseudo-Spekulation: David Friedrich Strauß als Dogmatiker im Kontext der positionellen Theologie seiner Zeit*, Munich: Kaiser, 1982.

Guardini, Romano, *Weltbild und Frömmigkeit*, Paderborn: Matthias Grünewald / Schöningh, 1996 (originally published by Kösel Verlag in 1955).

Guetta, Alessandro, *Kabbalah and Philosophy: Elijah Benamozegh and the Reconciliation of Western Thought and Jewish Esotericism*, trans. Helena Kahan, Albany: State University of New York Press, 2009.

Habermas, Jürgen, 'Der deutsche Idealismus der jüdischen Philosophen', in *Philosophisch–Politische Profile*, Frankfurt am Main: Suhrkamp, 1981, 39–64.

Philosophical–Political Profiles, trans. Frederick G. Lawrence, Cambridge, MA: MIT Press, 1985.

Hachiya, Toshihisa, *Paradox, Vorbild und Versöhner: S. Kierkegaards Christologie und deren Rezeption in der deutschen Theologie des 20. Jahrhunderts* (Europäische Hochschulschriften, Reihe XXIII, vol. 836), Frankfurt am Main: Lang, 2006.

Hannay, Alastair, *Kierkegaard: A Biography*, Cambridge: Cambridge University Press, 2001.

Hanssen, Beatrice, '"Dichtermut" and "Blödigkeit" – two poems by Friedrich Hölderlin, interpreted by Walter Benjamin', in Andrew Benjamin (ed.), *Walter Benjamin and Romanticism*, London: Athlone Press, 2002.

Harrelson, Kevin, *The Ontological Argument from Descartes to Hegel*, Amherst, NY: Humanity Books, 2008.

Harris, H. S., *Hegel's Development: Toward the Sunlight, 1770–1801*, Oxford: Clarendon Press, 1972.

Hegel's Development, vol. II: *Night Thoughts*, Oxford: Clarendon, 1983.

Harris, Jay, *Nachman Krochmal: Guiding the Perplexed of the Modern Age*, New York: New York University Press, 1993.

Hart, Kevin, 'The poetics of the negative', in Stephen Prickett (ed.), *Reading the Text: Biblical Criticism and Literary Theory*, Oxford: Blackwell, 1991, 281–340.

Hartlich, Christian and Sachs, Walter, *Der Ursprung des Mythosbegriffes in der modernen Bibelwissenschaft*, Tübingen: Mohr, 1952.

Harvey, James W., 'Hegel, Rahner and Karl Barth: a study in the possibilities of a Trinitarian theology', D.Phil. thesis, University of Oxford, 1989.

Henrich, Dieter, *Between Kant and Hegel: Lectures on German Idealism*, Cambridge, MA: Harvard University Press, 2003.

Hick, John and McGill, Arthur, (eds.), *The Many-Faced Argument: Recent Studies on the Ontological Argument for the Existence of God*, London: Macmillan, 1968.

Hirsch, Emanuel, *Christliche Rechenschaft*, ed. Hayo Gerdes, vols. I and II, Tübingen: Katzmann, 1989.

Geschichte der neuern evangelischen Theologie im Zusammenhang mit den allgemeinen Bewegungen des europäischen Denkens, 3rd edn, vol. V, Gütersloh: Gütersloher Verlagshaus, 1964.

Hodgson, Peter C., *A Study of Ferdinand Christian Baur: The Formation of Historical Theology*, New York: Harper & Row, 1966.

God in History: Shapes of Freedom, Nashville: Abingdon Press, 1989.

Hegel and Christian Theology: A Reading of the Lectures of Philosophy of Religion, Oxford: Oxford University Press, 2008.

Hühn, Lore, *Kierkegaard und der Deutsche Idealismus: Konstellationen des Übergangs*, Tübingen: Mohr Siebeck, 2009.

Hyppolite, Jean, *Genesis and Structure of Hegel's Phenomenology of Spirit*, trans. S. Cherniak and J. Heckman, Evanston, IL: Northwestern University Press, 1974.

Idel, Moshe, 'Jewish Kabbalah and Platonism in the Middle Ages and the Renaissance', in Lenn E. Goodman (ed.), *Neo-Platonism and Jewish Thought*, Albany: State University of New York Press, 1992, 319–51.

Kabbalah in Italy 1280–1510, New Haven, CT: Yale University Press, 2011.

Israel, Jonathan I., *Radical Enlightenment: Philosophy and the Making of Modernity*, Oxford: Oxford University Press, 2001.

Jaeschke, W., *Reason in Religion*, trans. J. Michael Stewart and Peter C. Hodgson, Berkeley: University of California Press, 1990.

Jamme, Christoph, *Einführung in die Philosophie des Mythos: Neuzeit und Gegenwart*, Darmstadt: Wissenschaftliche Buchgesellschaft, 1991.

Jamme, Christoph and Schneider, Helmut (eds.), *Mythologie der Vernunft: Hegels 'ältestes Systemprogramm' des deutschen Idealismus*, Frankfurt am Main: Suhrkamp, 1984.

Janowski, J. C., *Der Mensch als Maß: Untersuchungen zum Grundgedanken und zur Struktur von Feuerbachs Werk*, Zürich, Cologne: Benziger, 1980.

Johnson, Keith, *Karl Barth and the* Analogia Entis, London: T. and T. Clark International, 2010.

Jüngel, Eberhard, *Barth-Studien*, Gütersloh, Benziger, 1982.

   God as the Mystery of the World: On the Foundation of the Theology of the Crucified One in the Dispute between Theism and Atheism, trans. Darell L. Guder, Grand Rapids, MI: Eerdmans, 1983.

   Gott als Geheimnis der Welt. Zur Begründung der Theologie des Gekreuzigten im Streit zwischen Theismus und Atheismus, Tübingen: Mohr/Siebeck, 1977.

Kalkavage, Peter, *The Logic of Desire: An Introduction to Hegel's 'Phenomenology of Spirit'*, Philadelphia: Paul Dry, 2007.

Kärkkäinen, Veli-Matti, *The Trinity: Global Perspectives*, Louisville, KY: Westminster John Knox Press, 2007.

Kilby, Karen, 'Balthasar and Karl Rahner', in *The Cambridge Companion to Hans Urs von Balthasar*, Cambridge: Cambridge University Press 2004, 256–68.

Kirmmse, Bruce (ed.), *Encounters with Kierkegaard: A Life as Seen by his Contemporaries*, Princeton, NJ: Princeton University Press, 1996.

   Kierkegaard in Golden Age Denmark, Bloomington: Indiana University Press, 1990.

Koch, Carl Henrik, *Den Danske Idealisme*, Copenhagen: Gyldendal, 2004.

Kojève, Alexandre, *Introduction to the Reading of Hegel*, ed. R. Queneau and Allan Bloom, trans. J. Nichols, New York: Cornell University Press, 1980.

Kosky, Jeffrey L., 'The birth of the modern philosophy of religion and the death of transcendence', in Regina Schwartz (ed.), *Transcendence: Philosophy, Literature, and Theology Approach the Beyond*, New York and London: Routledge, 2004, 13–30.

Krüger, Malte Dominik, *Göttliche Freiheit: die Trinitätslehre in Schellings Spätphilosophie* (Religion in Philosophy and Theology, 31), Tübingen: Mohr Siebeck, 2008.

Kühn, Manfred, *Kant: Eine Biographie*, Munich: Beck, 2003.

Kühn, U., *Christologie*, Göttingen: Vandenhoeck & Ruprecht, 2003.

Küng, Hans, *The Incarnation of God: The Introduction to Hegel's Theological Thought as a Prolegomenon to a Future Christology*, trans. J. R. Stephenson, New York: Crossroad, 1987.

Lacoste, Jean-Yves, *Experience and the Absolute: Disputed Questions on the Humanity of Man*, trans. Mark Raftery-Skehan, New York: Fordham University Press, 2001.

Lacoue-Labarthe, Philippe, 'Poetry's courage', in Beatrice Hanssen and Andrew Benjamin (eds.), *Walter Benjamin and Romanticism*, New York: Continuum, 2002.

Lange, Dietz, *Historischer Jesus oder mythischer Christus: Untersuchungen zum Gegensatz zwischen Friedrich Schleiermacher und David Friedrich Strauß*, Gütersloh: Gütersloher Verlagsanstalt, 1975.

Lash, Nicholas, *A Matter of Hope: A Theologian's Reflections on the Thought of Karl Marx*, London: Darton, Longman and Todd, 1981.

Lewis, Thomas A., *Religion, Modernity, and Politics in Hegel*, Oxford: Oxford University Press, 2011.

'Religion and demythologization', in Dean Moyar and Michael Quante (eds.), *Hegel's Phenomenology of Spirit: A Critical Guide*, Cambridge: Cambridge University Press, 2011, 192–209.

Lincoln, Bruce, *Theorizing Myth: Narrative, Ideology, and Scholarship*, Chicago: University of Chicago Press, 2000.

Löwith, Karl, *Von Hegel zu Nietzsche: Der revolutionäre Bruch im Denken des neunzehnten Jahrhunderts*, Zürich: Europa Verlag, 1941; English: *From Hegel to Nietzsche: The Revolution in Nineteenth-Century Thought*, trans. David E. Green, New York: Columbia University Press, 1964.

Lukács, Georg, *The Young Hegel*, trans. R. Livingston, London: Merlin Press, 1975.

Macintyre, Alasdair, *After Virtue: A Study in Moral Theory*, 3rd edn, London: Duckworth, 2007.

Magid, Shaul, *From Metaphysics to Midrash: Myth, History, and the Interpretation of Scripture in Lurianic Kabbala*, Bloomington: Indiana University Press, 2008.

Malabou, Catherine, *The Future of Hegel: Plasticity, Temporality, Dialectic*, trans. Lizabeth During, New York: Routledge, 2004.

Marion, Jean-Luc, 'The withdrawal of the divine and the face of the father: Hölderlin', in *The Idol and the Distance: Five Studies*, trans. Thomas A. Carlson, New York: Fordham University Press, 2001.

McCormack, Bruce, *Karl Barth's Critically Realistic Dialectical Theology: Its Genesis and Development, 1909-36*, Oxford and New York: Oxford University Press, 1995.

'Karl Barth's version of an "analogy of being": a dialectical No and Yes to Roman Catholicism', in *The Analogy of Being: Invention of the Antichrist or the Wisdom of God?* ed. Thomas Joseph White, OP, Grand Rapids, MI, and Cambridge: Eerdmans, 2011, 88–144.

McCumber, John, *The Company of Words: Hegel, Language, and Systematic Philosophy*, Evanston, IL: Northwestern University Press, 1993.

McGrath, A., *The Making of Modern Christology 1750-1990*, Grand Rapids, MI: Zondervan 1994.

Mechels, Eberhard, *Analogie bei Erich Przywara und Karl Barth. Das Verhältnis von Offenbarungstheologie und Metaphysik*, Neukirchen: Neukirchener Verlag, 1974.

Milbank, John, 'Postmodern critical Augustinianism: a short summa in forty-two responses to unasked questions', in John Milbank and Simon Oliver (eds.), *The Radical Orthodoxy Reader*, London: Routledge, 2009, 49-50.

Radical Orthodoxy: A New Theology, ed. John Milbank, Catherine Pickstock and Graham Ward, London and New York: Routledge, 1999.

The Suspended Middle: Henri de Lubac and the Debate Concerning the Supernatural, Grand Rapids, MI: Eerdmans, 2005.

Theology and Social Theory: Beyond Secular Reason, Oxford: Blackwell, 1990.

Milbank, John and Ward, Graham, 'The radical orthodoxy ten years on – the return of metaphysics', in Michael Hoelzl and Graham Ward, *The New Visibility of Religion: Studies in Religion and Cultural Hermeneutics*, London and New York: Continuum, 2008.

Mittelman, Alan, *Between Kant and Kabbalah: An Introduction to Isaac Breuer's Philosophy of Judaism*, Albany: State University of New York Press, 1990.

Morgan, Michael L., *Discovering Levinas*, Cambridge: Cambridge University Press, 2007.

Mostert, Christiaan, 'From eschatology to Trinity: Pannenberg's doctrine of God', *Pacifica. Australasian Theological Studies* 10 (1997), 70–83.

Nancy, Jean-Luc, 'Myth interrupted', in *The Inoperative Community*, ed. Peter Connor, Minneapolis: University of Minnesota Press, 1991, 43–70.

Neugebauer, G., *Tillichs frühe Christologie: Eine Untersuchung zu Offenbarung und Geschichte bei Tillich vor dem Hintergrund seiner Schellingrezeption* (Theologische Bibliothek Töpelmann, 141), Berlin and New York: de Gruyter, 2007.

Norgate, Jonathan, *Isaak A. Dorner: The Triune God and the Gospel of Salvation*, London: T. & T. Clark, 2009.

O'Meara, Thomas, *Erich Przywara, S. J.: His Theology and his World*, Notre Dame, Indiana: University of Notre Dame Press, 2002.

O'Neill, J. C., *The Bible's Authority: A Portrait Gallery of Thinkers from Lessing to Bultmann*, Edinburgh: T. & T. Clark, 1991.

'The study of the New Testament', in Ninian Smart (ed.), *Nineteenth-Century Religious Thought in the West*, Cambridge: Cambridge University Press, 1985.

O'Regan, Cyril, *Anatomy of Misremembering*, vol. I: *Balthasar and the Specter of Hegel*, New York: Crossroad, 2013.

'Hegel and anti-Judaism: narrative and the inner circulation of the Kabbalah', in *The Owl of Minerva*, 28,2 (Spring) (1997), 141–82.

The Heterodox Hegel, New York: State University of New York Press, 1994.

'The Trinity in Kant, Hegel, and Schelling', in Gilles Emery, OP and Matthew Levering (eds.), *The Oxford Handbook of the Trinity*, Oxford: Oxford University Press, 2011, 254–66.

Ogden, Mark, *The Problem of Christ in the Work of Friedrich Hölderlin*, London: Modern Humanities Research Association for The Institute of Germanic Studies, University of London, 1991.

Oppy, Graham, *Ontological Arguments and Belief in God*, Cambridge: Cambridge University Press, 1996.

Pannenberg, Wolfhart, 'Die Subjektivität Gottes und die Trinitätslehre. Ein Beitrag zur Beziehung zwischen Karl Barth und der Philosophie Hegels', *Kerygma und Dogma* 23 (1977), 25–40.

'La doctrina de la Trinidad en Hegel y su recepción en la teología alemana', *Estudios trinitarios* 30 (1996), 35–51.

Jesus – God and Man, London: SCM, 1968.

Systematic Theology, trans. Geoffrey W. Bromiley, vol. I, Grand Rapids, MI: William B. Eerdmans, 1991.

Pattison, George, *Kierkegaard, Religion and the Nineteenth-Century Crisis of Culture*, Cambridge: Cambridge University Press, 2002.

The Philosophy of Kierkegaard, Montreal: McGill-Queen's University Press, 2005.

Petzold, M., *Gottmensch und Gattung Mensch: Studien zur Christologie und Christologiekritik Ludwig Feuerbachs*, Berlin: Evangelische Verlagsanstalt, 1989.

Phan, Peter C. (ed.), *The Cambridge Companion to the Trinity*, Cambridge: Cambridge University Press, 2011.

Philoneko, Alexis, *La liberté humaine dans la philosophie de Fichte*, Paris: Vrin, 1966.

Plant, Raymond, *Hegel: An Introduction*, 2nd edn, Oxford: Blackwell, 1983.

Plantinga, Alvin (ed.), *The Ontological Argument: From St. Anselm to Contemporary Philosophers*, Garden City, NY: Doubleday, 1965.

Pöggeler, Otto, 'Hegel, der Verfasser des ältesten Systemprogramms des deutschen Idealismus', in Jamme and Schneider (eds.), *Mythologie der Vernunft*, 126–43.

Pollock, Benjamin, *Franz Rosenzweig and the Systematic Task of Philosophy*, Cambridge: Cambridge University Press, 2009.

Powell, Samuel M., 'Nineteenth-century Protestant doctrines of the Trinity', in Gilles Emery, OP and Matthew Levering (eds.), *The Oxford Handbook of the Trinity*, Oxford: Oxford University Press, 2011, 267–80.

'The doctrine of the Trinity in nineteenth-century German Protestant theology: Philipp Marheineke, Isaak Dorner, Johann von Hofmann, and Alexander Schweizer', Ph.D. dissertation, Claremont Graduate School, 1987.

The Trinity in German Thought, Cambridge: Cambridge University Press, 2001.

Quash, Ben, 'Drama and the ends of modernity', in Lucy Gardner, David Moss, Ben Quash and Graham Ward (eds.), *Balthasar at the End of Modernity*, Edinburgh: T. and T. Clark, 1999, 139–71.

Theology and the Drama of History, Cambridge: Cambridge University Press, 2005.

Ravitsky, Aviezer, 'Rabbi J. B. Soloveitchik on human knowledge: between Maimonidean and neo-Kantian philosophy', *Modern Judaism*, 6,2 (May 1986), 157–88.

Reardon, Bernard M. G., *Hegel's Philosophy of Religion*, London: Macmillan, 1977.

Reijnen, Anne Marie, 'Tillich's Christology', in Russell Re Manning (ed.), *The Cambridge Companion to Paul Tillich*, Cambridge: Cambridge University Press, 2008, 56–73.

Rohls, Jan, *Protestantische Theologie der Neuzeit*, vols. I and II, Tübingen: Mohr Siebeck, 1997.

Theologie und Metaphysik. Der ontologische Gottesbeweis und seine Kritiker, Gütersloh: Mohn, 1987.

Rose, Gillian, *Hegel Contra Sociology*, London: Athlone Press, 1981.

Rupprecht, Eva-Maria, *Kritikvergessene Spekulation: Das Religions- und Theologieverständnis der spekulativen Theologie Ph. K. Marheinekes* (Beiträge zur rationalen Theologie, 3), Frankfurt am Main and Berlin: Peter Lang, 1993.

Schlitt, Dale M., *Divine Subjectivity: Understanding Hegel's Philosophy of Religion*, Scranton, PA: Scranton University Press, 1990, 2009.

Hegel's Trinitarian Claim: A Critical Reflection, Leiden: Brill, 1984; Albany: State University of New York Press, 2012.

Schulte, Christoph, *Zimzum: Gott und Weltursprung*, Frankfurt am Main, Suhrkamp, 2013.

Schütte, Hans-Walter, 'Subjektivität und System: zum Briefwechsel E. Hirsch (1888–1972) und P. Tillich (1886–1965)', in Christian Danz (ed.), *Theologie als Religionsphilosophie. Studien zu den problemgeschichtlichen und systematischen Voraussetzungen der Theologie Paul Tillichs* (Tillich-Studien 9), Vienna: Lit, 2004, 3–22.

Schweitzer, Albert, *The Quest of the Historical Jesus: A Critical Study of its Progress from Reimarus to Wrede*, trans. William Montgomery, London: A. & C. Black, 1910.

Seidel, George, *Activity and Ground: Fichte, Schelling, and Hegel*, New York: George Olms Verlag, 1976.

Shanks, Andrew, *Hegel and Religious Faith: Divided Brain, Atoning Spirit*, London: T. and T. Clark International, 2011.

    Hegel's Political Theology, Cambridge: Cambridge University Press, 1991.

Smart, Ninian (ed.), *Nineteenth-Century Religious Thought in the West*, Cambridge: Cambridge University Press, 1985.

Smith, Gary (ed.), *Benjamin: Philosophy, Aesthetics, History*, Chicago: University of Chicago Press, 1989.

Söderquist, K. Brian, *The Isolated Self: Truth and Untruth in Søren Kierkegaard's On the Concept of Irony*, Copenhagen: Reitzel, 2007.

Soloveitchik, Joseph B., *And From There You Shall Seek*, trans. Naomi Goldblum, Jersey City, NJ: Ktav, 2008.

    U-vikashtem mi-sham, Ha-Darom 47 (1979), 1–83.

Soulen, R. Kendall, *The God of Israel and Christian Theology*, Minneapolis, MN: Fortress, 1996.

Stepelevich, Lawrence S. (ed.), *The Young Hegelians*, Cambridge: Cambridge University Press, 1983.

Stewart, Jon, 'Hegel's philosophy of religion and the question of "right" and "left" Hegelianism', in Douglas Moggach (ed.), *Politics, Religion and Art: Hegelian Debates*, Evanston, IL: Northwestern University Press, 2011.

    Kierkegaard's Relations to Hegel Reconsidered, Cambridge: Cambridge University Press, 2003.

    'The paradox and the criticism of Hegelian mediation in philosophical fragments', *Kierkegaard Studies* (2004), 184–207.

    (ed.), *Kierkegaard and his Danish Contemporaries: Philosophy, Politics and Social Theory*, vol. VII, tome 1 in *Kierkegaard Research: Sources, Reception and Resources*, Aldershot: Ashgate, 2009.

    Kierkegaard and his Danish Contemporaries: Theology, vol. VII, tome 2 in *Kierkegaard Research: Sources, Reception and Resources*, Aldershot: Ashgate, 2009.

    Kierkegaard and his German Contemporaries: Literature and Aesthetics, vol. VI, tome 3 in *Kierkegaard Research: Sources, Reception and Resources*, Aldershot: Ashgate, 2008.

    Kierkegaard and his German Contemporaries: Philosophy, vol. VI, tome 1 in *Kierkegaard Research: Sources, Reception and Resources*, Aldershot: Ashgate, 2007.

    Kierkegaard and his German Contemporaries: Theology, vol. VI, tome 2 in *Kierkegaard Research: Sources, Reception and Resources*, Aldershot: Ashgate, 2007.

Stolzenberg, Jürgen, 'Hegel's critique of the Enlightenment', in Kenneth Westphal
(ed.), *The Blackwell Guide to Hegel's Phenomenology of Spirit*, Oxford: Wiley-Blackwell,
2009, 190–208.

Striewe, H., '*Reditio subjecti in seipsum*. Der Einfluss Hegels, Kants und Fichtes auf die
Religionsphilosophie Karl Rahners', Doctoral dissertation, Faculty of Philosophy,
Freiburg-im-Brisgau University, 1979.

Taylor, Iain, *Pannenberg on the Triune God*, London: T. & T. Clark, 2007.

Taylor, Mark C., *After God*, Chicago and London: University of Chicago Press, 2007.
   Altarity, Chicago and London: University of Chicago Press, 1987.
   Journeys to Selfhood: Hegel and Kierkegaard, Berkeley: University of California Press,
   1980.

Theunissen, Michael, *Der Begriff Verzweiflung: Korrekturen an Kierkegaard*, Frankfurt am
Main: Suhrkamp, 1993.
   Kierkegaard's Concept of Despair, trans. Barbara Harshaw and Helmut Illbruck,
   Princeton, NJ: Princeton University Press, 2005.

Thulstrup, Niels, *Kierkegaard's Relation to Hegel*, trans. George L. Stengren, Princeton:
Princeton University Press, 1980.
   Kierkegaards forhold til Hegel og til den spekulative Idealisme indtil 1846, Copenhagen:
   Gyldendal, 1967.

Toews, John Edward, *Hegelianism: The Path Towards Dialectical Humanism, 1805–1840*,
Cambridge: Cambridge University Press, 1985.

Toulmin, Stephen, *Cosmopolis: The Hidden Agenda of Modernity*, Chicago: University of
Chicago Press, 1990.

Wagner, Falk, 'Der Gedanke der Persönlichkeit Gottes bei Ph. Marheineke:
Repristination eines vorkritischen Theismus', *Neue Zeitschrift für Systematische
Theologie und Religionsphilosophie* 10 (1969), 44–88.

Ward, Graham, *True Religion*, Oxford: Blackwell, 2003.

Weiss, Daniel H., *Paradox and the Prophets: Hermann Cohen and the Indirect Communication
of Religion*, Oxford: Oxford University Press, 2012.

Wendte, Martin, *Gottmenschliche Einheit bei Hegel: eine logische und theologische
Untersuchung* (Quellen und Studien zur Philosophie 77), Berlin and New York: de
Gruyter, 2007.
   'Lamentation between contradiction and obedience: Hegel and Barth as diametrically
   opposed brothers in the spirit of modernity', in Eva Harasta and Brian Brock (eds.),
   Evoking Lament: A Theological Discussion, London: T. & T. Clark, 2009, 77–98.

Wenz, Gunther, 'Die reformatorische Perspektive: der Einfluss Martin Kählers auf
Tillich', in Hermann Fischer (ed.), *Paul Tillich: Studien zu einer Theologie der Moderne*,
Frankfurt am Main: Athenäum, 1989, 62–92.
   Geschichte der Versöhnungslehre in der evangelischen Theologie der Neuzeit, vol. I, Munich:
   Kaiser, 1984.

Westphal, Merold, 'Kierkegaard and Hegel', in Alastair Hannay and Gordon Marino
(eds.), *The Cambridge Companion to Kierkegaard*, Cambridge: Cambridge University
Press, 1998, 101–23.

Williams, Rowan, 'Balthasar, Rahner and the apprehension of being', in Rowan
Williams and Mike Higton (eds.), *Wrestling with Angels: Conversations in Modern
Theology*, London: SCM Press; Grand Rapids, MI: Eerdmans, 2007.

Williamson, George S., *The Longing for Myth in Germany: Religion and Aesthetic Culture from Romanticism to Nietzsche*, Chicago: University of Chicago Press, 2004.

Zager, W., 'Einführung', in D. F. Strauss, *Die christliche Glaubenslehre in ihrer geschichtlichen Entwicklung und im Kampfe mit der modernen Wissenschaft*, vol. I, Darmstadt: WBG, 2009, 5–37.

Žižek, Slavoj, 'The Fear of Four Words: A Modest Plea for the Hegelian Reading of Christianity', in Creston Davis (ed.), *The Monstrosity of Christ: Paradox or Dialectic?*, Cambridge, MA: MIT Press, 2009.

The Fragile Absolute, London and New York: Verso, 2000.

Index